D1592069

The First Black Boxing Champions

ALSO BY COLLEEN AYCOCK AND MARK SCOTT

Joe Gans: A Biography of the First African American World Boxing Champion (McFarland, 2008)

The First Black Boxing Champions

*Essays on Fighters of
the 1800s to the 1920s*

Edited by
COLLEEN AYCOCK *and*
MARK SCOTT

Foreword by Al Bernstein

McFarland & Company, Inc., Publishers
Jefferson, North Carolina, and London

LIBRARY OF CONGRESS CATALOGUING-IN-PUBLICATION DATA

The first Black boxing champions : essays on fighters of the 1800s to the 1920s /
edited by Colleen Aycock and Mark Scott ; foreword by Al Bernstein.
p.   cm.
Includes bibliographical references and index.

ISBN 978-0-7864-4991-0

illustrated case binding : 50# alkaline paper ∞

1. African American boxers — Biography.
2. Boxers (Sports) — United States — Biography.
3. Boxing — United States — History.
I. Aycock, Colleen.
II. Scott, Mark, 1962–
GV1131.F56   2011   796.830922 — dc22   [B]   2010044529

BRITISH LIBRARY CATALOGUING DATA ARE AVAILABLE

On the cover: Sam Langford, 1913 (Clay Moyle Collection)

Manufactured in the United States of America

*McFarland & Company, Inc., Publishers
Box 611, Jefferson, North Carolina 28640
www.mcfarlandpub.com*

Acknowledgments

So many people helped to make this collection possible. We apologize for listing your names only once, so many of you were repeatedly helpful.

Boxing historians Tracy Callis, Don Cogswell, Neil Rodriguez, Luckett Davis, Ben Hawes, J. J. Johnston, Brian Robertson, Harry Shaffer, and Bill O'Laughlin. Dan Cuoco, Executive Director of the International Boxing Research Organization (IBRO); Arnold Thomas of Melbourne, Australia; Hall of Fame matchmaker Bruce Trampler of Top Rank, Las Vegas, Nevada; Iceman John Scully, former 175-pound contender and current trainer; George Kimball, award winning boxing writer and author; Nash Entertainment and their films of *Amazing Sports Stories*. Dave Bergin of Pugilistica.com, Sergei Yurchenko of Pereslavl, Russia, Tony Gee of London, England, Chris LaForce of South Carolina, David Chapman of Seattle, Washington and Tony Hood of Sydney, Australia, Jan Phillips Mackey of Prescott, Arizona, and sports collector Gary Schultz.

Robert Axtell, professor of Exercise Science at Southern Connecticut State University; Kurt Sollanek of the Exercise Science Department at Southern Connecticut State University; historian Janet Thompson of Albuquerque, New Mexico; editor Jean Johnson of Bishop, California; Ed Matthews of Placerville, California; Angela Haag of the Central Nevada Museum at Tonopah; and Dr. Theresa Runstedtler, assistant professor, American Studies, University at Buffalo, who provided the very important copies of the French newspapers *L'Auto* covering the 1909 Jennette-McVey fight in Paris. To the remarkable staff members and curators of special collections at the Library of Congress, Bibliotheque Nationale de France, New York Public Library, Chicago History Museum, and the Office of the State Historian, Santa Fe, New Mexico.

A very special thanks to Dave Wallace, engineer extraordinaire, for his endless patience working with the photographs for this book.

Individual thanks from contributors goes out to the following: From Colleen Aycock to Jason Wallace and Neil Wallace, for their creative perspectives and work with very old manuscripts. From Clay Moyle to the relatives of Sam Langford — great-granddaughter Carol Doyle and great-niece Rosemarie Pleasant. From Peter Benson to Mamadou Niang, who generously shared photographs with him. A number of other individuals provided information in the course of Benson's research, including Oumou Ball and Oumar Ly. He also wishes to express his abiding gratitude to Pino Mitrani and Nathalie Simmonot, and to Philippe and Dominique Certain, who put him up in Paris during several trips he made to do research there, and whose warmth and gracious hospitality made his stay in the French capital a pleasure. From Mike Glenn for his late father, Charles Glenn, who shared his passion for sports with him. From Michael J. Schmidt to Suzanna Walter, his wife, for her tireless efforts in reviewing drafts and giving her non-boxing thoughts, and son Jordan Schmidt for his tireless research efforts and for listening endlessly in regards to this project. And to his younger son Alex "The Jet" Schmidt, who passed away at the age of 15; your everyday joy of life continues to inspire.

Finally, the editors would like to express their gratitude to Hall-of-Fame announcer Al Bernstein, for agreeing to write the foreword for this book. The year 2010 marked the thirtieth anniversary of his debut as a national broadcaster, so along with our sincere thanks, we'd like to offer our congratulations as well.

Table of Contents

Foreword by Al Bernstein

It is a gross understatement to say that boxers are a special breed of athlete. With the possible exception of mixed martial artists and bronco or bull riding cowboys, no sport demands more courage and fortitude. When you make a mistake in basketball you give up two points, in baseball a run or two, or hockey a goal. In boxing when you make a mistake you get punched.

Added to the physical nature of the sport is the uncertainty of the endeavor. First of all, there is no set schedule, so you may never get the fight you want or need to advance your career, and at times you may be forced into fighting more tough opponents than someone else — for less reward. Then there is the mercurial way in which judges often score boxing matches. Justice is not always served. Months of work on a fight and sweat and blood during the match can be trivialized and wasted by some incompetent or biased judges.

This is what all boxers face in their career, no matter how well known or skilled they may be. As difficult as that sounds, it was much harder for one particular group of boxers — the black boxers just before and just after the turn of the 20th century. For those men the usual difficulties were compounded by enormous racial bias.

Whether it was obtaining meaningful matches, getting a fair decision on a fight, or even preserving their personal safety when they fought, black fighters of that era faced many obstacles. To examine those boxers you simply have to look at things through that prism. But, all that having been said, it would be a mistake to simply see them as societal victims. Despite the disadvantages these men carved out many special moments in boxing history — even if those moments have not always been celebrated as much as they should be — until now.

This extraordinary collection of writing about the African American and other black fighters of that era will provide the first comprehensive, documented acknowledgment of the achievements of these great boxers. There have been some excellent books written on individual fighters, but this collection paints with a wider brush to include many of the top black fighters of that era.

Just as these great athletes put their own personal stamp on their boxing performances, so do the different writers who contributed to the present work. Many boxing and writing styles go into making this book special. Both inside and outside the ring the athletes profiled within provided intriguing stories. The importance of the stories in many cases transcends sport. Even the ones that don't are important to tell because without them the history of boxing is incomplete.

I am honored to be able to write this foreword in the same year I am marking my 30th year as a boxing broadcaster. Over those three decades I've talked to many African American boxers who understood and appreciated what these pioneers did for them by paving the way in this sport. One of the most eloquent on the subject was the late great Archie Moore, who was a conduit from those fighters to a more modern era. Many believe that Archie himself suffered from a "black quota" of champions, and that explains why he did not get a title shot for so long. He outwaited those forces and won his world title after he reached 40 years of age, and he still hung onto the crown for seven years. As a young boxer he met some of the great black fighters mentioned in this book and was happy to absorb their wisdom.

Many boxing people like to quip that these days the only color that matters in boxing is green. With some exceptions that statement is true, but those exceptions remind us how important it is to revisit in great prose a time when it was not true. This book does that, and a lot more. Enjoy the read.

Al Bernstein, elected to the World Boxing Hall of Fame in 2009, is the only broadcaster in history to serve in the roles of analyst, blow-by-blow announcer, host, and in-ring interviewer. He has called more than 60 major pay-per-view boxing telecasts, has served as NBC's boxing analyst at Olympic Games and has been the voice of boxing on Showtime since 2003.

Introduction

This collection of essays includes 15 detailed biographies on some of the first masters of the ring who achieved fame in the early days of boxing. Drawing from the world's émigrés and masses of poor, the prize ring was one of the few places where men of African descent could garner riches, achieve celebrity, and battle for supremacy in mixed ethnic contests. Much to the dismay of some racial theorists at the time, the black pugilists became masters of this fistic domain, breaking through the "color line" and challenging stereotypes that labeled them with the so-called "yellowstreak," or "shiftlessness," and a "brutish indifference to pain." These athletes were the first in the sports world to issue a *défi* to white supremacy, but few today, other than boxing aficionados, have ever heard of their remarkable stories.

When our biography of *Joe Gans: the First African American World Boxing Champion* was published, fight fans from all over the world thanked us, saying that the book was long overdue. Many were curious about the early black fighters. What happened to them? There were so many talented black men of the ring during that era, yet the questions kept piling up. We thought a book that would answer these questions was sorely needed; therefore we solicited historians who had devoted special attention to the boxers dedicated in this work.

The decades immediately preceding and following 1900 were unique in the world of athletics. Bare-knuckle boxing, in which bouts were held on a field and contestants wore spiked shoes, was giving way to a new sport — that of gloved boxing, fought on canvas with felt-soled shoes. Transitioning from the earlier sport to the new from 1882 to 1892, American John L. Sullivan became a global superstar. Professors of Boxing, as they were called, set up gyms to train men in the new "science." These training facilities attracted men of all social classes. Eminent citizens, as well as professional hopefuls, flocked to the gyms for instruction. Holidays were enthusiastically anticipated, where the festivities began with patriotic parades and ended with pugilistic contests. Boxing simply upstaged all other forms of recreation and entertainment. Nothing today compares to the booming popularity of the fistic entertainment a century ago.

For the early black battlers, a boxing career oftentimes meant stepping across social lines and through the ropes for the express purpose of hammering a white man. Men with exceptional courage and phenomenal physical skills and stamina risked death when they entered the ring for fights to the finish (often lasting more than 40 rounds) making the events more dramatic than Spanish bullfights. Unlike today's professionals, these early boxers not only fought to the finish but also in back-to-back fights, particularly when they were in immediate need of a paycheck. In traveling road shows, they had to face all comers, usually unknown volunteers who challenged them from the audience. The black fighters in this book often fought more bouts in their first few years of campaigning than today's boxers do in their entire professional careers. Their superhuman endurance simply captivated the sporting world. The famously popular and controversial battles of men stripped down to their "boxers," methodically and scientifically pummeling each other under the watchful eye of a referee, rocked a society coming out of the Victorian era.

The period when most of these fighters plied their trade during the 1880s to 1920s corresponded to the Progressive Era in America and the *Belle Epoque* in France. New discoveries and industrial progress created unprecedented optimism. Cultural and scientific expositions flourished, with each showcase of progress trying to out-progress the previous one. From the American Columbian Exposition of 1893 to the Paris Exposition of 1900, boxing was among the marvels of the new age. In Chicago Gentleman Jim Corbett demonstrated his scientific boxing moves, along with the strongman Sandow. It was a time when science, sport, and the arts fed off each other.

After decades of fascination with Darwinist theories on race, survival of the fittest, and competition, the struggles of the prize ring captivated the experts. The boxers were measured and compared. The scholars debated: Who was more game, the Danes or the Irish? Who was the more menacing, the most enduring? How did the modern fighters compare to the ancients? The artists searched: Who exemplified the perfect man? These were the questions of the period. And, interestingly enough, their answer, at one point, came in the form of black Peter Jackson. More Greek than a Grecian god posed on a slab of marble, the naked body of Peter Jackson was studied as the figure unsurpassed by any other — the perfect specimen of man. It helped that he spoke the Queen's English and sounded more intelligent than his American cousins. Jackson's reputation in the ring and as a gentleman preceded his arrival on the California coast, and John L. Sullivan knew he couldn't compete with Jackson, the 6-foot giant, so he avoided him like the plague.

Pictures of the boxers evolved with the new media of film. Thomas Edison, the American inventor par excellence, had formed the Edison Exhibiting Company, and his first film made in the Black Maria studio in New Jersey was of a boxing match. The first profitable films made in America were fight films. The interest was worldwide, with boxers becoming the first movie stars, public celebrities in ways only politicians or military generals had enjoyed before. Boxing entertainment was big business, and a tremendous amount of money exchanged hands through the boxers (their entourage, management, and promoters), theater owners, and new filmmakers, not to mention the gambling enterprises.

With this spirit of entrepreneurial progress came a paternalistic notion that the new middle class, now with extra spending money, needed to be directed away from pouring their hard-earned income into harmful populist entertainment such as boxing and "peep shows." The profitable sport sparked a backlash of social reactions. Church members at the grass-root level condemned local boxing matches, calling them immoral, barbaric, anti–Christian activities. These citizens took on roles as *Reformers* of society. They lobbied local governmental authorities to prohibit boxing matches, long considered illegal entertainment, but condoned by a political and economic power base controlled by saloon-types they viewed as immoral. Over the course of time in the United States, laws governing the sport were tweaked such that boxing exhibitions became legal, scientific displays of human prowess. Because boxing's influence reached as far and wide as the various churches, the Reformers' calls were eventually heard in Washington, D.C. Following the disappointing outcome to mainstream America in the battle between Jim Jeffries (the Great White Hope) and black Jack Johnson in Reno, July 4, 1910, the Reformers successfully convinced Congress to ban fight films, the very sight of which was judged harmful to the young and distasteful to a civilized society.

After the Civil War, the black population in America may have been led to believe that they had become free and equal citizens. But such was not the case. Black Americans were forced to take the lowest paid, most dangerous jobs and submit to the status of second-class citizens. Dangerous, yes, but the boxing ring offered financial and social rewards unlike any other line of work. Prior to the Civil War, Tom Molineaux, the Virginia slave, earned his freedom in a prize fight. Champions like Molineaux, and later George Godfrey and Peter Jackson, gave hope and inspiration to former slaves and their descendants. Is it any wonder that black men were willing to risk injury and death to earn glory in the prize ring? In America, and in as far-flung places as the Antipodes, theatrical black-faced entertainment, bordello music, and boxing were three professions destined to transcend the restrictive remnants of colonial history. Yet for patronage, the black fighters were still dependant on white society.

The rise of black pugilists clearly alarmed many in the white establishment, their prowess in the ring directly challenging ideas of white supremacy. Boxing was considered the one area of competition where individual superiority could be decisively established. In 1895, the editor of the *New York Sun*, Charles A. Dana, wrote, "There are two negroes in the ring today who can thrash any white man breathing in their respective classes ... George Dixon ... and Joe Walcott." Dana was referring to two master boxers from the British Commonwealth countries of Canada and Barbados. Within ten years, Dixon would die destitute, while Walcott's career ended early because of a gunshot wound. Indeed, tragedies seemed to lie in wait for most of the early black gladiators, in the same way that calamities attended the voyage home of Odysseus.

All of the fighters in this collection had to overcome the adversity that went with being a black prize fighter on a world stage. They were cheated, mistreated, and scorned throughout their careers. Such was the paradox for black fighters — the better they were, the more of a threat they posed, and the more likely it was that a backlash would come their way. As a result, these black battlers were known primarily for their "defensive" skills. White fighters would come on strong, thrashing and hammering their opponents, aggressive from the outset. Black fighters against white opponents could ill afford to come on with such aggression. As a result, they developed the full skills of ring generalship, frequently "carrying" their white opponents or allowing them to wear themselves out in the ring, finishing them painlessly at any point they wanted.

Whether in America, England, or France, black fighters were accepted until they defeated white fighters. Oftentimes when a black fighter prospered in the prize ring, those behind the scenes were working busily to cheat him out of his glory. As early as 1810, Tom Molineaux, a freed slave, seemingly defeated the white world champion in England, only to have the crowd and officials at ringside rob him of his victory. George Godfrey and Peter Jackson were methodically denied opportunities to compete against John L. Sullivan for the world heavyweight title. Joe Gans, the first African American World Champion, was crucified in the press and robbed of his rightful title ownership in the history books. Most of the stories told here ended in tragedy, and yet these men were able to stake their claims to fame in the short time they spent on earth.

America was not the only country where racism continued to play an insidious role. The acclaim given by the French press to Sam McVey and Joe Jennette in 1909 seemed to indicate that black gladiators would be given a fairer shake in France. Jennette was acclaimed in the French press as a "paragon of courage," while McVey was so popular that they called him "our Sam." The French seemed to love the black battlers, and many great fights with black battlers were staged in the land of Napoleon. However, the tragic fate of Battling Siki dispelled that notion of French magnanimity a little over a decade later. Siki, conqueror of the legendary George Carpentier, was lampooned as a clown after winning the world light heavyweight championship. A Shakespearean figure to match Othello, Siki's tragic end came a few years after his astounding victory over Carpentier.

By 1900 black ringmen dominated the sport of boxing. From 1900 to 1915 there were four black "insuperables": Joe Walcott, 1901–1905, Joe Gans, 1902–1908, Jack Johnson, 1908–1915, and uncrowned light-heavyweight Sam Langford, all casting a "black shadow across the boxing world." Before he died, early boxing historian Nat Fleischer rated the first three as the all-time greatest in their respective divisions. If these were the acknowledged greats, why is the public not more familiar with them?

In reaction to what many of the day called "the Ethiopian menace," white sportswriters and sport historians in the 20th century touted the legacies of Anglo-Saxon and Western heroism, deluding themselves, even in their own histories, by the simple selectivity of the victors' historiography. Though Achilles of Greece clearly slew the easterner Hector the Trojan, would the story of their fight have been written differently if Troy had won the war? Does anyone really know how the Gods on Mount Olympus laid their bets? History is, of course, written by the winners and the dominant classes of society. So for years the black titans of the prize ring were forgotten or trivialized. Mainly, it was simply taken as conventional wisdom that white boxers were superior despite all evidence to the contrary. The Progressive Era was the age of big ideas, big money, and of ballyhoo. If men could garner enough publicity and gain the ear of the popular sportswriter or the magazine editor, men like Pierce Egan, Richard K. Fox, Nat Fleischer, Billy Naughton or Damon Runyon, they could get better fights, larger purses, or more than a footnote in the history books. We are fortunate that there were writers who admired these boxers, men like Tad Edgren, Rex Beach, Grantland Rice, George Siler, and others who wrote of their epic feats in the ring. But unfortunately, if a boxer couldn't garner the ballyhoo, he was lost in obscurity, as the majority of so many good black fighters were.

Yet another reason for the obscurity of these boxers can be found in large measure in America's reaction to the flamboyant Jack Johnson. The holder of the heavyweight championship was seen as the emperor of masculinity. And Johnson's image of that masculinity threatened an establishment eager to maintain social segregation. Unfortunately, the ones who paid for Jack Johnson's victories and flamboyant behavior were men like Sam Langford, Jack Blackburn, and others who would never be given the chance to challenge white ring supremacy as long as the public remembered Johnson's reign of terror as heavyweight champion.

Johnson was considered such a menace to society that Congress banned film of his fights. In a letter to the editor of the Baltimore *Afro-American Ledger* dated July 30, 1910, John T. Jennifer wrote about the ban: "How questionable is that spasmodic piety, which is moving a number of cities, churches, and societies to cause the elimination of the fight pictures 'in the interest of good morals,' when nearly every day in some town or city a Negro is either lynched or burned in site and sanction of some of its 'best citizens.' Such barbarism has no protest from American churches. Such piety is too thin to conceal its motives." Unfortunately, many white readers never quite got the terrible truth: As many times as these men were stepping into the ring to pummel white men for the sake of entertainment, other black men were being hung or burned at the stake for the sake of a perverted justice. Such were the times when these black fighters stepped through the ropes.

Once Johnson had been defeated, America wanted to hear nothing more about black fighters. With his golden smile and provocative ways, the career of Jack Johnson all but spelled *finis* to the hopes of black boxers from 1915 until the 1930s, when the quiet, unassuming ways of Joe Louis led white, mainstream America to accept the idea of having a black fighter at the top of the boxing world, especially since his arrival on the scene coincided with America's need to counter the impression that it treated blacks much as Nazi Germany treated Jews.

In putting together this collection, we were very fortunate to find writers who had painstakingly researched their subjects in Canada, America, Australia, France and Senegal (Siki's home country). An appendix also includes the blow-by-blow newspaper coverage of several of history's most hotly contested ring battles, many of them often listed as among the greatest fights ever. For the first time, we have a translated account, directly from ringside, of the 1909 Paris fight between Joe Jennette and Sam McVey.

Finally, boxing has never been just about boxing. What happened inside the ring's ropes had a significance that extended beyond sports. These men were the foot soldiers in the war against racism. They created opportunity and developed sportsmanship. They became great trainers and teachers, some traveling the world, becoming emissaries not only for the new sport of gloved boxing, but for new social attitudes. Ultimately, history needs to credit them for paving the way for other black athletes and performers in the 20th century.

CHAPTER 1

Tom Molineaux: From Slave to American Heavyweight Champion

Bill Calogero

In 1810, Great Britain not only ruled the waves, her sons were the undisputed masters of boxing's prize ring. Admiral Nelson had sunk Napoleon's fleet at Trafalgar Square, and Tom Cribb, king of the heavyweights, had turned back all challengers in the world of fistiana.

America was a young, upstart nation. In 1812, England would send an army to North America to put down what it still considered to be the revolting colonists. Only after the defeat of the British at the Battle of New Orleans would America's status as a free country be firmly established. However, a large proportion of the American population had no freedom at all.

Men like Tom Molineaux, born into slavery, gained their freedom only in extraordinary circumstances. And Tom's life was one of the most extraordinary ever lived. Not only would he earn his prize of freedom in the boxing ring, he would become the first American to go to England and issue a *defi* to the British champion and fight one of the bloodiest battles in ring history. America had once again laid down the gauntlet to her former master, Great Britain.

When Lord Wellington said of Waterloo a few years later that it was "the nearest run thing you ever saw," he might well have added "except for the great Cribb-Molineaux fight." The story of Tom Molineaux is the amazing story of how a former American slave came to challenge the world's greatest fighter in the world's most powerful country.

For many of the champions who were born into destitution, boxing has been a way to escape poverty. However, for America's first great champion, Tom Molineaux, who was born into slavery, boxing was a means to life as a free man. After having gained his freedom from servitude, he was able to travel the world in search of wealth and fame, both of which he achieved to the degree possible during his age. There may have been American fistic champions before Molineaux, but history has left few records. We are fortunate that the very first reporter of modern sporting events, a nineteenth-century chronicler of the sweet science, Pierce Egan, personally interviewed Molineaux and reported his feats from ringside in England.

Molineaux's is a quintessential American story, an up-from-the-bootstraps tale in which an individual could rise out of abject poverty and, through skill and perseverance, challenge the world's best. Molineaux was perhaps the first black man to exemplify the American ideal that your place in life is not situated in birthright but created by your acts. Sadly, as is the case with many of our great sportsmen, Molineaux's story did not have a happy ending. And, as with many of these early champions, his remarkable feats go unrecognized in the history books to this day.

Tom Molineaux appears to have been from a family noted for its boxing prowess. Zachary Molineaux, Tom's father, was a slave who took the surname of his owner and fought in the American Revolution in 1776. *The Ring* magazine founder, Nat Fleischer, credited him as the man responsible for bringing bare-knuckle boxing to the United States. According to Fleischer, Zachary Molineaux won many fights during his slave life after the Revolutionary War.[1] Zachary had five sons, Elizah, Ebenezer, Franklin, Moses and Tom. Tom Molineaux was born a slave on March 23, 1784 in Richmond, Virginia, on the Molineaux Plantation. Life for Tom as a boy on the plantation was the same as it was for all the others, which consisted of long days of hard work. By the time Tom was 14 years old, his father had died and young Tom solidified his position around the plantation as a chief handyman. He had big, broad shoulders, a deep chest and a thick neck. His appearance showed that he was a very strong young man.[2]

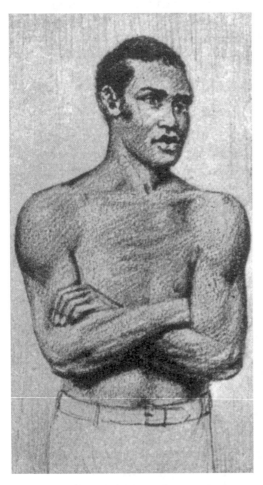

Molineaux set sail for England to issue a stout challenge to the British champion (Bill Calogero collection).

In 1801, when Tom was 17, Randolph Peyton, owner of a neighboring plantation, threw a party where he boasted that there wasn't a slave in any of Virginia's plantation families that could beat his slave, Abe, in a bare-knuckle contest. Tom's master, Algeron Molineaux, sent a message to all his slaves that he would grant freedom to any slave that could beat Peyton's slave Abe. Tom stepped forward and the match was set.[3]

The Molineaux family was one of the wealthiest plantation families and the result was that a considerably large amount of money was wagered on the outcome of the fight. So much money was bet on the fight that the Molineaux family would have been threatened with bankruptcy should Tom have lost. Algeron Molineaux didn't want to take any chances, so he hired Patrick Davis, a sailor from England on the ship *Margaret Elizabeth*, to help train Tom. After working with him for a short time, Davis told Algeron that he thought Tom was too docile and was not taking his training seriously. When learning of this, Tom was beaten and warned that the entire plantation was at stake. Master Molineaux upped the ante for Tom, promising him $500 along with his freedom for a victory. Tom's attitude changed. He resumed his training and did very well.[4]

When the time for the match came, Tom entered the ring in top shape, as did Abe. Once the bout began, Tom controlled it, giving Abe a brutal beating. He won the contest, pounding Abe into submission in less than five bloody rounds. True to his word, Algeron gave Tom the $500 and granted him his freedom. Tom didn't waste any time. He took nothing but the clothes on his back, his money and his newfound freedom, and left the Virginia plantation where he was born for good.[5]

It is not known exactly how he got there, or where he may have stopped along the way, but by 1804, Molineaux was in New York making his living as a professional fighter. He ended up in the Catherine Market area, where black men could fight each other and occasionally fight the English sailors who were on shore leave. The Catherine Slip during this time was one of the busiest ports in New York and was filled with a motley mix of fighters, seamen, street performers, businessmen and lowlifes. Fighting in America at this time was more of a "rough and tumble" style, devoid of skill or the science of boxing. The fights were brutal and were generally impromptu, staged when enough money was put up for the principals. It was here that Tom gained considerable notoriety and the reputation of a champion. Although no surviving printed accounts of any of these fights have surfaced, Molineaux must have been involved with enough of them to have the moniker "Champion of America" bestowed upon him.[6]

After beating all who dared to enter the ring against him and after speaking with the English sailors, who spoke of the popularity of prize fighting in England and the great amounts of money that could be made there, Tom took his title of Champion of America and set out for England to capture the world title.[7]

Exactly how Molineaux, who at this time was just about out of his ring earnings and didn't really know anyone, got himself hired on as a ship's mate on board the *Bristol* for its return passage to Liverpool, England is unknown. (The *Bristol*, with all of its manifest records, sank on December 16, 1819, off the coast of Wales at Porth Ysgo in Rhiw.)[8] What is known is that he arrived in London during the winter of 1809.

By the time he arrived in London, he was penniless. He visited the sporting houses and taverns boasting that he was the champion of America and could lick any man in England, including the heavyweight champion, Tom Cribb. Everyone thought he was out of his mind, this black man from America. After all, he was by himself without a penny in his pocket! He was told to seek out Bob Gregson, who was a popular heavyweight and owned Bob's Chop House, which was a gathering place for the fight crowd. Bob didn't see any future for Molineaux and decided to send him to "one of his own," another black fighter who was also born in America, Bill Richmond.[9]

After seeing Molineaux, Bill Richmond could tell he was in shape, but early on thought the same as Gregson did — no future. He did feel some sort of kinship towards the American, but thought that Molineaux may very well have been out of his mind. Being a smart businessman, Richmond thought that Molineaux was a novelty and figured he might be able to make a little money off of him, so he decided to take him in as his new fighter. After watching Tom train, he became even less impressed. His style was crude and he did not display the skills of a polished boxer. However, his physical makeup was impressive and Richmond thought that if he could break Tom of his American style of fighting and teach him some proper technique, maybe he could win a few fights on English soil. Richmond tried to teach Tom how to jab and to throw his right hand behind it. He also tried to break Molineaux of the way he was delivering his punches, which was in a downward motion, striking with the bottom of his clenched fist rather than landing a punch with his knuckles. This type of "hammer" punch was common in America, but would not fare well against

Early nineteenth-century artists were fascinated with ring engagements. French artist Theodore Gericault's famous lithograph *The Boxers* (1818) notes the hurly-burly of a Molineaux fight while a ringman reclines on the canvas (Bill Calogero collection).

the more scientific fighters in England. After working with Tom all winter, Richmond felt that Molineaux was ready for his first fight in England.[10]

Molineaux's initial fight in England took place at Tothill Fields in Westminster on July 24, 1810, against a 6-foot-tall, 210-pound Bristolean named Jack Burrows. Tom Cribb, the English Champion whom Molineaux wanted to challenge for the world title, trained Jack, who was virtually unknown. As a matter of fact, many referred to him as "The Bristol Unknown." By this time there was a considerable amount of interest in Molineaux, but of the three hundred spectators gathered to see "The New Black," as he was being called, none really knew what to expect. When Molineaux stripped his 5-foot-9-inch 196-pound frame to get ready for the contest, a collective sigh was heard. All in attendance saw Tom's muscles bulging underneath his glistening skin with every movement. There was no doubt that Tom was in top shape.[11]

The action-packed fight lasted for about an hour. Molineaux punished Burrows so thoroughly that it was impossible to distinguish a single feature on his face. Despite his crude style, Molineaux showed his strength and was declared the winner.[12] He received considerable attention from all of the spectators, who viewed him as a pugilist of promise.

Bill Richmond was pleased with Tom's performance, to a degree. The only reason Molineaux did not finish off his opponent sooner was due to his lack of technique. Despite working on the correct way to deliver a punch, Tom continued to use his "hammer blow," something Richmond meant to correct before his pupil's next fight. One other thing was accomplished during Tom's first fight on English soil: he got his first view of the English Champion Tom Cribb, whom Molineaux had come to England to fight in the first place. Cribb also had his first look at Molineaux and was not at all impressed. One person who was in attendance and who was extremely impressed with Molineaux was Lord George Sackville, the younger brother of the Duke of Dorset. He said that Molineaux was the equal of any man on the British Isles and offered to back Molineaux in his quest to unseat Tom Cribb as the English Champion.[13]

Molineaux continued to train and work on his technique with Richmond. He began to receive a lot of attention and enjoyed his celebrity status at Richmond's Horse and Dolphin Tavern. He received his first taste of fame from the diverse crowd that frequented the pub, which included the rich, the poor, the young and the old. What drew them all together was the love of sport. With his recent impressive victory, and the fact that Tom was an imposing black man who stood out no matter where he went, he became the "spice" of prizefighting. His performance added life to the sport, which was, at the time, experiencing a lull. He was viewed as being good for the game. At the same time, Molineaux became the focus of interest among the English women. Most women made no bones about the fact they had desires for "The New Black," and Tom loved every minute of it. He was having the time of his life, doing things that he had only dreamed of in the past. Bill Richmond knew that Tom's newfound celebrity could mean trouble, but did nothing about it.[14]

After Molineaux's English debut, Bill Richmond worked relentlessly to improve Tom's boxing skill while looking for a better quality opponent who would test his young fighter. He found the perfect opponent in Tom Blake, whose nickname was "Tough Tom." Blake was a sailor and was exactly what his nickname suggested, a real tough guy. He was an experienced fighter who possessed stamina, heart and strength, and would be a perfect gauge of how good Molineaux really was.[15]

Tough Tom had just returned from spending several years at sea and was as hard as nails, with a composition that was preserved by life on the sea. While at sea, he fought several fights and was eager to give "The New Black" a try. All that was preventing Blake from securing the fight was the 100 guineas forfeit amount required from each side. Once again, the Champion of England, Tom Cribb, got involved, putting up the money so the fight would take place. Less than one month after his first fight on English soil, Molineaux was set for his next fight at the Castle Tavern, a few miles from Margate at Epple Bay, on August 21, 1810.[16]

Because of Molineaux's first fight, his constant ridicule and calling out of Tom Cribb, along with his newfound fame, there was a considerable amount of interest in this fight. On the day of the fight, all types of vehicles (horse drawn buggies and carriages) as well as many fans on foot blocked the road on the way to the site of the fight. As it approached noon, Tough Tom made his entrance, seated in a colorful baronet's barouche. Molineaux was already at ringside waiting to get the fight started. (17)

Molineaux was seconded by Bill Richmond. Tough Tom had Tom Cribb as his second and Bill Gibbons as his bottle-holder. During the first round, there was immediate evidence of Molineaux's improved boxing skill. As the two combatants sparred with each other, Molineaux landed several devastating "hammer blows" to the back of Tough Tom's head, sending him down to end the first round.

During the second round, Blake came hard at Molineaux in an attempt to end the bout, but learned that although Molineaux was crude, he was no easy opponent. Despite receiving a solid punch on the jaw, Molineaux was not fazed; and by the end of the third round, Tough Tom was exhausted.

The fourth and fifth rounds saw Molineaux land many devastating blows to the face of Tough Tom, who in turn landed several solid shots to the body of "The New Black," though none seemed to affect him. By the beginning of the sixth round, Tom Blake was gasping for air, completely covered in blood and unable to hurt Molineaux whatsoever.

During the seventh and at the start of the eighth round, Tough Tom showed his fortitude, refusing to give in, despite the beating he was sustaining. The round and the fight ended abruptly when Molineaux landed a devastating punch to the head of Blake which sent him down and out and unable to recover in the time allotted, giving Molineaux his second victory on English soil.

After the fight, boxing fans felt that Molineaux not only had improved greatly from his fight a month before, but that Molineaux would give England's heavyweight champion a tough fight.[18]

The public began to talk of Molineaux as a worthy opponent for the champion, Tom Cribb. Many felt he could actually beat him. At this point, Cribb had been in something of a retirement because he felt there were no worthy opponents for him. Now, the public felt there was, but at first, Cribb stated that he had no intentions of coming back. When this comment spread throughout the boxing world, Molineaux made a statement that if Cribb would not fight him, then he should be considered the Champion of England. This was no joke. What started out as a search for a worthy opponent now became a concern. After all, Molineaux was an American, and to make matters worse, he was a black American. Now the honor of the country was at stake. Bill Richmond started a public campaign to have Tom recognized as the champion. While Richmond was working the public through the press, Molineaux could be found drinking and spending time with as many women as possible. He spent every penny he had on fine clothes and would frequently be seen walking down the streets with a pretty woman on each arm. He was not training and just couldn't say no to the offer of sprits or that of a fine woman. Finally, after much pressure, Tom Cribb agreed to fight Molineaux but demanded that the fight take place in December, which was longer than Bill Richmond wanted to wait. Cribb needed the extra time so he could get into shape. Both sides agreed, put up the required money and the fight was set.[19]

The fight took place at Copthall Common in East Grinstead, Sussex, which was about thirty miles outside of London, on December 18, 1810. The weather was terrible. The rain, which was a freezing rain, was described as coming down in torrents. Despite the unfavorable winter weather and the distance from the metropolis, over 10,000 fans came to witness this "World Championship Match-up." From royalty to people living in the streets, people of every type and social class trudged through knee-deep mud for over five miles to get a spot on the hillside where the fight would take place. The ring was formed at the bottom of a hill with a twenty-four foot area roped off. As soon as the ring was set and ready to go, which was a little after noon, the principals were ready to set-to. Molineaux was seconded by Bill Richmond and Paddington Jones and Cribb by John Gulley and Joe Ward. Cribb, and most in attendance, felt that the fight would not exceed fifteen minutes, with the English champion coming out of the contest the winner. Both combatants shook hands in the center of the ring and the fight was ready to begin.[20]

The first round was a feeling-out round. Both fighters landed a few shots. Molineaux landed a solid left followed by a hard right to the head of Cribb. Cribb had some problems

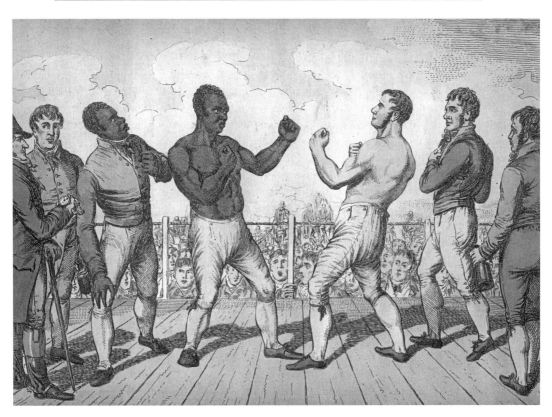

Engraving of Molineaux and Cribb in pre-fight pose as the official time-keeper (with cane) looks on. Molineaux is seconded by Bill Richmond (to the immediate left) and Paddington Jones; to the right of Cribb are John Gulley and Joe Ward. Caricatures such as this one, by an unknown engraver and published in October 1811, and those of English artist Thomas Rowlandson, influenced the twentieth-century American artist of boxing events, George Bellows.

finding the right distance, but landed a timed left under the eye of Molineaux. After an exchange of shots, Molineaux was thrown down to end the round.

The second round began with Molineaux landing a hard left to Cribb's head. Cribb answered with a powerful left of his own which landed on Tom's right eyebrow. To the astonishment of all in attendance, this punch had virtually no effect on Molineaux. Tom returned with a flurry of shots that opened up a cut on Cribb's mouth.

As the third round began, both fighters stood toe-to-toe and sparred. Cribb displayed the superior science, but Tom had improved significantly since his last fight with Blake. The round ended when a solid body shot thrown by Cribb landed under Tom's rib, sending him down on one knee.

The fourth round did not last long as Cribb landed a solid punch to Tom's face, and as a result of the ground now becoming wet and slick, Molineaux slipped down to end the round.

Everyone in attendance was treated to an action-packed fifth round. Both fighters landed devastating shots to the head and body. There were several exchanges that lasted over thirty seconds each, and by the time Molineaux slipped again from a jab, the crowd was on their feet cheering.

During the sixth, seventh, and eighth rounds, it became apparent that Tom Molineaux would not be an easy victory for Cribb. Although Cribb was landing hard punches, Tom was taking them and was not slowing down, and in return was starting to beat up on the champion.

By the time the ninth round began, both fighters were showing the signs of this extraordinary battle. Cribb's entire head was swollen and becoming disfigured. The top of Molineaux's head was also swollen, and blood was flowing freely from both boxers. Despite the damage on both fighters, this round continued at a fast pace. It ended when Molineaux landed a tremendous shot to the face of Cribb, which sent him down.

When the tenth round began, Molineaux actually started to show signs of tiring, but was able to rally and battered Cribb around the ring. Cribb was landing hard shots to the head of Molineaux, but they were not slowing him down at all. Cribb then began to throw punches at Tom while retreating, which was his specialty.

During the eleventh through the eighteenth rounds, the fight moved at a slightly slower pace, but both fighters were landing devastating shots to the head and body. During the fifteenth round, Cribb was leveled from a shot to his throat. During the seventeenth, Crib landed a body shot that sent Molineaux to his knees. The eighteenth round ended after a non-stop flurry that left both men exhausted. At the end, Molineaux went down from the impact of his own punch that he landed on Cribb's forehead.

By the time the nineteenth round began, both fighters were so disfigured and covered in blood that is was virtually impossible to tell them apart. It was astonishing to all those present that this fight was actually still going on. The brutality taking place before their eyes had never before been witnessed to this degree. During this round, Molineaux was on the attack as Cribb retreated backwards while trying to land jabs to the face of his aggressive opponent. Molineaux was able to get under Cribb's jab and pinned him against the ropes into a headlock and began pummeling him in the face. It was not looking good for the champion, as Molineaux appeared to be putting him away. Because he had him in the headlock, Cribb was not able to fall, which would have ended the round, so Molineaux kept pounding away to certain victory, which would have given him the title of World Champion.

This is where the first of two travesties took place. The fans were shocked at what they were witnessing. A black American was about to win the championship, and they could not let that happen. Almost two hundred spectators charged the ring. Many of them made it past the outer ring area to the roped off area and attacked Molineaux. They literally pried Tom's fingers to free his grip on Cribb, and in the process broke at least one of his fingers. As soon as he was free, Cribb fell to the ground, out cold. By the time order was restored, the ring cleared, and the fight was ready to continue, Cribb had recovered enough to come out for a few seconds to start the twentieth round, at which Molineaux sent him down quickly from a single shot to his head.

As the twenty-first round began, Cribb was coherent, and Molineaux started to show effects of the cold and freezing rain that had been falling since the beginning of the contest. Both landed hard shots, and the round ended when Cribb was thrown.

The twenty-second through the twenty-sixth rounds saw both fighters trying to catch their breath, but mostly sparring and occasionally landing hard shots to each other's head and body. By the time they came out for the twenty-seventh round, both were clearly weak but continued with heart that was truly amazing.[21]

When the two fighters started round twenty-eight, the overall consensus was, "how could they keep fighting?" Molineaux landed a devastating punch squarely on the face of

Cribb, sending him down and out. His seconds dragged the unconscious Cribb back to the corner in an attempt to revive him within the thirty-second time limit so he could come out for the twenty-ninth round. This is when the second travesty took place. When referee Sir Thomas Apreece yelled, "Time," Cribb was not able to continue. He yelled it again, and then again for a third time. Cribb was still out; and in all fairness, Tom Molineaux should have immediately been declared the winner. He was not. At that moment, one of Cribb's seconds, Joe Ward, leaped into the ring and accused Molineaux of having bullets in his clenched fists. Molineaux and his corner denied this, but Ward insisted, resulting in the referee demanding Molineaux open his hands for inspection. After doing so and finding that Molineaux did not have anything in his hands, Cribb, who had several minutes of extra time to recover, had regained his senses enough to come out for the twenty-ninth round.[22]

Cribb was still in serious trouble when the twenty-ninth round began, and it did not take much of a punch from Molineaux to again send the champion to the ground. At the start of the thirtieth round, Molineaux went after Cribb with all the power left in his body and once again battered Cribb around the ring. However, after landing a savage shot to the head of Cribb, followed by him grabbing the Champion and throwing him to the ground, Molineaux slipped and hit his own head on one of the ring posts, which sent him staggering back to his corner.[23]

When the thirty-first round began, Molineaux was still groggy from the fall and Cribb, known for his stamina, was able to land a powerful shot to the challenger's throat, sending him down to end the round.

The thirty-second round saw both men seemingly ready to fight again, but simultaneously, without exchanging a single punch, both fell from exhaustion to end the round.

From the thirty-third through the thirty-eighth rounds, neither man could do much. Both were beaten beyond recognition. Despite making it out for the thirty-ninth round and throwing a few punches at its conclusion, Tom Molineaux told his corner, "I can fight no more." Bill Richmond convinced him to come out for the fortieth round, but the game Molineaux fell from exhaustion and was counted out, giving Tom Cribb the victory.

This fight was the most ferocious and brutal fight to have taken place up to that time, and Pierce Egan felt that it was also the greatest battle he had ever witnessed. The amount of damage the combatants inflicted on each other is almost incomprehensible. The fight lasted for almost one hour. Both fighters had to be carried off and it took several days for each to recover enough to speak.[24]

Many people who were in attendance felt that Tom Molineaux lost as a result of foul play, and so did Tom himself. Although the pride of England was at stake, the taste of an improper result did not sit well with many boxing fans. As a matter of fact, most in attendance, and many who read about the great fight, felt a rematch was in order. After he healed enough to speak, Tom and his team published the following letter in the newspaper:

Pugilistic Challenge to Mr. Tom Cribb

Sir — My friends think that had the weather on last Tuesday, on which I contended with you, not been so unfavorable, I should have won the battle. I therefore challenge you to a second meeting, at anytime within two months, for such a sum as those gentleman who place confidence in me may be pleased to arrange. As it is possible that this letter may meet the public eye, I cannot omit the opportunity of expressing a confident hope that the circumstances of my being of a different color to that of a people amongst whom I have sought protection, will not in any way operate to my prejudice.

I am, sir, your most obedient humble servant, T. Molineaux.[25]

Tom Cribb was in no hurry to give Molineaux a rematch, despite the huge interest in the bout. Molineaux was the talk of the town and was one of the biggest celebrities around. His fame brought fortune, which he continued to spend on spirits, clothes and women. He was not training and began to believe that he did not need to. He thought he could beat any man alive. As much as Molineaux was enjoying his fame and new lifestyle, it was not cheap and he soon needed money. Bill Richmond needed to keep him busy as they continued to lobby for a rematch with Tom Cribb.

On May 21, 1811, Tom Molineaux stepped into the ring against a Scottish man from Lancashire, named Rimmer, in front of over 10,000 fans at Moulsey Hurst. Rimmer was a big man, but did not possess the skill to challenge Tom Molineaux. Molineaux used his power to punish Rimmer throughout the contest. With the exception of an incident that took place during the fight, Rimmer took a severe beating from start to finish. Because it was such a one-sided contest, the fans became agitated and stormed the ring at the conclusion of the fifteenth round, which resulted in a twenty-minute delay. Once order was restored, the fight resumed until Rimmer could not continue, giving Molineaux the victory in twenty-one rounds.[26]

It had been over six months since his controversial loss to the Champion of England, and after his victory over Rimmer, Molineaux was having a difficult time finding opponents willing to get into the ring with him. As a result, he and Bill Richmond continued to demand a rematch with Cribb. Because no one would fight Molineaux, and Cribb was not accepting the rematch challenge, Tom publicly stated, verbally and through the press, that he would claim the English title if Cribb would not agree to the rematch. Finally, Cribb, for the honor of England, agreed to fight Molineaux.[27]

The rematch was the biggest event that boxing had ever seen. It took place at Thistleton Gap on September 28, 1811. For the week leading up to the fight, there wasn't a vacant bed, a spot on the floor, in a barn, or even on the grass for anyone to sleep within miles of the fight site. Over 20,000 people were in attendance by noontime and the surrounding areas were mobbed with boxing fans trying to reach the site of the bout. When the two celebrities entered the ring, the applause exceeded anything of its kind.

Cribb was in top shape and although Molineaux looked like he was, truth be told, he hadn't trained seriously since the first fight. Both fighters met in the center of the ring and the fight began at 12:18 P.M.[28]

The fight began with Molineaux dominating, landing powerful shots to the face and head of Cribb. By the second round, Cribb was bleeding in several places, and by the beginning of the third round his right eye was almost swollen shut from the beating he was taking from the challenger. In the fourth and fifth stanzas, Molineaux seemed to be having his way with his opponent, landing devastating shots to the head and body. Cribb's blood flowed in steady streams, while Molineaux did not show any signs of damage.

When both fighters came out to start the sixth round, Molineaux was exhausted. The lack of training finally caught up with him. Cribb worked the body of his opponent with several hard punches, eventually dropping the tired challenger to end the round. Still huffing and puffing, Molineaux came out for the seventh only to be met by several hard shots to his head and to receive a devastating punch to the pit of his stomach, which sent Tom down again. In the eighth round, Molineaux could hardly lift his hands, and consequently took a severe beating, including a powerful right hand from Cribb that broke his jaw. The ninth round was much of the same, and it became evident that Tom was finished. Molineaux came out for the tenth round, but took more of a beating and was dropped to end the

Rural Sports, a Milling Match — Thomas Rowlandson's depiction of the 1811 Molineaux-Cribb fight.

round. He barely made it to the eleventh round, and could hardly stand. It only took a few punches for Cribb to knock Molineaux out cold. The total time of the contest was nineteen minutes and ten seconds.

Despite looking like the superior man physically, Tom's lack of training and his excessive drinking and womanizing had finally caught up with him, and the result was another loss at the hands of the champion of England, Tom Cribb.[29]

Following his second defeat to Cribb, Molineaux was not the same fighter. His drinking actually increased, he engaged in street fights, and failed to take any care of himself. He had a falling out with Bill Richmond that resulted in spending time in prison for what was noted as an unpaid debt. Afterward, he went on an exhibition tour that featured boxing and wrestling matches. He had three more significant fights.

On April 23, 1813, he won a twenty-five round decision over Jack Carter; however, it was a strange fight, indeed. Uncharacteristically, Molineaux acted afraid, running around the ring, yelling and screaming as if out of his mind. He made accusations that Carter was biting him and that his seconds were out to get him. Everyone in attendance was perplexed to say the least. After going through this for twenty-five rounds, all of a sudden, Carter passed out, resulting in a victory for Molineaux.

On May 27, 1814, he fought William Fuller twelve miles from Glasgow. Many noticed a compete change in Molineaux. He was not only a shell of himself in the ring in terms of his boxing ability, but his lifestyle had altered his appearance. This was not the same man who fought for the World Title in 1810. There was a lot of action in this fight. Molineaux landed several hard shots to the face of Fuller, which had him disfigured after the first round. The fight lasted only two rounds, but it took sixty-eight minutes for Fuller to end it when he landed a solid shot on Tom's face that knocked him out cold.

On March 10, 1815, he fought George Cooper in a lackluster performance. Molineaux was not able to defend himself and took a beating that lasted twenty minutes before Cooper was declared the winner.[30]

After the Cooper fight, he went to Ireland. While he was not fit to fight, he was met with great curiosity. He traveled through towns putting on boxing exhibitions or teaching boxing for whatever money he could get. His health was rapidly declining. He was suffering from the contagion of tuberculosis or what was called "consumption." His alcohol abuse and complications from disease had given his skin a yellow tinge. His eyes became sunken and his formerly fine-tuned muscles were now those of a fat and flabby man three times his age. Before long, he was unable to care for himself and had to rely on others to keep food in his stomach, clothes on his back and a roof over his head. In 1818 he ended up in Galway where his condition worsened. As much as he tried to keep teaching the science of boxing, his health prevented him from earning a living wage on a consistent basis. Three black soldiers that were members of the 77th Regiment of Foot Band befriended him.[31]

Tom Molineaux died on August 4, 1818, in a storage closet, penniless at 38 years old. At the time of his death, his disease had ravished his body. His once Herculean physique had been reduced to a skeleton, unable to walk. The only people at his side at the end were the three soldiers whom he had befriended only a few months prior to his death.[32]

Tom Molineaux's life history has been incomplete, a result of the poor record-keeping during his lifetime in the United States, made even more difficult because he was a black man during a time when most people did not consider him an equal. While there is now a great deal of intrigue about the early boxing great, facts are difficult to come by. An essay written by Lindsey Williams in the early 1980's claimed that George Washington introduced Tom Molineaux to Prize Fighting during the final years of his life.[33] According to author Bill Paxton, George Washington was at one time the Amateur Bare-Knuckle Boxing Champion as a sixteen-year-old teenager. If Washington had indeed taken an interest in the young Tom Molineaux, it would have occurred during the last years of the President's life when Molineaux was fourteen or fifteen.

Tom Molineaux is an important part of American history as well as world boxing history. He was a man who won his freedom in the prize ring, traveled around the world without friends or money, had no formal education, yet he accomplished more than most ever dreamed. He was blatantly robbed of the World Title, but it goes deeper than that one fight. The fact that he is virtually a forgotten man is even more of a travesty than his ring record. But we can correct the way his accomplishments are remembered, especially in the organizations that are in place to chronicle boxing's history and to distinguish its champions.

While the early British press recognized Tom Molineaux as an American Champion, based upon his accomplishments in the ring, Americans have done little to recognize him as the first champion. Today, the International Boxing Hall Of Fame and the Bare Knuckle Boxing Hall Of Fame both recognize Tom Hyer as the first American Champion, in 1849. They also recognize George Godfrey as the First Black American Champion, in 1879. However, Tom Molineaux left the United States in 1809, making him the first American to fight for the heavyweight championship, the first American to fight in an international championship fight, and the first African American to fight for a championship. And he accomplished these feats 70 years prior to George Godfrey, 40 years prior to Hyer, and 50 years prior to the international heavyweight bout in England between British Tom Sayers and American John C. Heenan. Without the illegal interference of the hostile British crowd, Tom Molineaux would have been recognized as the first black world heavyweight champion, a century before Jack Johnson. Considering that Molineaux used the prize ring first to win his freedom in a fight to the finish and then, ultimately, to challenge the Champion of England who many believed to be the best fighter up to that point in time, Molineaux's accomplishments place him in the top rung of boxing's immortals.

NOTES

1. Nat Fleischer, *Black Dynamite, Vol. I*, Chapter II, page 20. Nat Fleischer takes his information from Pierce Egan's statement in *Boxiana*, "Unknown, unnoticed, unprotected, and uninformed, the brave Molineaux arrived in England: descended from a warlike hero, who had been the conquering pugilist of America, he felt all the animating spirit of his courageous sire, and left his native soil in quest of glory and renown."

2. Fleischer, 34.
3. *Ibid.*
4. Fleischer, 34–35.
5. *Ibid.* See also, the International Boxing Hall Of Fame website, *www.ibhof.com* under Enshrinee information for Tom Molineaux.
6. "Molyneux V. Cribb First Fight for World's Championship," *Boxing News,* December 8, 1925; and Kevin Smith, *Black Genesis: The History of the Black Prizefighter 1760–1870*, Ch. 3, 29–30.
7. Mike Glenn, *The Integration Of Sports History: The Mike Glenn Collection, Vol. 2*, 12.
8. Information on "The Bristol" is located at: *http://www.rhiw.com/y_mor/shipwrecks/the_bristol.htm*, January 10, 2010.
9. Fleischer, 36.
10. Smith, 30.
11. Smith, 30–31.
12. *Ibid.*
13. Pierce Egan, *Boxiana, Vol. I*, 317.
14. Smith, 32.
15. Smith, 33.
16. Egan, 317.
17. Smith, 34.
18. Fleischer, 38.
19. Egan, 317–319.
20. Smith, 36–37.
21. Egan, 354–355.
22. Egan, 355–360.
23. Glenn, 17.
24. Smith, 43.
25. Egan, 361–362.
26. Smith, 44.
27. Fleischer, 40.
28. J.B. McCormick, *The Square Circle: Stories of the Prize Ring*, 61.
29. Smith, 51–52.
30. Fleischer, 41–42.
31. Smith, 58–59.
32. Egan, 418–419.
33. Williams information came from M.L. Weems (former Rector of Mt. Vernon Parish), *The Life of George Washington with Curious Anecdotes*, M. Carey & Son: Philadelphia, 1818.

CHAPTER 2

George Godfrey: First Colored Heavyweight Champion

Tony Triem

More often than not today, the name "George Godfrey" recalls the Leiperville Shadow (Philadelphian fighter Feab Smith Williams, managed by early boxers-turned-trainers, Bobby Dobbs and Jack Blackburn), a leading black heavyweight contender and sparring partner of Jack Dempsey in the late 1920s. Williams, who like his mentor, carried the title "Colored Heavyweight Champion," adopted the fighting name, "George Godfrey," in tribute to the earlier heavyweight fighter from Canada during the era of John L. Sullivan. The original George Godfrey, known as "Old Chocolate," would go down in the history books as the first American Colored World Heavyweight Champion, forever known as the man John L. Sullivan refused to fight.

Godfrey entered the field as boxing transitioned from bare-knuckle prizefights to gloved boxing events. He fought throughout the 1880s and 1890s, and wore everything from skin-tight gloves to 2- and 4-ounce gloves. At 5'10½" and weighing not more than 175 pounds, George Godfrey was never much bigger than a light heavyweight by today's standards, but was so quick, clever, and especially game, that he fought anyone, regardless of weight. Sadly, we will never know if he could have been the world heavyweight champion, without the color factor, because he was never allowed a title fight when he was at the top of his game. Boxing in America during this time was largely segregated by race, and although Godfrey fought many of the top black and white heavyweights of his era, he was denied the ultimate opportunity to cross the color line to contend for a title outside his race. For years he challenged white boxer and champion John L. Sullivan. However, despite claiming he would do so any time a sufficient purse could be raised, Sullivan consistently refused to fight Godfrey, or any other black man.

George Godfrey was born on March 20, 1853 (although some sources incorrectly state 1852) in Charlottetown, Prince Edward Island, Canada, in a neighborhood known as "The Bog."[1] A poor part of Charlottetown, the area had a high concentration of blacks, almost all of whom were descended from slaves brought to the Island in the 1780s as a result of the American Revolution. The Bog was notorious for its poverty and minor crimes such as bootlegging and prostitution. A member of Godfrey's mother's family, Peter Byers, was hanged for theft in 1815, and the year after Godfrey was born, his father was convicted of petty larceny, serving two weeks in jail for stealing a cow.[2]

Godfrey left Prince Edwards Island in his youth, around 1870, and traveled to Boston, Massachusetts, thereafter calling the Hub City home. (Boston has long been called the Hub City by New Englanders who consider it the hub of the universe.) Godfrey found work as a porter in one of Boston's silk importing offices. By 1879, at the late age of 26, he had taken up boxing and began fighting competitively during what was still known as the bare knuckle era.[3] At that time he could not afford to support himself through prize fighting, so he worked during the day as a beef carrier for the Boston Market. He did all of his training and fighting at nights. Later, he married a white woman and worked as a carpenter while he still tried to make it in the fight game.[4]

The origin of Godfrey's fight name is difficult to fathom because he was not especially aged by today's standards and was so light skinned that his subsequent heirs considered their race to be white.[5] However, 26 was considered old for one first entering the sport in the late 1800s, and Chocolate was a common epithet for blacks of the period. A similar ring name, "Little Chocolate," was given to George Dixon — a smaller, contemporary black boxer from Halifax.

Boston was noted for the sport of boxing, and Godfrey was followed to the area by several other black fighters from the Bog, notably George (Budge) Byers, a prominent turn-of-the-century middleweight. Godfrey's fame as a boxing star would rise in the eastern horizon simultaneously with white boxers John L. Sullivan and Jake Kilrain.

George Godfrey in boxing pose, circa 1882 to 1885 (Tony Triem collection).

Godfrey was trained by noted black professional, Professor John Bailey, who ran the Hub City Gym in downtown Boston.[6] At Bailey's club Godfrey was first matched with John L. Sullivan in 1880. The match earned Godfrey a great deal of notoriety. Both fighters hailed from Boston, both claimed that they could lick anyone in the fight business, and consequently, both headed for a showdown. On September 21, 1880 Sullivan and Godfrey agreed to a fight to the finish at Bailey's Gym. What occurred that night would be debated for years to come. It appears that both fighters were dressed and ready to fight; but once the police were informed of the fight, the bout was halted before the first round. Godfrey would go to his grave claiming that Sullivan conspired with police to have the bout cancelled so that Sullivan would not have to face him and risk losing.[7] Sullivan would later say that he would never fight a black man. Godfrey would spend the rest of his fighting life challenging Sullivan, but the Boston Strong Boy never answered the challenge.

George Godfrey's career interactions with another heavyweight white boxer, Jake Kilrain, had different results. On January 15, 1882, in Boston, early in both of their careers, Godfrey fought Kilrain to a draw in three rounds. Kilrain won their second three-round match on May 16, 1883. The two would not fight again until March 13, 1891.

The week after the first Kilrain fight, in 1882, Godfrey traveled to New York to fight Professor Charles Hadley, a noted black boxer. The two fought to a draw. Again, Godfrey met the Professor in New York in a tournament for an official title, in a contest beginning February 7, 1883. The best black boxers were invited to a tournament sponsored by boxing enthusiast and newspaper publisher, Richard K. Fox, to contend for a *National Police Gazette* Belt for the "Colored Heavyweight Champion." Nat Fleischer mentioned this belt as being for the "heavyweight championship of the colored race."[8] This event was apparently the origin of a title which would be used well into the 1920s. Godfrey won the title and successfully held the Colored Heavyweight Championship, defending it for five years against the likes of McHenry Johnson, whom he fought three times. Godfrey maintained the title until he was bested by Australian Peter Jackson when he came to the United States in 1888.

Lithograph depicting John L. Sullivan (Library of Congress Prints and Photographs Division).

The second half of Godfrey's career would find him in the ring with stellar heavyweights Peter Jackson in 1888, Jake Kilrain in 1891, Joe Choynski in 1892, and Peter Maher in 1894. Far older than his opponents, Godfrey would lose to these distinguished men of the ring. It is an interesting fact that, unlike others whose stars fade after they begin to lose, Godfrey's reputation became all the more heroic during the latter part of his ring career. He was the one man during this era whose name was synonymous with gameness. His bouts in the ring displayed tremendous courage and sportsmanship. And for these reasons, many younger fighters looked to him for their education and training.

Most of the heavyweight battlers were relocating to the California fight center. While Nat Fleischer credits W. W. Naughton, sportswriter for the *San Francisco Examiner,* for inviting Australian Peter Jackson to the United States, it is not clear if the scribe brought him to the United States or simply helped to arrange a fight after he arrived in California.[9] When Jackson arrived, San Franciscan promoters began trying to arrange a marquee fight. First choice John L. Sullivan refused to fight the newcomer. Sullivan's career was riding high, and although the Champion of the Pacific Coast, as Sullivan was billed, was thought to be unbeatable, he refused the purse said to be a fortune offered by the California Athletic Club. Organizers sent for George Godfrey as their second choice (a choice which explains just how good Godfrey really was.) Patrons of the sport would not be disappointed.

According to the *San Francisco Chronicle,* August 25, 1888, "It is doubtful if any contest that ever took place in San Francisco attracted as much attention from ring-goers and the lovers of sport generally as that between the colored pugilists, Peter Jackson and George Godfrey, in the gymnasium of the California Athletic Club last night. The records of both men are already familiar to every one who pays attention to the achievements of professors of the manly sport."[10]

In brief exhibitions prior to the match, spectators were favorably impressed with Jackson's boxing abilities. They witnessed everything rumored about the "champion of champions:" he was "clever as old Jem Mace, with all the dash and reach essential to a first-class heavy-weight pugilist. The local men pitted against him were totally unequal to the task of making him extend himself, and all his exhibitions were no more than pleasant exercise just barely conducive to perspiration."[11] More than anything, Jackson was a curiosity: he could speak like an English gentleman and fight like an African lion. Unlike the American heavyweight gladiators of the period who rushed at their opponents head-on and who timed their punches and defensive head movements, Jackson was faster, more clever, and had more pugilistic tools in his arsenal.

Professor Charles Hadley, noted boxer and teacher, ran a gym in New York. The win in the Richard K. Fox–sponsored tournament against Hadley gave Godfrey the title of Colored Heavyweight Champion (Tony Triem collection).

The California Athletic Club set the purse at $1,500, which it offered to the winner, and gave Godfrey $400 for travel and expenses. Jackson's training quarters were set up at Tiburon, by the seashore, and Godfrey went into seclusion in San Leandro at Joe Deaves' hostlery.[12]

The preliminaries began at 8 o'clock with a full house. Billy Jordan served as master of ceremonies, which meant that he brought in the two chairs for the corners, placed gloves on each chair, and introduced the first match between Young Brady and Professor Gagan. A second match between Young Hartz and Billy Madden brought some heavy hitting that thrilled the attendees. However, the last preliminary battle between Kineally of the Olympic Club and Tom Johnson was so tame that many hissed the boxers.[13]

On August 24, 1888, precisely at 9:05 P.M., Billy Jordan held up the 4-ounce mitts that would be used in the marquee event between Jackson and Godfrey. Godfrey was attended by Arthur Chambers and Tom Cleary, and Sam Fitzpatrick and Young Mitchell served the Australian. Godfrey looked perceptibly smaller than most Californians had expected from his ring notoriety. His hair was cut close to his scalp and his mustache was stubby.

Peter Jackson appeared in several drawings for the *National Police Gazette* from 1894 to 1900.

There was a slight delay after Godfrey appeared and the spectators grew impatient. At 9:15 P.M. the tall Australian pugilist entered the ring, wearing white tights and black laced shoes.

Hiram Cook had been chosen referee, W. W. Naughton timekeeper for Jackson, James Corbett timekeeper for Godfrey and Dave Eisner timekeeper for the club. Billy Jordan introduced the pugilists: "George Godfrey of Boston," proclaimed Mr. Jordan, and a faint cheer went up. "Peter Jackson of Australia," said Mr. Jordan, and a great shout shook the gymnasium.[14]

Referee Cook ordered the men to shake hands. They shed their robes and walked to the scratch. The difference in size was discouraging to the Bostonian's friends. Jackson towered three or four inches above Godfrey and weighed 190 pounds to Godfrey's 165 pounds. Their contrasting styles were immediately noticeable when they squared off. Jackson held his guard low, and Godfrey held his hands high with his feet wider apart.*

In the beginning of the 1st round, each fighter exchanged light punches to measure their reach. Then Godfrey rushed the Australian, electrifying the crowd. When Jackson tried to lead, Godfrey stopped the punch and returned a solid hit on Jackson's jaw and followed it up with a right that the reporters said would have dropped an ox. The

See the complete round-by-round report of this fight in the Appendix.

exchanges in the opening round were so fast and furious, with such savage rushes by Godfrey that many thought a kayo was eminent. Outsized, but not outclassed, Godfrey weathered the storm of Jackson's methodical precision and machine-like punishment.

Jackson came out in the 2nd round on the offensive, working his opponent to the ropes with a left to the chin and a right to the ribs. While Jackson punished Godfrey along the ropes, the Bostonian never flinched. Away from the ropes, Godfrey tried to spar at long range but could never reach the taller man. One rally resulted in Godfrey being hit on the jaw and sent to the floor. Godfrey led time and again, but was hit in the face and ribs repeatedly with Jackson's straight left. Reporters said that there was more savage fighting without flinching in these first two rounds than in any full-length fight the club had seen previously.

The first clinch of the fight occurred in the 3rd round, and after light sparring, Jackson landed a blow so hard that many thought Godfrey's shoulder had been broken. By the end of the round, Godfrey was bleeding from his injured shoulder and a cut to his mouth.

Both men landed hard punches in the 4th and 5th rounds. Godfrey came to the scratch of the 5th spitting a mouth-full of blood. Godfrey was hit so hard on the left eye during infighting in the round that the eye bled for the rest of the fight. Reporters busily dictated comments for the wires that fighting such as this had never before been witnessed in the ring. While Godfrey appeared "fairly slaughtered, he fought like a tiger," and Jackson's shorts were soaked with blood.[15] The end would have come had not Jackson's wind given out as the round ended.

With the fight less than half over, Godfrey came out for the 6th round gamely smiling and bleeding. Again, Jackson methodically worked his man to the ropes. Godfrey braced himself and continued to fight like a tiger through the next round. His endurance was beyond compare and the tide seemed to favor him in the 8th. He was able to dodge Jackson's swings in the 9th and 10th rounds with his clever defenses.

How Godfrey's courage held out when Jackson drove him to the ropes and beat him to a pulp in the 12th round was beyond anyone's comprehension. His superhuman endurance, ducking and fighting, kept Godfrey in the fight for the next three rounds.

By the 16th Jackson was out of breath, unable to deliver the *coup-de-grâce*, and Godfrey "was bleeding at every pore."[16]

Godfrey came out gamely for the 17th round, but Jackson had it all his own way. Godfrey "staggered like a drunken man and was barely able to lift his hands, even for defense, but the end of the 17th round found him still on his feet."[17] When Jackson forced him to the ropes and hit Godfrey squarely over the heart, the Colored Heavyweight Champion of American dropped his hands and ended the fight.

Godfrey was able to walk to his dressing room, disappointed that he could not win. His friends drove him to the Hammam baths on Dupont Street, where he spent the night.[18] Jackson left the hall and was given a champion's welcome by his friends, and hailed as the new wonder on American soil.

After the fight, few would consent to a go with Jackson, while Godfrey, who was considered unbeatable prior to the Jackson fight, would have many offers. The newspapers noted Godfrey's successful career and how the professor of boxing had beaten "some of the best men in the pugilistic business including Joe Lannon, Dominick, George LaBlanche, Jack Ashton and Ed Smith."[19] After his winning bout in 1890 in Providence, Rhode Island, against Patsy Cardiff, who was considered one of the cleverest heavyweights of the day, Godfrey was in line to meet Jake Kilrain.

On March 13, 1891, only a few days shy of his 39th birthday — considered very old for a prize fighter — Godfrey met Jake Kilrain of Baltimore for a fight to the finish with a purse of $5,000 at the California Athletic Club. The fight would go a brutal 44 rounds. Godfrey was greatly outweighed, and, as the papers noted afterwards, he had no real chance of victory from the call of time.[20]

Kilrain had been trained for the battle and was now seconded by Bill Muldoon. The betting odds were 4 to 3 in Kilrain's favor, largely due to the fact that Kilrain's backers were more numerous. Godfrey's seconds were Frank and Jack Steele, with Peter Jackson the bottle holder. Both fighters were 5'10½", but Kilrain weighed 192 to Godfrey's 173 pounds.[21]

When time was called at 9:53 P.M., Godfrey assumed his usual form, with weight on his back leg and left arm extended. Kilrain stood more casually. The men came together, inflicting shots to the ribs and numerous blows to the face. Kilrain was more inclined to rush his opponent, while Godfrey blocked Kilrain's leads with patient science.

In the 3rd, Godfrey led with a rush. Kilrain landed a good left on Godfrey's cheek. But Godfrey just smiled and evened things up by giving Kilrain a light bruise under the left eye.

In the 4th, both men swung powerfully and guarded successfully, with Kilrain landing a punch in the chest that caused Godfrey to moan.

While Godfrey retained his cool demeanor, Kilrain lost his, twice in the 5th putting Godfrey into a head lock, causing the crowd to cry foul. By the end of the 6th, Godfrey had taken several of Kilrain's lefts to the cheek, cutting a swath in his temple.

In the 7th, Godfrey dodged most of Kilrain's punches and took his time responding, eventually scoring with a lefthander.

The fight progressed slowly for the next half hour, each combatant landing blows over

Sullivan (left) and Kilrain in Richburg, Mississippi, in 1889 for the last bare-knuckle title fight (Library of Congress Prints and Photographs Division).

time that dazed their opponent, although the papers noted that Godfrey appeared to be receiving most of the punishment.

By the 23rd round reporters noted that "Godfrey had up to this time taken punishment sufficient to wear out any pugilist, but the contest apparently was no nearer termination than half an hour before. He continued to receive punches in the mouth, jaw and ear with perfect equanimity that seemed to nonplus the doughty Baltimorean."[22]

Not until the 26th round did Kilrain punch Godfrey to the ropes, hammering him until the bell rang. But Godfrey still went to his corner smiling.

From the 27th to the 35th rounds, the fight was nothing more than an endurance contest. Both men landed punches, but the manner in which Godfrey absorbed more of the punches precluded Kilrain from an easy win.

In the 36th round "Kilrain started in to force matters, and encouraged by cries of the spectators he threw Godfrey to the floor. He then proceeded to knock him about the ring and drove him into his corner, over and against the ropes until it seemed impossible for the Negro to stand. Twice he fell into the chair and once he fell helpless through the ropes, and just before the gong sounded he sank helpless to the floor, all but out. He rose two seconds before the gong sounded amid uproarious applause and so great was Kilrain's exhaustion he could not touch the man who needed but a touch to go down."[23]

By the 37th round, Kilrain was too weak to end the fight, and neither fighter was able to do much damage. The next few rounds passed uneventfully.

But in the 40th round, Kilrain came out with renewed energy and began his long, two-handed drive for Godfrey's head. "The latter stood feebly against the ropes unable to do anything, taking whatever punishment, Kilrain had strength to administer."[24] Godfrey fell through the ropes landing on his head. He struggled courageously to get back into the ring, but only managed to get his head over the ropes. At that point, he was counted out and carried to his chair by his seconds. The crowd cheered wildly, but it was not for the victor's late win, rather Godfrey's gameness in the face of inevitable defeat.

Where Godfrey had to give up twenty pounds to Peter Jackson and Jake Kilrain, in his fight against Joe Lannon the next year, he would not give up as much poundage. Lannon would only weigh in ten pounds heavier, at 185 pounds, than Godfrey's 175, although reporters said Lannon looked heavier.[25]

Godfrey went into the fight with Lannon favored to win. Godfrey had Howie Hodgkins, Frank Steele and Jim Godfrey, his brother, in his corner, and Lannon was helped out by Jack Barnett, Billy Mahoney and Dan Murphy. Charley Johnson was the time-keeper for Lannon and Tom Kenny for Godfrey. All those men were Bostonians, except Johnson, who was the backer of John L. Sullivan. Al Smith was the referee.

The fight lasted only four rounds. It was said to have been a grudge match, and as a result, the boxers went on the attack from the outset. Godfrey smiled throughout, even when Lannon landed a vicious punch, a gesture that Godfrey always used in his matches and one that Jack Johnson would later imitate. In the last round Godfrey knocked Lannon down, and fell with him as they clinched, wherein Godfrey scored two good licks before they went down. Lannon was plainly groggy as he tried to rise from the knockdown. Lannon was thoroughly exhausted from Godfrey's blows to his ribs and face. Just before the end of the round Godfrey rushed his man to the corner, smashed him against the ropes and punched him repeatedly. After the gong sounded Godfrey continued to punch and landed a stiff right hander to Lannon's ribs. The spectators cried "foul," and Lannon tried to fight back, but he was too exhausted to have any effect on Godfrey.[26] Godfrey escaped with only a small cut over his left eye. After the men went to their corners, Lannon's seconds claimed the decision, and refused to allow their man to return for another round. The referee would not allow the claim of foul, and gave the verdict to Godfrey. Lannon's friends protested, but to no avail.

Godfrey would fight and lose a fifteen-rounder to Joe Choynski in 1882 and a six-rounder to Peter Maher in 1884. He would fight once in 1885 in Baltimore and win on a foul in the 9th when his younger opponent became frustrated after being knocked about the ring and even floored once. He concluded his ring career with a fifteen-round draw against Nick Burley in Boston, Massachusetts.

His fighting career spanned 17 years, from January 1, 1879 to March 5, 1896. He had a ring record of 22 wins, with 17 of those wins coming by way of knockout. He lost 6 times, and of those 6, he was knocked out 5 times. He had 14 draws with 3 no contest bouts for a total of 45 fights. Some sources state Godfrey had 100 bouts, but those fights have not yet been confirmed. Historians suggest that Godfrey's temperate habits played a role in his long, successful career.

Godfrey continued giving boxing exhibitions, returning to Prince Edward Island for this purpose a few years after his last fight. He also opened a gymnasium and boxing school on Hanover Street in Boston, turning a profit and investing carefully in property in the area.[27] Throughout his life he was known for being hardworking, thrifty and economical, leaving his children a sizeable fortune after his death.[28] He died in his home October 17, 1901 (some sources say August 18) at the age of 48 after suffering from what was at the time reported as "dropsy."[29] Dropsy, an accumulation of fluids causing swelling of the ankles, was more likely the result of congestive heart failure.

By today's standards, Godfrey's life was cut short, but in 1901 the average life expectancy for a black man was only 35 years of age.[30] "Old Chocolate" was revered by the leading citizens of Boston, who signed on for his courses in the "manly art," and the fans and professionals who witnessed his phenomenal gameness during the era of John L. Sullivan. But by 1920 when the title Colored Heavyweight Champion was no longer in use, George Godfrey was largely forgotten by a newer generation of boxing fans looking to crown a heavyweight champion.[31]

NOTES

1. "George Godfrey," BoxRec.com 2009, accessed December 15, 2009. http://boxrec.com/media/index. php?title=Human:46632

2. Ibid.

3. "George Godfrey," African American Registry, Web. *http://www.aaregistry.com/show.php*, Accessed January 15, 2010.

4. "Birthday of Famous 'Old Chocolate,'" *Chester* (Pennsylvania) *Times*, March 20, 1915.

5. "George Godfrey," BoxRec.com 2009, accessed December 15, 2009. http://boxrec.com/media/index. php?title=Human:46632

6. Kevin Smith, *The Sundowners*, 509–510.

7. Ibid.

8. "Professor Charles Hadley," BoxRec.com, 2010, Accessed January 10, 2010. *http://boxrec.com/list_ bouts.php?human_id=40008&cat=boxer*. In addition, Nat Fleischer mentions this belt in *Black Dynamite*, 98.

9. Nat Fleischer, "Peter Jackson," *Black Dynamite, Vol. I*, 137.

10. "GODFREY GIVES UP: Jackson Batters Him for Nineteen Rounds: Game and Exciting Fight to the Close: The Bostonian Is Badly Injured by the Australian's Heavy Blows," *San Francisco Chronicle*, August 25, 1888.

11. Ibid.

12. Ibid.

13. Ibid.

14. Ibid.

15. Ibid.

16. Ibid.

17. Ibid.

18. Ibid.

19. "Pugilist Talk," *Bismarck Daily Tribune*, May 12, 1891.

20. Ibid.

21. "Jake Kilrain VS George Godfrey: The Balti-

morean wins In Forty Four Rounds," *The Daily Republican* (Fresno, California), March 14, 891.

22. Ibid.

23. Ibid.

24. Ibid.

25. "Godfrey Defeats Lannon: Four Rounds Settled It: Godfrey Comes Out the Victor in the Fight with Lannon," *Fitchburg* (New York) *Daily Sentinel*, May 17, 1892.

26. Ibid.

27. Smith, 511.

28. "Birthday of Famous 'Old Chocolate,'" *Chester* (Pennsylvania) *Times*, March 20, 1915.

29. "George Godfrey," BoxRec.com, 2009. Accessed December 15, 2009. http://boxrec.com/media/index.php?title=Human:46632

30. In 1901 a white male lived, on average ten years longer than a black male. By 2006, African Americans still lived five fewer years than white Americans, 69.5 years for black males, and 75.8 for white males. Lance Chilton, "African-Americans Still Face Disparities in Health," *Albuquerque Journal*, Health, C3, January 18, 2010.

31. "Birthday of Famous 'Old Chocolate,'" *Chester* (Pennsylvania) *Times*, March 20, 1915.

CHAPTER 3

Peter Jackson: Heavyweight Champion of Australia

Bob Petersen

Peter Jackson was the best fighter of the 1880's, and today is still considered one of the best heavyweights in history. In 1886, Jackson won the heavyweight championship belt of Australia. Going to the United States in 1888, he defeated all comers and won the "Colored Heavyweight Championship of the World" by defeating George Godfrey in San Francisco. Hoping for a fighting paycheck, Jackson ventured across the Atlantic in 1889, where he beat Jem Smith, champion of England, in a non-title fight. His career stalled in the United States when world champion John L. Sullivan refused to fight unless Jackson paid him an appearance fee of $30,000 for a bout in Texas. Whether he would have met Jackson, even if the outrageous sum could have been raised, is doubtful. Jackson's wish to become undisputed champion of the three fighting countries, England, Australia, and America, was thwarted when, upon his return to the States, Sullivan's successor James J. Corbett also avoided his challenges. Well past his prime, but still considered a formidable opponent, Jackson's pleas fell on deaf ears in America. Unable to secure profitable matches, and then with his health wrecked by tuberculosis, he returned to Australia sick and penniless.

Jackson was the most important heavyweight black fighter before Jack Johnson. William Phelon from Cincinnati wrote in 1913 that "Peter Jackson, who flourished about 1890, was probably a shade better pugilist than Johnson—in all probability the best fighter of the negro race. He had fully as good a defense as Johnson, and rather neater footwork; he had a better left hand, and a right that was as effective either for long-range boxing or for infighting; his generalship was quite equal to that of Johnson, and his gameness was heroic." He added that "in my own opinion Johnson is hardly the equal of that other black wizard, Peter Jackson."[1] Phelon was a baseball journalist but interested in boxing, and though he may have seen Jackson and Jack Ashton punching a ball in Cincinnati in 1890, his opinion is not conclusive.

But others also considered him better than Johnson, including the only man who trained both Jackson and Johnson. In early 1909 Sam Fitzpatrick talked with Frederick Hornibrook, English boxing aficionado. Hornibrook wrote in the 1940s: "I was fortunate enough to have a long chat one day with Sam Fitzpatrick who was Johnson's trainer and incidentally knew more about the psychology of negro pugilists than any man living as he had trained Peter Jackson, Joe Walcott and Johnson. I asked him, explaining that it was not for publication, which he thought was the better man — Peter Jackson or Johnson. He replied, 'Peter Jackson was the best man in the world and would have beaten Johnson.' I asked him why, and I shall always remember his answer —'Peter was a heavyweight but he was like a featherweight on his feet. Johnson, on the other hand, is a flat-footed boxer who makes men come to him and then possesses this wonderful defense. Peter's left hand would have been too quick for that defense and he would have made Johnson come to him.'"[2] Fitzpatrick's opinion deserves consideration.

Jackson has had a vast and enduring reputation, though he had few big fights. In 1890 Richard Fox published a book of 57 pages called *Lives and Battles of Famous Black Pugilists* (cover) and *The Black Champions of the Prize Ring from Molineaux to Jackson* (title page). It took the story from 1810 up to the defeat of the champion of England in November 1889 by Peter Jackson, the "Colored Heavy-Weight Champion of the World." As late as December 1894 it was advertised in the *National Police Gazette* with a woodcut of Jackson, who had by then

Peter Jackson photograph in the "Fine Specimen of Physical Development," published in *The College of Life: or, Practical Self-Educator,* by Henry Davenport Northrop, Joseph R. Gay, and I Garland Penn, 1900 (Colleen Aycock collection).

moved to England.[3] He has figured in almost every general history of boxing since.

Unlike Johnson, Jackson did not write an autobiography or leave any personal papers. We have many photographs but no movies of Jackson, because James J. Corbett declined to make an Edison kinetograph film with him, and then within three weeks boxed Peter Courtney on camera. Jackson's life story must be pieced together from newspaper reports and official documents.

Jackson was born on September 23, 1860, on a sugar plantation called Estate Orange Grove near, Christiansted on the island of St. Croix in the Danish West Indies (since 1916, the Virgin Islands of the United States).[4] His parents, Joseph and Julia, returned to Frederiksted, the second largest town on the island, soon after Jackson's birth. There in St. Paul's Anglican Church on August 31, 1861, he was christened Peter James Jackson by clergyman John DuBois. He did not know his date of birth, usually saying July 1861, and did not consult the baptismal register when he returned briefly to St. Croix in 1894. He was well educated in the St. Paul's parish school, acquiring a good English accent.

His parents and his eldest brother Samuel all died before 1880.[5] In 1878 he quit an economically devastated St. Croix, going to New York to join his elder brother James. But James had left the address at which Jackson sought him, so Peter signed on as a seaman on the *H. J. Libby*, which sailed from New York to Calcutta and then to Java. In Java it was loaded with raw sugar and sailed on to Sydney, where it arrived on February 19, 1879, and discharged its cargo at the new sugar refinery.

Peter Jackson in cloth cap (bottom left) and his brothers James (with wife) and Felix, together with residents of the plantation at Estate Orange Grove (Compagnie), St. Croix, in early October 1894 (*The Referee*, February 27, 1918).

During his professional career Jackson said nothing about these events; but amid persistent murmurs that he hailed from Jacksonville, Florida, he played variations on the story he told the *Louisville Courier-Journal* in March 1890, which was that: "I was born in the West Indies, at Nassau, in 1861, and I went to Australia with my parents in 1866, when I was five years old. My father and mother were respectively cook and stewardess on a sailing vessel. They carried me to Sydney, New South Wales." Nassau never appeared elsewhere in the saga, and Joseph and Julia had at least eight children by the census of 1870, Peter being the second youngest. His parents' voyage was imaginary; in fact, Jackson had been cook and steward on the *H. J. Libby*. Veteran journalist Will Lawless knew better. "Peter was the only member of his family to leave St. Croix, West Indies," he wrote in 1933, "as can be seen by a picture in my possession, showing himself and members of his family outside the home where the great colored champion was born. The photo was taken upon Peter's visit after many years absence."[6] Jackson told reporters what he wanted them to hear. A woman from the *San Francisco Examiner* asked him if he sang, and when he answered "no," she said she wanted plantation songs with banjo. Next would have come watermelons and chicken and razors. Actually, Jackson had good baritone, but he had assessed this reporter's attitudes.

Early in 1880, Jackson jumped ship in Sydney Harbor with a sailor from Baltimore and began walking north to Newcastle, from where boats loaded with excellent coal were constantly sailing to San Francisco. They were picked up by a horse-bus and taken to the

Greengate Hotel where they were given employment by the Waterhouse family, Jackson on boats plying the harbor and along the coast of New South Wales. He was introduced to Greengate's culture, where bare-knuckle fighting was popular. After some months he moved to the city, where he studied scientific boxing from teach-yourself books and joined a gymnasium. In November 1880, Jackson's talents were noticed by Larry Foley, the bare-knuckle champion of Australia, who engaged him as a roustabout at his White Horse hotel.

The story of Jackson's younger days was obscured by a book by A. G. "Smiler" Hales published in 1910 called *Romantic Career of Peter Jackson, his fights re-told* on the title page and with the running title of *Peter the Black Prince, a tale of love and sport.* A second version appeared in 1920 as *Romantic Career of Peter Jackson: His fights re-told*, while a third version appeared in 1931 as *Black Prince Peter: the Romantic Career of Peter Jackson.*[7] The three versions are all much the same. Hales hardly knew Jackson, and relied on newspaper archives and a few interviews with people who had known him well. In 1933 Will Lawless described the book as "an absolute scream." Hales invented a tale about Jackson's arrival in Australia which, for the lack of other books, was necessarily adopted by other biographers. Hales' book has been read not as the *vie romance* it is but as exciting biography. Even the Peter Jackson entries in the *Australian Dictionary of Biography* and *American National Biography* were corrupted by Hales' fiction.[8] It also tainted Chapter 18, on Jackson's career, in volume 1 of Nat Fleischer's *Black Dynamite* (1930). Fleischer's fifty pages are still worth reading, though he repeats some of Hales' nonsense. On the word of reporter "Hype" Igoe, he also says that entertainer Ernest Hogan ("The Unbleached American") was at Jackson's deathbed. Hogan must have told Igoe this as a joke. On July 13, 1901 he was not in Australia but working the Cherry Blossom Grove in Manhattan with his usual success, according to the *New York Dramatic Critic.*

After the Fleischer chapter there was nothing on Jackson's life beyond rehashed sports-magazine articles until the Englishman Tom Langley published *The Life of Peter Jackson, Champion of Australia* in 1974.[9] Langley said he read Hales' *Black Prince Peter* "over fifty years ago;" and by invoking the Hogan anecdote showed he had also read Fleischer. Langley's book starts with stories about Jackson's family and his youth in St. Croix which, when verifiable at all, prove to be false. Many later passages in the mere 78 pages contain fantasies, not research. To be blunt, a good third of Langley's biography is inexplicably invented and the book is better forgotten.

The best accounts of Jackson's early life appeared in newspapers but until the advent of microfilm these were almost inaccessible to historians. One article, in the March 3, 1889, *San Francisco Examiner*, probably by W. W. Naughton, was called "Peter the Pugilist: He Deserted Orange Groves to Make His Mark in a Prize Ring." The other, an article called "From Orange Groves to the World's Pugilistic Championship," appeared on March 27, 1901 in the Sydney *Referee.* It was written by Will Corbett, the *Referee's* boxing editor and Jackson's friend, in collaboration with Jackson himself. Although longer than the *Examiner* article, it was still silent on certain important matters. Then in 1918 and 1919, the *Referee* published 71 weekly episodes by Corbett entitled "Life and Boxing Skill of Peter Jackson," taking him from birth to burial. This biography utilized Australian documents for the most part, plus information Corbett had gathered from Jackson personally in 1900.

In 2000 the first new material on Jackson since 1919 appeared in Clark's article, "Up Against the Ropes: Peter Jackson as 'Uncle Tom' in America," which traced his acting career and tried to assess its reception by audiences.[10] In 2005, after several preliminary studies, I published a full biography of Jackson entitled *Gentleman Bruiser.*[11] It supplemented and corrected the previous biographies, stressing that Jackson never fought with bare fists after his Greengate months, gloves being Jem Mace's truest gift to Australian boxing. Most importantly, it showed that Jackson and Slavin were not hostile to one another, and their famous fight in 1892 was not a grudge match, but a reluctant battle between two friends who needed the money. Meanwhile, Patrick Myler scotched the rumor that Jackson ever fought Billy Warren.[12] Pollack's *John L. Sullivan* (2006) and the *Life of Jem Mace* by Gordon (2007) provided fresh details about Jackson's career.[13]

Reliable websites like the *Cyber Boxing Zone* and *Boxing Record Archives* list all of Jackson's encounters, set bouts and casual exhibitions, and we can enumerate the important ones. In his early years we can count two fights against Billy Farnan in Melbourne and Sydney, which he lost, and one win against Tom Lees in Sydney which made him (gloved) champion of Australia, Larry Foley presenting him with a recycled silver belt. The only other Australian whom Jackson considered worthy, his former pupil Frank "Paddy" Slavin, would not fight him. His other pupil, Bob Fitzsimmons, was still a debutant. The visiting Jack Burke refused in 1888 to fight a black man. Jackson had effectively no contenders, so he left Sydney for the United States and England.

PETER JACKSON,
Australia's Representative for the World's Championship.

Jackson arrived in San Francisco on May 12, 1888 and began giving exhibitions with the Australian ex-patriot Con Riordan, while looking to fight George Godfrey, the "Colored Champion of the World." Eventually, Americans challenged him; and his managers, most notably L. R. Fulda of the California Athletic Club, looked around for definitive bouts. Because prizefighting was frowned upon, even in San Francisco, men joined clubs in order to attend the fights as members. The C.A.C. brought Godfrey over from Boston for a title match with Jackson, Jackson won Godfrey's title, which he never had to defend and gave up in 1897. Another win over California's idol Joe McAuliffe made Jackson "Champion of the Pacific Slope" for a few years, and his defeat of Patsy Cardiff from Peoria in 1889 confirmed his prowess.

From San Francisco he went

Jackson, the national hero. Immediately after defeating Slavin in London, Jackson was confidently expected to be the contender against John L. Sullivan. The depiction of the kangaroo and emu is one of the earliest uses of the Australian national icons in a sporting contest (*The Sportsman*, Melbourne, June 7, 1892).

"The Ex-Champions of the Roped Arena." Peter Jackson, champion of Australia, is heralded along with other great champions of the ring. Only in fine print in the article below the illustration is it mentioned that "Peter was never a world champion, but his friends insist to this day that he had championship stuff in him and might have fought his way to the top had the fates been more propitious" (*San Francisco Examiner*, May 2, 1897).

to Chicago where he found a manager, Charles "Parson" Davies, and to New York. From there he went to England at the invitation of the Earl of Lonsdale, of Lonsdale Belt fame. In London he fought Jem Smith, the champion, and won — but in a non-title bout. Back to the United States, he fought his way back to San Francisco, with routine fights and exhibitions paying his way. The only opponent who played a part in his later life was Denver Ed Smith, whom he fought in Chicago in May. In mid–1890, boxing being stagnant in California, he returned to Sydney, and was pulled in a carriage through the streets to a fervent welcome. He toured to Adelaide with Albert "Young Griffo" Griffiths, and to Melbourne, where he fought Joe Goddard in an eight-round competition judged a draw. Then he returned to San Francisco where he ran a bar for a while.

Jackson fought James J. Corbett on May 21, 1891.[14] The two men were at their peak, generally. The year before, Corbett had beaten Kilrain, who had fought Sullivan, and Jackson had beaten all opponents across America and in Australia. The following year, Jackson

Jackson sparring with Joe Choynski at San Leandro near San Francisco, January 1889 (original in Mitchell Library, Sydney, Australia).

would defeat Slavin, the champion of England, and Corbett would defeat Sullivan, the world champion. But Jackson had sprained his ankle seven weeks prior to his fight with Corbett, going on crutches until April 21, and had therefore been late starting training. Advised by his trainer Sam Fitzpatrick not to enter a ring so soon, he apparently thought that his being proactive would bring about a short match and damage his ankle very little. Corbett had seen Jackson fight at least once when he acted as timekeeper at the Godfrey bout, though in his 1925 memoirs Corbett denied having set eyes on him before. Jackson had never seen Corbett fight. Mostly, Corbett danced away when Jackson attacked. In a self-justificatory letter to the *San Francisco Examiner* of May 24, Corbett wrote: "I cannot recollect a single time when I took the lead." The fight lasted for sixty-one rounds, the last thirty rounds degenerating into a walking-around match. Both men were exhausted, Corbett's hands were damaged and Jackson's ankle swollen to the size of his thigh. After four hours, the match was declared "no contest" and all bets were off because the California Athletic Club despaired of either man's winning. The fighters were paid only about half what a draw would have brought them. An acrimonious scandal broke out in the press. What was not revealed at the time was that the California Club could not cover the bets — the club went bankrupt soon thereafter.

Two things can be said about the Corbett fight. In his 1925 memoirs, Corbett told a racist story about Jackson's revealing an African fear of entering the ring second, so he agreed they would enter simultaneously and then tricked him, only pretending to enter so that Jackson would start with bad luck. There was nothing in the reporting of 1891 about Corbett's ploy, indeed the *San Francisco Call* described Corbett seated and being cheered before Jackson entered. The juicy story was enacted in the movie *Gentleman Jim,* mocking Sullivan for his *Irish* superstition. Secondly, a poster of Corbett and Jackson as the combatants of May 21, 1891, is occasionally reproduced in books, but it was issued by the *National Police Gazette* on May 10, 1894, for their scheduled contest that month, showing them "in fighting attitudes." They never assumed those attitudes because the May 1894 fight somehow evaporated. The poster also showed them both in slips, which Corbett affected but Jackson never donned in a fight. Corbett never fought Jackson again. The *New York Times* reported on January 23, 1893, that "Corbett says he will meet any man in the world, barring no color or nationality." But over the next five years he fought only three men: Charles Mitchell (English), Tom Sharkey (Irish), and Bob Fitzsimmons from New Zealand.

In 1892 in London, Jackson fought Slavin for the first time in a ring, thus reasserting his Australian championship. Then he returned to San Francisco to again run a bar for a while. He played "Uncle Tom" in a touring company from February 1893 until March 1894, with each performance including boxing. During his career he exhibited wherever he could, in Australia, in America, in England, in Paris. The money was not in the fights but in the exhibitions. Starring in *Uncle Tom's Cabin,* he sparred with Joe Choynski on evenings and during matinees across half of the United States. Many, many people saw Jackson in action and were enraptured.

Disgusted after years of waiting for Corbett, unable to fight him again, he went via St. Croix in 1894 to England, where he stayed until 1897, sparring with various partners all over Britain and in Paris. In 1896 he and Bob Fitzsimmons were on tours, and coincided in Cardiff for their first meeting since the old days with Larry Foley. They may have sparred. The next year Fitzsimmons won Corbett's title. Jackson was said to be drinking a lot and wasting all his money on slow racehorses and fast women. He was depressed and sometimes didn't show at the theater.

In September 1897, Mrs. Bob Fitzsimmons forbade the new champion of the world to fight again, and the title was thrown open to all comers until Fitzsimmons reassessed the situation. Feeling hopeful, Jackson left all his enterprises in England and returned to San Francisco. Here he spent his money, caught tuberculosis, and fought Jim Jeffries in March 1899.[15] He lost that fight, his first loss since Farnan in 1884, and he predicted Jeffries would become the next champion of the world.

Months passed and Jackson became an alcoholic. Friends bundled him out of California, to British Columbia from where he could spar his way across Canada and on to New York. In British Columbia he had three pathetic fights against Jim Jeffers, the last at Vancouver on August 23, 1899 which he lost. He never fought again. Slavin, who now was living in Victoria B.C., embarked with Jackson for the Klondike, intending them to give exhibitions for the miners. But at Skagway Jackson collapsed, and Slavin shipped him south, back to Victoria. He was convalescent for months in Denver Ed Smith's hotel until W. W. Naughton of the *San Francisco Examiner* paid his passage back to Australia. Jackson had a dozen big fights in all. His fight with Jim Jeffers in Vancouver B.C. was important only because it was his last.

Jackson was very popular in Australia, more so in Sydney and, because of inter-city rivalry, less in Melbourne, where Slavin, in defiance of reality, was always declared to be the Australian champion. Jackson was popular in Britain, where the Earl of Lonsdale introduced him to the National Sporting Club and its other titled members. He was the only boxer allowed to enter the club whenever he liked, and he was the only boxer whose portrait (by Alfred Dickman Bastin) was displayed for years in the club.[16] Prince Eddy, Prince Albert Victor of Wales, Queen Victoria's grandson and Heir Presumptive to the English throne, shook his hand enthusiastically at the Newmarket races in 1898.[17] His season exhibiting with Dai St. John at the Folies Bergére was a triumph. He was fully expected by its organizers at the Sullivan-Corbett match in New Orleans in 1892, decreed the only man of his race permitted in the auditorium, and with accommodation reserved for him at the Senate Club. But he did not go to New Orleans, He saw St. Louis and he had visited Louisville in 1890. Then he had been to New Orleans in January 1891 to see his ex-pupil Fitzsimmons fight Jack "Nonpareil" Dempsey, and that was enough of Dixie for him. After that he refused to fight in the South or even travel there.

The African Americans were not certain of what attitude to assume in regard to Jackson. This was two decades before the founding of the National Association for the Advancement of Colored People, and Booker T. Washington had not yet delivered the "Atlanta Address." African American pastors and ministers and teachers were taking leadership positions. In the quest for respectability, boxing was pushed to the low end of sport. In those dreadful years the African American bourgeoisie were urging education and the creation of a middle class led by decent clergy, but they were forced to accept that the best advertisement around for black talent was a prize-fighter. Moreover, Jackson was a boxer who had learned at school how to use his "shalls" and his "wills," and who had the habit of quoting Shakespeare. The *Freeman*'s journalist James Vena called Jackson "the man pre-eminent in elevating a calling frequently debased by its other representatives."

Given the sadly incomplete state of African American newspaper files, it is hard to estimate just how popular Jackson was, but the papers that remain are favorable. They always sent around a reporter when he was in town. Some African American newspapers began to promote boxing and sporting columns at just this time. The *Cleveland Gazette* paid attention to sports from 1889, noting the doings of George Dixon, of Peter, of the Cuban Giants baseball team, etc. The *Freeman* introduced a sporting column in April 1890, apparently just so it could announce: "Peter Jackson does this generation a service by proving that a man can be both a prize-fighter and a gentleman." Ike Hines had in his famed Professional Club in New York a room covered with portraits of black achievers. As James Weldon Johnson described it in 1912: "There were pictures of Frederick Douglass and of Peter Jackson, of all the lesser lights of the prize-fighting ring, of all the famous jockeys and the stage celebrities."[18]

In the 1890s, organized sports were developing among African Americans, colleges like Tougaloo and Howard University fostering track and field sports, and creating baseball and football teams. Intervarsity competitions were set up. Before any YMCA for African Americans had moved along from spiritual exercises to athletic, and forty years before any Texas YMCA existed for them, some young men in Austin, Texas, led by Professor E. L. Blackshear, set up an athletic organization for African Americans in October 1892. They promoted all kinds of manly sports and called themselves "The Peter Jackson Club."

On July 19, 1890 the *Freeman* wrote a paragraph which revealed the moral and political dilemma of many African Americans when they considered Jackson's success, saying: "In these two qualities, courage and pluck, the most civilized nations have flattered themselves they had no equals. Especially the negro has been regarded as deficient in the traits names, and he was thought inferior because he was lacking in them. But now, what shall we say? ... Is the colored race to step in and steal the laurels from white folk in this way? If so, perhaps those to whom only brute force can appeal as an argument may begin to respect the negro as a man and brother." The African American bourgeoisie had spent so much time trying to shuck off the darky image which included gambling and prize-fighting — and now the most famous black man, not just in the United States but across the world, was a boxer.

However, "Old Sport" of the *New York Age* spoke more generally for African Americans. In August, 1891 he took the positive line of saying about George Dixon, Harris "Black Pearl" Martin, and Jackson: "I don't care what it is, if one of the race is best at it, it helps."

In 1895 Jackson achieved lasting fame among African Americans when his portrait from a Taber photograph of 1888–1889, clearly showing his squinting left eye, appeared in Northrop, Gay and Penn, *The College of Life*: or, *Practical Self-Educator*, "embellished with hundreds of superb engravings." Plate Number 6 showed Jackson bare torso, arms folded, and (almost alone among his images) full faced, and was captioned, "Fine Specimen of Physical Development, PETER JACKSON, Athlete."[19]

Jackson went to St. Louis in April 1890 to spar with Jack Ashton, but the police vetoed the demonstration. As a sporting event, the visit to St. Louis was a failure, but it apparently marked the peak of his success in African-American society. For days beforehand, the *St. Louis Post-Dispatch* reported: "The colored population is worked up over the coming of Peter Jackson." Five hundred gathered at the depot for a wild welcome.

Jackson was given a lunchtime reception in the Union Bethel Hall, with prominent gentlemen present. Welcome was extended by the most famous African American to come out of St. Louis, and one of the best known African Americans in the United States. This was James Milton Turner, a prominent educator whom President Grant appointed United States ambassador to Liberia, and who served there from 1871 to 1878 under Grant and President Hayes. After 1890 he turned to actively promoting black Freemasonry.[20] It cannot be pretended that everywhere Jackson was greeted by such eminent blacks, but evidence suggests that wherever he went the locals rolled out their best red carpet. Yet still, apart from Frederick Douglass himself, scarcely one African American had a higher profile than Turner. That he should have been asked to officiate at a banquet for a boxer, and that he should have agreed to do so, is a measure of how highly Jackson was regarded.

The Sydney *Referee* suggested the next year that Jackson himself should emulate Douglass and lead his people. It even suggested that he should make his home in the South! The sports editor in 1891, who was "Smiler" Hales, apparently did not realize that Jackson was a West Indian and subject of the King of Denmark, and not an African American. Jackson lived eighteen years in the Danish West Indies, and afterwards lived in Australia for eleven years all told, and in England for four. He was in the United States on five occasions for a total of just over six years, and the purchase of the Danish West Indies by Woodrow Wilson in 1916 did not retroactively make him an African American. Moreover, when Jackson spoke of retiring, it was to Australia, or to England, never to below the Mason-Dixon Line. Jackson was staying at good hotels in the years when Frederick Douglass, the Ambassador to Haiti, if traveling by train, was obliged to sit in the caboose. J.W. Johnson reported in his autobiography that "Frederick Douglass had a picture of Peter Jackson in his study, and he used to point to it and say, 'Peter is doing a great deal with his fists to solve the Negro question.'"[21]

The St. Louis visit raises the issue of Freemasonry. In 1911, Jack Johnson was initiated into Lodge Forfar and Kincardine, No. 225 in Scotland, an event oddly not noted in G. C. Ward's book *Unforgivable Blackness*.[22] This was immediately telegraphed to the *New York Times* on October 29 and caused such a scandal, with American lodges threatening to boycott the Grand Lodge of Scotland, that Johnson's membership was cancelled and Lodge Forfar and Kincardine itself temporarily suspended. The ostensible reason was not Johnson's race but his being by profession "the champion brute of the world"; technically, along with messy paperwork, this may have been the case. Normally in America, black Freemasonry was quite separated from white, and while Voorhis showed that there were a number of isolated cases of black Freemasons in white lodges in the nineteenth century, presumably none were boxers.[23] After all, without any outrage from America, another Scottish lodge had in 1903 initiated Egbert Williams and the other black males from the *In Dahomey* theatrical company.

Jackson's pastor and teacher at St. Paul's, DuBois, was chaplain to the Frederiksted Lodge. Another man in Jackson's life, Larry Foley, joined a lodge in 1885 though he was a Catholic, but soon lapsed, maybe after priestly pressure. How many other Masons Jackson met is unknown, but the upper class in England favored Masonry, and Prince Eddy, until his sudden death, was being groomed to head English Freemasonry. And then Jackson met Turner. As Kremer reports, it was that very year, 1890, that Turner became a Freemason, being initiated into the Widow's Son Lodge in St. Louis.

Turner's act may have inspired Jackson to this limited extent, that some months later, back in Sydney, Jackson also was initiated into Freemasonry, in Balmain at Lodge General Gordon, No. 166 United Grand Lodge of New South Wales. There was a brouhaha about his initiation. There were irregularities with his sponsorship, because he was on a visit from the United States and not strictly a resident of Balmain. The Master of Lodge General Gordon was called on "to explain the circumstances under which the initiation of a pugilist took place in the said lodge, and to produce nomination and other papers in respect of the occurrence." But it seems to have been mainly the question of his occupation, not his race. Jackson, like Johnson twenty years later, was a boxer. As the Masonic paper the *Australian Keyhole* wrote on February 3, 1891, "Is a pugilist a man and a brother?" The Freemasons debated it, but according to official records, Jackson was initiated on October 1, took the Second Degree on the 14th before leaving for Melbourne to face Goddard, and the third on the 23rd; and Brother Jackson's membership was never revoked.[24]

After the months convalescing with tuberculosis at Denver Ed's, Jackson arrived in Sydney on April 15, 1900. He could do little. He did not fight in Australia, though he did referee a couple of fights and he was master-of-ceremonies at a few other events. He trained another St. Croix fighter, Peter Felix, who claimed to be some sort of cousin, for his match on July 16 with Bill Doherty. Felix would not follow his trainer's advice, and lost. Jackson made walk-on appearances in a circus. But the most important thing he did was impart his memories to Will Corbett. A few episodes were published before Jackson died, but the biography was then abandoned for almost twenty years.

It was decided to send the consumptive to Brisbane, but despite good care in a hospital, the air in Brisbane was too humid and so, with special permission from Queensland's Chief Secretary, the incurable Jackson was sent out west to another hospital in the dry atmosphere of Roma. Despite good nursing from a competent doctor and a dedicated nurse he faded, reading the weekly installments of Corbett's biography but finally dying on July 13. "Corbett understands me — if I should ever see him again," were his last words.

Jackson was interviewed almost everywhere he went, and his doings and sayings attracted more newspaper attention than those of any other black man of the period. His appearance was as impressive to his public as were his performances. Nobody ever mentioned his squint, and most of his photographers disguised it. A well-known contributor to the *New York Herald* said while *Uncle Tom's Cabin* was playing New York City: "If I were a sculptor, and wanted a model of a perfect figure to illustrate the happiest possible combination of strength and agility — a between of Hercules and Mercury — I would choose Peter Jackson."[25] There were portraits of him (the *National Police Gazette* sold them for 10 cents) and many cigarette cards illustrating Jackson in defensive poses. One was by John Woods of the Bowery, the pugilists' cameraman, but the best one was taken by the most fashionable photographer in New York, Napoleon Sarony.

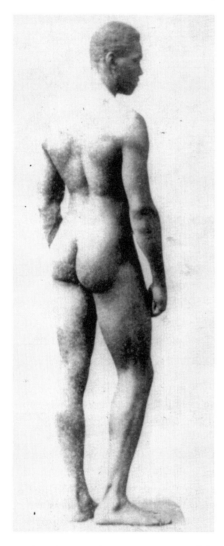

This photograph reappears as one of the "Three Graces" in the *San Francisco Examiner* in 1894, illustrating in neoclassical style the perfect physique — that of a boxer and obviously that of Peter Jackson, the most intriguing and studied figure of the age (photograph by Isaiah Taber, San Francisco, May 1889; original in Mitchell Library, Sydney, Australia).

In San Francisco, Isaiah Taber had a photographic studio and shop for many years. Peter patronized Taber, who in turn sold Peter's images to his fans and others. In May 1889, after the McAuliffe fight, Peter was measured by a doctor who (for some reason) urged him to get photographed nude. Taber took at least two photographs, one a profile shot in a pleated loincloth looking Egyptian, and another stripped for a three-quarters rear shot.

In Sydney only two months later, the nude photograph in half-tone appeared in the *Dead Bird*, a naughty-sporty paper, with the comment: "The portrait which adorns our fifth page will be readily recognized, even without the name on the pedestal, as that of our champion boxer, Peter Jackson, and we venture to assert that never has there been given to the world a more beautiful sample of reproduced living statuary.... The marble man should blush to hear himself called a fine shapely man after seeing it, and Australia should be proud to have fed and reared such a model as our champion."[26]

The two Taber photographs of Jackson nude anticipate by some seven or eight years the famous "Nubian Series" by F. Holland Day, shown and discussed in *Race Men* by Carby and conventionally called the first "artistic" photographs of black men.[27] In his book on Carl Van Vechten's photography, Smalls says that after the Civil War the dangerous and threatening black body had to be domesticated

THE THREE TYPES OF MANLY FORM.
[Jackson and Sandow, from photographs by Taber.]

"Three Types of Manly Form." In a discussion of aesthetic beauty, experts of the day remark that Peter Jackson approaches the more "elegant proportions" than does Sandow, the strongman (Langford illustration, *San Francisco Examiner*, May 20, 1894).

by "sexualizing, classicizing, eroticizing, primitivizing and feminizing."[28] Six feet and a half an inch tall, and weighing 200 pounds in 1889, Jackson's pugilist's body was threatening and dangerous, but Taber's portrait did not do any of those things to domesticate it.

In May 1894 the picture made a reappearance in the *San Francisco Examiner* alongside one of the body-builder Eugene Sandow, who was in San Francisco for the Midwinter Exposition that spring. He had been hailed as having the ideal male body. Jackson was featured in *Examiner* articles which discussed the perfect man. The paper asked San Francisco painters and sculptors whether Sandow's body or Jackson's represented the ideal male physique. Jackson and Sandow themselves both contributed to the coverage. Jackson saying apropos of using classical sculptures as the standard of beauty: "The inclination nowadays, of course, is to compare alleged perfect men with the old Grecian athletes and Roman gladiators. I think these ancients must have looked better in statues than they did in the flesh."

The articles were illustrated by an engraving of male figures posed like the Three Graces: the Apollo Belvedere at center, with on his left Sandow in sandals and his trademark fig leaf, and on his right Jackson in the resurrected nude pose of 1889. It was surprising that a black man should be brought into such a debate. Even more surprisingly the connoisseurs announced, in the words of John Stanton from the School of Design, "Peter Jackson to my mind approaches the nearer the elegant proportions of the old Greek statues than Sandow.

The lines of his contour of figure are more finely drawn, more delicate than those of Sandow."[29] It was very strange to hear a black man declared more Greek than a white! Most surprising of all, Hearst's *Examiner* made no mention of Jackson's race except for one word in one subtitle, and the whole debate was conducted in terms of body types: Herculean versus Apollonian. Although Hjalmarson's *Artful Players: Artistic Life in Early San Francisco*

Tomb of the great Peter Jackson, dedicated in May 1903, located in the General Cemetery, Toowong, Australia. The inscription in the marble reads: "This Was A Man" (photograph by Mr. Arnold Thomas, 1992).

(1999) managed to discuss Sandow as the perfect man without mentioning Jackson, the incident was not forgotten among African Americans.[30] Seven years later, his obituary in the *Freeman* said "Jackson in his prime was said to have been the finest specimen of physical manhood in the United States and he posed before a number of artists and sculptors."

His portrait, carved in Carrara marble by the monumental mason Lewis Pages, adorns his grave. He was buried not in tiny Roma but in Brisbane, where his remains could be more easily visited. The interment was in the General Cemetery at Toowong on July 16, 1901. Money collected by Corbett bought an elaborate tomb which was unveiled in May 1903. Antony's tribute to Brutus was inscribed on it: "This Was A Man."

Six years later, on February 17, 1909, the day that Jack Johnson was in Brisbane, departing Australia, heading for Vancouver and home, the new heavyweight champion of the world visited Jackson's grave. The *Brisbane Courier* reported that "when lunch was over, the champion and his wife, with a couple of friends, motored to Toowong Cemetery, and there, on the quiet picturesque hillside, the living champion spent a few moments in silent contemplation of the sport where rested the mortal remains of the dead. It was an impressive sight indeed to see the splendid form of the living gladiator bending for a moment over the tomb of he who was Australia's fistic idol, and the solemnity of the occasion swept his now famous smile from Johnson's face."[31] Johnson had been in Australia before, though not in Brisbane. In 1913 he told a French interviewer that "after my fight with Burns I stayed in Australia until February; during those few months I had quite a few adventures."[32] Johnson left no word about his pilgrimage to Toowong Cemetery. Maybe the man who managed both fighters, Sam Fitzpatrick, had told him more than he wanted to hear about Peter Jackson.

NOTES

1. W. A. Phelon, "The Kings of the Roped Arena; the Greatest Boxing Champions of All Time, in Three Parts, Part I," *Baseball Magazine* (February 1913); 34–49.

2. F. A. Hornibrook, *The Lure of the Ring*, 3.

3. On these matters see Guy Reel, *The National Police Gazette and the Making of the Modern American Man, 1879–1906*, and Edward Van Every, *The Sins of New York; as 'Exposed' by the Police Gazette*.

4. Dr. George Tyson and his team have now put all the individual records from all the Danish censuses of St. Croix on *Ancestry.com*. Peter Jackson appeared in one census only: 1870.

5. They do not figure in the 1880 census.

6. W. Lawless, "Solar Plexus," "A Page of Pugilistic History, I," *Boxer and Wrestler*, July 14, 1933, 3.

7. The dates were ascertained from the accession stamps on the British Library copies.

8. R. Broome, "Peter Jackson," *Australian Dictionary of Biography*, Vol. 9 (1891–1939), 458–459; J.M. Carroll, "Jackson, Peter," in J.A. Garraty and M.C. Carnes (eds.), *American National Biography*, Vol. 11, 761–762.

9. Tom Langley, *The Life of Peter Jackson, Champion of Australia*.

10. Susan F. Clark, "Up Against the Ropes: Peter Jackson as 'Uncle Tom' in America," *Drama Review*, 44, I (Spring 2000), 157–182.

11. Bob Petersen, *Gentleman Bruiser: A Life of the Boxer Peter Jackson, 1860–1901*.

12. Patrick Myler, "Untwisting the Cyclone," *The Ring* (August 2003), 50–54.

13. Graham Gordon, *Master of the Ring: The Extraordinary Life of Jem Mace*, A. J. Pollack, *John L. Sullivan: The Career of the First Gloved Heavyweight Champion*.

14. Accounts of the fight are in: Petersen, 207–217; Armond Fields, *James J. Corbett: A Biography of the Heavyweight Boxing Champion and Popular Theater Headliner*, 43–47; Patrick Myler, *Gentleman Jim Corbett: The Truth Behind a Boxing Legend*. 40–45.

15. James J. Jeffries, "Life and Fights: Colorful Story Told by Himself," the *Referee*, 1927; Chapter 7 on Jackson fight in *Referee*, August 16, 1927.

16. For the respectable but dull artist, see Jeremy Wood, *Hidden Talents: A Dictionary of Neglected Artists Working 1880–1950*.

17. Andrew Cook, *Prince Eddy: The King Britain Never Had*, 176–177.

18. Reproduced in 1930 from his *Autobiography of an Ex-Coloured Man*, in James Weldon Johnson, *Black Manhattan*, 75.

19. If squint he had, it dated either from adulthood and after a head punch, in which case he would have had double vision, or from childhood and his vision had adapted. See: H. D. Northrop, J.R. Gay, and I.G.

Penn, *The College of Life: Practical Self-Educator, A Manual of Self-Improvement for the Colored Race Forming an Educational Emancipator and a Guide to Success.*

20. G. R. Kremer, "The World of Make-Believe: James Milton Turner and Black Masonry," *Missouri Historical Review*, 76, 2, January 1982, 50–71.

21. James Weldon Johnson, *Along This Way: The Autobiography of James Weldon Johnson*, 208.

22. Geoffrey C. Ward, *Unforgivable Blackness: The Rise and Fall of Jack Johnson.*

23. Harold V.B. Voorhis, *Negro Masonry in the United States*; W. H. Grimshaw, *Official History of Freemasonry Among the Colored People in North America.*

24. Information kindly supplied by Br. G. Cumming of the Masonic Centre Library, United Grand Lodge of NSW and ACT (Personal communication, 7/30/2005).

25. *New York Herald*, "Sportsman," April 17, 1894.

26. *Dead Bird*, July 20, 1889, 5.

27. Hazel V. Carby, *Race Men*, 55–58.

28. J. Smalls, *The Homoerotic Photography of Carl Van Vechten*, 81.

29. *San Francisco Examiner*, May 27, 1894.

30. Birgitta Hjalmarson, *Artful Players: Artistic Life in Early San Francisco.*

31. *Brisbane Courier*, February 18, 1909.

32. Jack Johnson, *My Life and Battles*, translated from *Ma Vie Et Mes Combats* by C. Rivers, 75.

CHAPTER 4

George Dixon: World Bantamweight and Featherweight Champion

Mike Glenn

George Dixon, a pioneer of the modern sport, is considered by many to be the finest bantamweight and featherweight fighter in history. The man dubbed "Little Chocolate" followed the path blazed eighty years earlier by Tom Molineaux, the first great athlete in American history, who traveled to England to fight the British champion. Unlike his predecessors, Dixon successfully won the championship fight across the pond in 1890 and was acknowledged as a world title holder. In the ring Dixon was characterized as "a fighter without a flaw" and with uncommon endurance — as evidenced by his fighting up to 70 rounds.[1] He was a scientific boxer with uncommon defensive skills. To sharpen those skills, he invented shadow boxing and the suspended punching bag which have become a fundamental part of every boxer's training.[2]

Dixon was a man of many recorded "firsts." He was the first Canadian-born world champion. He became the first boxer to win two world championship titles (paperweight and bantamweight) and go on to win three (including the featherweight) — all three titles acknowledged in 1938 by boxing historian Nat Fleischer.[3] Dixon was also the first champion to lose his title and then to regain it. Dixon fought over a period of 20 years with 27 title fights to his credit; some historians count as many as 33. Either number gives Dixon the record for most title fights. Sportswriters of his day said, "He had everything," including fame. Nat Fleischer stated, "I doubt that there ever was a pugilist who was as popular during his entire career as was Little Chocolate."[4] Even more important to history, Dixon was one of the first sport celebrities to become a force for social change on American soil.

Unlike those of many of the early black boxers, Dixon's history-making accomplishments were noted during his lifetime. In 1897, founding Cincinnati *Enquirer* sport editor J. B. McCormick, known as "Macon," recorded his 50-year experiences at ringside. The scribe said of Dixon, "There were brave men before Agamemnon and there were Negro pugilists before Dixon, but none of them ever succeeded in breaking down the race prejudice against black men as he has.... Dixon not only succeeded in getting fair play for himself and other Negroes when pitted against white men, but he also succeeded in getting men of Celtic origin to manage himself and other fighters like Peter Jackson and Frank Craig. This was an achievement which would have been regarded as impossible a generation ago."[5] In his conclusion to "George Dixon, The Fistic Marvel, A Colored Feather-Weight Champion to Whom the Negro Race is Greatly Indebted," Macon maintained, "Take him all for all, however, I regard him as the most marvelous little fighter the ring has ever known.... The colored race will be ungrateful indeed if it does not rear a monument to him when he dies."[6]

George Dixon was born July 29, 1870, in Africville, Nova Scotia, a Black-Canadian community in Halifax. His mother was black and his father was reported to be a white British soldier.[7] He engaged in his first fight, a three-rounder in Halifax, when he was 16. His boxing interest, however, didn't become a vocation until the Dixon family moved to Boston, the fistic Mecca of America at that time due in large part to the popularity of its hometown champion, John L. Sullivan. Working in Boston, Dixon was apprenticed to a photographer who took set pictures of professional boxers. Inspired by these colorful and statuesque men, Dixon entered the ring for a career. He was discovered by Boston local Ben Benton, known as "Rob Roy."[8] Dixon would later be managed by former boxer Tom O'Rourke, who would then remain his life-long handler.

Fighting at 5'3" and under 100 pounds, Dixon got his break and gained regional recognition as a paperweight when manager Benton matched him on May 10, 1888, with top-level boxer Tommy "The Harlem Spider" Kelly. Kelly put his 105-pound championship on the line in this bout with George Dixon. The fight ended in a draw. Soon afterward Spider Kelly retired from the ring, leaving claim to the paperweight title to Dixon. Since several states never recognized a paperweight champion, Dixon's title recognition at the time was limited; but in late 19th-century record books, Dixon was acknowledged as the title holder.[9]

Dixon's early matches with Benton as his manager foreshadowed the many long and difficult battles that would take him to the top of the championship ladder. A series of encounters, with Hank Brennan, beginning on June 21, 1888, will remain in the annals of boxing history forever. Although Dixon was also fighting out of Boston, he fought a man dubbed the "Pride of Boston," who was his mirror image in ability and intensity. Fans were aware of the skills

An undated photograph of George Dixon in fighting form.

of the equally matched artists as well as their rivalries. Despite the fact that Dixon had a knockdown in the fight to his credit, the match ended in a draw. The furious action of the combatants delighted the crowd so much that they demanded a rematch. On December 4th of the same year, these two pugs, now more determined than ever, battled at a frenzied pace, trading blows consistently to the head and body and charging ahead at all costs. The referee, perhaps hating to see either fighter injured or defeated, stopped the fight after nine rounds of punishment. Again the verdict was no decision.

A third engagement for the warriors was set for December 28. A heavy snowstorm enveloped Boston but did not prevent hundreds of fans from gathering at the Athenian Club to see the final battle of the now-storied trilogy. They were not disappointed. Even though Dixon was slightly favored, Brennan seemed to have a surfeit of confidence. Brennan had trained hard for the fight and was convinced that his abilities had improved such that he had surpassed Dixon in skill. A confident and determined opponent is never an easy foe. In a classic attempt to gain a psychological edge, Brennan entered the fight without the benefit of his corner men. Brennan counseled the referee, "All I want is a square deal from you. My fist will do the rest."[10] Dixon discovered the greater challenge late in the fight — a time when legs get weary and competitors concede. Despite a puffed eye and a swollen face, Brennan "came through with a rush in the last five rounds." When the referee once again declared the fight a draw, the crowd turned into a mob and stormed the ring in support of their heroes. After calmer heads prevailed inside, the crowd went outside and started fights that required intervention by the Boston riot police.

A fourth battle between the two gladiators was set for October 14, 1889. In the interim, Dixon fought and won four contests that seemed to be warm-ups for the upcoming part IV of the Dixon-Brennan rivalry. In the fourth encounter, Brennan had his seconds in place and checked his ego at the door. From the outset through the first seven rounds, Brennan rushed with left hooks and right uppercuts that kept Dixon on the retreat. In the eighth round, Dixon attacked with punches that closed Brennan's left eye. Refusing to back down, Brennan took the aggressive stance in the ninth round with his powerful body blows. Both fighters were cut and bleeding freely, but they battled courageously through the next thirteen rounds without retreat. In the 23rd round Brennan led with powerful rights, but he was outdone by Dixon's counterpunches that knocked him to the floor. With uncommon endurance, Brennan returned to form in the 24th round. At the end of the 26th round, referee Drouhan declared the fight a draw. Once again police had to chase away mobs of angry fans to protect the referee and the contestants. Boxing history has never recorded another display of such intensely fought matches between two fighters that yielded no winner.

By 1889 Dixon had learned that the path to success included valleys of despair as well as peaks of jubilation. On June 3, 1889, he suffered his first defeat to George Wright, a non-contender who should have given Dixon little problem. An unintentional low blow by Dixon gave the victory to Wright on a foul. Dixon was heartbroken but bounced back quickly. He defeated Eugene Hornbacker, a top contender, with a kayo in the second round to earn a date with the bantamweight champion. It would be the longest fight of his life, and at the age of 19.

Champion Cal McCarthy agreed to fight George Dixon for the bantamweight title on February 7, 1890 in Boston. Dixon knew that it would be difficult to defeat the current champion and equally difficult to overthrow a system that devalued his triumphs and overvalued the efforts of his white counterparts.

Nat Fleischer described the 21-year-old McCarthy as an aggressive pugilist who tired in late rounds. As far as this fight was concerned, Fleischer was partially correct. McCarthy pursued Dixon all over the ring in the early rounds. However, in the ninth round, momentum shifted and Dixon knocked McCarthy to his knees. In the tenth round Dixon staggered the champ. By the twelfth round McCarthy had raised a lump over Dixon's left eye. Dixon's quickness and endurance seemed to play a greater role as the fight progressed. As Fleischer described it, "Dixon fought fairly, but every time he landed a crushing blow to the opponent's body, the champion attempted to wrestle or toss him otherwise rough him against the ropes."[11] In the 62nd round, McCarthy went down on his knees from a right to the chin. When he got up, he rushed the Boston lad and pushed his head through the ropes, but was admonished by the referee for his rough work. Fatigued beyond reason, both fighters accepted a draw in the 70th round. The fight lasted for an eternal 4 hours and 40 minutes. Nat Fleischer reflected on the fight's aftermath, "McCarthy was in far worse shape than his challenger who was up and around Boston at 8:30 in the morning after the contest, showing no marks except a little lump over his left eye."[12]

Despite the disappointment of not being declared the world champ, Dixon and his manager maximized the verdict. They claimed a share to the title and set their aims on consolidating the title. Following the path of earlier great Black boxers, Dixon traveled to England to fight Nunc Wallace, the British champion of fighters weighing 115 pounds or less.

On June 27, 1890, one month shy of age 20, Dixon fought for the world championship title of the bantamweight division. Apparently, the British felt that their champion, Wallace, was actually the world champion. Therefore, a fight against a man who had a share of the American championship could accurately be called a championship bout. The fight was held at the Pelican Club, an exclusive London establishment that maintained a formal dress code. The attire of black tie and tails was worn by everyone. Even the referee was required to adhere to these strict standards. George Dixon, the only person in the club with melanin in his skin, had to feel like his predecessors Richmond and Molineaux almost a century earlier. Like them, Dixon was a lone black American against the British Empire. This time the results were different. Wallace, in the opening rounds, led the attack as Dixon maneuvered defensively. In the fourth round, Dixon attacked but received an uppercut that brought him to his knees. Up quickly from the canvas, Dixon landed a right and a left that sent Wallace down to the floor. In the sixth round, Dixon closed one of Wallace's eyes and gave him a multitude of punches to the body. Dixon's superior speed was obvious; his superb conditioning was a surprise. Wallace, unable to match the quickness of Dixon, wrestled and held on at every opportunity. Wallace did everything and anything to survive the onslaught of punches. In the 18th round, Dixon forced Wallace to the ropes and went to work on Wallace's body. A helpless Wallace called it quits. The English people, O'Rourke, and many others marveled at the new bantamweight champion of the world. George Dixon had accomplished a deed that no other American fighter had been able to achieve; he traveled to England and defeated an English boxer for an international title. Tom Molineaux, Bill Richmond, John L. Sullivan, and John Heenan had all failed in similar quests.

Dixon returned to America from England and received a hero's welcome. However, when it came time to defend his title against a white challenger, Dixon still faced the racism and discrimination that ruled all aspects of American life. Stereotypes, customs, habits, beliefs, laws, religion, education, history, and science were all used to support white dominance as the natural order. Anything that challenged these long-standing, false assumptions challenged the American system and caused discomfort. Sports officials were probably no more prepared to be impartial than the lawmakers who created Black Laws, that only applied to black people, or all white juries that exonerated lynch mob leaders. Canadian historian Charles Saunders described Dixon's bantam title defense against Johnny Murphy in Providence, Rhode Island, on October 23, 1890. The 40-round fight was brutal. Saunders explained: "Dixon as a black man fighting in front of white audiences was often at a disadvantage. A perfect example could be seen at the fight against Johnny Murphy. Dixon won the fight, but had to fight near the center of the ring to stay away from the ropes where fans could hit his legs with blackjacks and slug shots. Black boxers were encouraged to fight like lions against each other but like lambs against Caucasians.... They were often coerced into losing deliberately to white opponents, or at least doing nothing that would cause a white foe undue distress."[13]

Dixon still had unfinished business. Although Little Chocolate had beaten Wallace, the British champ of the little guys, American Cal McCarthy was still considered the American champion at 115 pounds, and Abe Willis, at the same weight, was called the Australian champion.

Dixon revisited Cal McCarthy on March 31, 1891 at Troy, New York, in what was publicized as the world featherweight title. At that time Dixon weighed between 112 and 115 pounds. In the third round, Dixon tried to end the fight by knocking McCarthy out. Dixon backed him to the ropes with alternating body and headshots that eventually knocked McCarthy to the floor. While referee Dunn was counting, Jack McAuliffe and Billy Madden, McCarthy's seconds, dragged their fighter to the corner and cared for him. Tom O'Rourke yelled and screamed at the referee to declare Dixon the winner. "This is not a bare-knuckle, London Prize Ring rules battle," he shouted. Referee Dunn responded, "Aw keep quiet, Tom. Dixon will win in another round. What difference does it make?"[14] Ultimately, the referee was correct. Dixon did win the fight and the title of featherweight champion of the world in New York that day, but it required 22 rounds to complete the task.

Most considered Dixon as the featherweight world champ, but the Australians disagreed. It should be stated that during this time period, the smaller weight categories were in flux with various title championships just coming into being. Many boxing experts of the day considered Abe Willis to be the true featherweight champion and George Dixon to be only the bantamweight champion. However, many thought British Wallace to hold title to both bantam and featherweight championships. A championship featherweight fight between these two champions would determine the title for the record books.

On July 28, 1891, Dixon defeated Abe Willis for the featherweight world championship. San Francisco's Athletic Club hosted the international title bout with 8,000 fans in attendance. George Dixon, at 21-years-old, weighed 114 pounds, and his challenger Abe Willis tipped the scales at 113 pounds. The winner would receive 75 percent of a $5,000 cash prize. Dixon took control early with quick jabs and punches to set the tempo. At the end of the round, Willis had a lump above one of his eyes. In the fifth round, Dixon knocked Willis out cold and jumped over the ring to celebrate. O'Rourke claimed that Dixon was the bantamweight and featherweight champion of the world. In 1892, Dixon brought more "weight" to his claim by beating Fred Johnson, Wallace's successor to the British featherweight title, in 14 rounds.

A watershed moment in the history of boxing in America occurred during a three-day boxing carnival beginning September 5, 1892. It would mark the end of the heavyweight title reign of one of the most iconic men of the ring. John L. Sullivan would lose to Gentleman

Jim Corbett. The Carnival of Champions would also deal a death blow for interracial championship fights for another decade. New Orleans hosted the Carnival that showcased title bouts in three divisions: featherweight, lightweight, and heavyweight. On September 5, the lightweight bout featured the champion Jack McAuliffe against Billy Mayer. On September 6, the featherweight bout featured the champion George Dixon against Jack Skelly. It would be the first public, legal series of championship fights featuring an interracial match in the

Dixon and Skelly depicted in the *New Orleans Times Picayune.* Headlines for September 7, 1892, read "Black Wins." Drawings such as this gave reading audiences images prior to action photography.

South. On September 7, the heavyweight bout featured the champion John L. Sullivan against Gentleman Jim Corbett. For the first time, all of the matches were fought under the Queensberry rules which mandated three-minute rounds with one-minute rest breaks, the standard used today. These rules also outlawed wrestling and bare knuckles. Prior to this birth of modern boxing, prize fighting was illegal in many states. Matches were often held in secret places that had a lookout or someone who would pay off the local police. Since the South was racially divided during this time, mixed public matches were supposed to be illegal. However, the private Olympia Club hosted the event as a way to bypass the Jim Crow laws.

Indoor lights were used for the first time during the spectacular event. A $17,500 winner-take-all prize awaited the victor of the George Dixon–Jack Skelly fight. Dixon negotiated 850 seats (at $6.00 per seat) in the gallery for blacks. Over 400 black fans watched the historic match in the same setting with 4,000 whites. Technically, Jack Skelly was an amateur who should not have been matched against Dixon. However, several white fans believed a white boxer could beat any black boxer. Some even thought a white boxer could simply look sternly into the eyes of the black boxer and bring fear and trepidation to his being. Their calculations were inaccurate. Dixon entered the ring at 118 pounds and annihilated the amateur (who weighed 116) to the delight of black fans and to the consternation of the whites. Historian Arthur Ashe informed, "In some quarters of the city black citizens celebrated for two days." Stories from ringside were reported over the wires, "The occupants of the colored gallery made a great noise and kept it up until R.M. Frank, the official time keeper of the club, called for order."[15] *The Chicago Tribune* wrote, "White fans winced every time Dixon landed on Jack Skelly. The sight was repugnant to some of the men from the South. A darky is alright in his place here, but the idea of sitting quietly by and seeing a colored boy pummel a white lad grates on Southerners."[16] The *New Orleans Time-Democrat* gave a southern point of view: "What with bruises, lacerations and coagulated blood Jack Skelly's nose, mouth, and eye presented a horrible spectacle ... some even turned away their heads in disgust at that face already disfigured beyond recognition ... it was a mistake to match a Negro and a white man a mistake to bring the races together on any terms of equality, even in the prize ring ... it was not pleasant to see a white man applaud a Negro for knocking another white man out."[17]

After the Carnival of Champions, the Olympia Club did not permit any more matches to be fought there which ignored the color line. The reaction to the Dixon victory may have reinforced the color line in the heavyweight division and in other sports as well.[18] But Dixon's victory on that historic occasion cemented his position as a pioneer of American boxing. In addition to defeating a white fighter in the segregated South, Dixon had claimed equality for the fan base by using his status for the benefit of black attendees, a request that was unheard of at the Olympic Club in New Orleans or anywhere else in the South at that time.[19]

Through all of these and other experiences, Dixon gained respect and sophistication. In March of 1893, Richard K. Fox, esteemed editor and owner of the *Police Gazette Newspaper,* awarded the featherweight championship belt to Dixon as he was acclaimed to be a pioneering scientific boxer under the Queensberry rules.

Throughout his career, Dixon identified with the plight of black people, despite his privileged status as a renowned athlete. He contributed to causes that fought racism in this country and abroad. Dixon was a noted stylish dresser who freely spent money and loved to have a good time. He was always willing to give a handout to those in need when he had the money. In 1893, he wrote his autobiography, which was well received. The following

John L. Sullivan,
—THE AMERICAN CAFÉ—
ColemanHouse.

1177 BROADWAY.
75 ROOMS—BY DAY OR WEEK.

Dante's Inferno Exhibition Company, Proprietors.   Capital Stock, $50,000. Incorporated 1898.

Telephone: 953 Madison Square.   New York, Dec. 29th 1899

Ben: Benton Esqr

                        My dear Benton
You can state that McGovern will beat
Dixon sure and inside of 10 rounds. that is
as sure as your name is Ben Benton take my
tip for that although Dixon is a great little
colored boy this is the time he will meet his
waterloo although it will be no credit to any
one who does defeat him because he has gone
a fast clip like myself. But never mind
that McGovern could beat him in his best day,
and I do not want you to think I am prejudiced
predjudiced I am far from being such this boy
McGovern is a wonder of the nineteen century
as before I am. Yours Truly
                        John L Sullivan

In a pre-fight press statement (solicited from boxing celebrities), John L. Sullivan wrote to George Dixon's former manager and newspaper scribe, Ben Benton, predicting that Dixon will meet his "waterloo" when he defends his featherweight title against Terry McGovern on January 9, 1900. Sullivan alludes to his legacy by reminding Benton that he is "far from being" prejudiced (letter reprinted by Harry Pegg, *Boxiana Review*, Issue No. 9, 1973).

World fighting celebrities posed in front of Professor Jimmy Kelly's Gym at New Dorp, Staten Island. Front row, seated left to right: Joe Gans, Joe Walcott, and George Dixon. Standing, left to right: Professor Kelly, unidentified trainer, Gans' manager Al Herford, unidentified trainer, and fighter Harry Lyons (Gary Schultz collection).

year he toured the country with a vaudeville group and athletic company called the George Dixon Specialty Company. His group performed in front of packed houses all over America. Dixon was the idol of millions of fans, both black and white. Dixon found the competition of sports often forced white fans to, at least temporarily, drop racist attitudes and positions. Black fans adored him unconditionally. That love was only slightly challenged when Dixon fell in love with a white woman, Kitty O'Rourke, his manager's sister. Kitty was to be his second wife. He was previously married to a black woman. While traveling with his touring company, Dixon often stayed at a "Colored boarding house" while his wife was put up in a local whites-only hotel.[20] Nevertheless, it was the sport of boxing, Dixon's profession, which allowed him to break through racist barriers and stereotypes. Through his example of dignified excellence, Little Chocolate challenged the prevailing bigotry of the period and created a model of inclusion that would be followed by athletes, entertainers, and human rights activists to come.

On October 4, 1897, Dixon experienced a disappointing loss that he turned into a stepping stone. Solly Smith, whom Dixon had previously defeated, won the 20-round match on decision. Tom O'Rourke complained that his fighter had been robbed. Dixon felt the loss of his title so deeply that he broke down in the dressing room with only his manager to console him.[21] On November 11, 1898 Dixon redeemed himself by knocking out Dave Sullivan, the man who defeated Solly Smith, to become the first man to lose his title in the ring and to regain it.

In the year 1900 Dixon slowed down, losing a step and consequently his championship.

George Dixon Memorial Fountain, dedicated to the popular champion on August 28, 1908, in New York (Bain News Service, George Grantham Bain Collection, Library of Congress).

The 14-year veteran of the ring fought "Terrible" Terry McGovern, an outstanding fighter in the prime of his career. Dixon started at his typical frantic pace and kept McGovern focused on defense. In the fourth round the momentum changed and McGovern took control. Dixon was floored eight times in the eighth round. After the bell sounded, O'Rourke called off the fight. McGovern gave Dixon another chance, on June 23, 1900, but Dixon could not recapture the essence of his earlier days. Again McGovern was announced the winner.

Like many boxers, Dixon fought too long. Macon commented that "it was safe to say" he had fought 600 battles by 1897.[22] Dixon's manager reported 800 for his boxing career, a number that was passed on by Nat Fleischer.[23] Dixon continued to fight for five more years after losing the title. He won most of his matches, but could not earn the same level of income. Despite the apparent limitations and the need for an adjustment in his lifestyle, Dixon continued to live the high life as he knew it. As he began drinking more and training less, he lost all of his wealth. With nowhere else to turn, he received help from an unlikely source, John L. Sullivan. The former heavyweight champion had been a heavy drinker who liked to party and came to the aid of Dixon. Sullivan, a fighter who drew the color line, refusing to fight black fighters, was speaking out against drinking. He befriended Dixon who was appreciative to the very end. Dixon said that Sullivan was the only man in pugilism who hadn't turned him down. Dixon complained that even his manager, Tom O'Rourke, turned away when his fighting days were over.

Only two years after he was knocked out by Tommy Murphy in two rounds in Philadelphia, George Dixon passed away in New York City at the age of 37. The date was January 6, 1908. After his retirement from the ring, few knew of his whereabouts. The glamorous, friendly, record-setting sport icon had dropped into homeless obscurity. A few days prior to his death George was accompanied by an unnamed black friend and a white friend to Bellevue Hospital, suffering from an acute case of inflammatory rheumatism, a painful condition of the muscle tissue. The next day his condition worsened and he continued to deteriorate until he died. His body was taken to the city morgue and embalmed.[24] The sporting members of New York were shocked and saddened by the news. His friends arranged for Dixon to lie in state in one of the club rooms of the Longacre Athletic Club on west Twenty-Ninth Street. Members of the athletic club paid for his burial expenses, after which a committee of club members debated whether to provide for either a gravestone or a memorial. They ultimately decided that a city memorial to the most popular and accomplished boxer of the generation would be more fitting.

New York boxing announcer Joe Humphreys and boxers Terry McGovern and Young Corbett collected donations for the George Dixon Memorial Fountain, a New York public fountain — one side for horses and the other for the public — on the corner of Thompson and Broome streets. The monument was completed on August 28, 1908. On the wall of the fountain was a permanent wreath encircling the words: "In memory of George Dixon, erected by his friends, 1908."[25]

Athletes are continuously challenged to prove they have exceptional prowess and courage. Once levels of achievement have been reached, there is an endless panoply of competitors and pundits who believe someone else is more deserving of the accolades. George Dixon triumphed over the adversaries who considered him too small, too black, and too flamboyant.

Dixon served as a role model for all athletes by accepting the challenges and creatively using them to enhance his skills and expand his fame. Becoming the first multiple titleholder in pugilistic history, the first to lose and regain his world title in the ring, and the first black athlete to be crowned the best in the world are no small feats. We can easily marvel at anyone who is generally conceded to be the finest bantamweight and featherweight in history. Above all else, we are captivated by his pioneering proof that you can never measure the *heart* of an athlete by size or color.

NOTES

1. Nat Fleischer, *Black Dynamite, Vol. III, The Three Colored Aces: Story of the George Dixon, Joe Gans and Joe Walcott and Several Contemporaries*, 6.

2. Charles Saunders, *Sweat and Soul: The Saga of Black Boxers from the Halifax to Caesar's Palace*, "The Colour Line," 22.

3. Nat Fleischer, *Ring Record Book and Boxing Encyclopedia*, 31.

4. Fleischer, *Black Dynamite*, 6.

5. J. B. McCormick, *The Square Circle: Stories of the Prize Ring*, 230–231.

6. McCormick, 234.

7. McCormick, 231.

8. Ibid.

9. Fleischer, *The Ring Record Book*, 31.

10. Fleischer, "King of Paperweights," *Black Dynamite*, 15.

11. Fleischer, 23.

12. Fleischer, 24.

13 Saunders, 29.

14. Fleischer, 34–35.

15. "White vs. Black: The Color Line Not Drawn in Fistic Ring," *Hamilton* (Ohio) *Daily Democrat*, September 8, 1892.

16. Arthur Ashe, *A Hard Road to Glory: A History of the African-American Athlete*, 23–30.

17. Ibid.

18. Ibid.

19. Ibid.

20. Ocania Chalk, *Pioneers of Black Sport*, 128.

21. Nat Fleischer and Sam Andre, *A Pictorial History of Boxing*, 276.

22. McCormick, 234.

23. Fleischer, *Ring Record Book*, 31.

24. "George Dixon Dead: Former Pugilistic Wonder Succumbs to Heart Disease at Bellevue," *New York Times*, January 7, 1908.

25. "Sports to Erect Monument to George Dixon," *Washington Post*, January 8, 1908; "A Memorial Erected to the Late George Dixon," *Lowell Sun* (Mass.), August 30, 1908.

CHAPTER 5

Bobby Dobbs: Lightweight Challenger and Father of Boxing in Germany

Kevin Smith

In 1923, sportswriter Damon Runyon reported that Bobby Dobbs was one of the leading lightweights of his time, an old-timer, "now an old, old man — just how old nobody knows."[1] Bobby Dobbs always lied about his age. Or possibly, he never truly knew what the exact date of his birth was. In 1905 he told a group of English writers that he was 45 years old. Later in 1917, Lawrence Sweeney of the *Boston Globe* ran into Bobby at a fair in Old Orchard Beach, Maine, where the retired pugilist told the sports writer that his sister had recently recovered a family bible that listed his birth date as 1858. Others cite 1869 as Dobbs' birth date.[2] In 1930 Dobbs, then living in Charleston, South Carolina, told census takers that he was 70 years old. Ten years earlier he had told them that he was 46. All of this of course was Bobby Dobbs being Bobby Dobbs. He seemed to like the fact that no one could pin down his age, or even his place of birth. He frequently changed and re-arranged the facts, seemingly playing a game of "guess what" with whoever made inquiries into his personal history. He changed the facts, depending on his mood and where and with whom he was speaking. Denver, Ogden, Knoxville, Atlanta were all cities claimed by Dobbs, at one time or another, to be the host of his natural born birth. And for years on in, those who have written or spoken about the incredible Dobbs were never quite sure what the facts were. I think that's the way Bobby would have liked it.

According to U.S. census records, Robert W. Dobbs was born in Cartersville, Georgia in January of 1868.[3] He was the first of three children born to Gib and Harriet, both former slaves who, having gotten a late start to their "free life," did not have their first child until well into their 40's. Gib had grown up on the Dobbs estate, where he had labored for nearly his entire life as a cotton picker and general farm worker, and had probably known Harriet for years. They married in 1867 and shortly thereafter had their first child, a son they named Robert. Gib continued to work the fields of the Dobbs estate, now as a paid hand, and as soon as young Bob turned ten, he too, took to the fields. When Robert set out onto his worldly life is unknown. He liked to claim that he was on the road and fighting as early as 1875, but this could not have been the case. The Federal Census of 1880, places Bob, age 12, in Cartersville living with his parents and his two sisters, Sarah and Roseanne. Again, Dobbs' memory, or more aptly, his imagination, leads one to consider his autobiographical story-telling more as fancy fiction than fact. In that vein, it is nearly impossible to truly know when he "left off from the farm."

Dobbs evidently did some traveling and some fighting as early as the mid–1880s. Bat Masterson, who was the sheriff at Dodge City in the late 1870s and then again in the mid 1880s, claimed in 1910 that he remembered Bobby fighting around Dodge City during that time.[4] Bat, who settled in Denver in the early 1890s where he became involved with the fight game as a manager and matchmaker, more than likely had his dates and locations confused. Dobbs was floating around Colorado in the early 1890's and more than likely Masterson ran into the colored lightweight at Denver during that time.

In 1890, Bobby landed in Ogden, Utah where he began his career as a prizefighter in earnest. He came to Utah to play baseball for the Ogden Nine, a local team of semi-professional ball players that barnstormed throughout Utah playing against other local teams. Bobby played left field for the Nine and batted in the two hole. Dobbs played ball for the Ogden Nine

Bobby Dobbs, master boxer, in fighting stance (Kevin Smith collection).

throughout the summer of 1890.[5] He was a reliable defender and a speedy runner. He could also hit a bit. However, his real talent was fist fighting. His first known (or traceable) bout took place at Ogden on August 5, 1890. Dobbs won with a knockout over John Moore in four rounds. And thus, one of the more brilliant and interesting careers in the history of pugilism began.

Dobbs spent the first season of his career jumping back and forth between Utah and Colorado, getting his knuckles dirty and building a reputation. The good sports of Ogden liked Dobbs immensely and even at this early stage of his career, his charismatic and cheerful disposition earned him friends of all kinds. His first fight of significance was against Dan Egan, the Montana Kid, who had something of a name in the game. Bobby met Egan for the first time in November of 1890, and despite proving the Kid's master, lost on a foul in the tenth round. The two men were re-matched a month later and fought a clean ten-round draw. These decisions aside, Bobby was praised for his panther-like quickness and his ability to hit hard with either hand. He was a good self-promoter and found work rather easily. Having backers in Colorado and Utah who were both confident in his ability and well heeled in cash, Dobbs fought frequently for the next year and a half. In 1892 he ventured out to the West Coast and was promptly knocked out by California Jack O'Brien in two rounds in San Francisco. Bobby had controlled the fight until running into a left hook, and many described O'Brien's win as a "fluke." Dobbs offered no excuses. In a letter to his fans in Ogden he stated clearly, "I offer no excuses. I have learned that no man should be taken lightly. I was in top shape and possibly a bit over confident. I offer no excuse for my defeat other than the fact that I lost. I shall not take such liberties again."[6] The "liberties" that Bobby spoke of were in essence a lack of concentration. After handling O'Brien easily in the first round, Dobbs let up a bit and began to take things easy, figuring he had the fight in control and could take out his opponent when he chose. A short left hook settled the value of that thinking.

Bobby rebounded from his defeat by winning a few minor bouts before earning a rematch with his conqueror. This time he took no chances. Fighting with focus and determination, Dobbs wiped the floor with O'Brien and knocked him cold in three rounds. His lesson had been learned. And as he would demonstrate throughout his career, if Bobby Dobbs was anything, he was a student of the game. He studied pugilism as if it were an art form, learning the ever-so-fine aspects of the game — those little things that separated the pugs from the contenders and the contenders from the champions. Of course, it would also help that Dobbs would fight professionally for over two decades, making him a virtual model of experience. This determination, combined with his ability to absorb detail, made him a virtuoso of sorts — for no ordinary fighter could have survived as long as he did in such a brutal and unforgiving game.

Dobbs, invigorated by his return victory, continued to make a name for himself, basing his operations in San Francisco and beating back a number of good lightweights. A match with Minnesota's Charley Johnson was the breakthrough that catapulted Dobbs from a western phenom into a nationwide name. Fighting gracefully with brutal force that had become his style, Bobby waged a savage war with Johnson before finishing his game opponent in the 41st round.[7] A draw with black middleweight Charley Turner led to a match with newly arrived Australian welterweight Jim Barron, a grim faced, stocky welterweight. Dobbs boxed brilliantly for the first round-and-a-half until running into a sledgehammer of a right hand. He wobbled and fell as if drunk. In a letter to his Ogden friends Bobby described the incident:

He (Barron) was standing in front of me, holding his hands high near his head and I decided to soften his underside. I whipped a left and then a right to his stomach and heard him grunt, like they hurt. But he kept his hands up and I thought I would oblige him with more. He whipped another right in there and then the roof fell on my head. I don't know what he hit me with but I saw black for a moment and then realized I was on my back. It took a second or two to remember where I was and what I was doing. I could not feel my legs, like they had been cut from my body, but I could see them out in front of me. I tried to stand but could not find my balance. I stumbled around the ring for a moment, but beat the referee's count. I was not steady cause I could not feel my legs. I don't know where Barron was but the referee started waving the fight off and came over to me. I asked him what's what and he says that the fight's over. I said "Did I win?" He says that my corner "threw up the sponge." I looked over and I saw Lloyd and Johnson come in the ropes and start walking towards me with long faces. I ask them the same thing I asked the referee and they tell me that I was a goner. Lloyd says, "You should be happy we saved you — you was dead out!" I told them I was awake but that I could not feel my legs — that I could have continued, but they said they couldn't know what was what. I was mad at first but then realized that I should have never gotten hit like that. Barron was strong but he was not a boxer — not a boxer of the ability of some of the other men I have beaten. I have asked him for a rematch — here is hoping to the fact that he fights me again.[8]

As with his loss to O'Brien, Dobbs realized that he had only himself to blame for the loss to Barron. He called it carelessness, but it could have just as easily been described as a fluke. Bobby didn't let it affect him. He knew he would have better days. He also knew that he had to learn from what happened against Barron; learn to never let that happen again — not to a lesser man.

Bobby rebounded from the loss to Barron by taking the measure of the famous Harris Martin, better known in fight circles as the "Black Pearl." Martin was a number of years past his best when he came to San Francisco to match up with the black lightweight from Ogden, but nonetheless a stiff challenge for the still-learning Dobbs. The Pearl was the heaviest man that Bobby had yet faced, and combined with his pedigree as a tough-as-nails skin-fighter, who throughout his career boasted an impressive ability to absorb tremendous amounts of punishment, served to provide the young Dobbs with a very tall task. The men were scheduled to fight to the finish with 5-ounce gloves, but Bobby proved too elusive and too clever for the cruder and slower Martin. Having made a career out of out-slugging his opponents, the Pearl, once his famed stamina had given way, was really no challenge at all for the lighter Dobbs, who darted in, out and around for 15 rounds before settling in and finishing his exhausted foe in the 18th frame. Still, the match proved to be quite a feather in Bobby's cap, for it was thought before the fight by many pugilistic authorities that Dobbs had not the weight, chin, nor pedigree to take the measure of the far more experienced and larger Martin. As he would throughout his career, Bobby Dobbs proved the "experts" wrong.

Bobby remained out in the Western states, honing his craft in a number of lesser bouts of the four- and six-round variety and building on his growing reputation by knocking out some higher quality men in longer and better-publicized matches. In Minneapolis he took the measure of Iron Bark Jim Burge in 20 rounds and then knocked out lightweight Billy Lavigne, the brother of the lightweight champion George Lavigne, in five rounds.[9] The victory over Lavigne gave Dobbs his first true national reputation, the result of the fight being carried in newspapers across the country, and Billy being touted as a comer in the lightweight division. With this publicity firmly in hand, Dobbs was signed on by Boston-based fight manager Ben "Rob Roy" Benton, who immediately brought his new charge East to join his troupe of boxers which, at the time, included Dan Creedon, Tom Tracey and Dick Moore.

Bobby met Benton in Chicago where the former was immediately put through the paces in a series of exhibition matches. His first such fight in the Windy City was against the sturdy black welterweight Frank O'Neal. Dobbs struggled a bit with the weight and rough infighting of the Chicago fighter but did little to damage Benton's enthusiasm for his new charge. A few similar short-round, "try out" type, preliminary matches followed before Dobbs and Benton headed off for the latter's vacation estate in Eastport, Maine, for a bit of rest and recuperation. While in Eastport, Bobby trained faithfully and took part in a few six-round bouts, the most notable being a rough draw with Andy Watson, the superb West Indian lightweight. For some reason both men had a personal dislike for the other, and it showed in the ferocity of their six-round tussle in the small Maine seaport. A few days later the two rivals headed up into St. John's, Nova Scotia, where they resumed their hostilities for another six rounds. Bad blood was plentiful, and both men were accused of fighting foul. Their feud would not be limited to the ring however. When both returned to Boston, Watson to his usual haunts and Dobbs with Benton to begin his eastern campaign, they met up on a West End street corner and had a fist fight. Both were thrown in jail, but released without further incident.[10] Three days latter, the feud still fresh in their minds, they were at it again, this time in the back alley of a popular watering hole. Friends broke up the scuffle, but the owner of the establishment informed police that real trouble was brewing between the two men and that if the authorities did not intervene one of them might end up dead. Benton saw this personal matter as bad for business and urged Dobbs and Watson to meet at the sporting offices of the *Boston Post* to make a forfeit for a finish match. Why not get paid for hurting one another, thought Benton? Watson agreed, and on the evening of September 5, 1894, the two fighters, Dobbs flanked by his manager and Watson by a few friends, met at the offices of Benton (who also worked for the *Post*) to hash out the details of their official grudge match. The meeting did not go smoothly. First Dobbs, and then Watson, threw pointed barbs at the other until a scuffle broke out. Bobby reportedly bit Andy on the arm and then hit him with a cane. Watson responded by punching Dobbs hard on the ear, knocking him to the floor where the West Indian then set upon him with an assortment of kicks and stomps. Andy's friends pulled him off Dobbs and escorted him from the building. Needless to say, arrangements for the match were never completed.

In order to cool his fighter's heels, Benton sent Bobby back up to the St. John's area, where the latter performed nightly in a small theatre show. After a few weeks the crowds dried up, and Bobby sent word to Benton that he was out of money and wanted to return to Boston. Ben sent Dobbs to Maine instead where he once again was sent out on a small touring set, this time, traveling from small town to small town, where sometimes he was forced to fight in small tents and barns. Dobbs was miserable. He again sent word to his manager that he wished to return to the city, but Benton told him that he had to stay on the tour so that he could "honor the agreement" signed by himself (Benton) and the tour's manager and owner, John Bently. Bobby fumed, and after a few mores shows, took what little money he had and purchased his own fare to return to Boston. Once in the Hub, Dobbs made his own arrangements to fight John Butler, another good, black lightweight, at the latter's home stomping grounds in Lynn, Massachusetts, for a $500 purse. By this time, however, Benton had caught wind from Bently that Dobbs had left the tour and set out to seek his damages. Ben had Dobbs arrested, on charges of debt evasion, and sought out an injunction to have Bobby repay him the $300 he stated that he "lost" when the latter left the Maine tour. Dobbs was furious by the charge and stewed in the cooler for a few days while he adamantly refused to pay up. Finally, with the date for his match with Butler drawing near, and his $500 purse in jeopardy, Bobby admitted that he did not have the money to pay Benton and signed a "debtor's promissory note" agreeing to pay Benton when the funds became available. What Dobbs did not mention to the judge or the court was his bout with Butler in Lynn or the $500 purse that was to come with it. Benton, a man who was well-in-the-know in local Boston boxing circles, eventually found out about the match and was infuriated. He had a judge issue a warrant for the arrest of Dobbs and planned to take every measure to ensure that the planned Butler match did not take place. On the night of September 27, 1894, Ben Benton, along with the Middlesex County sheriff, a few of his deputies, and a warrant for Bobby Dobbs' arrest, were all present at the Kirkland Athletic Club awaiting the arrival of the western prizefighter. John Butler stood in the ring while the crowd clamored for the appearance of Dobbs. Bobby, who had been hiding out for days at the home of Bob Allen, finally and brazenly appeared at 8:45 P.M. in his full boxing gear, ready to fight. As soon as he stepped into the ring however, he was greeted by Benton, the sheriff, the deputies, and a warrant for his arrest. Dobbs went quietly.[11]

Bobby returned to Boston and somehow escaped punishment. He claimed once again that he did not have the funds to pay Benton and took a "poor debtor's oath" to avoid another stint in jail. Just why Benton would have prevented Dobbs from earning his $500 against Butler in Lynn does not makes sense. If Benton had allowed Bobby to fight, the latter could have surely been made to pay his debt. As it was however, Dobbs had little more than the shirt on his back and no means to make money. Benton, who still maintained that he was, by contract, Dobbs' manager, told him that he could work the debt off by returning to the tour in Maine. Bobby had other ideas.

Dobbs took off for Philadelphia where he signed on with Howie Hodgkins, who managed Joe Walcott (when Tom O'Rourke and Walcott were bickering, that is). Hodgkins immediately found him a four-round tilt with Frank McClean — also known as the Cuban Wonder. Benton published threats to have Dobbs arrested if he chose to go through with the scheduled fight, but at some point must have decided Bobby Dobbs was no longer worth his efforts. For his part, Dobbs looked rusty and overmatched when he stepped into the ring with the Wonder, losing a four-round decision and igniting a storm of criticism from the press. The *Boston Globe* wrote, "Another western wonder has imploded, as Dobbs the Minneapolis lightweight showed far worse than his reputation in a four-round tussle with Frank McClean in Philadelphia the other night. Frank had things all his own way despite the fact that he claimed he had a bad right hand from a fight he had just a fortnight before."[12]

Dobbs did not offer excuses but instead turned inward, determining that he would not confront the papers publicly. He felt he was being slighted and judged unfairly, not only in reference to his fight with McClean, but also in his episodes with Ben Benton. The McClean fight had been simply an exhibition in Bobby's mind, nothing more than an opportunity for him to stretch his muscles and keep busy while he waited for bigger and better fights. He did not realize beforehand, that his entire reputation balanced on his performance against McClean. He had spent the better part of the past two months fighting in small venues, against nondescript opponents on a "take on all comers" tour in Maine and Canada. The bout in Philly seemed to be little different. But the Benton drama infuriated Dobbs even more. It was the wily manager who pulled Bobby East, promising him big matches for big money. What happened instead was that Dobbs found himself fighting for small change, at the whim and mercy of a manager who seemed to care little about getting his charge a well-paying gig. His dealings with Benton and his eventual solution to the issue demonstrated the resolve that Bobby had. He was no one's servant, and he certainly was under no man's charge. He stood up to Benton and freed himself from a situation that he found not to be in his best interest. That he risked his own personal liberty was of little consequence. A few nights in jail were a hell of a lot better than a few years of being at Benton's beck and call.

In the late fall of 1894, Bobby Dobbs was in a no-man's land. The good reputation that he had built up the long and hard way in Colorado, Minnesota and California was virtually worthless as stretches of small-time bouts, inactivity, unimpressive performances and legal problems had tarnished his name in the East. Fortunately, not everyone had given up on Bobby Dobbs. In a stroke of luck he was matched against the famous lightweight Billy Vernon, the Haverstraw Brick-maker, in New York. Dobbs knocked him cold in the fourth round of a fight that he was losing. This impressive KO of the usually durable Vernon forced Eastern sportsmen to reconsider their initial assessment on Bobby, and placed him back on the doorstep of contendership. A return to Philadelphia saw Bobby's match-up with Bull McCarthy end when a rumble in the crowd interrupted the proceedings, but a knockout over Jimmy Fox in four rounds kept the train on track.

Howie Hodgkins took Bobby back to Boston where the local fans were still interested in seeing the crack colored man from the West fight (they had been deprived of that pleasure by the poor management of Ben Benton). Dick O'Brien, a very good middleweight from Lewiston, Maine, was signed as an opponent, the men scheduled to box on April 19, 1894 at the Farragut Club for a scheduled 25 rounds. Dick was a good, stand-up boxer and a strong puncher, and had championship aspirations of his own in the 158-pound division. Why Hodgkins would allow his lightweight — Dobbs had not yet weighed over 142 pounds for any fight and could easily scale down to the 133 lightweight limit — to fight a heavy middleweight is not known. It was a match that seemed to reek of poor piloting. But Dobbs had fought bigger men before, was trained to the minute, and seemed to have confidence that he could give away some fifteen to twenty pounds and still prove to be O'Brien's master. He was wrong. From the start, Dick demonstrated that he would make the fight a rough-and-tough power play. Using his extra weight and muscle to maneuver the lighter Dobbs around the ring, the Maine middleweight immediately took control of the fight. He knocked Dobbs down several times in the first ten rounds and punished his body with digging shots when in close. Bobby tried to fight back as best he could, but he was quickly losing his strength. In the thirteenth round, as his body began to give out on him, Dobbs made one final effort to crash the defense of the sturdy O'Brien. He launched a furious and desperate assault that had some of the Maine man's supporters concerned, but in the end, left little impression on the outcome of the fight. Dobbs spent the next several rounds simply trying to survive, but that strategy proved unsuccessful as well. Finally, in the middle of the 18th round, after Dobbs had been knocked to the canvas for the 13th time, the referee stepped in and awarded the fight to O'Brien. Bobby Dobbs had given too much away. That a good big man will always beat a good small man was true in this instance. Dobbs simply could not cope with the extra strength that O'Brien's larger frame afforded him. It was not a test of skill, but instead a test of strength, one that Bobby could not have hoped to have won.

The next year of Bobby Dobbs' fistic career would see him matched up with some of the best men in the lighter weight divisions. He remained on the East Coast and fought a plethora of all-time great men, the names of Joe Walcott, Pepper Griffin, Andy Watson, Philadelphia Jack O'Brien, Billy Hill, Hugh McWinters, Martin Judge and a host of others gracing his ledger. He beat most of them above and drew with several others. His January 16, 1897, draw in Philadelphia with Joe Walcott, then the scourge of welterweights everywhere, deserves particular mention. Dobbs fought Walcott tooth-and-nail and proved a tartar to the future welterweight king. Not only did the Barbados Demon struggle with Bobby, but many of newspapermen and fans in attendance credited Bobby with a newspaper win in their six-round battle.[13] Dobbs' three-bout series with O'Brien, a four-round win and four- and six-round draws, also deserves notice. Philly Jack, the future light heavyweight king, was young and inexperienced, but his pedigree even then was first class. Consider that after loosing to Dobbs in 1897, O'Brien would lose only two more times over the course of the next ten years, all while fighting at the highest level of competition. There were small setbacks for Dobbs during this time as well. He looked tired and out of shape in dropping a six-round decision to Austin Gibbons in Patterson, struggled again with Frank Mclean and fought tooth-and-nail for 10 rounds with tough old friend Billy Hill, the famous "Pickaninny." But despite these minor setbacks, Bobby was fighting with regularity, and constantly rebuilding what had been a damaged reputation at the beginning of the 1896 season. However, it was Dobbs third to last fight of 1897 that would earn him his greatest accolades, and in the end, the victory which would ultimately prove to be his finest hour.

Joe Gans today is considered one of the best, if not the greatest, lightweights who has ever slipped on a pair of boxing gloves. In September of 1897 he was being touted as the Colored Lightweight Champion of the World and considered one of the better lightweight men in existence. He was earmarked for the championship and figured to have little trouble with the up and down Dobbs. The two colored lightweights met at the Greenpoint Athletic Club in Brooklyn on September 27, 1897, and Bobby Dobbs could not have been more ready. The first four rounds were nearly void of any action, as both men circled one another looking for openings. In the fifth however, Dobbs, who was described as being taller and more well-muscled than Gans, drove his shorter opponent to the ropes, where he worked his punches almost exclusively to the Baltimore man's ribs. These punches would have a dramatic effect on Gans as he struggled to fight Bobby off and could not seem to time the rushes of his taller foe. The fight itself was not a technical marvel but an illustration of what planning and determination can do for a fighter. Dobbs worked the body of Gans for the most part of the middle seven rounds, forsaking any type of head punches in order to rake and pound the ribs and stomach of Joe's slight build. Dobbs resorted to clinches and infighting. While Gans complained about the clinching, the body work of Dobbs paid huge dividends as Gans never seemed to recover the strength and speed that had been sapped from his body by the fierce attack. The fight remained competitive until the end, but when the gong sounded it was clear who had won.[14]

Dobbs' defeat of the well-known Gans skyrocketed him into a new fistic realm. When before he had come East, he was considered a phenom, and then after his arrival a disappointment, Bobby Dobbs was now a full-fledged contender. The newspapermen spoke of him in glowing, superhuman terms; matchmakers and promoters alike sought his services and flooded him with offers and guarantees. And as with all good black contenders, other contenders and their managers started staying clear. Dobbs finished off his season with a few more wins, and then began his 1898 campaign much in the same manner as he had ended his previous one, by winning frequently. Prior to the fall of 1898 Dobbs took part in seven contests, winning six, three by KO, two by foul, and fought a 4-round draw with Paddy Sheehan. Among his victims during that stretch were the very capable Dick Case, Jack Fox, black middleweight Charley Peaker, and the always entertaining Billy Ernst — not exactly a Hall-of-Fame crew, but still a solid group of boxers. Despite his success, Bobby was after bigger game and bigger purses. He challenged all and sundry, trying in one way or another to find a match against a big-name opponent that would give him the opportunity to net a large sum of money. He would be frustrated, however, as managers of rival lightweight and welterweight contenders shied away from Dobbs as if he were a contagious disease. The problem was Bobby's drawing capacity (which in essence affected the amount a man could demand in purse money). Although good, it did not warrant the risk involved by taking him on. Another issue was Bobby's somewhat inflated self image. He often demanded outlandish purses and enormous guarantees which in most cases simply priced him out of fights altogether. Weeks soon turned into months and Bobby was at a crossroad. He contemplated signing up for a few minor fights he had been offered in rural Pennsylvania when he got a cable from English manager John S. Barnes, an acquaintance of Frank Craig's, requesting his signature on a contract. Barnes' bait was a twenty-round match with England's famous lightweight Dick Burge for a purse of 250 pounds with a side bet of 300 pounds. Dobbs wasted little time contemplating his options.

When Bobby arrived in London he was greeted by Frank Craig, who had been in England for well over five years. The Coffee Cooler had made himself quite a healthy sum of money in Britain and told Bobby that he could do the same. Frank assisted Bobby in

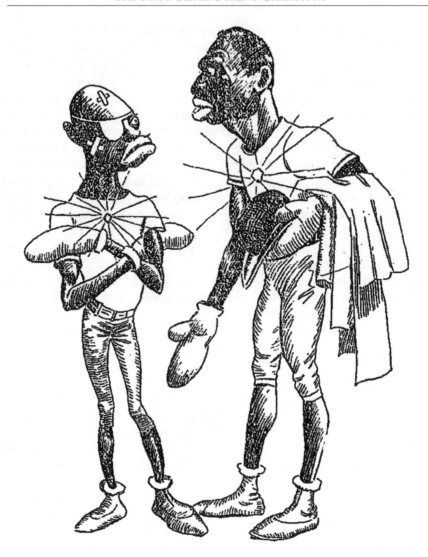

Frank Craig, the "Harlem Coffee Cooler" says to Bobby Dobbs in a cartoon after their return to America, "Jes stop an' tink wot bloomin chumps we was to leave Hengland. We might er got to be Princes of Wales over dere, hinstead of eatin' at sandwich wagins" (Kevin Smith collection).

getting acquainted with the local area, hiring sparring partners and setting up his friend with proper quarters. Bobby trained as usual, with a fervor and dedication that marked nearly everything that he did. The British liked the look of Dobbs, his long, lithe frame drawing deep gasps of admiration from any onlooker who spied him in training. Soon he was the talk of London. As the English had loved Peter Jackson and Frank Craig, so too would they be enamored with Bobby Dobbs.

The Burge-Dobbs battle took place at Newcastle on Tyne on December 12, 1898, and was ugly from the start.[15] Bobby was trained to the minute and looked ready for a long, hard fight. Burge, on the other hand, seemed dry, uninterested and undertrained, a slight paunch visible around his midsection. The two men wasted little time in getting to work when the initial bell opened the contest. Burge seemed to be in control early, pushing and mauling Dobbs in the clinches and working him over with short hard shots to the ribs and back. Bobby fought back with his own assortment of inside blows, and the fight turned ugly. Both fighters, along with their seconds, repeatedly claimed fouls as both Dick and Bobby began to get personal with an variety of low blows, kidney punches, head butts and elbows. The referee sent out warnings to both men, but the fight remained a free-for-all. In the fifth frame, however, Dobbs began to use his superior foot and hand speed, and brought the fight off the ropes into the middle of the ring. Bobby's new tactics, along with his hard training, immediately began to pay dividends and by the end of the round Burge was noticeably winded. Dobbs controlled the action for the next round and a half and started to settle in to a comfortable pace of domination. In the eighth, Burge and Dobbs fell into a clinch and moved together to the ropes. Dick then hollered with pain and indignation, claiming that Dobbs had again fouled him. The referee disagreed and ordered the Englishman to fight on, but Burge wouldn't. The fight was then awarded to Dobbs.

Burge and his backers caterwauled about the Newcastle fight for several weeks, claiming that Dobbs was a dirty fighter and had won only by using "foul American tactics" to gain the victory. Bobby shrugged off these comments and offered to fight Burge again anytime he chose. Dick offered no answer. The British press was of the opinion that Bobby's victory was both a clean and notable one, offering him praise for defeating the heavier Englishmen. "Dobbs," wrote British journalist Henry Thatcher, "is about the best bit of a 10 stone man that we have seen in quite some time. It is my opinion that we have no one here to deal with him properly and that even Lavigne would have trouble with this coloured wonder."[16] The love affair had begun.

As the New Year began, John Barnes continued to offer Dick Burge a rematch with Bobby but the former had no real interest. Burge, who would later do a stint in jail for fraud and then upon his release run the famous Ring at Black Friars, was a heavy drinker and the thought of putting himself through the grind of training, the kind that a match with Dobbs would require, most likely did not appeal to him. Barnes and Dobbs could have cared less — there were other fights to be had. In February, Bobby knocked out Jerry Driscoll in 14 rounds at London and then went on a short tour of Northern England.[17] Afterward he was matched with Scottish lightweight champion Pat McDonald at Glasgow, but the fight was prevented by police who arrested both fighters and charged them with disturbing the peace. The charges were quickly dropped, the matter smoothed over and the fight eventually rescheduled for two weeks later. In the end, all the machinations were hardly worth the trouble as McDonald lasted but a mere round and a half before being knocked cold. A subsequent 14-round demolition of Jerry Mitchell would follow and then it all stopped. Bobby Dobbs was a hero in England, a second Frank Craig, the superior of any man near his weight in Europe. But, when one reaches such a lofty status, fights become harder and harder to come by. No lightweight in Great Britain wanted to step into the ring with Bobby Dobbs, nor did any welterweight. It was simple as that. There were no fights to be made.

About this time, Dick Burge's name resurfaced in the sporting sheets. He was attempting to recover the funds that he had put up to cover the side bet in his match with Dobbs and he was taking his case to the court of public opinion. Unfortunately for old Dick, his sob story about being fouled in his bout with Dobbs found little sympathy in public opinion. When Burge realized that he wasn't getting anywhere, he decided to drop a bomb on the boxing world. He announced that his match with Bobby had been rigged — or it was supposed to be anyway. According to Burge, he and his backers met with Barnes and Dobbs to work out a deal in which Bobby would "get knocked" out in the third round. The men all agreed to pool their money, split the betting proceeds and pay Barnes and Bobby and extra 500 pounds for their efforts. Burge stated that Dobbs agreed and the two men even met in a hotel room to rehearse the fake. In the third frame of the fight, Bobby was to come at Burge, take a punch to the temple and go down and out. Burge claims that he was instead double-crossed. He went on to state that Dobbs trained long and hard for the fight, while Burge, thinking the fight predetermined, did next to nothing to prepare, and when the bout went into the middle rounds he was in no condition to fight on. Bobby and John Barnes denied the "fix" story and called Burge's story nothing but an excuse. Most of the public sided with them.

Dobbs arrived in New York on August 24, 1899, on board the steamer *Barbarosa*. Things having dried up across the pond, Dobbs was lured back to the states by William A. Brady, James Jeffries' manager, who had been touring Britain with the latter for a few weeks. The first bout upon Bobby's return to the U.S. was a 25-round battle with future Welter-weight champion Matty Matthews at Coney Island. Dobbs gave away ten pounds to his big rival but won the fight's early rounds. He knocked Matthews down twice but was show-ing signs of weariness by the 10th frame. He fought off his fatigue and seemed to have a new lease on his wind, fighting toe-to-toe with Matty and hurting him with a good left hook in the 15th round. Throughout the fight both men were using rough-housing tactics, holding and hitting, elbowing and wrestling. Referee George Siler warned Dobbs three sep-arate times to stop his holding and hitting tactics in the clinches, but Bobby paid him little attention. Dobbs went into the 24th with a mouth full of blood and Matthews hit him a dozen times in the face. In the 25th and last round, when Dobbs once again put his elbow into Matthews' throat in a clinch, Siler stepped in and disqualified the English champion.[18] The fact that Matthews was just as guilty of fighting dirty seemed to have escaped Siler's notice. This is not to say that Dobbs could not "get rough" when he chose; he could and would. Even back in his days around Ogden and San Francisco, Bobby was never one to shy away from using the rough stuff if he felt it served his purpose. He undoubtedly fouled Matthews and most likely deserved to be disqualified. However, it was not as cut and dry as Siler made it seem. Matthews had weight, age and the home turf advantage over Bobby, and he used every one of these assets to his advantage. He also made frequent use of his elbows and head when infighting. Still, it must be noted that the Bobby Dobbs of September 1899 did not seem to be the same fighter who had left the U.S. just months before as the scourge of lightweights everywhere. His legs seemed to lack spring, his punches steam and his defense was almost sloppy. Fistic experts everywhere thought that Bobby Dobbs had gone back, not one step, but two.

Dobbs would do little to change this impression as he lost two of his next three fights, both in uniquely disturbing fashion. In Buffalo he dropped a dreadful 20-round decision to another future welterweight king, Rube Ferns. That Dobbs struggled to land on a man he had handled and knocked out less than a year and a half before certainly pointed to an evident decline in his skills. He then struggled with a virtual unknown named Fred Darnell, who was a last minute replacement, before finally knocking out his frisky foe in the eigh-teenth frame of a severe battle. But his next match would prove to be the icing on the cake, or more pointedly, the nail in the coffin. Fighting a practically one-armed Joe Walcott, who claimed he entered the ring against Bobby with a fractured right hand, Dobbs seemed feeble and far from world class. The Barbados Demon smashed the taller Dobbs around the Broad-way Athletic Club ring for five rounds before knocking him cold, dead-to-the-world out, with a left hand hook to the point of the jaw. It was an embarrassing loss and one that virtually sealed the lid on Dobbs' championship hopes. "Bobby Dobbs, the ebony hued Minneapolis boxer," wrote the *Milwaukee Journal*, "had better take the first steamer back to England. Before Bobby crossed the pond a year ago, he was rated as one of the most dangerous lightweights in the country and he proved that he could fight a bit by walloping Dick Burge and Pat McDonald, the best England had to offer in the 140-pound class. Dobbs is said to have set up a mighty speedy clip after these victories. However, the London pace may have been too much for Dobbs. It is said by those who saw his clumsy mill with Rube Ferns in Buffalo, that Bobby fought like an old woman. Dobbs no doubt now realizes that he made a big mistake when he listened to William Brady's hot air and left the old country, where the pugilistic going is easy and where a successful pug — especially if he be of African descent — treads a path of roses."

Dobbs had no doubt made a mistake. But his reputation in England, when he arrived in that country and especially after his victories there, virtually guaranteed him no bouts. He was rated as too tough, too big a challenge for most men to risk their reputations on. In 1898, Bobby was the lion that no one wanted to try and cage. After beating Gans, he couldn't get matches in the U.S., so he went to England under the tutelage of Jack Skelly.[19] Once there, he beat Burge, Driscoll and McDonald and sure enough, he had dried up the courage of all of Britain's 10-stone men. It was only natural that he returned to the U.S.— and that he did, with horrendous results.

The one positive factor in the demise of Bobby's skills and reputation was that he could find steady work. He was now deemed vulnerable and became a much easier pill to swallow for fellow welterweights, managers and matchmakers alike. For the next two years Bobby would find himself in Memphis, Rochester, Baltimore, Chicago and Philadelphia, fighting a plethora of good men with less than stellar results. He was knocked out twice by former victim Joe Gans in 1901, quit to Martin Judge, fought a dirty and ugly affair with Bob Long and had a three fight series with Young Peter Jackson. These were long, hard fights against the ironmen of the lighter divisions and Dobbs struggled to remain competitive. At this point in his career he was seemingly treading water, hoping that the sting in his punches and the bounce in his legs might return so that he could catch lightning in a bottle just once. He was now an old fox, using a mixture of moxy, style and a big bag of old tricks to stay in pace with the young lions. It was a race that Dobby could not win.

It was during this time, what would have appeared to have been the end of Bobby's fighting career, that the latent teacher and physical culturalist in him seemingly came to life. While settled in Baltimore, Dobbs opened a gym where he taught a series of classes on the rudiments of boxing. The classes were exclusively for "students of color" and focused not on the combative aspects of boxing but rather on the art of the sport and its benefits as a physical exercise. People flocked to Bobby's gym and several community leaders embraced his teachings as being good for the morale and physical vigor of the young black community. In April of 1902, Dobbs organized, ran and took part in a large field day that featured live music, food, drink and sporting events. The guest list included prominent social, political and religious black leaders from Washington, DC, Baltimore, New York and Chicago. The attendance at the event swelled to nearly 3,000 over the course of the five days it ran. Dobbs demonstrated his physical prowess by placing first in the 100 yard dash and second in the 1500 yard race. His team won the tug of war as well as the baseball series and Bobby fought over 30 exhibition rounds with a plethora of students. It was grand event that was hailed by the *Afro-American* as being the finest event the city had known in years.

By the late fall of 1902, the fight venues of America held little hope for Bobby Dobbs. He was considered past his time and to be fighting as an "opponent" only. The big money had eluded him and now he was looking for greener pastures where he could graze. England seemed to be the perfect fit.

Bobby Dobbs, his past glories remembered, returned to jolly old Britain in November of 1902.[20] Once there he immediately set about to find matches and reclaim his title as the champion of England. For the next seven years he would remain a mainstay in British rings. He lost as often as he won, but with each passing year, he became more and more of a legend. He liked to tell the English reporters that he had been fighting for 25 years, forgetting the fact that he was only 37 years old at the time. But as was always the case, Bobby never cared too much for the personal facts. The inflation of his age only added to his accolades and to his pocket book. The older he seemed to the public, the more amazing his feats in the ring seemed, and thus the bigger the purse. Dobbs was a hustler, and hustlers didn't need to check their facts — those got checked at the door. No, Bobby had to make his living, and if that meant lying a bit to inflate a gate, well then so be it. Nobody ever bothered to check.

The near-decade that Dobbs spent in Britain saw him remain competitive — certainly more competitive than he could have hoped to have been in the States. And despite the fact that he did lose often, even occasionally getting himself knocked out, Bobby scored some impressive and quality wins during these years. His most notable victims for that duration were Australian Billy Edwards, Charlie Knock, George Roache and Billy Chester. These men were not world beaters, but good professional fighters and Bobby, while nearing forty, still had enough guile to defeat them.

By the time 1910 had rolled around Dobbs tired of England and set off for Copenhagen, at the request of Magnus Olsen Bech, a former circus strongman who was running a tent circus in that city. Bech had arranged two fights for Bobby, the first being with Holgar Hansen, a welterweight of great popularity, and the second with Johannes Jørgensen, better known as Jim Smith, perhaps the most famous of Danish boxers. Before Dobbs had ever stepped into a Copenhagen ring he was thought of as a star. His reputation in England had reached Denmark and despite their rabid loyalty to their own fighters, the sports fans of Copenhagen considered Bobby a physical marvel. On the night of July 10, 1910, their hearts were certainly with Hansen but their wallets were with Dobbs. Breaking merely a small sweat, Bobby bewildered, bedazzled and knocked Hansen out with ease, all the while earning both the respect and admiration of the crowd. The Danish paper *Dagbladet Politiken* reported the next day, "The Negro Bobby Dobbs showed that he was fully worthy of his world reputation. He carried his elegantly built body with an agility and superior ease that made a great impression on the audience. Not once did he make a movement that wasn't calculated in advance. With a confidence in his blocks and precision in his hits he showed himself a master in his art and aroused sympathy that rose every minute, because it was evident that he had no intention of inflicting on his opponent unnecessary harm, but only waited for the right moment to put him out of action."[21] Championed as the best fighter they had ever seen, the good, sports-loving folks of Copenhagen also saw in Dobbs a level of sportsmanship that they both appreciated and cheered. After Bobby had knocked Hansen out, he then carried his stricken foe to his corner and helped Holgar's corner men revive him, scolding them when they attempted to use iced water to snap their man back into consciousness. It was an act that earned Bobby a loud ovation from the sold out house. He returned the gesture by bowing to all four corners of the building.

Dobbs, ever the businessman, decided to capitalize on his popularity and opened a small boxing school in the northern section of town. His club was well attended and his classes swelled with new students daily. He appeared for a number of weeks in a theatre show where he simply shadowboxed and went through some training stunts. But Bobby also insisted on speaking about the importance of diet, abstinence from tobacco and liquor and daily exercise at both his public engagements and his private classes. He fully believed in the power of fitness, both physical and mental, and stressed that he was only able to keep boxing at his advanced age, because he had been following these cardinal rules for years.

Dobbs fought Jim Smith under the canopy of Bech's big top and again proved his mettle. Smith was bigger and better than Hansen, and before the match, was thought to be the one man in Copenhagen who could give the old black pugilist a run for his money. As it turned out, he wasn't any better, but simply a better punch absorber, lasting twice as long as Holgmar, but taking twice the beating. Unlike Hansen, who Dobbs knocked cold, Smith

Bobby Dobbs vs. Holger Hausen, December 10, 1910, Germany (Bains News Service, George Grantham Bain Collection, Library of Congress).

did not go quietly. That is to say, he did not go down from one punch. Heavier and more durable than his countryman, Smith did not buckle under Bobby's quick, whiplike punches but instead had to be chopped down slowly like a big tree. It was an uneven affair, and an exhibition neither as clean nor as pretty as the one Copenhagen had seen Dobbs give little more than a month before. The Smith fight was far more gruesome and far more brutal — and in the end signaled the end of Dobbs' stay in Copenhagen.

After his mastery over Smith, few fights were to be found in Denmark. If the Danish champion could not beat him, who could? With his earning potential all but limited to his gym, Bobby decided to again move on. He latched on with one of Bech's traveling circuses and headed off for Germany.

Landing in Berlin, Bobby found the Germans a stout and strong group. Unlike the Danes, they did not seem to know or care much for boxing. The black prizefighter again saw an opportunity to make some real money and opened the Anglo-American boxing club in the middle of Berlin. Almost overnight, boxing became the rage in Germany; the royal family of Wilhelm even getting acquainted with the art through first hand tutoring from none other than Professor Dobbs. Through his introduction of the sport of boxing to the Germans, Bobby earned a unique place in the country's sporting history. On December 2, 1910, he took part in the first successful prizefight ever to be held on German soil. Ironically, his opponent, the 25-year-old Dick Green of Chicago, also happened to be an American.[22] Dobbs knocked Green out in 12 rounds and Berlin fell at his feet. Soon he was the toast of the town, entertained by political powers, land barons and even elegant women, who found his dark skin and sharp wit entirely delectable. In March of 1911, Dobbs fought an exhibition bout with another black American, Billy Gordon, with two royal princes (nephews of Kaiser Wilhelm), before a sold-out crowd at the largest theatre in Berlin. Germany seemingly thought that Bobby Dobbs had invented the wheel.

As with all fads, the 1911 boxing craze in Germany quickly came to a crashing end. Dobbs began losing clients and looked to new ways to keep his buying public's attention. He attempted to introduce the sport of boxing on horseback to German audiences, but after demonstrating the ludicrous idea to a small group of socialites, who seemed confused and disinterested, Bobby decided that fighting in that form had no future.

Bobby did what he always did — he moved on, this time heading back to Copenhagen, where he matched up with the famous Dick Nelson. Nelson had begun his career in Copenhagen, but had seasoned himself in the United States, facing off and winning against a number of top flight men. His record included welterweights and middleweights of championship class, and men like Dixie Kid, Leo Houck, Mike Glover, Kid Henry and Young Loughrey exchanged punches with the well-versed Dane. Nelson was no Holgar Hansen and his pedigree was far and away the highest that Dobbs had faced in years. The two men met on November 26, 1911, at the Danish Sporting Club and it was clever battle from the start. But Dobbs, despite holding his ground with pride, simply did not have enough left in the tank to keep the younger Nelson at bay. At the end of 20 rounds, Bobby Dobbs was adjudged the loser.

Bobby Dobbs was inventive. In 1911 he introduced a group of German aristocrats to boxing on horseback. The idea never took off (Kevin Smith collection).

Bobby stayed on in Europe until the outbreak of World War One in 1914. In 1912, Dobbs popped up in Vienna, where he stayed 20 rounds with the stocky, well built Waldmar Holberg and then in 1913 he showed up in Budapest, Hungary, where he knocked out Jack Meekins in 10 frames. But by the time the "guns of August" had sounded Dobbs decided that it was time to beat it out of Europe. He immediately went to the American Embassy in Budapest and requested assistance in booking passage for the U.S.

Bobby Dobbs returned to the country of his birth in 1915. Landing in New York, Dobbs immediately attempted to find some promoter who would put him on. Most laughed at him, citing the fact that he was far too old to be taken seriously as a boxer. Somehow he talked the management of the Olympia Club into allowing him to go on in a ten-round match and Dobbs acquitted himself well, winning a ten-round verdict from the 142-pound Joe Cassidy. Despite his decent performance, Bobby could not find subsequent matches. Looking for ways to earn a living, he sought out an old theatrical promoter and friend, Herr Rachman, whom he had met in Berlin a number of years before the war. Rachman, who had left Europe for much the same reasons as Dobbs, was managing big-time wrestlers in New York at the time, most notably the world champion, Waldek Zbyszko. He hired Bobby to work with his stable of gargantuan grapplers as a conditioner, but despite Dobbs' known affinity for healthy living and exercise, his game was boxing, not wrestling.

Dobbs fought as the unidentified "Masked Marvel" in a traveling carnival in Savannah, Georgia, 1919 (Kevin Smith collection).

The gig lasted for about a year before Dobbs once again got wanderlust and headed down into the southern states.

Dobbs ended up in Savannah, Georgia, where he once again became aligned with a traveling circus. This time his tour was more of the stage variety with Bobby going through his workout and then challenging all comers to stay four rounds with him on the stage for a ten-dollar reward. The catch was that he performed not as Bobby Dobbs the famous lightweight, but instead as "The Masked Marvel." (This would lend one to believe that while working with Rachman's wrestling stable, Bobby had picked up some of their theatrical flair.) For several days, Bobby turned back the challenges of several local pugs and soon the Savannah sports were becoming embarrassed. One night they planted their local champion, KO Lew Williams, in the audience, instructing him to accept Dobbs' challenge when it came. Somehow Bobby sniffed out the ruse and instead of presenting his normal defy, he challenged Williams directly — offering to fight him in a true boxing match over the course of ten rounds for a $500 dollar purse. A bit stunned by being usurped, Williams agreed.

Williams was a damn fine welterweight and a phenom in his native Georgia. The bout with Dobbs would turn out to be his last in the South, the black welterweight setting off for New York shortly afterward, where he hoped he could make a name for himself. The promotion of the fight was interesting. Dobbs appeared daily at the local theater, where he went through his stunts with his face hidden behind a cloth mask. He spoke only in German, claiming to have come from a "far off place" and told reporters, through a translator of course, that he would reveal his true identity only if Williams defeated him. The interest in the "Masked Marvel" was high and many theories were bandied about as to who this strange fighter really was. No one ever suspected that it was Bobby Dobbs.

The night of the fight, Savannah's fight populace turned out by the hundreds, nearly 2,000 packing the Pekin Theatre and hundreds more being turned away at the door. As it turned out, the fight was of little interest. The Masked Marvel was no match for Williams, the latter being too young, too strong and too quick for his mysterious opponent. In the ninth round, Dobbs, beaten and bloodied, held his hands up and motioned Williams to stop coming forward. In 1919, Dobbs told Dan Saunders of the *Boston Globe* what happened next. "I pulled off my mask and grabbing that young fellow by the hand I said in English to him, 'You win, I am done.' When I spoke English to him he was so startled I thought he would run out of the ring. When the spectators, who thought I could only speak German, heard me talking in English they became sore at being fooled by me and I figured it best for me to slip quietly out of the theatre. No more Masked Marvels for me."

The Williams fight is the last recorded bout of Bobby Dobbs' professional boxing career. What had begun in anonymity could be said to have ended in it as well. Bobby was not done with the sport however, far from it. He headed back north, into New York and Philadelphia where he began training fighters.

His first students of note were Eddie Dorsey, a very good black lightweight, Blacksmith Russell, a fair heavyweight and a lightweight billed as Bobby Dobbs Jr., supposedly the son of Bobby Dobbs. (While some records indicate that Bobby and his wife Luvinia had a daughter named Lillian, born in 1906, no evidence has been found of a son.) Dorsey was the best of the lot but he parted ways with his famous teacher in early 1920. Bobby returned briefly to South Carolina and attempted to open a gym in Charleston but the venture proved to be a quick failure. Through a letter-writing campaign to a series of northern managers Bobby found employment in Pennsylvania latching on with James Dougherty's stable. Under the employ of "The Baron of Leiperville," as Dougherty was known, Bobby trained welterweight star Bobby Barrett, lightweight Alex Hart and heavyweight contender George Godfrey. Dobbs was an active teacher and frequently acted as a sparring partner for Hart and Barrett. The cagey veteran did not have much left in the tank, but still proved to be shifty and elusive. He also remained proud. While preparing George Godfrey, the "Black Shadow" of Leiperville, for a bout with Rough House Ware in Philadelphia in 1923, Bobby was the subject of an article written by Damon Runyon. "For all his years," Ruynon wrote, "vanity is still strong in Bobby Dobbs. He keeps his hair closely shaved so as no grey hair will show. And he cannot see very well but still disdains glasses. Until recently he sparred with all of Dougherty's boxers. Bobby could not see a punch until it had almost struck him, but instinct would prompt him to block it. Across the breast of his sweater he has his name painted in big letters. It is common for seconds to wear the names of the fighters that they are training on their sweaters. Not Bobby Dobbs. He wears his own name."[23]

And so it was that Bobby remained in the game for the rest of his life, or pretty well close to it anyway. In the late twenties he hopped back and forth between New York,

Philadelphia and Charleston. His wife, whom he married in 1902 at Baltimore, still lived in Charleston as did his recently widowed daughter Lillian, her husband having been killed in a tragic train accident. From time to time Dobbs would take a job as a locker room attendant, or athletic masseur, but he never strayed too far from the game he loved. Over the course of the last decade of his life his name would occasionally pop up in the press, the story usually about some big, new black fighter he had found in the South that he hoped to match with some contender. Unfortunately, those men never made their marks as fighters, nor did Dobbs as a trainer.

In April of 1930, Bobby was reported to be a patient at the Metropolitan Hospital on Welfare Island in New York, admitted due to what was simply described as complications from old age. What was more likely is that he was suffering from some type of disease. In June he was well enough to return to Charleston, where he lived out the remainder of his days in the charity ward of Charleston City Hospital.

BOBBY DOBBS

The professor of boxing dressed as a gentleman (Kevin Smith collection).

Bobby Dobbs was reportedly buried in a pauper's field without a headstone. Despite reports to the contrary, he was only 62 years old.

Bobby had an amazing career. At the height of his powers he was a slick, quick and a complete pugilist. His chin was dented a few times, but in over 180 recorded professional prizefights, many against top tier men, he was only truly knocked out six times. He was a master of his craft, who despite losing his physical tools rather quickly, remained competitive well into his late 30's. He was a tremendous showman and businessman and could sniff a moneymaking opportunity from a mile away. He was charming and likeable and often times got into trouble with women. (In 1901, while Bobby was fighting in Memphis, a white Scottish woman by the name of Edna Roe appeared in Pittsburgh claiming to have traveled from Edinburgh in order to marry Bobby. She was quietly convinced to forgo her plans for interracial marriage and placed under the care of the YWCA). He was a complete athlete, who even in his era of rather rudimentary exercise beliefs, stressed the importance of abstinence from alcohol and tobacco, a daily exercise routine, and a good diet. He was a teacher who fancied himself a role model, not only for young men of his own race, but for young men of all races. He sparred with princes, boxed on the back of a horse, fought in front of royalty and spread the good name of American boxing throughout the world. He was a black man who moved freely and willingly throughout the world, learning languages and cultures and assimilating as if he were a dignitary. He fought in over a dozen countries and made friends and allies across the globe. And despite not being as old as he always claimed, Bobby was always an old soul — one who was wise and learned beyond his years. In the end it did not matter how many years he had been roaming the earth, because the time he did spend was jam-packed with life.

NOTES

1. "Kings of Ring All Trained at Leiperville, Pa," *The Davenport Democrat and Leader*, December 7, 1923.

2. Boxrec.com, "Bobby Dobbs."

3. 1880 U.S. Federal Census Records, Burton County, Georgia.

4. "Masterson Recalls Dobbs," *Afro-American Baltimore*, August 13, 1953.

5. "Sporting Matters," *Ogden Standard Examine*, June 7, 1890.

6. "A Letter from Dobbs," *Ogden Standard Examiner* March 28, 1892.

7. "Dobbs Defeats Johnson," *Los Angeles Times*, October 31, 1892.

8. Untitled, *Ogden Standard Examiner*, October 28, 1892.

9. "Dobbs — Lavigne," *Omaha Daily World,* March 20, 1894.

10. "Sporting Miscellany," *Boston Globe*, September 26, 1894.

11. "Sporting Miscellany," *Boston Evening Transcript— Boston Globe*, September 28, 1894.

12. "Sporting Miscellany," *Boston Globe*, October 23, 1894.

13. "Ring Notes," *Philadelphia Inquirer*, January 17, 1897.

14. "Dobbs Defeats Gans," *Philadelphia Inquirer*, September 28, 1897.

15. "The Dobbs — Burge Contest," *National Police Gazette*, December 20, 1898.

16. "The Ring," *Police News*, January 1899.

17. "Bobby Dobbs Won," *The Saint Paul Globe*, May 30, 1899.

18. "Bobby Dobbs Was Playing it Foxy," *Scranton Tribune*, September 16, 1899.

19. "Bobby Dobbs Beats Bob Kane," *Kansas City Journal*, February 24, 1898.

20. "American Bobby Dobbs Lost in London, Syracuse, NY *Post Standard*, November 21, 1902.

21. "Dobbs," *Dagbladet Politken*, July 11, 1910.

22. "Dobbs Beat Green," *New York Times*, December 3, 1910.

23. "Kings of Ring All Trained at Leiperville, Pa," *The Davenport Democrat and Leader*, December 7, 1923.

CHAPTER 6

Joe Gans: World Lightweight Champion

Colleen Aycock

At the time Joe Gans began boxing professionally in 1891, no American-born man of African descent had ever held a world title in the sport of gloved boxing. Canada's first champion, George Dixon, won the world bantamweight title in England a year earlier in 1890. For the most part, American-born black fighters were constrained by a racial barrier in their home country, limited as they were to fighting for black titles created for their race by a white establishment. Popular heavyweight champions John L. Sullivan, Jim Corbett, and Jim Jeffries had drawn public attention to the racial color line in sport, refusing to grant black contenders world title fights and encouraging white fighters on other continents to do the same. By 1900 Joe Gans was one of the top challengers for the lightweight title, and somehow he seemed less threatening than other contenders for a crown. While he had spent over a decade in the professional ranks, as a challenger for the lightweight laurels in 1902 he was simply not predicted to win, in part because he had lost to the champion, Frank Erne, in 1900. However, the boxing establishment in New York was still so fearful of staging an interracial championship fight in the United States that it ultimately moved the lightweight title fight between Joe Gans and title holder Frank Erne from Buffalo, New York, to Ft. Erie, Canada, where the question of race was less problematic. In what was then the shortest title fight to date, Gans captured the world crown in a 100-second kayo in the first round, making him the fourth American, lineal world lightweight champion of gloved boxing. Gans' glory, however, seemed about as short-lived as his title match until an unknown promoter in a Nevada mining camp brought him out of homelessness to compete for the largest purse to date.

Gans gave as his birth date, November 25, 1874, Baltimore.[1] However, his true genesis is buried in obscurity. What seems certain, from statements made by his boyhood friend Eubie Blake, is that he was born Joseph Saifuss Butts, named after his father who was reported to be a top "colored" professional baseball player.[2] Gans' birth mother may have died when he was four; and unable to care for a child as a single parent, his father gave Gans to a foster parent, Maria Jackson Gant.[3] Mrs. Gant may have been related to Gans' mother in that her husband was frequently referred to as Gans' "uncle." Gans never referred to Maria Gant as his "aunt," but chose to call her "mother," illustrating his bonded attachment to her throughout his life. Joseph was called by the name "Gant" during his boyhood and early ring battles; but during the year 1894 when various news reports referred to him as the boxer "Gans" (occasionally spelling it Gantz) the name stuck, and Gans and his later children adopted it as their surname.[4]

Joe Gans, the "Old Master." This photograph was taken at the Goldfield fight in Nevada, 1906 (Gary Schultz collection, photograph restored by Jean Johnson).

The Gant home in the Greenwillow section of Baltimore was known as "The Bottom." Mrs. Gant's occupation was listed in the census as a washerwoman, a difficult job, one loathsome even to workers in the lower classes who elected to send their laundry out. It is clear that Mrs. Gant became a stalwart working model for the young boy, grounding him in an independent work ethic with spiritual ties to the church. (Gans had close friendships with the ministers of the church and selected the Whatcoat Methodist Episcopal Church as the setting for his funeral.) Throughout his professional career, Gans delighted in surprising his mother with substantial portions of his earnings which she carefully saved, a wise decision in that he often had a difficult time keeping a fifty dollar bill in his pocket and away from the gambling tables.[5] Like many of the sporting men of his age, Gans loved the saloons full of exciting characters playing card games and dice.

Gans was educated at the elementary school serving the Greenwillow area of Baltimore, after which he worked as an oyster shucker at a fish market in the historic harbor area of the Chesapeake. The work was tedious, the weather during the oyster harvests harsh, and the danger of accidents enormous. But through the experience, Gans' hands were conditioned for the tools of his later chosen profession.

While working at the harbor, Gans was exposed to the excitement of boxing. In 1885, fistic marvel and Colored Heavyweight Champion George Godfrey of Boston met Billy Woods at the Front Street Theater near the market in Baltimore. Both Godfrey and John L. Sullivan were Boston celebrities, and along with Jake Kilrain, the three heavyweight careers coincided. Kilrain, Baltimore's adopted hometown hero at the time of his great fight with Sullivan, walked the streets and trained in Baltimore for the last bare knuckle title contested in America, in 1889. During the 1880s and 1890s, boxing gymnasiums and local athletic clubs directed by Professors of Boxing were popping up in cities across America, encouraging young recruits, employing all ethnic races, and attracting professionals for club promotions. During these years, the rough-and-tumble sport of prize fighting was transitioning into professional boxing; and much like other rigorous careers, such as dock workers, stevedores, or hod carriers, it drew enormous numbers of men from a variety of ethnic backgrounds eager to market their physical strength. In addition to paying the bills, boxing turned the strongest competitors into celebrities and gave the youthful high aspirations.

Gans was known to don the mitts and spar with the other boys working the markets

By 1896 young sports had many fistic idols to look up to. This early tobacco card was titled "The Lightweights" (photograph by Alfred S. Campbell, Elizabeth, N.J., 1896).

of old Baltimore. It has been reported that Caleb Bond, proprietor of a fish market and Gans' first manager, so-to-speak, discovered the lad's talent and encouraged his training with the gloves in the store's basement.[6] In an interview given to a reporter for the *Trenton Evening Times* before he died, Gans said that his boss, his boss' brother, and he had chipped in money to buy a $5 set of boxing gloves. After Gans became too good to fight the other boys around the market, they made him fight two boys at a time. "My first fight was to a finish with another kid. My boxing with two boys at a time had taught me how to block and dodge and lead so that I won my first real fight."[7] Like many of the boxers trying to start a professional career, Gans frequented the gyms and boxed as an amateur in clubs and vaudeville shows which were entertaining the working classes around Baltimore. After Gans gained fame in 1906, reporters noted that he first won respect in the ring at the Monumental Theater in two *battle royals,* tawdry gambling spectacles where several young black men were put into a makeshift ring and made to battle it out until only one warrior remained standing. While these early battles are seldom reported in newspaper coverage, this form of entertainment was common for novices wishing to gain visibility and for older pugs needing a paycheck.

In 1891, at age 17, Gans' amateur life came to an end when his boxing prowess caught the attention of local Baltimore gambler, restaurateur, and boxing entrepreneur Abraham Lincoln Herford, who sported the name "Al." Herford approached Gans with an offer to

One of the earliest pictures of Joe Gans (right) with his lifelong cornerman and stablemate, Young Peter Jackson, also managed by Al Herford of Baltimore (Gary Schultz collection).

provide the young boxer with professional management after he had witnessed Gans' performance in Bill Muldoon's traveling carnival when the popular amusement came to Baltimore.[8] New York impresario William Muldoon had been the first major star of American wrestling. He had served in the Union Army in the American Civil War and in the French Army in the Franco-Prussian War of 1870, afterward serving in the New York Police Department. He became a professional Greco-Roman wrestler and boxer in the early 1880s, an actor in the mid 1880s, trainer for John L. Sullivan in the 1889 bout with Kilrain, a sporting man in and around the rings, and, later, the first chairman of the New York State Athletic Commission. His road show, called "Muldoon's Variety and Athletic Combination," in 1891 included the formidable Charlie Smith, known as the "Black Thunderbolt," and Fred Morris, "Muldoon's Cyclone." Al Herford reported that Gans was boxing in the show and had been forced to take on three consecutive opponents from Muldoon's troup, at $2.50 per fight. Gans had handily beaten the first two boxers, but the third was a ringer, a mean slugger they called "Pick," or "Old Pickaninny." Gans stayed the two rounds and "then kicked," as Herford recalled the event in 1904. Gans threw in the towel, citing that he wasn't being handled fairly.[9] Herford then volunteered his services to Gans as manager. From that point on, Herford remained Gans' manager for thirteen years before abandoning him, as managers did at the time (and still do when they can no

An undated photograph of Joe Gans in street clothes (Gary Schultz collection).

longer arrange fights for big money)—ironically failing to see Gans' largest paydays.

By 1894 Gans was mentioned in the Baltimore sporting columns as a "Colored Champion." He had won a medal in the lightweight division by beating Buck Wilkie in a contest held at the Monumental Theater when a traveling show called the "Pastime Athletic Club" came to town. The Baltimore sportswriter invoked another black champion in his description of the contest, "More than one imitator of the mighty Peter Jackson was sorer and weaker than he was last night."[10] The contest continued the next night, but it was reported that Gans was defeated by Paul (Kangaroo) Johnson.

Before the end of 1895, Gans was fighting top-notch fighters and hailed by state and regional titles, colored lightweight champion of Maryland and colored featherweight champion of the South.[11] (During this period the featherweight and lightweight classes were frequently used interchangeably.) The first lengthy press article describing a Gans fight occurred on March 6, 1895, when Gans appeared on the undercard for a Bob Fitzsimmons fight arranged by Al Herford at the Monumental Theater in Baltimore. Fitzsimmons was a three-time world champion and his appearance drew a large crowd. But when his opponent failed to show for the bout, the sportswriters had nothing to report the next day but Gans' preliminary fight as being the best on the card. Gans' fight against Soloman English ended when the police stopped it in the ninth round as a result of the sound beating Gans was giving English.[12]

In November of 1895, Gans was pitted against Albert Griffiths, aka "Young Griffo," world-class pugilist from Australia who had contended in the previous year with American featherweight and lightweight champion icons George Dixon, Jack McAuliffe, and Kid Lavigne. The Gans-Griffo bout was scheduled for ten rounds and resulted in a draw. Griffo contended that it was previously arranged by Herford for him to let Gans "stay" the ten rounds. Regardless, the newspaper reported that Gans landed more punches and Griffo's punches, while "vicious blows," landed short.[13] The draw with the noted Griffo gave the young phenom national attention. The two would meet again in two years with Griffo sincerely acknowledging Gans' fighting prowess.

In his final fight of 1895, Gans fought George Siddons of New Orleans at 125 pounds for the Colored Featherweight Championship of the South. The papers noted that Gans deserved the title due to his more scientific, methodical approach in the ring. Gans used the early rounds to study his opponent's movements, reactions, and punches, and to measure his reach. Then he knocked Siddons out in the seventh.[14]

By 1896 Gans' matches included those with top white fighters of the Gay Nineties, which were covered in the national news. His fight with Mike Leonard (the "Adonis of Boxing," as he was called) in a fistic carnival in San Francisco that included heavyweight Jim Jeffries gave Gans the publicity he needed on the West Coast where he was touted in the newspapers as being a recognized fighter on the East Coast.[15]

After fighting in traveling carnivals, local theaters, private clubs, various contests, and then traveling out West, Gans had already fought a career's worth of bouts. Some estimated that he had accumulated at least 60 wins, some as high as 150, by 1896. To put this record in perspective, in the first five years of his professional life, Gans had already won more fights than Joe Louis or Muhammad Ali would win in their entire careers. Compared to fighters of today who often have Olympic notoriety as a launching pad to lucrative careers, the road that brought Joe Gans to glory was as hard as the oyster-shell streets of Baltimore where he spent his childhood. Nat Fleischer would say, "No fighter had ever faced a tougher field in the journey to the title."[16]

By 1896 both Frank Erne of Buffalo and Joe Gans of Baltimore were rising stars chasing a title belt, much like heavyweights Godfrey, Sullivan, and Kilrain a decade earlier. As top contenders, Gans and Erne had been matched first in 1896, but Erne reneged and refused to fight Gans.[17] It would be four more years before Gans would get another chance to take on Erne. The two fighters were the same age and same height, at 5'6". Both had turned professional in 1891. Although Gans never challenged his friend George Dixon for the featherweight title, Erne did, and beat Dixon in 1897. Both Gans and Erne were known as "scientific boxers." Both had drawn against George Siddons and Young Griffo. (It is also interesting that both would lose to Terry McGovern in 1900.) But in 1898 Erne, not Gans, would get the chance to fight the title holder, Kid Lavigne, for the world lightweight crown.

Elbows McFadden (left) insisted his tactics were never foul. Here he is illustrating the block of a left lead by capturing the opponent's arm and "straining" his elbow (*Blocking and Hitting* by McFadden, Richard K. Fox Publishing Company, 1905).

Erne's draw with Lavigne would set in motion a large field of qualified contenders eager to prove that they deserved a shot at the lightweight title. In addition to Erne and Gans, contenders included Kid McPartland, Dal Hawkins, and Elbows McFadden. Gans would fight Kid McPartland three times, once after he won the title; but it was their first battle in 1898 and its 20-round decision that would gain Gans national recognition as a top contender.[18] After Erne's failed attempt to gain the crown, Erne came back in his first fight of 1899 to beat Dal Hawkins.

Gans would lose to one of the top contenders, Elbows McFadden, on April 14, 1899, in New York in a 25-round scheduled bout that lasted 23 rounds. Gans had been sick for the bout (he was frequently bothered by intestinal catarrh or irritable bowels), and, with the exception of when he was dying of tuberculosis, this bout was one of the most brutal lickings he would ever take. Gans came out in his signature form, dancing around his opponent; so light and crafty was his footwork that he seemed to be able to dodge the best of the punchers. McFadden was a slugger who walked straight into his man to attack his body at close range. By the fifth, McFadden had suffered a punch to his right eye and mouth and both were swollen. Normally, Gans had his opponent winded by this time, but by the seventh, McFadden had survived. The eighth through tenth rounds were so furiously fought they would drain both men of their energy. After the thirteenth (with twelve more rounds to go), Gans went to his corner as blood dripped from his mouth and nose. At the end of the eighteenth, both had battered each other against the ropes. Both fought on viciously until the end of the twenty-second. Gans finally fell in the twenty-third round, as a result of repeated head and body shots. As he was falling, McFadden sent a right into Gans' chin that left him helpless on the floor, blood flowing around his head. The loss to one of the meanest and toughest competitors — he didn't get the name "Elbows" for nothing — was a setback to Gans' title aspirations in 1899.[19] Erne would beat McFadden in May, setting Erne up for another chance at Kid Lavigne. On July 3, Frank Erne would win the lightweight crown.

In order to get a shot at Erne, Gans would have to beat Elbows McFadden. On July 28, 1899, with both fighters seeking opportunities against Erne, Gans and McFadden would have another punishing go at each other, this time finishing a 25-round match with a draw. The two would fight a rubber match that year in New York on October 31. The fight would be reported as "one of the best ever seen" at the Broadway Athletic Club.[20] McFadden was known as "The Greatest Defensive Boxer in the World" for his wicked blocking tactics.[21] Against the head of Joe Hopkins in a bout in New Jersey, McFadden had broken three bones in his right hand. For two years he proceeded in the fight game, remarkably as a one-handed puncher, who wielded his right elbow as cleverly as if he had a useful right hand.[22] In doing so, he developed several off-beat offensive skills with his elbows that became notorious. Later, as a Professor of Boxing, he always maintained that "there are other things beside your hands that you can use in a fight and they ain't foul, either, although some people think they are."[23] Like Gans' previous fight with McFadden, the October fight went the distance of 25 hard-fought rounds.

This third fight between Gans and McFadden had so much publicity, that the newsmen were afraid the final results would set off riots. Back in Baltimore, Al Herford's brother, Maurice, was hosting an event for the sporting men. They would be brought the round-by-round fight results via a runner to the Associated Press office. Bets were running 100 to 80 on McFadden. At the end of the eleventh round, the messenger came in with the news bulletin: "They are even up to the twelfth round." The Baltimore gamblers wondered if

Gans could be given a fair shake by the referee. The messenger went to the office for the results of the next round and was told that Gans was defeated. After giving the news to the gentlemen, he was sent back for the exact words of the bulletin. This time he was told that Gans was given the decision by the referee, that the verdict "was too hot a message for the whites."[24] Gans had, in fact, won the fight by decision, a fact that the boxing community could apparently take more easily than the rest of society. The win allowed Gans' manager Herford to challenge Erne for the lightweight title, providing he could come up with a side-bet of $5,000, a fortune in those days that few expected Herford to raise — but one a gambler and boxing manager couldn't afford to turn down.

Erne agreed to meet Gans March 23, 1900, in a title bout, but the outcome would not favor Gans. The fight was described as a furiously fought battle when Gans sustained a wicked gash over his eye that temporarily blinded him. Gans went into the 12th round ahead when he was head-butted, which cut his eye so badly below the brow that his eye protruded out of its socket. Blood gushed and Gans was blinded. The ring doctor forced the eyeball back into place, and the referee ordered Gans to keep fighting. These were tough times, but the best men of the ring were expected to rise above mortal trifles. Gans, however, refused to continue and asked to have the bout stopped.[25] The consensus about the cut, reached later, was that it was the result of a head butt, not a blow by a glove, and that in fairness Gans should have been given the verdict.[26] Unfairly, Gans was declared the loser, the newspapers trumpeted, "Gans Quits!," and Nat Fleischer reported many years later that Gans couldn't stand the "gaff," or spear, a statement questioning the man's fortitude.[27] Herford would definitely have to do some clever wheeling-and-dealing to get Gans another chance at the title

Gans demonstrates his fighting moves (photograph by Charles Dana, San Francisco, Gary Schultz collection).

Despite the prejudice against black boxers, Gans had earned recognition as a top professional by 1900. J. J. Johnston states in *Images of Sport: Chicago Boxing*, "At the time, the two best boxers in America — unquestionably — were Joe Gans and featherweight champion Terry McGovern."[28] To receive another chance at the top, Gans had to agree to "lay down" against the formidable McGovern. After the Erne loss and then the Chicago fiasco, the newspapers crucified Gans and nearly ended his career.[29]

Although most historians say

that McGovern was not involved, the evidence shows otherwise, and Gans took the blame for the big fix in Chicago in 1900. The managers of the two fighters held surreptitious meetings before and after the fight.[30] McGovern probably agreed to step aside and not challenge Erne for the lightweight title, and in exchange, Gans would give him a win. "Terrible" Terry had beaten George Dixon in June of 1900, and one month after that fight, he had beaten Frank Erne — a fight for which Erne would have wanted a rematch in his title quest. McGovern would be Gans' key to Erne. The Gans-McGovern fight would only add to McGovern's streak of wins until the end of 1901. While Gans was extremely articulate, he was stage-shy and certainly no actor for the cameras on that Friday, the 13th of December, in Chicago. As the film indicates, his sharp offensive and defensive skills became nothing more than feeble paws at McGovern's punches until he went down in the second round. The next morning, all parties to the fight found themselves in court before the judge. While no one was jailed as a result of the fix, the fight caused such an uproar by a group of Chicago social reformers that city councilmen were pressured into banning public boxing in the Windy City, a ban that existed for over twenty years.

The title loss to Frank Erne, a draw with McFadden, and then the disastrous fight with Terry McGovern at the end of 1900, in which Gans was stopped in two rounds, might have discouraged a lesser fighter.

Gans battled back. Between the years 1900 and 1902, before his second title shot, Gans continued to show that he was a worthy contender. He fought some of the best fighters of the era. He knocked out Joe Youngs, who had only recently lost the welterweight crown. Dal Hawkins, Young Griffo, and Bobby Dobbs, all vicious punchers, were defeated by Gans' fast mitts. Gans would fight Dal Hawkins three times. His return bout with Griffo was no walk in the park. Fleischer describes the Gans-Griffo match of July 10, 1900: "Gans piled the blows in there until Griffo's face was battered and bathed in blood, but the plucky fighter stood up and took the gaff, only to be knocked down again. Gans simply laid his blows all over his man after that, and with a heavy right on the jaw made Griffo totter blindly toward the ropes. The sponge from Griffo's corner and the referee simultaneously prevented further blows. The time of the round was 1 minute 38 seconds."[31] Gans had already accomplished a stellar group of wins, yet his greatest exploits were still ahead of him.

Following the loss to McGovern, Gans fought 19 times without a loss over the next 14 months, which set up a rematch with Erne on May 12, 1902. This time it was all Gans as he stopped Erne in one round to win the world lightweight title. Gans had noted in the previous bout with Erne that the Buffalo boy had a habit of feinting and pulling his head back about a foot before throwing a left. Gans practiced this timing with Harry Lenny, and fashioned an effective counter, a right cross to the chin.[32] Gans actually took Erne down with a right, although it wasn't after one of his trademark feints for which he had prepared.

Saturday night before the Monday fight, the odds had shifted slightly to favor Gans, 10 to 9. The 5,000 seat house in Ft. Erie was sold out. The wire reports told the story:

Gans-Erne Lightweight Title Match, Ft. Erie, Canada, May 12, 1902.

They came out and sparred away briskly. Gans led his left for the face twice, but missed. Then he led with both hands for the face. Erne ducked and they clinched. Then Erne tried his left, but it was too high. He next tried a straight left but the shifty Gans side-stepped.

There was a slight mix-up and Gans had the better of it. When they got out of the mix Gans sent his right to the ear hard. There was a quick exchange, when the Baltimore boy sent both hands to head, and Erne looked dazed.

Gans now felt out his opponent with a left punch to the face, drawing blood from Erne's nose, Erne seemed fully dazed now and Gans rushed in and banged him right plump on Erne's jaw.

Frank fell slowly to the floor with mouth and nose bleeding. He rolled over on his abdomen and was counted out before he could attempt to regain his feet. The time of the round: 1 minute and 40 seconds.[33]

Gans' lightweight title defenses, including top-ranked fights in the welterweight division, brought great popularity to the man now called the "Old Master" and drew attraction to the smaller classes from 1902 to 1908. A lack of public attention had occurred in the heavyweight division during this period when Jim Jeffries retired and no new white blood infused the heavyweight ring. Jack Johnson would win the crown in Australia in 1908; but prior to Johnson's reign, Gans' popularity was at its zenith. He would become a star movie attraction for three of the Miles Brothers' eight fight films as the new motion picture industry began to develop on the West Coast.[34] His reputation, however, was not impervious to attack.

During Gans' title reign (he never lost a title defense from 1902–1908), members of the San Francisco sporting society were not keen on having a black man wear a crown. It was common knowledge that many of the fights during these socially turbulent decades carried with them handicaps or deals that favored the white fighter. The truth was that if Gans fought unleashed, no one could beat him. After 1902, the boxing establishment in San Francisco was eager to replace Gans with a white champion. When he defended his title there against popular native son Jimmy Britt on October 31, 1904, a deal was struck between the managers of the fighters that was the beginning of an orchestrated attempt to remove Joe Gans from the limelight. Only a short time before Gans entered the ring to fight Britt, manager Herford told Gans that he had arranged a deal with Willus Britt, James Britt's brother and manager. For the upcoming fight, Gans was told to let Britt have a good showing for five rounds. For this Britt was to receive $11,000 of the purse and Gans, $2,000 and a promise of a rematch. Gans was furious, but followed Herford's commands. A few months after the Gans-Britt fight, the *San Francisco Examiner* concluded that although Gans had won the match on a technicality from a foul, the real winner and champion was Jimmy Britt, for his better showing.[35] While Gans protested and explained the raw deal in the press, it did little good. Gans would be shunned, as California boxing fans became more interested in a new line of lightweight fighters. Chicago referee and sportswriter George Siler reported on January 22, 1905, that when Herford and Gans arrived on the West Coast expecting a match between Gans and Jimmy Gardner, they found that it had never been arranged. Siler said, "And now they are baiting their hooks for a return bout with Jimmy Britt." He went on to explain that promoters Aleck Greggains and Morris Levy's fight cards were full until March and that they would not be eager to make a match with Gans or his "Baltimore manipulator." "After Gans' poor showing with Britt, promoters are taking a chance on the attitude the public will assume when he appears again. There will surely be little betting until Herford declares with which man he wants to win."[36] Gans was being punished for Herford's missteps. By July 15 of 1905, Herford would be back in San Francisco for a Britt fight, but his charge would not be Joe Gans. Herford would match Kid Sullivan with Britt in San Francisco for a 20-round bout and a purse of $15,000.[37]

It should be noted that Gans never abandoned his title ownership in any newspaper story during this period. Depleted of income, he was simply forced to take on heavier fighters in order to get a paycheck. Even after Gans and Herford separated, reporters in

"YOU JOE! BRING HOME DAT BACON!"

As soon as the Gans-Britt rematch was set, the San Francisco press began its racially charged pre-fight publicity. This grotesque caricature of Gans and his mother mocked her famous telegram sent to the Goldfield match. The telegram made the phrase instantly famous (drawing by Robert Carter, *San Francisco Examiner*, September 1907).

California still wanted to tarnish Gans' reputation. Commenting before the Gans-Nelson fight in 1906, the *Oakland Tribune* reported, "The whole affair has a very nasty look. In the first place Al Herford is still the actual manager for Gans. Some time ago they were supposed to have parted forever, but I know that Herford has something on Gans that compels the Coon to do anything he says."[38]

From 1902 to 1908, Gans was continually referred to as the Lightweight Champion. Only in San Francisco did ring promoters attempt to start a new line of champions, perhaps the first that specifically crowned a fighter as the "White Champion." There they promoted Jimmy Britt, and his successor, Oscar Nelson, as the "White Lightweight Champions," a title that on the West Coast was supposed to be more enviable perhaps than the world title. The boxing establishment outside of California, of course, knew that Gans still held the world lightweight championship — regardless of color.

Sadly, there still exists some confusion regarding Gans' continuous 6-year title lineage in a few of the modern record books as a result of this episode in California. Nat Fleischer incorrectly stated in *Black Dynamite, Vol. IV* in 1938 in a tangential aside to his discussion of Langford, repeating Britt's claim to the title taken directly from the *San Francisco Examiner*, that "Gans had ignored a challenge from Jimmy Britt to fight for the lightweight crown at the class limit of 133 pounds, and Britt in consequence had claimed the title, [although] Joe had never been defeated with the championship at stake, the championship he won by kayoing Frank Erne in 1902."[39] It is as though Fleischer realizes this absurdity and rationalizes in his next sentence: "Gans had simply let the title go by default temporarily and devoted his time to boxing welters."[40] Gans had taken on welterweights prior to the Britt lightweight title fight. Gans fought black welterweight champion Barbados Joe Walcott one month prior to the Britt fight. Although Gans received the "newspaper decision," Walcott kept his welterweight title with an official draw. The operative words in Fleischer's strangely worded explanation are *default* and *temporarily*. How does someone give up a title by *default* and then, only *temporarily*? This is likely where the confusion lies in many modern accounts misrepresenting Gans' title lineage as going from 1902 to 1904 and then from 1906 to 1908, rather than as a continual lineage from 1902–1908. If Gans had abandoned the title by default and Britt acquired it in 1904, then surely Fleischer would have listed Britt (and Nelson who followed him) as lightweight champions in his *Ring Record* books. Those names do not appear. Fleischer lists Frank Erne as the lightweight champion immediately before Gans, with Erne losing to Gans in 1902. Fleischer lists Battling Nelson as the lightweight champion immediately after Gans lost to him in their second fight in 1908.

Newspaper reports outside of California during the years between 1906–1908 refer to Gans as the lightweight champion, but his pitiful pleas to the fight establishment in San Francisco in those years to recognize him as the true lightweight champion, or to match him in a fight there, fell on deaf ears. It is interesting to note that all newspaper reports *prior* to the first Gans-Nelson fight in Goldfield in 1906, *including* the *San Francisco Examiner*, refer to Gans as the world champion and Nelson as the challenger.

Like most fighters of the day, Gans lived from fight paycheck to fight paycheck, and after 1904 he was considered damaged property. Unable to find fights, he was driven into poverty. Gans gave his own interview to the *San Francisco Examiner*, exposing the management scheme that had forced the boxer to fight to orders and explained his unusual showing in several noted fights, including the fiasco involving Jimmy Britt. But according to the press, his statements only proved how crooked he was.[41]

By 1905 no white pugilist wanted to fight Gans. He moved as quickly as a cat, as did

Rex Beach, a popular author of the day, compared the sound of Gans striking the bag to a "Gatling Gun." Gans destroyed nine bags during his short training period in Tonopah, Nevada, for the Gans-Herman fight. December, 1906 (Gary Schultz collection).

After the successful Goldfield fight, the city of Tonopah sponsored the next Gans title fight, hoping to reap similar economic rewards. A giant indoor arena was built specifically for the event of January 1, 1907. A blizzard prevented many from attending. While it proved a great entertainment venue, the building shown here was demolished by 1910 (Gary Schultz collection).

many of the black fighters of his era. He had seen it all in the ring, and his opponents claimed he knew what they would do before they themselves knew. Gans was cool in the ring, focused, and calculating. His brilliant defensive skills were thrilling to watch. His hands were lightening fast. He would catch and block his opponents' punches, as if he knew what they were going to throw at him. He evaded punches by fractions of an inch. He countered equally well with both hands, able to squeeze through the slightest of openings to land combinations to his advantage. His punch was so strong that when in training he would go through as many as nine leather bags in a few days. One writer remarked that his punches to a body bag shook the training camp, exploding like a Gatling gun. His hand and footwork were all calculated to save energy during the longer matches. His endurance was remarkable until his last fighting years, when his stamina was compromised by tuberculosis.

By 1906 Gans still was unable to attract fights and a much-needed paycheck. For a period of 12 months from 1905 to 1906, the only man who would fight Gans was Mike "Twin" Sullivan. The duo would fight three times, once in Baltimore and twice in California. The second bout in January of 1906 was billed as a championship match for the welterweight title; and while Gans won the fight, Californians were not eager to give him the laurels.

Reporting to the *Washington Post*, George Siler explained, "The Joe Gans–Mike 'Twin' Sullivan contest, which will be decided under the auspices of the Hayes Valley Club, is not causing much interest on the coast, or anywhere else for that matter, *despite* the fact that the battle should be a corker. The direct cause of this is attributed to Gans' last fight on the coast — that with Jimmy Britt.... It does not appear right that Gans [who] was, practically, lead about by the nose by his white manager, should be made to bear the brunt of that battle, while Britt, who undoubtedly, transacted his own business and was equally as guilty of wrongdoing as was Gans, should not be made accountable. Gans' color and unsavory reputation is against him."[42]

By the middle of 1906, however, the colors of gold and money trumped those of race. Nevada gambler Tex Rickard knew virtually nothing of the ring at that time (although he would go on to become one of the shrewdest, most successful fight promoters in history). What he wanted to do was to promote Goldfield mining stocks to encourage continued investments in the city's economy.[43] (A Gans fight three months later would be promoted in Tonopah, Nevada, to herald that city's mining stock.)[44] With a few calls to his friends at the major California newspapers, Rickard learned that Gans, while penniless and living off the generosity of friends in San Francisco, was the best boxer available. Rickard had already tied down Bat Nelson, the most popular white fighter. The stage was set in Nevada for a showdown.

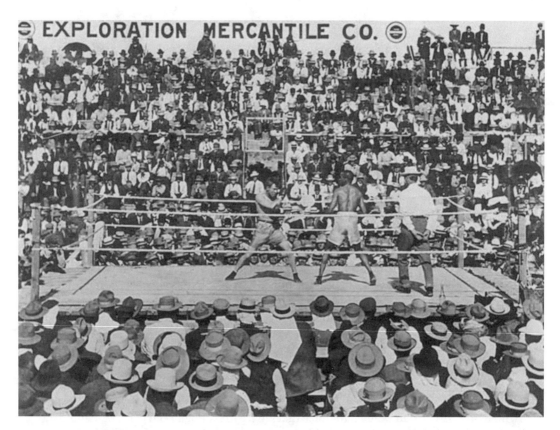

Gans and Nelson battle it out for 42 rounds before the huge Goldfield crowd in 1906. Gans named his popular hotel in Baltimore after this famous battle (Tony Triem collection).

With only his "good luck" worn leather boxing shoes, Gans borrowed train fare to get to Goldfield, Nevada. There he solidified his rightful place in pugilistic history when he beat white lightweight champion Battling Nelson September 3, 1906, in a grueling, record-setting 42-round battle to the finish. (See the appendix for the round-by-round newspaper coverage.) The long fight was brutal to both combatants. Gans had been forced to reduce to a weight that caused severe dehydration. During the fight, his seconds tried to refresh

ROUND 3   DANA PHOTO

Gans loses his title in 1908 when he gives a rematch to Battling Nelson (photograph by Charles Dana, Colleen Aycock collection).

him but he is seen in the Miles Brothers' film throwing up between rounds. Nelson, frustrated, resorted to infighting in clinches, and was repeatedly warned by the referee to refrain from foul head-butts. The battle was viciously fought in the early rounds, and by the end of the 42nd round, the men were drained of all energy. Frustrated, Nelson leveled a blow below the belt that forced Gans to his knees, to be declared the winner on a foul. The spectators were in favor of the referee's call; long had they booed and hooted Nelson's foul tactics during the protracted match. It should be noted that Nelson went to his grave insisting that the blow was not a foul, and stating that he had in his possession a hand-written note from Gans while on his Baltimore deathbed addressed to Nelson attesting as much.[45] It is highly unlikely that Gans wrote such a note to Nelson, and none has surfaced to date.

Badly weakened by tuberculosis, but still eager for the large purses that the big fights would bring, Gans lost the rematch to Nelson in the 17th round in Colma, California, on July 4, 1908, in front of ten thousand spectators. In Baltimore, three thousand fans had gathered at his Goldfield Hotel to hear the returns from the wires. The crowd was silenced each time they learned that Nelson had knocked Gans down for three nine-counts, in the 12th, 13th, and 16th rounds, and two eight-counts in the final round before the blow that kept him down for good.[46] Again on September 9, 1908, Gans met Nelson in a rematch. While Gans lasted 21 rounds, the outcome was the same. The famous trilogy of title fights between these two battlers comprised a total of 80 rounds.

Smart enough to use his $11,000 in winnings from his first match with Nelson (although it was less than the money given to the loser), Gans established the Goldfield Hotel in 1907, a saloon in Baltimore intended to provide income for his family after he left the ring. While it was estimated that Gans would make almost $100,000 during 1907 from his fame after the Goldfield battle, newspapers were also quick to point out in 1907 that he had gambled all his money away and was left broke.[47] The truth was that between 1907 and 1909, Gans would sink $50,000 into hotel expenses and renovations of the Goldfield. During two months of 1907, Gans would bring home almost $30,000.[48] In 1908, Gans would earn $84,000 in ring bouts and theatrical exhibitions. Tragically, Gans would enjoy only two-and-a-half years of the hotel's vibrant life after getting it up and running. The Goldfield was the hopping entertainment center of Baltimore, attracting clientele both black and white, high society and low. Every major entertainer who passed through Baltimore would make the hotel a port of call. There Eubie Blake, the great ragtime musician, would begin his own professional career working a 12-hour daily shift on the piano for $55 per week.[49]

Gans would spend the majority of his remaining funds and most of 1910 chasing remedies to improve his health. Incurable tuberculosis would take him to Prescott, Arizona, but before he left he made one final public curtain call at the Gayety Theater in Baltimore. Battling Nelson was appearing at the theater in an exhibition as champion. Gans was not a part of the production, but when introduced, he made a "short address in which he told of the great prowess of the mighty Dane. Gans was given a grand ovation. The parting of Gans and Nelson, as the former left the stage was most pathetic. Both men visibly showing the human affection. In the eyes of both were tears."[50] The following day, Gans left for Arizona. He succumbed to tuberculosis only one year after his last fight.

As with many of the great black battlers, the places they so grandly built up at one time have been lost to history. Goldfield, Nevada, is a ghost town today. It is easy to imagine the place a hundred years ago when thousands of people gravitated to one old baseball field turned into a magnificent stadium for 10,000 fans of a boxing match. Upon entering Goldfield's city limits, the visitor sees a stone marker announcing the town's cherished

An early training gym reported to be Gans' at 1413 Etting St., Baltimore (photograph by Colleen Aycock, 2010).

boxing heritage, quite unlike Gans' hometown Baltimore, where there is scant indication of recognition of its native son.

Walking the streets of the old port at Fells Point and feeling the icy sting from a light rain caught by the Baltimore wind, one can imagine the life at the busy fish market where Gans worked a hundred years ago and the sounds that swelled the air. Gans' hotel is gone, along with his mother's property on Argyle Street where he died. His old training gym at 1413 Etting Street sits abandoned, the sounds of fighters hitting the bags silenced. Prescott, Arizona is also a place filled only with ghostly reminders of the champion. The home where Gans recuperated on Virginia Street has been demolished, but its Victorian counterparts remain largely intact. The nearby train depot sits empty now — with its own ghosts, not the least of which was the memory of Gans casting his eyes toward Baltimore in his last public interview before he boarded the train for his long trip back through Chicago to his Maryland home.

Accompanied by Prescott physician Dr. Harry Southworth, Gans would make it to Baltimore on August 5, and attend to his family and finances before he died on August 10, 1910.[51] His last days were noted by every major newspaper in the country, and his death was a day of mourning for people of all races and walks of life. Thousands of people (some estimates as high as 10,000) filed past his casket at Whatcoat Methodist Episcopal Church, at Pine and Franklin streets in Baltimore. Baritone Nelson Tunstall of New York sang at the

Former Maryland boxing commissioner Earl Savage, standing by Gans' gravestone, says a few words to members of the Veteran Boxers Association, Ring 101, of Baltimore as they lay a wreath at Gans' grave, August 10, 2010.

funeral. Wagons full of flowers preceded a hundred plus hacks carrying mourners to Gans' final resting place at Sharp Street Cemetery, today known as Mount Auburn Cemetery, Baltimore.[52]

One hundred years later, there is no visible, fitting memorial to Baltimore's native son in the Monumental City. There are no streets, parks, or public statues noting the first American-born black boxer to achieve world recognition. Earlier in the century, H. L. Mencken noted, "It always amazes me how easily men of the highest talents and eminence can be forgotten in this careless world." He offered to contribute "$100 in cash money whenever a sufficiently reliable committee opens subscription books."[53]

Were it not for the Veteran Boxers Association International Ring 101 of Baltimore, Gans' grave at Mt. Auburn Cemetery, slowly sinking into the soft earth, may have fallen into ruin. Spearheaded in 2005 by Ring 101 President Frank Gilbert, a drive was made to restore the grave lot and monument to its original grandeur. Today, two Hall of Fame Ring members, Gene Wagstaff and Earl Savage, maintain the gravesite.[54] A wreath-laying ceremony by Ring 101 commemorated the centennial of Gans' death (August 10, 2010). Officiating at the ceremony was Bishop Joseph Gans, of Washington, D.C., namesake relative of Joe Gans.

Thirty-two years after Gans' death, newspaper man Bill Moran of Nevada said, "There can be only one Greatest Fighter Who Ever Lived," and the "daddy of them all, the champion of all races, was a coffee-colored Baltimore boy named Joe Gans, who demonstrated with his two hands the perfect coordination that man is capable of developing between mind

Maryland Hall-of-Fame members, International Ring 101, who maintain Gans' gravesite with the author. Left to right: Gene Wagstaff, Colleen Aycock, Frank Gilbert and Earl Savage (photograph by Dave Wallace, August 1, 2009).

and muscle."[55] Gans was a good, clean fighter. While he won five fights on fouls, he lost no bouts on fouls. And where he won on fouls, it was usually after a multitude of fouls had been committed against him. Gans accumulated over 150 wins and over 100 kayos, but he gained immortality in the sports history books for his 42-round battle with Oscar "Battling" Nelson. It would be the longest title fight in gloved boxing, the longest fight to be filmed, the first "Fight of the Century" promoted by Tex Rickard, considered the father of Madison Square Garden, and the promotional spectacle that would spark the last gold rush on the American frontier. Gans was such an iconic draw for the early movie industry that it shifted early film experiments from boxing reenactments to documentaries. In addition to his boxing legacy, Gans would take his winnings from the longest fight and open the first "black-and-tan" club, the Goldfield, in Baltimore, a precursor to the great jazz clubs. There he would start the music career of the great Eubie Blake.

For both George Dixon and Gans, despite all of their ring prowess and the science they brought to boxing, their greatest achievement, and perhaps boxing's legacy to American culture, was crossing the color line. One of the most recognized and influential men of the cloth, the Reverend Francis J. Grimke of Washington, D.C., speaking in his famous discourse after the great "Fight of the Century," noted, "It is generally conceded ... that Booker T. Washington has done much good and will do much for the colored race for its uplifting, its education, for making its members citizens in a true sense of the word; but with all that, in the entire course of his life work he never did one-tenth to place the black man in the

Gans' original headstone (undated photograph, Tony Triem collection).

front rank as a gentleman as has been done by Joe Gans."[56] The sport of boxing, and its
early African American masters, accomplished that.

NOTES

1. Prior to his lightweight title win, newspapers quoted his birth year as 1874; however during his later bouts, it appears as though the newspapers tried to make him appear a younger fighter by quoting his birth year as 1876.

2. "Gans Takes Final Count," *Baltimore Sun*, August 11, 1910.

3. Ibid.

4. According to the "Local Smoker and Sparring Matches" listed in the *Baltimore Sun*, Gans is referred to as Gant on 11.28.1893, as Gantz on 2.13.1894, and as Gans on 4.20.1894.

5. When Gans came into a surprise windfall of $6000 while in Nevada from mining stock given to him by gamblers after the Goldfield fight, he immediately sent the proceeds to his foster mother. He used the money from his Goldfield and Tonopah prize fights to buy property in Baltimore. See Colleen Aycock and Mark Scott, "The Joe Gans–Kid Herman World Box-

ing Title Fight: New Year's Day, 1907, Tonopah, Nevada," *Boomtown History III*, Jean Johnson, ed., Amargosa, Nev.: Nevada Boom Town History Event, 2010.

6. L.S., "Les Champions du monde: Joe Gans Fut le Quatrieme Champion du Monde (Poids Legers)," *La Vie au Grand Air*, N.d., 2047–2049.

7. "White Plague Winner of Fight with Joe Gans," *Trenton Evening Times*, August 10, 1910. The *Syracuse Herald* reported Gans' forays into the battle royals in "Gans' Pugilistic Career," October 7, 1906.

8. "How It Came to Gans: Herford Tells How the Oyster City Man Started Out," *Oakland Tribune*, November 5, 1904.

9. Ibid.

10. "Colored Champions," *Baltimore Sun*, June 27, 1894.

11. "Elliott Knocked Out: Joseph Gans, the Clever Colored Man, Does it by a Strange Blow," *Baltimore*

Sun, October 22, 1895, and "Gans Knocks Out Siddons: The Dangerous New Orleans Lad Stays Nearly Seven Rounds," *Baltimore Sun*, November 29, 1895.

12. "Gans Whips English," *Baltimore Sun*, March 7, 1895.

13. "An Imitation Fight," *Baltimore Sun*, November 19, 1895.

14. "Gans Knocks Out Siddons," *Baltimore Sun*, November 29, 1895.

15. "Beau Brummel of Fistdom," *San Francisco Examiner*, May 19, 1897.

16. Fleischer, 143.

17. "Gans in Quick Time: The Match that Failed," *Baltimore Sun*, May 13, 1902.

18. Fleischer, 145–147.

19. "Joe Gans Bests George M'Fadden," *San Francisco Examiner*, November 1, 1899.

20. Ibid.

21. Ike Swift, "Something Else," in *George McFadden*, 8–11.

22. Ibid.

23. "Joe Gans Bests M'Fadden," *San Francisco Examiner*, November1, 1899.

24. "Excited Crowd of Sports: How a Flash Bulletin Put Them All in a Panic," *Baltimore Sun*, November 1, 1899.

25. Nat Fleischer, *The Ring Record Book and Boxing Encyclopedia* (1961 ed.), 282.

26. "The New Champion: What He Told Harry Lyons," *Baltimore Sun*, May 14, 1902.

27. Fleischer, *Black Dynamite, Vol. III*, 151.

28. J. J. Johnston and Sean Curtin, *Images of Sport: Chicago Boxing*, 19.

29. "M'Govern Wins a 'Fake' Fight," *Chicago Times Herald*, December 14, 1900.

30. "Herford and Gans to Go to Chicago," *Baltimore Sun*, October 22, 1900.

31. Nat Fleischer, *Black Dynamite, Vol. III*, 64.

32. Ibid., 155.

33. "Gans in Quick Time," *Baltimore Sun*, May 15, 1902.

34. Dan Streible, *Fight Pictures: A History of Boxing and Early Cinema*, 166.

35. W. W. Naughton, "Lightweight Laurels Belong to Boxer James Edward Britt," *San Francisco Examiner*, January 10, 1905.

36. George Siler, "Jimmy Gardner Takes Exception That He Side-Stepped Joe Gans," *Salt Lake Tribune*, January 22, 1905.

37. "Sporting News," *Racine Daily Journal*, June 15, 1905.

38. "The Knave," *Oakland Tribune*, August 19, 1906.

39. Nat Fleischer, *Black Dynamite, Vol. IV*. "Langford," 129.

40. Ibid.

41. "Charges Local Boxer Deceived His Friends: Baltimorean Thinks Britt's Reputation Will Suffer When Truth Comes Out," *San Francisco Examiner*, February 18, 1906.

42. George Siler, "Siler Revives Gossip of the Gans-Britt Fiasco Which Put the Negro Pug 'in Bad' with the Public," *Washington Post*, January 14, 1906.

43. Colleen Aycock and Mark Scott, *Joe Gans: A Biography of the First African American World Boxing Champion*, Ch. 14 "Epic Battle in the Nevada Desert."

44. Colleen Aycock and Mark Scott, "The Joe Gans — Kid Herman World Boxing Title Fight: New Year's Day, 1907, Tonopah, Nevada," *Boomtown History III*, Jean Johnson, ed., Amargosa, Nev.: Nevada Boom Town History Event, 2010.

45. Harry Pegg, "Battling Nelson" *Boxiana Review* No. 9, 1973.

46. "Joe Gans Knocked Out: Down at Joe's Hotel," *Baltimore Sun*, July 5, 1908.

47. "Gans' Earning Capacity for This Year May Reach the Tremendous Sum of $100,000 and Upwards," *Philadelphia Press*, January 6, 1907; "Joe Gans is Broke," *Milwaukee Free Press*, February 21, 1907)

48. "Gans Taking Home $30,000," *Milwaukee Free Press*, October 2, 1907; "$25,000 to Throw Fight," *New York Times*, September 5, 1906.

49. Al Rose, *Eubie Blake*, New York: Schirmer Books, Macmillan, 1979, unnumbered page between 44 and 45.

50. "White Plague Winner of Fight with Joe Gans," *Trenton Evening Times*, August 10, 1910.

51. "Gans Takes Final Count," *Baltimore Sun*, August 11, 1910.

52. "Joe Gans," Obituary, Baltimore, *Afro-American*, August 13, 1910.

53. H. L. Mencken, "Days of Innocence: Master of Gladiators," *New Yorker*, April 25, 1942, 18–20.

54. Nicole Fuller, "Grave of Baltimorean Who Boxed Decades Ago Is Restored, Courtesy of Modern-Day Admirers," *Baltimore Sun*, October 27, 2005.

55. Bill Moran, "The Greatest Fighter Who Ever Lived? This Writer Lauds Joe Gans, Old Master," *Nevada State Journal*, September 27, 1942.

56. Francis J. Grimke, "The Atlanta Riot: A Discourse Published by Request," Washington D.C., October 7, 1906.

CHAPTER 7

Dave Holly: "Challenger of the World"

Douglas Cavanaugh

*I can lick Battling Nelson a good deal easier than I can Dave Holly. I have
met Holly three times and I know he is a hard man to beat.* —Joe Gans

In every professional sport there exists the story of the athlete whose contribution gets
overlooked, whose own accomplishments are eclipsed due to the charisma or achievements
of his more flashy contemporaries. The most famous example of this phenomenon would
be baseball great Lou Gehrig, who found it next to impossible to come out of the long
shadows cast by his Yankee teammates Babe Ruth and Joe DiMaggio. In pro football Tommy
Nobis was considered by insiders to be one of the greatest linebackers of his era. Unfortunately, his "era" also featured Dick Butkus, Ray Nitschke, Willie Lanier and Jack Lambert;
four Hall of Fame linebackers, each of whom has a claim to being the finest ever to play
the position. Speaking of football, fans remember well the exploits of the Ram's "Fearsome
Foursome" defensive line, but how many realized that in addition to high-profile members
Deacon Jones, Merlin Olson and Rosey Grier, there was also Lamar Lundy, who was considered an outstanding lineman in his own right?

If the sadly neglected career of Dave Holly proves anything it is that boxing is not
exempt from this same phenomenon; that even the finest of fighters can get lost in the
shuffle and be overlooked by history, irrespective of achievements. In the case of Holly many
factors contributed, not the least of which is that he was a big fish in a huge pond, as vast
and deep as it was wide. He fought during one of the toughest stretches in the history of
the lower weight classes (1900–1910), a period during which could be found a dispropor-
tionately large number of outstanding ringmen plying their trade. Among them were fighters
destined for greatness in boxing's pantheon, their names reading like a veritable who's-who
of the Hall of Fame: Joe Gans, Battling Nelson, Packey McFarland, Abe Attell, Jack Blackburn, Sam Langford, Joe Walcott, Dixie Kid, Freddie Welsh, Jimmy Britt and Ad Wolgast.
With opposition of that caliber battling for the same spotlight, it is little wonder that Holly's
star has been eclipsed, his career overlooked and underappreciated.

Dave Holly was born on March 2, 1881 in Westchester, Pennsylvania. Though later
domiciled in Camden, New Jersey, Holly fought almost exclusively out of Philadelphia,
where he contested 100 of his 128 recorded bouts and possibly more. He was a clever boxer-
puncher who fought out of a crouch and possessed a shell-like defense opponents found

difficult to penetrate. He began his career in the no-decision era with a string of kayos and newspaper victories over largely forgotten local fighters. But since the "City of Brotherly Love" was a major fight Mecca (then as now) it must be assumed that these men were far from being pushovers. His most frequent opponents in the early years were a pair of toughies named Vernon Campbell (eight bouts) and Jimmy Hill (five bouts). He also fought a six-bout series with famed iron man Joe Grim who, staying true to form, managed to finish every one of their skirmishes defiantly on his feet.

In 1902 — his second year as a pro — with less than fifty fights under his belt, Holly traveled to Lancaster, Pennsylvania, to take on the great Joe Gans, world lightweight champion and a veteran of over one hundred career bouts. Their ten-round engagement on October 13 resulted in Holly being floored three times and thoroughly outclassed throughout. Knowing he was in over his head Dave ran, crouched, clinched and did everything in his power to stay the distance with his legendary opponent. Afterward he announced to the crowd that he was "only an amateur" compared to Gans, whom he called "A scienced [sic] man and a champion."[1] This bout was significant in Holly's career because not only did it signal the beginning of a series of fights between himself and Gans, but also heralded the start of his battles with several of the outstanding "colored" fighters of the era. The second series began five months and ten fights later when he was matched against a fellow up and comer named Jack Blackburn. The tall, rangy Blackburn, who would do time in prison for murder and later gain fame as the trainer of heavyweight champion Joe Louis, took a six-round newspaper win in what would be the first of five hotly contested fights between the two over the next several years.

Dave Holly took on the greatest fighters of the era.

Spike Sullivan, brother of Featherweight Champion Dave Sullivan, was next on the list. A seasoned pro, Spike was a fan favorite, a tough little Irishman who had fought top level opposition such as Dal Hawkins, Tommy White and George "Elbows" McFadden and gave as good as he got against all of them. But what had really endeared him to fight fans was his gallant stand against lightweight champ Joe Gans. Hopelessly outclassed, Spike had nevertheless torn after Gans from the first gong and never stopped trying to batter his elusive foe. The referee stopped the bout in the fourteenth round, declaring Gans the victor but at the same time making Sullivan something of a hero to everyone.

Sullivan and Holly met on September 13 in Philadelphia. Spike was installed as the favorite and for the early rounds it seemed justified, as he got the better of the action, jabbing Holly and going hard to the body. But Dave bided his time and in the fourth round opened up on his opponent, belting him about at will. In the fifth Spike was dropped by a body blow and floored three more times in the sixth and final round.[2] This bout, though a no-decision affair, was an obvious win for Holly, whose stock in the lightweight ranks was raised considerably as a result. It was his most high profile fight to date and newspapers gave it considerable coverage, thus insuring that he was now regarded as a serious contender for the lightweight crown.

Gans no doubt heard about Holly's victory and was impressed enough to again try out this kid whom he'd bested so easily the previous year. He agreed to a six-round bout to be fought in Holly's adopted hometown of Philly on October 23, 1903. It proved to be a far cry from their first encounter. The vastly improved Holly had learned his trade and this time forced the action on Joe, who fought a careful, defensive fight. The end result was a newspaper draw, though some reported a close win for Holly.[3] Sportswriters praised both men for the high level of skill displayed and called the bout "a revelation to those gathered at ringside."[4] A rematch was fought six weeks later, December 7, again in Philadelphia. This time Holly's aggression cost him as he suffered two flash knockdowns in the first two frames. But he was up quickly and went after Joe with such liveliness that he managed to shade most of the remaining rounds. The *Philadelphia Item* scored it as a win for Gans, but other sources thought Holly deserved a draw despite the knockdowns.[5]

Dave Holly in fighting pose.

The year concluded with a six-round newspaper win over Jack Blackburn and a twelve-round beating administered to tough Belfield Walcott, brother of welterweight champ Joe Walcott. Then on April 11, 1904, he traveled to Cambridge, Massachusetts to meet a hot young local who was beginning to make some noise in fistic circles. His name was Sam Langford, "The Boston Tar Baby." Despite having been a professional a mere two years, Langford was already giving a good account of himself against the game's top lightweights, having twice fought Jack Blackburn and dueling with Joe Gans a mere twenty-four hours after Holly last fought him. In fact he had scored a convincing fifteen-round decision victory over "The Old Master" in the non–title affair. So Holly made a rare foray out of his native Pennsylvania to deal with this newcomer.

Langford was made a pre-fight favorite and from the first gong the long-armed Boston boy fought aggressively, snapping his jab and hooking hard at his more experienced foe. He was successful for the first few minutes of action, but his now-seasoned Philly opponent had an answer. He began boring up under Langford's reach and working from the inside with sharp counters, his crouching, shell-like defense blunting Langford's return volleys. Ultimately Holly proved too difficult a puzzle for young Sam to solve. In front of his home-town admirers Langford was served a thorough ten-round lacing, losing a clear-cut decision to the invader from Philly. The final round saw him holding on for dear life as Holly poured it on in an attempt to finish him.[6]

Joe Gans was taking note of all the commotion and once again emerged from his native Baltimore to do battle with the man who was quickly becoming the most obvious opponent for his crown. The fight, in Philadelphia on June 27, 1904, took up the usual pattern of Gans on the defensive and Holly forcing matters. Dave slipped most of Gan's leads, hammering him with uppercuts and never allowing the champ to get set. Holly's onslaught was so fierce that he had Gans bewildered, the *New York Evening World* noting Gans' clinching at the finish to be so intense that "the referee could hardly separate the two men."[7] The Philadelphia papers gave the decision to Holly, noting that it was his fight "from beginning to end." Furthermore, based on the last few bouts between the two it appeared that Holly had managed to "solve Gans' clever style."[8] Still, a title bout would not be forthcoming. The Philadelphian was still too dangerous and would have to wait another two years for his shot. "I can lick Battling Nelson a good deal easier than I can Dave Holly," Gans said later, "So you can see what I think of Holly. I have met him three [sic] times in limited bouts and I know he is a hard man to beat."[9]

The next six months would be a whirlwind for Holly and an entire career's worth of hard fights by modern standards as he faced practically every top black lightweight and welterweight around, including Jack Blackburn, Dixie Kid, George Cole and Rufe Turner. His bout with Jack Blackburn (their third) on August 26 was a close affair, Jack getting a shade by using an educated left to control the fight. Nonplussed, Holly immediately went after former welterweight champion Joe Walcott, the famed "Barbados Demon." He had already trounced Walcott's brother Belfield and didn't figure Joe, now long in the tooth, would pose much more of a problem. The bout took place on September 10, 1904, in Philadelphia.

Showing little respect for the aging great, Holly tore after him at the opening bell. Walcott bided his time, letting his opponent expend his energy while he looked for openings and opportunities to exert his advantage in experience. But after several clinches in which his ribs were ceaselessly pounded the old champ became irritated over his foe's aggression and lack of respect. Summoning the old strength that had allowed him to battle heavyweights, Walcott grabbed Holly in a clinch, threw him backward to the floor and then took a vicious swing at his fallen antagonist. Dave got the message and though he continued to force matters he now focused as much on making the still-dangerous Walcott miss as working his body. Most sources reported it as a close win for Holly, but some thought that the old warhorse deserved a draw.[10]

Three fights versus Sam Langford and two against Dixie Kid followed in close succession, the first Langford bout taking place a mere two weeks after the Walcott set-to. Sam showed marked improvement since their initial encounter, using a sharp left jab to close Holly's eye and control him from the outside, while Dave continued to be the master in the trenches. It was judged a draw after fifteen fast and furious rounds. Their next bout, a six-rounder in Philadelphia, was also judged a draw by the newspapers- now referring to Sam and Dave as "bitter rivals."[11] The final bout, held in Salem, Massachusetts, in 1905, saw Langford finally get the best of the series. Outweighed by thirteen pounds, Holly was given a thorough trouncing in fifteen rounds.

The bouts with future Hall-of-Fame welterweight Dixie Kid saw each man take a six-round newspaper decision in what were described as bloody encounters. The *Philadelphia Item* reported Holly as giving his larger foe a "sound beating" in their first fight.[12] The return bout five weeks later was reported as a win for the Kid. Both were all-action fights, which pleased the fans greatly and elevated the status of both combatants.

But the fight Holly really wanted — a title shot against champion Joe Gans — still evaded him. Gans had been clamoring for a bout against Battling Nelson (who had been inexplicably claiming the lightweight championship) for some time. Since there was a plethora of viable contenders for both men the Nelson camp was content to avoid Gans. Joe decided that the best course of action was to eliminate all possible roadblocks to a bout with Bat and when Holly beat the highly regarded Rufe Turner he became the next obstacle to be dealt with. This time the Baltimore native would make clear the answer to the question of superiority between himself and the muscular Philadelphian.

The lightweight championship title fight between champion Joe Gans and challenger Dave Holly took place in Seattle, Washington, on July 23, 1906. The opening rounds looked promising for Holly as he pressed the "Old Master," opening a gash over his eye and eventually swelling it shut. Undeterred, Joe remained focused on blunting the body attack, which he knew from experience was Holly's main weapon. He did so by offering nothing but elbows and forearms whenever his antagonist went to the midsection. By the middle rounds Gans' sharp punches began to exact their toll. Holly's left eye was swollen shut and his right badly gashed. In a reversal of tactics he reverted to a defensive stance while Joe took on the role of stalker. The bout dissolved into a dreary affair with an estimated 145 clinches throughout. Though his blows had done damage, Gans saw that his iron-jawed opponent was not going to fall from headshots. In yet another role reversal the champion became the body puncher, raking Holly's ribs and kidneys with deadly precision.

The challenger was in deep water now and both men knew it. Gans had been a veteran of twenty-round fights before his opponent had even had his first pro bout; Holly had gone twenty rounds only once and that being in his previous fight with Rufe Turner. He was fading fast and in the final round Gans tried to finish him. He unloaded heavy blows, which staggered Holly, but Dave fought back hard unleashing volleys of his own. At the final bell the decision was clear-cut in the champion's favor.[13] In one final ironic note to a fight that was full of ironies, Gans drew the color line afterwards stating that he didn't want to face black opponents like Dave Holly anymore but instead wanted Bat Nelson and the paydays concomitant to fighting white opponents.[14] He stayed true to his word and never again fought another black fighter.

His title hopes dashed, Holly spent the rest of his ring career losing more than he won. In his very next bout on October 11 he once more faced Jack Blackburn, who by now was at the zenith of his powers and claiming the lightweight championship for himself. Though a dubious claim at best, what was not questionable was that he had developed into one of the deadliest fighters in the game[15] which he proved by administering a savage six-round beating to the faded Holly. It was a newspaper decision and the last time these two greats would face each other in the ring. Holly then faced Sailor Burke, a fighter who had the distinction to be the first to ever knock out iron man Joe Grim. The much larger Sailor, who would go on to fight heavyweight champion Jess Willard, would also have the distinction of being the first to ever drop Holly, flooring him twelve times in three rounds until the

Einey, meeney, miney, mo,
Fight a nigger, yes or no.
If he's very apt to win
Draw the line and let him go;
Einey, meeney, miney, mo.

White title holders "draw the color line," especially if they thought a black fighter might win. Here Marvin Hart, acting heavyweight title holder, draws the color line against Jack Johnson (from the *Tonopah Daily Sun* [Nevada], July 13, 1905).

police finally intervened. Subsequent kayo losses to Jeff Clark — the celebrated "Joplin Ghost" — and unheralded Heywood Briggs convinced Holly to finally hang up the gloves for good.

The fact that he could boast wins over such incredible opposition as Joe Gans, Sam Langford, Joe Walcott, Jack Blackburn and Dixie Kid probably did little to soothe the disappointment Holly felt over never having won a world title. Thus he retired to his home in Camden, New Jersey and quietly went into the sign painting business. Two years after he left boxing on July 15, 1912, Holly was bitten by a stray dog. He was treated at the hospital and released, thinking little of it. On July 19 he traveled to Philadelphia to second for his friend, heavyweight contender Joe Jennette in his bout with Battling Jim Johnson. A few days afterward he suddenly took ill, dying the following morning on July 25 from blood poisoning. He was 31 years old.[16]

NOTES

1. "The Boxing Show," *Lancaster Daily Examiner,* October 15, 1902.

2. "Dave Holly Beat Spike Sullivan." *Evening World* (NY), September 11, 1903.

3. "Gans and Holly in Fast Bout," *Philadelphia Bulletin,* December 8, 1903.

4. "Gans vs. Holly," *Philadelphia Public Ledger,* October 23, 1903.

5. "Holly and Gans Draw," *Philadelphia Bulletin,* October 24, 1903.

6. "Dave Holly Won from Langford," *Evening World* (NY), April 12, 1904.

7. "Gans Goes Up Against a Surprise in Holly," *Evening World* (NY), June 28, 1904.

8. "Holly Outpoints Gans," *Philadelphia Public Ledger,* June 27, 1904.

9. "This Match Has Class," *Seattle Sunday Times,* July 22, 1906.

10. "Holly and Walcott Draw," *Philadelphia Record,* September 11, 1904.

11. "Langford and Holly Fight a Draw at Baltimore," *New York Sun,* October 2, 1904.

12. *Http://boxrec.com/list_bouts.php?human_id= 11016&cat=boxer,* Accessed January 18, 2010.

13. "Gans is Master of Dave Holly," *Seattle Post-Intelligencer,* July 24, 1906.

14. "Joe Gans is Here Ready for Match," *Seattle Post-Intelligencer,* July 11, 1906.

15. "Blackburn a Good One," *Los Angeles Times,* February 12, 1906.

16. "Dave Holly Dead," *Philadelphia Record,* July 26, 1912.

CHAPTER 8

Joe Walcott, the Barbados Demon: World Welterweight Champion

Michael J. Schmidt

As a child of the sixties my boyhood heroes included, amongst others, Muhammad Ali, Joe Frazier, Jerry Quarry, Bob Foster and Carlos Monzon. In later years this expanded to the likes of Marvin Hagler, Roberto Duran, Larry Holmes, etc. But after reading about the exploits of Joe Gans, I became a follower of the "old timers," as boxers in the 1800's and early 1900's are so fondly referred to.

Anyone who has been in the "squared circle" or partaken of the "sweet science" will no doubt remember how easy sparring first looked before you actually put on those old leather gloves for the first time. The simple act of holding up your hands after a few rounds became a problem, having not first learned the fine art of pacing yourself through a few rounds with the local boxing club legends. It was with amazement that I read of the exploits of Joe Gans, who fought beyond forty rounds in temperatures that were unbearable and without the aid of modern day gloves or rules. He also took on bigger, heavier men for twenty rounds or more. The "old timers" had caught my attention indeed.

Any fighter with a moniker of "The Barbados Demon," who had a propensity of beating much bigger foes, had to inspire even the remotely curious. Joe Walcott was a man legendary for taking on foes much bigger than he was and is considered today one of the all time greats.

Joe Walcott was a force to be reckoned with, who fought from 1890–1911, and compiled a record of ninety-two wins, twenty-five losses, and twenty-four draws.[1] Walcott reigned as World Welterweight Champion from 1901 to 1904. He challenged foes ranging from lightweight to heavyweight and is reputed (along with others) to have coined the phrase "The bigger they are, the harder they fall." A test of any boxer's position in the pantheon of all-time greats surely must include an examination of his opponents and notable fights. The list of Walcott's prominent opponents is a virtual who's who of boxing hall-of-fame representatives. His opponents included legendary fighters, "Mysterious" Billy Smith, George "Kid" Lavigne, Joe Choynski, "Philadelphia" Jack O'Brien, Dixie Kid, Joe Gans, and Sam Langford.

Reports of Walcott's date of birth vary. The two most cited dates are March 13, 1873, and April 1, 1872, in Barbados. Prospects for a young man such as Walcott on the Island were limited in a culture still influenced by colonialism. Slavery had been abolished some thirty-nine years earlier. However, decades after, free men continued to work without pay in exchange for living accommodations provided by plantation owners as part of a four-year "apprenticeship."[2]

Walcott was only fifteen when he signed on as a cabin boy on a sailing ship bound for Boston. Flogging or whipping of seamen was allowed in the British Navy well into the 1940s, and it was in this hardened setting that young Walcott made his journey into fistiana. Walcott's legendary ability to outbox much larger foes began aboard ship. "While at sea, Joe had engaged in several rough-and-tumble fights with men much larger than himself and discovered that his natural great strength enabled him to give most of them tough arguments."[3] Upon his arrival in Boston, Massachusetts, one can only imagine the adventurous spirit of a remarkably strong youth.

Walcott spent the days during his teenage years in Boston working various menial jobs, including those of cook, mover and porter. Boxing, of course, would be a way for Walcott to establish himself in a rough-and-tumble setting for which he was apparently well-versed. "Boxing, is at best, a reminder of man's savage past. It is also one way for the poorest, the most desperate man, to slug his way into being somebody."[4] Evenings for Walcott were spent at the gym, learning to box and wrestle; and Boston was the perfect place to learn the sweet science.

Joe Walcott, the "Barbados Demon," stood 5'1½" tall, but what he lacked in height he more than made up for in power, reach, and stamina.

The "Boston Strong Boy," John L. Sullivan, rose from the streets there to win the most coveted sport championship of the time, world heavyweight champion, and ruled from 1882 until 1892. A portion of this reign, of course, was as a bare-knuckle fighter. Sullivan was as big a sporting name as there was at the time. He barnstormed the country during 1883 and 1884, promising purses sometimes as high as one thousand dollars for any man who could last four rounds with him. "Sullivan made 195 appearances in 136 cities and towns over the course of 238 days. No one, not even a presidential candidate, had undertaken such an ambitious tour before."[5]

By the time Walcott arrived in Boston, boxing had already become a focal point. "During that time, Boston became a hotbed for boxing and featured such distinguished boxing clubs as the Cribb Club and the Casino Athletic Club in the South End. Prizefighters came from around the country to Bean Town because it was now the place for good matches and good purses."[6] Such was the talent-rich boxing area of Boston that a young Walcott was entering. (Over a period of seven years, 1901–1908, the World Welterweight Championship was held by four Boston area fighters, including Walcott.) Other boxing luminaries in and about Boston when young Walcott entered the field included, among others, George Dixon and the legendary Jake Kilrain, who gave boxing lessons at the Cribb Club.

Various photographs of Walcott depict an extremely thick and powerfully built man, and it is easy to envision his successes in the squared circle. Walcott stood all of five feet, one-and-a-half inches, not much taller than most bantamweights. He weighed in the area of 142 pounds, but he had incredibly long arms and an amazing eighteen-inch neck and an expanded chest measurement of 41 inches.[7] Comparatively speaking, these measurements are remarkable. Walcott's neck size was equal or greater than that of every heavyweight champion until Joe Frazier, with the exception of Jim Jeffries, Marvin Hart, and Primo Carnera.

Short statured Walcott was known as a giant killer. In this drawing by Edgren for Fleischer's *Black Dynamite, vol. III*, Walcott appears to leap up at his opponents.

His expanded chest measurement was one inch less than the great heavyweight champions, Ezzard Charles, Rocky Marciano and Floyd Patterson. Walcott was described as having "amazingly long, thick muscular arms, broad bulky shoulders between which a bullet head sat deep on a short neck."[8] He was an incredible puncher and used his short stature to advantage by becoming a ferocious body puncher. "Men who fought him were handicapped sorely. Naturally, for all his opponents were taller, and their blows usually landed on his shoulders, or on top of that granite skull."[9] It did not take young Walcott long to make his mark in the boxing-rich Boston area.

As an amateur, Walcott knocked out a local amateur heavyweight champion, Pat Reilly, in the first round; and on another occasion, knocked out two opponents in the same night, both of whom outweighed Walcott by twenty pounds. On this particular evening good fortune came Walcott's way. In the crowd was legendary bantamweight champion George Dixon who was so impressed by Walcott that he introduced him to his manager, Tom O'Rourke. "Walcott was added to O'Rourke's roster of boxers from his position in Boston as an elevator operator at the American House Hotel."[10] Walcott's ring exposure was rapid as he toured with Dixon, fighting on undercards of the well-known Dixon, with O'Rourke being a manager mainstay for years to come.

Early records, which possibly excluded many bouts, show Walcott engaging in anywhere from twelve to twenty fights in 1892. The bulk of these fights took place in Boston and Philadelphia. In August 1893 boxing scribes began to take further note as Walcott blasted out Australian lightweight champion Jack Hall in one round in New York. At this point in his career, Walcott was on a proverbial roll. From August 1893 through December 1895, Walcott engaged in nineteen fights without a loss. Included in this string of victories were some very tough battles with undefeated Australian welterweight champion Tommy Tracey and undefeated New England welterweight Dick O'Brien. The bout with Tracey epitomized Walcott's boxing style. "Gradually, yet surely, Walcott's cruel bombardment of the body weakened the Australian, until it became evident that it was only a question of how long he could stand up under the punishment. When Walcott switched his attack from body to head, Tracey was already a beaten man. In the 19th round the colored boy drove him to the ropes and smashed a right on the jaw that sent the game boxer from the Antipodes down and out."[11] Walcott at this time was making a name for himself as a very tough fighter to deal with and one who would dish out out severe punishment to his opponent.

Walcott's style was that of a punching machine bent on destruction by way of an unrelenting swarming offence which eschewed self-preservation. Comparisons with future fighters conjure up a boxing cocktail of Henry Armstrong, Jake Lamotta, Rocky Marciano , Joe Frazier, and Aaron Pryor. Somewhere in all of these men's background, or psyche as it were, was some demon that formed a personality prepared to go to depths of unfathomable pain and exhaustion to render out their own version of social or personal justice or, perhaps, some personal vindication. What early developmental upbringing, or early personality traits, would drive a person to engage in battle at such levels? Each fighter, of course, would have his own inner stories to tell in that regard. George Vecsey, in writing on a young Cassius Clay, describes one particular instance of a fighter's reason for engaging in such a trying sport:

> Some men become boxers because they are used to fighting in the street; because they are poor; because they see boxing as a chance to put food in their stomachs. But Cassius was not poor; he was not desperate for material things. "I think boxing was an escape all right" said a social worker who knew young Cassius. "It seemed to be kind of a release for him. I think at first it was kind of fear of his father. There was tension there in that family although none of them will ever admit it."[12]

What level of pain and endurance, Dante's inferno as it were, was Lamotta entering into in his battles with Sugar Ray Robinson? Marciano exhibited similar grit in his battles with Ezzard Charles, as did Frazier with Ali, Zale against Graziano, and Pryor in his tremendous battles with the great Alexis Arguello. What demon drove these fighters to the outer limits of pain and extreme physical and mental endurance?

Perhaps Ralph Wiley, writing in the introduction to Arthur Ashe's book, *A Hard Road to Glory*, sums up the primordial elements of boxing's best: "Boxing is no game. It is more than and less than a game, but not simply a game. Even to call it 'sport' stretches credulity. Boxing is both an obsession and a reminder, having to do with man's ability to survive, and to defend himself against the savages lurking within, and eventually to best himself, and It."[13] In this context it is readily apparent, in reviewing the Barbados demon's fights, that Joe Walcott was prepared to endure whatever pain was necessary and, in turn, to inflict whatever level of pain upon an opponent as was necessary. Pulitzer prize winning author Norman Mailer, writing in *King of the Hill*, succinctly describes the depths of immense physical, mental, and perhaps spiritual pain that a prizefighter of Walcott's aggressive style would experience: "Like men who climb mountains, it is an exercise of ego which becomes something like soul — just as technology may have begun to have transcended itself when we reached the moon. So, too, great fighters in a great fight travel down subterranean rivers of exhaustion and cross mountain peaks of agony, stare at the light of their own death in the eye of the man they are fighting, travel into the crossroads of the most excruciating choice of karma as they get up from the floor against all the appeal of the sweet swooning catacombs of oblivion...."[14] Walcott proved the worth of his legend in a number of engagements where he would make that journey described by Mailer to transcend what the ordinary mind could imagine as possible.

In Hall-of-Fame fighter Mysterious Billy Smith, the Barbados Demon met an opponent equal to the task in terms of unrelenting mayhem by way of speed, slugging, and stamina. This fighting style was coupled with a fighter who, in Smith, was prepared to foul repeatedly to obtain the upper hand to the point of losing on fouls some ten times in his career. Sun Tzu's classic *Art of War* would aptly describe Walcott and Smith's approach in their fights against each other in that "the clever combatant imposes his will on the enemy, but does not allow the enemy's will to be imposed on him."[15] These two immovable greats would attempt to impose their will, to the utmost, upon each other.

Mysterious Billy Smith, welterweight champion from 1892 until 1894, first met Joe Walcott on March 1, 1895. The fight resulted in a fifteen-round draw. The two fighters would end up fighting each other a total of six times, with Walcott holding an advantage with three wins, one loss, and two draws. It would be a grave disservice to leave the account of these two protagonists' battles simply in terms of wins, losses, or draws. Smith was not prepared to give quarter to Walcott's unrelenting aggressiveness. Images of epic battles of Ali vs. Frazier, Robinson vs. Lamotta, Marciano vs. Charles, Zale vs. Graziano, Pryor vs. Arguello, and Gans vs. Nelson certainly come to mind comparatively, in the context of these two men. The greatness of each of these boxers of course was inextricably tied to their opponents. Each brought out the best in the other. Such was the case of Smith and Walcott, and in turn, George Lavigne and Walcott.

The first fight between Walcott and Smith was important to both fighters in that it was billed as an eliminator to see who would have the right to fight for the world welterweight Championship. Neither man disappointed the spectators that particular evening. The first five rounds sum up the flow of the battle: "In the first two rounds, Smith received many hefty wallops to the stomach, blows he didn't relish. On two occasions he doubled up with right hand smashes that sank almost wrist-deep in the mid-section. The next three rounds found Smith the aggressor. He sent his left frequently to Joe's face and battered Joe's body with effectiveness. Yet Walcott fought back viciously and gained the third session."[16] Back and forth went the epic battle. At one point the referee had to admonish Smith for using a strangle hold! In the end, although it was apparent that Walcott had been worn down, he finished the fight in the final minute with one last furious rally.

The second bout between Walcott and Smith, on April 14, 1898, was no less vicious a battle, again ending in a draw. It was a testament to the rough-and-tumble nature of Smith that each fighter was forced to place the sum of two hundred and fifty dollars forfeiture against personal fouls. Again, both fighters in this bout engaged in punishing each other with tremendous body blows, the bout changing repeatedly with ebbs and flows. On December 6 of the same year, Walcott and Smith engaged in another tremendous battle. "The fans were treated to thrill after thrill as the fighting demons slashed away at each other with scarcely a let up."[17] Smith set a furious pace, knocking down Walcott in the eleventh round twice, only to see Walcott saved by the bell. In turn Walcott almost had Smith down in the nineteenth round. The two fighters continued to batter each other at an incredible pace, with Smith ending the fight in nonstop punching fashion. After the furious punching affair, Smith was awarded the twenty-round decision.

Walcott and Smith would meet in two more epic battles, in May and September of 1900. In the May fight, which continued the furious ebb and flow of the previous fights, Smith suffered a serious and painful rib injury such that the doctor in attendance was asked to inject cocaine to alleviate Smith's pain. As strange as this may now seem, cocaine was the preferred antidote to pain and readily available during the time. In fact, in the 1860s it was sold in France as a mix in wine, and until 1914 it could be bought over the counter in drug and department stores. Coca-Cola, introduced in 1886, contained one part cocaine — an estimated nine milligrams of cocaine per glass — until 1903. Like women who became addicted to the drug as a result of its common use during childbirth, it can be assumed that many of the boxers were introduced to the drug following injuries during their ring bouts.

Walcott won his battle against Smith by way of a decision after twenty-five rounds. Their next match, much to the dissatisfaction of the spectators, ended in a foul-plagued victory for Walcott. In fact, Smith allegedly hurt his hand, but after repeated warnings from the referee for flagrant fouls including head butting, Smith, having taken a sound beating, simply turned to his corner and quit. The last bout that the two engaged in took place in May of 1903, and it was evident that Smith was no longer the force that he had been previously, as he was stopped in the fourth round. In fact during this period of Smith's career he lost five of what would be his last six fights.

It is a testament to the Barbados Demon's durability that following the first physically taxing battle with Smith, he fought another four times in 1895, winning three in a row before facing another Hall-of-Fame fighter, George "Kid" Lavigne. The Saginaw Kid, as he was otherwise known, was sometimes referred to as a tornado in the ring with tremendous punching power and stamina. The two met on December 2, 1895, in the first of two matches. The sheer savagery was equal to the first Smith fight. By this time, Walcott's reputation was preceding him. It was a condition of the fight that he not only reduce down to the lighter weight of 133 pounds. Also terms were set such that if Walcott did not stop Lavigne inside of fifteen rounds, he would be deemed the loser.

A few weeks before Christmas 1895, at the Empire Club in Maspeth, Long Island, a packed house of spectators bore witness to fifteen brutal rounds between two legends of boxing. Through the first five rounds, Walcott battered Lavigne, at times joking between rounds. Whether the result of Walcott's having to come in at the lower weight, or Lavigne's withstanding an early onslaught with a pace that Walcott could not maintain, it became obvious that Walcott was growing weary as Lavigne mounted his own blistering attack through rounds six and seven. As was the case in many of Walcott's greater challenges, the tide turned again and again during the bout, and in the eighth round, a Walcott punch closed one of Lavigne's eyes. The tenth round bore witness to Lavigne's ear being hit so hard and so often that it swelled up like a cauliflower and was sliced open with blood pouring out. "A torrent of gore was spattered over both fighters and on those of the spectators who were sitting on the fringe around the ring. Then came another smash that cut the ear almost off, and it dangled on Lavigne's neck, held by a few bloody tendons."[18] What followed in the ensuing rounds would not be believable in a Hollywood script, as the Saginaw Kid not only mounted a furious comeback but had Walcott ready to quit in the fourteenth round. The bout ended in the fifteenth round, with both fighters trading blows back and forth. Both men had gone to the extreme, physically and mentally, in a battle where they both suffered intense punishment. Lavigne was declared the winner of one of boxing's great epic battles. Boxing scribes would later describe the fight as the greatest fight the world had ever seen.[19] The punishment meted out to Lavigne and his ability to absorb it were nothing short of miraculous. Both of Lavigne's eyes were swollen shut, his left ear was all but falling off, and his mouth was grotesquely swollen.

The Demon and the Saginaw Kid would square off once again in a rematch for the lightweight championship of the world on October 29, 1897, in San Francisco before a packed house of ten thousand fans, giving tribute to the boxers' now legendary first fight and the anticipation of another great fight:

> The doors leading to the galleries of the big building were thrown open as early as 5:30 P.M.; and as those who held tickets admitting them to that portion of the pavilion acted on the rule of "first come; first served," the so-called easy seats filled up. The crowd upstairs was a good-natured one and settled down for the long wait which they knew they would have to endure. The seats on the main floor began filling at 7:30, and when the first preliminary was called an hour later, every chair had its occupants, and men and boys were perched upon the beams of the great arched roof overhanging the ring. The arrangements made by the Occidental Club for the comfort of the public were most elaborate. A squad of fifty policemen guarded the entrance and kept back the surging crowd which thronged the streets in the vicinity of the pavilion. The ushers were attired in Turkish costumes of the most fantastic colors.[20]

Lavigne's legendary ability to absorb punishment while executing a non-stop attack was again on display. Clearly, as later victories showed at the welterweight level, Joe Walcott was not at his powerful best as a lightweight, and most certainly not when up against an indomitable force such as Lavigne, who would show time and time again in his career an almost inhuman ability to take punishment. The weigh-in for the fight took place at six P.M. with Walcott weighing well below his ideal weight at 135 pounds. As before, both combatants employed their non-stop, aggressive punching style. Entering the fifth round, it was becoming apparent that Lavigne was not being slowed down by Walcott's punches and was taking control of the fight. In the seventh round, reported as one of the fastest-paced rounds seen, Lavigne pummeled Walcott on the ropes. By the ninth round Walcott was a spent force. "Lavigne rushed Walcott to the ropes in the ninth and repeatedly put his right over the heart. The blood streamed down over Walcott's face from a cut on the forehead received in a hot rally. Walcott seemed tired and clinched in every exchange. In going to his corner he was unsteady in his walk."[21] The tenth round saw Walcott taking more severe punishment. "Lavigne landed right and left on the jaw and on the heart several times without return."[22] By the eleventh round Walcott was taking a beating with little by way of offensive response. Walcott's manager Tom O'Rourke threw in the sponge, signaling the end of the fight after the eleventh round. At the end of the fight, fans of the Saginaw Kid surged into the ring, but Walcott was hastily taken from the ring by his manager O'Rourke. Two months after the second Lavigne fight, in a testament to Walcott's physical durability, the Demon entered the ring against Tom Tracey in Chicago, fighting to a draw.

During the period of 1896 while training for a fight with "Scaldy" Bill Quinn, Walcott was introduced to a young man by the name of Jack Johnson, future heavyweight champion of the world. It was the beginning of a long-term friendship. Walcott took a liking to the young Johnson and employed him as a sparring partner. Johnson, at the time, was untrained in the "sweet science," but Walcott felt, after having sparred with Johnson, that his future was bright and that he showed considerable promise. Years later toward the end of Walcott's career, Johnson reciprocated the favor by employing the Demon as a sparring partner, second, and advisor.[23]

From early 1899 through August 27, 1900, Walcott was unbeatable, winning seventeen consecutive fights before losing to Tommy West in August 1900. West had given Walcott a tremendous battle to a draw back in December, 1896, in which Walcott had gone down from "the force of a right smash to the jaw."[24] During this period, given Walcott's winning streak, it was difficult for him to obtain fights. The West fight is significant in highlighting the problem that great fighters of the time had and illustrates why fight outcomes were sometimes "arranged." In the eleventh round Walcott simply held up his hand, insisting that he had broken his arm and quit. Manager Tom O'Rourke would later admit that "If Walcott hadn't pulled up that night both he and his manager would have wound up on slabs in the morgue."[25] In fact, up to the point of stoppage, Walcott had the fight very much his way, punishing West through eleven rounds.

Walcott and his manager began to challenge much heavier opponents including Tom Sharkey, James J. Corbett, Bob Fitzsimmons and even James J. Jeffries.[26]. While perhaps this could have been seen as a publicity stunt born out of an inability to obtain proper fights with opponents at a natural weight, a final review of the Demon's record and reputation as a "giant killer" proves otherwise. Quite clearly Walcott was prepared to take on opponents who held extraordinary physical advantages over him.

In the case of Tom Sharkey, who had twice gone the distance with James J. Jeffries, one of Walcott's sparring sessions with Sharkey was stopped when Walcott floored Sharkey.[27] Early in his career, Walcott scored a first-round knockout over one- hundred-eighty-pound Tom McCarthy. Tommy West was a middleweight who had fought seventeen rounds with Tommy Ryan for the middleweight championship. Other "big men" on Walcott's record included Philadelphia Jack O'Brien, a future light heavyweight champion; middleweights Jack Bonner and Joe Grim; light heavyweight champion George Gardner, good enough not only to become champion but to have gone twenty rounds with Jack Johnson; the legendary Sam Langford; and heavyweights John "Sandy" Ferguson and Frank Childs. Fittingly, years later Walcott expressed the wish that if he was in his prime he could have met Primo Carnera. "That big fellow's got a lantun jaw, an how I loved to crack them lantun jaws. They always fold up."[28].

Perhaps no single fight solidified the Barbados Demon's reputation against big men more than his fight with Joe Choynski in February of 1900. Choynski was a legitimate heavyweight challenger. His record includes going twenty-eight rounds with Jim Corbett, a draw with Bob Fitzsimmons, and a knockout over a young Jack Johnson. Other legends Choynski faced included Philadelphia Jack O'Brien, Marvin Hart, Jim Jeffries, who Choynski held to a twenty-round draw, and Kid McCoy. "Joe Choynski was considered by boxing experts as one of the greatest uncrowned boxing champions in the long and celebrated history of the heavyweight division."[29] Choynski's second fight with Corbett took place on a barge moored in San Francisco Bay, and was legendary for its brutality. Barge fights, in years gone past, were not uncommon. In short, they were held as a means of avoiding police authorities in order to stage fights that otherwise would not be deemed to be legal on land. One of John L. Sullivan's first well-known fights against John Flood in New York was held on a barge anchored off Yonkers. These types of bouts were vividly portrayed in the movie *Hard Times*, starring Charles Bronson, where Bronson portrays a bare-knuckle fighter, previous rail-riding hobo, engaging in bouts in abandoned warehouses and out of the way locales for on location "purse" money collected by the promoters. Such was Choynski's fighting nature that, suffice to say, he was a force in the squared circle.

For the Choynski fight Walcott weighed 147 pounds to Choynski's 173 pounds. Choynski was a prohibitive betting favorite at three hundred to thirty, but this hardly reflected what occurred early on. The first round set the tempo for a terrible beating rendered by Walcott. "In the first round Choynski was floored five times. The first time he measured his length on the canvas floor he was hit with a right under the jaw. Another hard right in the vicinity of the solar plexus put him down a second time, a right cross on the jaw was the cause of his third fall, and a left on the jaw put him down for the fourth time."[30] By the seventh round Choynski was defenseless, and after he was dropped from a powerful right hand, referee Charley White stepped in to stop the fight.

To give a sense of the magnitude of Walcott's accomplishments in fighting bigger foes, by comparison of weight differential and height, and in particular by way of weight differential such as in the Choynski fight against a top fighter, is not easy. Various "dream" matchups come to mind in an attempt to illustrate Walcott's boxing feats: Jose Napoles vs. Bob Foster, Sugar Ray Robinson as a welterweight vs. Ezzard Charles while a light heavyweight, Emile Griffith vs. Floyd Patterson, or perhaps Sugar Ray Leonard vs. Michael Spinks. The absurdity of these "dream" matches, as nothing more than that, only gives more credence to how amazing Walcott's accomplishments were.

While the balance of 1900 and 1901 after the Choynski battle bore a spotty record for Walcott against tough opposition, December of 1901 marked another benchmark in the Demon's career when he won the world welterweight championship from James "Rube" Ferns. The Barbados Demon's Christmas present came one week early on December 18th, 1901 in Fort Erie, Ontario, a town situated directly on the Niagara River and a short distance from Niagara Falls, Canada, as he blasted out Ferns inside of five rounds. Unfortunately for Ferns, the battle that he engaged in was a one-sided affair in favor of Walcott, and considering some of the epic battles that Walcott had already had, the bout with Ferns was otherwise anticlimactic. By the third round it was apparent that Ferns was out of his depth as Walcott began to dominate, and in the fifth round the referee stopped the contest after Ferns had been dropped for the second time. Walcott was the new welterweight champion of the world!

Walcott engaged in ten fights the subsequent year of 1902. It is evident that his reputation as a "giant killer" was forcing him out of his weight division to obtain fights, even though he was now welterweight champion. The bulk of his fights that year were against bigger men, excluding his one title defense against Tommy West, which Walcott won by a fifteen-round decision on June 23. Included in the list of "big men" that Walcott engaged that year were middleweights Jimmy Handler, Young Peter Jackson, Billy Stift, George Gardner, light-heavyweight Philadelphia Jack O'Brien, and more significantly, heavyweights Fred Russell and Frank Childs. Walcott did not fare well against O'Brien, who simply out-boxed Walcott while refusing to engage in long toe-to-toe action. As reported, "O'Brien's footwork was marvelous."[31] Such was not the case in the Demon's bout against Fred Russell, who by all reports stood well over six feet tall and weighed some 215 pounds. Such was the size disparity that Walcott had to literally jump six inches off his feet to land head blows! While the bout was ruled a draw, it was apparent that Walcott manhandled Russell and had his way with his opponent, including a knockdown in the first round. The results would not be the same in Walcott's last bout of 1902, against heavyweight Frank Childs, in October.

Frank Childs was a legitimate force in the heavyweight division, having lost but five out of forty-nine fights leading up to the Walcott fight. He would later engage the legendary Jack Johnson in two bouts, including one immediately after his tussle with Walcott that went a tough twelve rounds. While the two fighters appeared to be evenly matched over the first two rounds, Walcott did not come out for the third round, claiming he had injured his right arm. A review of Walcott's record would appear to legitimize the claim of injury. After the Childs fight, Walcott did not engage in another contest for five months.

The remainder of 1903 was an exceptionally busy year as Walcott engaged in sixteen bouts over a ten-month period. It is to be noted, as was the case with many fighters during this generation, and up through the fighters of the 1940s, that the level of Walcott's activity was, in comparison to modern-day fighters, incredible. This level of activity for fighters of yesteryear was not uncommon. As an example, over a three-year period, the legendary "Old Mongoose" Archie Moore, who would end up engaging in some 237 fights, fought 44 times! The inimitable Sugar Ray Robinson, on two separate occasions, engaged in over 18 fights in one year! Willie Pep, who fought an incredible 242 fights in his career, engaged in 30 fights over a two-year span. In comparison to Walcott's busy year, consider that portion of the all-time great Sugar Ray Leonard's career immediately prior to his winning the welterweight title, during which he had 16 fights over a period of 12 years, the same number as Walcott had in only tenth months! In the case of Thomas "The Hit Man" Hearns, after winning his welterweight championship from knockout specialist Pipino Cuevas, it would take some six years to accumulate 16 more fights. In the case of the legendary Jose Napoles, it would take some four years to tally 16 fights. This was to be Walcott's busiest year short of 1892, when he had engaged in sixteen recorded fights. Walcott's only loss that year was to another heavyweight, John "Sandy" Ferguson, by way of a fifteen-round decision. This was perhaps the last great year of Walcott's career.

In the ensuing year of 1904, Walcott was to fight ten times, winning twice, losing four times, and drawing four times. Certainly the list of opponents that year showed, once again, that the Demon was prepared to take on any and all opponents. This perhaps, in part, contributed to his more than losing record during that span. Included in the list that year were middleweight Young Peter Jackson, the aforesaid John "Sandy" Ferguson , a heavyweight who had lost on points to Jack Johnson, and matches against the legendary fighters Sam Langford, Joe Gans, and Dixie Kid, to whom Walcott relinquished his title on April 29,1904.

The welterweight bout with Dixie Kid would live on for many years in infamy leading to the confusion as to who was the legitimate welterweight champion. Aaron Brown, otherwise known as the "Dixie Kid," fought 152 fights over the span of a twenty-year career. Although he had a reputation as a scientific boxer with an innate ability to counterpunch, a style that was problematic for Walcott, his record also shows 55 knockouts among his 79 wins. Coupled with his skills as a boxer, he was able to avoid punishment and to take a punch. His only knockout losses were at the hands of the great Sam Langford. "The Dixie Kid was in a class by himself as a wizard of ring craft. He was one of the most cunning fighters of his period."[32] Included in the Dixie Kid's wins was a very notable one-punch, fifth-round knockout against the legendary French fighter Georges Carpentier, who would later gain further fame in heavyweight fights against legends Jack Dempsey and Gene Tunney. It was Carpentier's only defeat over a span of 25 fights, and the Dixie Kid obtained the result in most certainly more convincing fashion than either Dempsey or Tunney would later manage.

What transpired in the fight itself between Walcott and Dixie Kid was nothing short of amazing in its twists and turns of skullduggery, with the end result providing a look at the "darker" side of boxing. In a fight that Walcott apparently was winning, the referee ruled a disqualification win for the Dixie Kid in the twentieth round. The proverbial shenanigans began before the fight when the scheduled referee was replaced on the day of the fight. After complaints by Walcott's manager, the promoter took the unusual step of promising Walcott the not-so-small sum-of-the-day of $2,500 if, in the opinion of the promoter, the result was unfair. When the referee ruled the disqualification, so irate was Walcott's manager and one of the promoters that they both leapt into the ring and pummeled the referee, knocking out several of his teeth.[33] A number of spectators then jumped into the ring and also started pummeling the referee. The police were forced to use their clubs as further fights began to break out.

The next day O'Rourke demanded a rematch, which was granted. A check in the amount of the agreed-upon $2,500 was handed over to Walcott, and little mention of the result was given in the press thereafter. In fact, very few recognized the Dixie Kid as welterweight champion, and his management did little to dispel this notion for many years thereafter, which in itself raised many questions. Rumors abounded that the referee had bet on Dixie Kid. The two boxers would fight some twelve days later, to a hotly contested twenty-round draw. Curiously, many ring record reports of Walcott's career omit this bout. Nat Fleischer gives a detailed account of the rematch in Volume IV of *Black Dynamite.* Unfortunately for Dixie Kid, the peculiar nature of the first bout left most of the public and press under the impression that the Demon remained as welterweight champion even though he had been disqualified, rightfully or wrongfully, in the first fight. Certainly from a later historical point, Dixie Kid was given recognition after the first fight as the champion. Of other historical note is the fact that the first bout appears to be the first on record of one black contestant winning a title from another.

Having fought Dixie Kid in two tough battles, twelve days apart, the rest of Walcott's 1904 fighting campaign is further testimony to his incredible durability. On May 23, 1904, eleven days after engaging Dixie Kid, Walcott went up against heavyweight giant John "Sandy" Ferguson, whom he had engaged in a battle the previous year, losing a fifteen-round decision. Walcott was outweighed by some fifty pounds. The fight ended in a draw. For Walcott two more fights ensued in June and one in July. What then followed was an amazing month in September to round out the 1904 year whereby Walcott fought all-time legends Sam Langford on September 5 and Joe Gans on September 30th. Amazingly, Walcott saw fit to sandwich a fight in between the Langford and Gans fights by fighting Dave Holly to a six-round no decision on September 10. The fight with the great lightweight Joe Gans was billed as being for the Welterweight Championship of the World.

Langford and Walcott fought to a draw on September 5th, 1904. How good was Langford? Boxing historian Burt Sugar, referred to Langford as the greatest non-champion in the history of boxing, and rated him the sixteenth greatest fighter of all time. Avoided by heavyweight champions from Jack Johnson to Jack Dempsey, suffice to say he was a tall order for the Demon. The fight was staged at Lake Massaesic and drew the summer resort crowd. Although Walcott dealt out his fair share of punishment, the general consensus was that Langford had won. As reported by the *New York Illustrated Post,* "Joe Walcott, world welterweight champion and Sam Langford of Cambridge, Massachusetts, fought a vicious fifteen-round draw at the Coliseum. The fight was witnessed by a fair-sized gathering. The spectators were much displeased by the decision, as the rounds story was one clearly in favor of Langford."[34] Perhaps no greater tribute could be given the Demon than from a fellow legend as Langford was to comment on Walcott years later: "He was the hardest hitter I ever met. Never before or never since then have I been hit as hard and as often as that night, and I never landed more blows on a fighter in fifteen rounds than I hurled

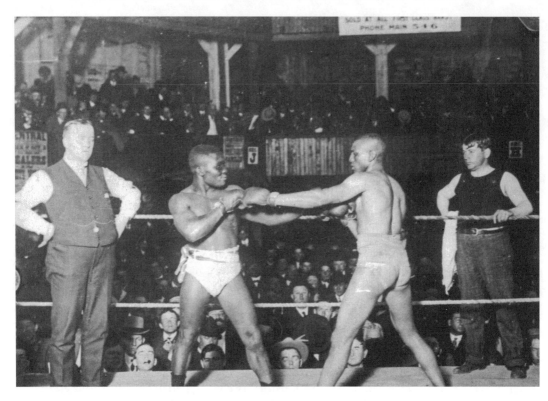

Gans (right) and Walcott square off in San Francisco (Gary Schultz collection).

into Joe Walcott that night."[35] Once again Walcott had engaged a bigger and stronger foe, and to good effect.

Twenty-five days later, Walcott was back in the ring with another all-time-great ring legend, Joe Gans. Ranked fifteenth by Burt Sugar in his all-time greatest list, many historians rate Gans the greatest lightweight of all time. The fight itself ended in a twenty-round draw. From all reports Gans won the fight. The early portion of the fight saw Walcott aggressively forcing the action in an ebb-and-flow battle, but the final two rounds were the tell-all. "In the nineteenth round, Walcott was almost finished when a powerful smash to the jaw put him in distress, and for the rest of the round, Gans battered him around the ring. The Baltimore Wonder outfought his opponent, landing blow after blow with telling effect throughout the session. The twentieth and last round was a repetition of the preceding."[36] Perhaps the follow-up headlines in the *San Francisco Examiner* on October 1 best summed up the end result: "Gans Outpoints Walcott, But Referee Calls it Draw: Ruling Makes Crowd Frown." The two best fighters in their respective weight divisions, and two of the greats of all time, had met with Gans proving superior. Walcott was to allege that he had broken his arm early in the fight. Although it would be fair to question why Walcott took this fight so soon after the draining fight with Langford; either way, the fact remains that Gans clearly edged Walcott in their battle.

The year 1905 marked the only year in Walcott's twenty-one year career that he did not engage in a bout. In fact the hiatus was for some twenty months! Certainly the strain of Walcott's two fights with the Dixie Kid and two fights in September of 1904 with Langford and Gans would have caused more than an ample amount of physical wear-and-tear. No doubt Walcott's loss of his title and mediocre record that year would have had its mental effects as well.

Sam Langford (left) and Joe Walcott (right). Photograph taken in Jim Toland's Gym, Boston, Massachusetts, 1931 (Clay Moyle collection).

Walcott was now 33 years old, an age not kind to most fighters and certainly not for someone with the mileage that Walcott had on his body at that time. Perhaps even more importantly were three other factors for what appeared to be a grand champion in decline. First, was the fact that Walcott was known not to enjoy training and to cut corners whenever possible. "Joe Walcott was always a hard fighter to handle. The 'Barbados Demon' hated to work. When he was not out on the road he would jog away from the training quarters, kicking up no end of dust and pawing through the turf like a man out for ten miles. But as soon as he got to sleep after a refreshing nap he would rise, pour water over himself to give the appearance of profuse perspiration, throw dust over the damp clothes and pull up in front of the training quarters like a stranded whale. It took Joe's trainers a long time to tumble to Joe's system but when they did they flexed him plenty. They tied him behind a dogcart and drove miles and miles."[37] In the early years, by the sheer volume of fights he had, this may not have been much of a factor, but as Walcott reached into his thirties, no doubt his lack of proper training diligence did not hold him in good stead. A second factor in his decline was that, given his stature and financial position, Walcott was now enjoying the high life. "Walcott was in funds at the time and lived like a lord. He displayed diamonds and flashed a big bank roll which he spent liberally, for he was ever a care-free, jovial chap to whom money meant little, except for the pleasures it brought him."[38]. Clearly at this point in his career, Walcott had retirement in mind. It was reported in late 1905 that Walcott commented that "like Mr. Jeffries" he had retired.[39] Lastly, was the tragedy that occurred at a dance hall in Boston. Walcott was showing a close friend a revolver he had purchased. The gun accidentally discharged — the bullet passing thru Walcott's hand and striking his friend in the head. Walcott's friend died and Walcott was left with a badly damaged right hand. This subsequently left him unable to close the hand tightly. The injury was severe enough that it was first thought that some of Walcott's fingers would need to be amputated. Walcott was overcome with grief. He did not resume his ring career until mid–1906.

On October 16, 1906, the Barbados Demon relinquished his welterweight title to Billy "Honey" Mellody by fifteen-round decision. Although Walcott floored Mellody in the first round for a nine count, Mellody's youth won out as he was able to survive the early rounds and, by all accounts, outbox the Demon in the later rounds. An immediate rematch took place the following month, and the physical wear-and-tear the old warrior had taken was vividly apparent. The fight was stopped after round twelve with Walcott having suffered a broken right hand and a broken arm. Although the Demon was to fight on up until 1911, including a busy fourteen fights in 1908, he clearly was but a shell of his former self. Walcott was to fight 31 times from September of 1906, including the Mellody fights. Of those telling 31 fights, Walcott would win only seven times.

Retirement years were not kind to Walcott. During his heyday, Walcott owned a very nice home in Malden, Massachusetts. Early 1900 pictures show a small but wealthy town, straight out of a Norman Rockwell image. Walcott's home was a short distance from Mystic River and the center of town. Given his world-famous stature as a fighter, Walcott would have stood out in Malden. Famous future residents of Malden include the academy-award-winning actor Walter Brennan, NFL football player Dan Ross, Earle Gardiner, lawyer/author of the Perry Mason mysteries, and boxer Dana Rosenblatt, a 1990's fighter whose only blemish on a 37–1 record was a loss to Vinny Pazienza. Unfortunately for Walcott, his lifestyle and squandering of money did not allow him to retire comfortably in such splendor as the scenic locale of Malden.

"Shadow of a Great Fighter Now Pushes Broom at New York [Madison Square] Garden," January 18, 1930 (image and caption used with permission of Zanesville, Ohio, *Times Recorder*).

Boxing can, and more often than not does, prove a cruel long-term taskmaster to fighters, especially for men such as Joe Walcott, who exert, over many years, every physical and mental portion of themselves to rise to the level of champion. As the years passed, Walcott was to take various jobs, including that of fireman on a freight steamer, a porter, and custodian at Madison Square Garden. By 1916 he was described while arriving on an Australian liner, employed as a stoker, as a penniless, down-and-out, ragged pitiful figure whose downfall was attributed to drink, women, and dice.[40] It was ironic indeed that the young man who had arrived in Boston, working on a ship, had come full circle.

Later reports in 1918 had Walcott working as a fireman on a freighter. "Walcott is an old man now, not old in years for he is only (forty-five) but old because of the physical strain he endured while in the ring."[41] Indeed some years later in 1927, the great George "Kid" Lavigne in writing an article about his two bouts with Walcott for the *Lincoln State Journal* commented, in reference to the physically debilitating nature of the bouts, "I am credited with two victories over Walcott but I feel I lost the championship thru those fearful struggles. I never had the same legs, wind or vitality after that last Walcott fight."[42] By the late 1920s and early 1930s various newspaper reports depicted Walcott as a "broom pusher"[43] and custodian, picking up crumpled programs between the seats at Madison Square Garden.[44] In 1924 Walcott was sent to jail in Boston for three years for assaulting a man. In January of 1930 the great writer Edward J. Neil painted the following vivid picture in words:

> Madison Square Garden is a dim, cool place in the afternoon, full of shadows that blot the outlines of the battle ring and fuse the endless rows of empty seats into banks of dusk. Footsteps echo loudly, folks usually talk in whispers in the amphitheatre that by night blazes with light and rocks to the roars of fight frenzied multitudes. There are dim figures too, in the corridors, mostly twisted old fellows with mops and pails of suds, washing floors for a meager hourly wage. There are others dusting the walls, wiping the glasses in huge pictures that show the likenesses of the late Tex Rickard, John L. Sullivan, Dempsey, Fitzsimmons, Corbett, Jack Johnson, Joe Gans and hosts of almost forgotten warriors of the ring. Only one of the chatmen hangs to himself, whistles occasionally, chuckles at his work. He's a short, chunky, happy negro with arms that stretch down to his knees. His shoes are almost without form, his trousers baggy, misshapen. A gray checkered coat sweater, fitting his arms all right, stretches down to his knees in incongruous fashion. Diligently he wipes pictures and woodwork with a dirty cloth. A shapeless cap on the back of his black hairless head, a grin on his wide, flat features. Yet this happy, harmless negro, 38 years old and glad of the chance to work at menial tasks is Joe Walcott, the Barbados Demon, perhaps the greatest fighter that ever lived.[45]

By 1932 it was reported that Walcott was living in an unlighted basement, maintaining himself on small sums of money earned as a referee and boxing instructor in Harlem.[46] It was during this time that Walcott was admitted to a psychopathic ward and diagnosed with hardening of the arteries and senile psychosis, a diagnosis that he would vehemently deny publicly.[47] The great champion was only in his fifties at the time.

While the Barbados Demon Joe Walcott's demise is variously listed as October 4, 1935, his death was shrouded in mystery. It was not until some years later that some light was shed on the fate of the Demon. Walcott had simply disappeared in September of 1935, and friends, although searching for months, were unable to verify his whereabouts. Writers of the day, and most specifically Jack Cuddy of the United Press, put out requests for information and some seven years later a response was received. A letter was received from a man in Massillon, Ohio. The following was reported: "*The Cleveland Plain Dealer* of Dec. 11, 1935 carried an article under your by-line concerning the mysterious disappearance of Joe Walcott, who was Hollywood bound in the company of one Mr. Morris Watnick. According to your

The second Madison Square Garden — this one designed by Standford White with a 32-story tower above the sports arena. The bronze statue of the Roman goddess Diana that stood above the tower was designed by Augustus Saint-Gaudens (photograph by Underhill).

article Mr. Watnick last saw Walcott when he gave him a quarter in Mansfield to go out and get Watnick a bromo."[48] Apparently Walcott had made his way to Massillon, Ohio where he was struck by a car while walking along the roadside. Watnick, a young man, was acting as Walcott's manager at the time. It was thought that perhaps someone would be interested in making a movie about Walcott and hence Watnick and Walcott were en route to Hollywood. At the time Walcott was not identified and his body was not claimed. Years later the undertaker involved gave a description that matched that of Walcott. This was hardly a fitting end to a one-time great, world champion, left unidentified for years after death, and described at the end of his life as an "ancient, broken-down, black fighting man, who looked like a chocolate Dr. Fu Manchu with his shaved head and drooping mustache."[49] Walcott had traveled the globe fighting only to end up the unidentified victim of a car accident on a lonely highway.

A brief review of Walcott's record, not from an opponent or win-loss perspective, but from a geographical, fight-location perspective, can't help but leave one waxing philosophically as to what big or small part of the legend of Joe Walcott was perhaps left behind on a gym wall, an old newspaper, a conversation with an old-time trainer or cornerman, or perhaps some youthful boxing fan who "shook the hand that shook the hand of." Aside from legendary fighters from the locations of New York and Boston, the list of which is endless, other locations where Walcott fought bring obvious connections to future well-known greats: Brockton, home of Marciano and Hagler; Lowell, home of "Irish" Micky Ward; Easton, home of Larry Holmes; Chicago, home Tony Zale; Louisville, home of Muhammad Ali; Toronto, home of George Chuvalo; Philadelphia, home of countless greats, including Joe Frazier, Bennie Briscoe, Bernard Hopkins ... and so the list goes on in relation to Walcott's many travels during a long and great ring career.

It is of interest what happened to some of the Walcott saga's main protagonists: the great George Dixon, dead at the young age of 38, having passed away two days after having been admitted to the New York Bellevue Hospital and having spent the last two years of his life drinking heavily. Joe Gans, dead at the age of 35, from the ravages of tuberculosis. Dixie Kid, dead at the age of 50, found unconscious beneath a slum tenement window under circumstances leading to unanswered questions of whether it was an accident or suicide. Mysterious Billy Smith, dead at age sixty-six, of uremia after a lengthy illness. George "Kid" Lavigne, dead at 58, of heart disease. Sam Langford, dead at 72, after years of eye problems and eventual blindness, and suffering from malnutrition and cerebral arterial sclerosis; and finally the great Jack Johnson, dead at age 68, having boxed until the amazing age of fifty, and having won 17 fights in a row after losing his heavyweight crown. In a cruel and ironic circumstance, given Johnson's racial problems during his prime on life's stage, Johnson died in a car accident brought on in part by his speeding away from a restaurant that would only serve him if he would sit in a back room.

Perhaps the great ring historian and founder of the venerable *Ring* magazine, Nat Fleischer, summarized Walcott's position in boxing best back at the time of an article he authored in 1926:

> No man in the last 30 years has had a more wonderful, more colorful ring career than did the Barbados negro, whose remarkable fighting ability, whose terrific hitting power and whose ability to stand the most terrible blows without flinching made him the marvel of the age. I have seen the greatest fighters that have flashed along the pugilistic horizon for more than 40 years. I have managed and trained or instructed many more ring marvels. Yet I feel and can honestly say that for his weight and height Joe Walcott was the greatest fighter of them all. Strictly

speaking, there were few, less than a handful of Supermen of the Ring, but when one records the history of such fighters it wouldn't be complete without the name of Joe Walcott rated among them.[50]

Fleischer, in later years, would rate Walcott the number one welterweight of all time, followed by Mysterious Billy Smith, Jack Britton, Ted "Kid" Lewis and Sugar Ray Robinson.

One must, of course, give consideration to Sugar Ray Robinson not only as the greatest welterweight of all time but also as the greatest fighter of all time. The best of Robinson, in his prime years as a welterweight, unfortunately were never video archived. At one point Robinson's record was an incredible 128 wins, 1 loss, and 2 draws, including a 91-bout winning streak. The only fighter remotely comparable, by the record, was Willie Pep, who at one point held an astounding 134 wins, 1 loss, 1 draw record. Bert Sugar, writing in *Boxing's Greatest Fighters*, ranked Walcott 26th . *The Ring* magazine rated Walcott as one of the top 100 greatest punchers. The International Boxing Research Organization ranked Walcott as the 4th greatest welterweight and the number 22 pound-for-pound fighter ever, one ranking ahead of the great undefeated heavyweight champion, Rocky Marciano.[51] (Voting was submitted on the basis of a points system whereby extra points were awarded for higher placed votes and lesser points in descending order of vote position.) Sugar Ray Robinson was ranked, pound for pound, first. In tribute to Walcott two of his adversaries made the list with Sam Langford rated sixth, and Joe Gans ranked eleventh.

Arguments among fight fans and experts abound when it comes to all-time-great rankings and comparisons. The usual comments arise during fun-filled, verbal exchanges including trying to compare fighters of different era's by way of dream matches, one era to another era, level or quality of opponent, old time styles vs. modern styles, training techniques, fight activity levels, and experience gained therein, ranking by era or by "pound for pound." Certainly in the heavyweights' case, comparative size differences between modern day giants and fighters of yesterday are debated. Fittingly, and in glowing tribute, Arnold Cream would take Walcott's name years later and would go on to win the world heavyweight championship in 1951 as Jersey Joe Walcott.

Close to one hundred years have passed since the magnificent Barbados Demon Joe Walcott retired, and it can be said without argument that he is still mentioned in the lists of all-time great fighters and discussions today. The Demon of boxing lives on.

NOTES

1. Roberts, James B., and Alexander G. Skutt. *The Boxing Register: International Boxing Hall of Fame Official Record Book*. Ithaca, NY: McBooks Press, 2006, 206.

2. Michener, James. *Caribbean*. New York: Ballantine Books, 1989, 485.

3. Fleischer, Nat. *Black Dynamite: Vol. 3, The Three Colored Aces: Story of George Dixon, Joe Gans, and Joe Walcott*. New York: C.J. O'Brien, 1938, 201.

4. Vecsey, George. *Frazier/Ali*. New York: Scholastic Book Services, 1972, 7.

5. Hauser, Thomas. *An Unforgiving Sport*. Fayetteville: University of Arkansas Press, 2009, 11.

6. Smith, Kevin. *Images of Sport: Boston's Boxing Heritage*. Charleston, SC: Arcadia, 2002, 8.

7. *National Police Gazette*, October 27, 1894.

8. Fleischer, *Black Dynamite, Vol. 3*, 196.

9. Ibid.

10. Ashe, Arthur R. *A Hard Road to Glory*. New York: Amistad: 1988, 8.

11. Fleischer, *Black Dynamite, Vol. 3*, 204.

12. Vescey, 13.

13. Ashe, xvii.

14. Mailer, Norman. *King of the Hill*. Chicago: Signet, 1971, 17.

15. Tzu, Sun. *The Art of War*. United London: Filiguarian Publishing, 2006, 31.

16. Fleischer, *Black Dynamite, Vol. 3*, 225.

17. Ibid., 228.

18. Ibid., 215.

19. "Sportograph," *The Cedar Rapids Evening Gazette*, October 29, 1914.

20. "Walcott is Whipped," *The Daily Tribune*, Salt Lake City, Utah, October 30, 1897.

21. Ibid.

22. Ibid.

23. "Brief and Breezy," *The Lethbridge Daily Herald*, February 17, 1910.

24. "Walcott and West Fight," *The Galveston Daily News*," December 10, 1896.

25. Sugar, Burt Randolph. *Boxing's Greatest Fighters*. Guilford, Conn: Lyons Press, 2006, 84.

26. *National Police Gazette*, October 13, 1900.

27. Fleischer, *Black Dynamite, Vol. 3,* 198–199.

28. Lank, Leonard. "Facts and Figures," *The Ring*, July, 1953.

29. Somrack, F. Daniel. *Boxing in San Francisco*. Charleston, SC: Arcadia, 2005, 29.

30. "Walcott is a Winner," *The Daily Tribune* (Salt Lake City), February 24, 1900.

31. "In the Sporting World," *The Daily Northwestern*, April 12, 1902.

32. Fleischer, Nat. *Black Dynamite. Volume 4, Fighting Furies: Story of the Golden Era of Jack Johnson, Sam Langford and their Negro Contemporaries*. New York: C.J. O'Brien, 1939, 253.

33. Ibid., 259.

34. *New York Illustrated News*, September 6, 1904.

35. *Halifax Herald*, August 18, 1924.

36. Fleischer, Nat. *Black Dynamite. Vol. 3*, 259.

37. *The Racine Daily Journal*, May 15, 1907.

38. Fleischer, Nat. *Black Dynamite. Vol. 3*, 259.

39. *The Anaconda Standard*, November 24, 1905.

40. "They Were Good Fellows When they had the Coin," *Bismarck Daily Tribune*, October 26, 1916.

41. "Now a Fireman: Joe Walcott is Shoveling Coal on an Ocean Freighter," *The Fort Wayne News and Sentinel*, March 2, 1918.

42. "Lavigne's Second Bout with Walcott," *The Lincoln State Journal*, December 26, 1927.

43. "Shadow of a Great Fighter Now Pushes Broom in New York Garden," *The Times Recorder*, January 18, 1930.

44. "Welters Lure $100,000 Gate by K.O. Punch," *San Antonio Express*, December 18, 1929.

45. "Walcott Labors in the Garden," *The Kingston Daily Freeman*, January 22, 1930.

46."Joe Walcott In Hospital," *Fitchburg Sentinel*, August 22, 1932.

47. "Former Negro Champ in Psychopathic Ward," *Middletown Times Herald*, August 22, 1932.

48. "Solution Looms To Mystery of Missing Walcott," *Olean Times-Herald*, October 14, 1942.49. "Letter from Mr. 'F' Revives Unsolved Joe Walcott Case," *The Morning Avalanche*, October 15, 1942.

50. "Joe Walcott Was One of Ring's Supermen," *Oakland Tribune*, December 9, 1926.

51. *I.B.R.O., Journal #91*, September 27, 2006.

CHAPTER 9

"Dixie Kid" Aaron Brown: World Welterweight Champion

Cathy van Ingen

At the beginning of his career, Aaron Brown often fought using the ring name "George White," but it was under the moniker "Dixie Kid" that he became legendary. Despite Dixie Kid's stardom on an international stage, he remains a mysterious figure in boxing history. Dixie Kid is perhaps best known for his controversial win over Joe Walcott in 1904, where he claimed the welterweight world title on a foul. Aaron Brown was a skilled pantomime in the prize ring, turning ring clowning into an art long before Muhammad Ali. Brown's trickster style provided flashy entertainment for audiences and had his opponents paying in flesh.[1] Dixie Kid was a veteran of over 150 bouts and held the highly disputed welterweight championship title for four years.[2] Dixie fought the world over, taking on headliners in the welter and middleweight divisions. He squared off against the best in the profession, including Battling Siki, Young Peter Jackson, Larry Temple, Kid Norfolk, Kid Brown, Joe Walcott and Sam Langford. Born in Fulton, Missouri, December 23, 1883, Dixie Kid began his professional career at the age of sixteen, yet he never achieved great fame in his own country but rather in Europe. Dixie Kid's story is also a sad tale of cocaine addiction ruining great ring talent. In his later years, Dixie Kid returned to the U.S. where his life remained derailed by his addiction and poverty. Dixie Kid died on April 6, 1934 at the age of 51, seven months after a failed suicide attempt in Los Angeles, California, the state in which he launched his professional career and also won his disputed 1904 championship.[3] He was inducted into the International Boxing Hall of Fame in 2002. Nat Fleischer, boxing historian, author of fifty-three books on the subject, and founder of *The Ring* magazine in 1922, ranked Dixie as the fifth best all-time welterweight.

Following other historians who revive the memory of previously overlooked black fighters, the focus here is to chronicle some of the ring battles of a champion who reigned in an era of racial segregation and to explore how this highly charged backdrop forced black boxers to negotiate an often tentative path between the deadening weight of white anxieties and their own athletic prowess.[4] Aaron Brown, like many black fighters who boxed when the thick walls of segregation divided the sport, also faced daily indignities and the ever-present threat of violence. In 1903 Civil Rights activist W. E. B. Du Bois published *Souls of Black Folks,* proclaiming that "the color line" would be the defining problem of the twentieth century. Indeed, even the Kid's boxing moniker reflects this problematic color line and the casual racial epithets of the Jim Crow era. "The Dixie Kid" was also the name of a

Dixie Kid in fighting pose, 1914 (Tony Triem collection).

popular "plantation" song sympathetic to the concept of slavery which had been sung in blackface minstrel shows since the mid–1800s.[5] The lyrics, which were sung in an exaggerated version of African American vernacular, told the story of a freed black slave who despite his new freedom longed for the "safety" and "comfort" of the plantation of his birth. During Aaron Brown's career, newspaper coverage of "the Dixie Kid" would include both reports from the roped arena and reviews of "The Dixie Kid" song performed at minstrel shows, by white children's choirs and university glee clubs.

The most highly regarded black fighters in the twentieth century were known as tricksters of style, fighters like Jack Johnson, Muhammad Ali, and Sugar Ray Robinson.[6] Journalists covering his bouts described Dixie Kid as a master of the ring, someone who knew "all the tricks of his tricky trade."[7] Nat Fleischer, the preeminent chronicler of boxing history, is no exception, referring to Dixie Kid as one of the greatest "tricksters" and fighters of his day. It is well noted that Fleisher's work in *The Black Dynamite* series is often laced with fabrications and distortions. Boxing historian Kevin Smith details the brazen plagiarism in Fleisher's writing, most notably lifting text directly from Richard Fox's (1897) *The Lives and Battles of Famous Black Pugilists*.[8] Despite these notable flaws, Fleischer devotes an entire chapter to Dixie Kid in *Black Dynamite, Vol. IV*, one of the only boxing texts to do so. Fleischer notes that Dixie Kid was an inventive boxer, "in a class by himself as a wizard of ring craft. He was one of the most cunning fighters of his period."[9] His trickery involved masterfully feinting, sidestepping, ducking, slipping and counterpunching. Dixie Kid, according to Fleischer, also introduced the technique of sliding along the ropes and launching himself, in catapult fashion, towards his opponent. Other strategies he employed included feigning fatigue and staggering back to the ropes, or doubling over in pain after a body shot. When his antagonist rushed forward to finish him, Dixie Kid would lash out and hit his surprised opponent with a stiff right or left.[10]

Fleischer claims that Dixie Kid blocked few punches but instead used his lightning-quick footwork to back away or sidestep punches. He often faced opponents with his hands down by his side, leaving his head an open target inviting attack. Dixie Kid would then bring up a right hand uppercut that often finished an opponent. He also loved to follow a right upper cut with a left hook. However, Dixie Kid's real strengths lay in his adaptability; he was, according to Fleischer, "As changeable as the weather — that's how Dixie Kid was."[11] Dixie could fight using any style, stand tall when needed, be flat footed at next glance, dance in the ring, or draw on any one of his many ring tricks. Considered by Fleischer to be a master of feinting and jabbing, other ringside journalists would report that his best work was done at close range, where he not only made an artistic specialty of his uppercut,

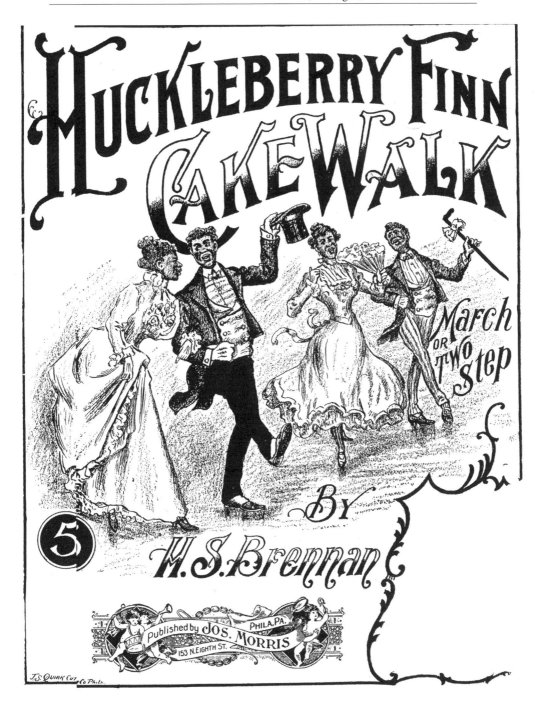

The *cakewalk* crossed over as a mainstream American entertainment. The high-spirited music inspired ragtime, the popular music of the period.

The Dixie Kid" was a popular ragtime song in Jim Crow America.

he also put in damaging punches to the body, and that "many of his shortest fights have been won by a hard right or left to the stomach delivered at very close range."[12]

Dixie began his pugilistic career in 1899 by knocking out his opponent in the first round. He carried power in either hand and his record shows a knockout percentage that was staggering in his early years.[13] Yet, despite his early success, Dixie Kid toiled in relative oblivion. Dixie, like many other black boxers, found it difficult to secure any measure of visibility and land the more lucrative matches with the best white talent. He was forced to fight in countless curtain raisers, fighting his way through all the second and third-rated fighters. As one sports scribe proclaimed, "These he disposed of in short order, knocking them out in from one to eleven rounds."[14]

Dixie Kid began his professional career on the Pacific coast "at a time when fighters were as thick as flies around a molasses barrel."[15] Prior to his ascension in the boxing world, Dixie struggled with meager paydays. He worked odd jobs when he could, and for a time was employed as a bootblack.[16] When desperate, he was not above engaging in thuggery to make ends meet. On July 1 1902, the *Los Angeles Times* reported that Aaron Brown, "who is known in sporting circles as a prizefighter who is hard to kill," was booked on a robbery charge and spent time in a city jail.[17] He and an accomplice were charged with "rolling" a man one Saturday evening and taking his watch, some coins, and other personal effects. The two were held on $1,500 bail until the hearing.[18] This was Dixie's first encounter inside a courtroom, but it would not be his last. After achieving some of the stardom he so desired, Dixie faced a fraud charge in London, and towards the end of his career, several drug-related charges in Scotland during the Roaring 20s.

On April 29, 1904, in San Francisco, Dixie Kid earned a title fight with the welterweight champion, the Barbados Demon, Joe Walcott. In his fifteen fights prior to the Walcott bout, Dixie Kid won thirteen by knockout. There would, however, be no knockout or even knockdowns in this meeting. The fight was stopped in the twentieth round by referee James "Duck" Sullivan, who awarded the title to Dixie Kid on a foul. Mayhem ensued after the questionable stoppage as Walcott's manager and one of the promoters entered the ring swinging at Sullivan. Walcott's manager managed to punch Sullivan in the mouth, knocking out several teeth.[19] A brawl broke out at ringside among spectators who had wagered on the bout and were dismayed with the result. The police were required to step in to regain order. To complicate matters, it was discovered that Sullivan, who was a late substitute as referee, had bet on Dixie Kid. Given the questionable result of this bout, Dixie Kid's status as world champion was never fully reported or widely recognized. The Walcott-Kid bout had been the first title championship to be won on a foul, and as Arthur Ashe observed, it was also "the first time a title held by a black boxer was lost to another black boxer."[20]

Less than two weeks later, Walcott and Dixie Kid met again, and Dixie held him to a draw in twenty rounds. After the rematch, Dixie's right to the title remained in dispute in a weight division that was plagued with problems. In 1910, six years after Dixie Kid was crowned champion on the West Coast, an East Coast daily ran the following, "The most astonishing development in the history of pugilism is the fact that for six years George White, known in the ring as the "Dixie Kid," has been the welterweight champion of America and no one has been aware of it."[21] It was not uncommon for boxers of this era to claim titles and masquerade as world champions. Two years after the 1904 bout, Walcott lost twice to Billy "Honey" Mellody who thereafter claimed the title. Dixie Kid and "Honey Boy" were at odds over what became a much-abused title. After the Dixie Kid-Walcott bout, Dixie Kid continued to take matches in New York, Philadelphia, Baltimore and other eastern U.S. cities. After winning the title, Dixie Kid did not meet defeat at the hands of any welterweight. It is now generally accepted that he was champion until 1908 when he outgrew the division, and Mike "Twin" Sullivan defeated Jimmy Gardner in a 25-round bout in Los Angeles to claim the crown.[22]

Whether recognized as champion or not, Dixie Kid continued to dominate fights. In 1905, Dixie fought in Baltimore against black heavyweight fighter Larry Temple, the "Quaker City Terror." The reporter covering the bout wrote that Dixie Kid "gave the cleverest exhibition in the ring seen here since Joe Gans' days," claiming Dixie was a "master of sparring, cat-like agility of foot movement, and ring generalship, "Dixie" made Temple look like a poor imitation of a boxer."[23] Temple, who was fifteen pounds heavier, tried to use his weight advantage to wear down Dixie with "bull-like rushes." In signature style, Dixie sidestepped each attack and delivered a well-timed left, repeatedly punishing Temple. Despite reports that Dixie Kid clearly dominated the fight, the bout was called a draw. Spectators stood in disbelief at the result, and according to a report in the *Oakland Tribune*, yelled 'Dixie!' until they were hoarse."[24] This article also mentions that Dixie's wife and child watched the bout from the main floor of the hall. This is the one of few mentions of his family life in the white press. Census records from 1910 indicate that Dixie had married a woman named Sophie Woods from Mississippi, with whom he eventually had three children: a daughter born in Paris, and two sons born in London between the years 1911 and 1913.[25] The identity of his wife and child in 1905 are unknown.

After the bout with Larry Temple, Dixie Kid fought twice more in 1905, once against George Cole, and a final bout against Joe Grim, a Philadelphia Italian famously known during this period as "the human punching bag." Grim, a welterweight, challenged fighters of all weight categories saying, "No one can knock me down." Few did. His notoriety came neither from his boxing skills nor quick thinking, but from his remarkable courage and endurance. Remarkably, after the Grim bout, there is a long gap in Dixie Kid's fight record. According to available records, he did not fight again until September 10, 1908.

What happened to Dixie Kid for the remaining ten months in 1905, and why did he disappear altogether in 1906 and 1907? *The Boxing Register*, the official record book for the International Boxing Hall of Fame, claims that Dixie spent time serving a prison sentence for assault.[26] This is a plausible explanation, but not one that is widely supported by media sources of the era. In 1992, after Mike Tyson's rape conviction, a journalist listed famous fighters who also did battle in courtrooms. That article claims that there is only one boxer who was ever jailed while world champion—Dixie Kid, who, the article claims, went to prison in 1904 for killing a man. Since Dixie was still actively fighting in 1904 and the early part of 1905, this explanation is faulty.[27] Curiously, Nat Fleisher does not address Dixie's two-and-a-half-year absence from the ring nor provide any explanation for the fighter's idleness. Fleisher simply states that Dixie "took the measure of Joe Grim in a six round tussle," and then casually mentions his next opponent as Cub White, without any mention that the White bout did not occur until 1908.[28] Here historians are confronted with significant problems of evidence. Given the current lack of credible sources, it is difficult to completely unravel the mystery of Dixie Kid during this time. One plausible explanation is that some of Dixie Kid's fights continue to be missing from the historical record, including one report claiming that Dixie Kid traveled to Europe for the first time in 1905. If true, it is likely he continued boxing.[29] A 1906 newspaper mentions that black welterweight Billy Yourall, who was gearing up for a fight, had recently beaten Dixie Kid in six rounds.[30] The *Pittsburgh Post* also claims that in 1906 Dixie Kid fought and lost a six-round newspaper

DIXIE KID DEFEATS LEWIS IN LAST ROUND

Willie Holds His Own Until Negro Floors Him, but Stays the Limit of Bout.

What prestige Willie Lewis lost in his last several bouts in this city he regained last night in his ten-round mix-up with the Dixie Kid at the National Sporting Club. The colored chap was the winner without any possibility of doubt, but Lewis's forcing of the pace almost throughout the entire ten rounds made the bout one of the liveliest and most satisfactory ever seen in this city.

Dixie Kid's fights made boxing and sport headlines (*New York Times*, September 10, 1910).

decision to Ed Givens in Pittsburgh.[31] Neither of these bouts are recorded on Dixie's official record at this time, but would account for his whereabouts in early 1906.

When Dixie Kid did return to the ring in 1908, he fought in five consecutive "no-decision" bouts, including one against Jeff Clark, the uncle of former 1950s' heavyweight champ Joe Walcott. Despite what is presumed to be a long layoff from boxing, Dixie successfully resumed his career in 1909 with seven knock outs in twelve battles and had, according to Fleisher, his best year in the ring.[32] Dixie also had his first of two meetings with heavyweight legend Sam Langford that year. As great a fighter as Dixie Kid was, he was never able to put a serious dent in Langford. In their first meeting on September 28, 1909, Dixie Kid, who was much lighter than Langford, managed to slip and block the majority of Langford's dangerous swings. In the third round, Dixie landed a series of punches to the Bostonian's body and jaw which slowed Langford down momentarily. However, in the next two rounds, Langford punished Dixie Kid, sending him to the canvas. At the end of the fifth, Langford landed a heavy body blow. When the bell rang to start the sixth round, the Kid's corner ended the fight taking a loss to avoid the inevitable knockout.[33]

Despite having an active record, it was difficult for Dixie to get bouts with new opposition. During these years the color line continued to haunt Dixie Kid, costing him numerous opportunities in the ring. A bout was cancelled between Dixie and Jack Gardner, a white welterweight, scheduled for November 1909 at The Phoenix Athletic Club in Memphis, Tennessee. A black newspaper, *The Freeman*, reported that white and colored fighters would no longer fight each other at the club, stating that, "The line has not barred the ebony scrappers from taking part in bouts pulled off by the club, but they must mix it among their own color."[34]

Dixie Kid often faced the same black opponents multiple times, such as Willie Lewis, whom Dixie fought frequently. On Nov 18, 1910, Sam Langford worked Dixie's corner for one such bout. Langford predicted that if Dixie Kid followed his instructions, he would surely stop Lewis.[35] Indeed, Dixie had soundly beaten Lewis weeks before. Perhaps Dixie Kid took the matchup lightly as he reportedly "wore a smile that was hard to knock off" during the bout.[36] In the seventh round, Dixie Kid reached into his bag of tricks to feign fatigue. Then, just as the bell rang to end the round, he smiled and landed a right on Lewis' ribs. The fight ended in a draw. The tame performance, which drew hisses from the crowd, disappointed onlookers who felt that both fighters failed to land good blows.[37]

Aaron Brown's brother George also earned a living as a professional boxer. Sometimes fighting as Dixie Brown, George Brown was a reasonably successful welterweight, although he never achieved the greatness of Aaron. On one occasion, George Brown was matched against Kid Williams, a Baltimore fighter, at Sharkey's Athletic Club in New York. The bout was a substitute for a Dixie Kid-Sailor Chuck Carlton match that was cancelled for unknown reasons.[38] Sharkey's was a popular entertainment club and bar, owned by former heavyweight "Sailor" Tom Sharkey. Until 1920, boxing was largely outlawed in New York State. However, a loophole allowed fights to occur in athletic clubs, which many bars then became. The club would grant "membership" to boxers only for the duration of their bouts. Sharkey's is perhaps best known as the setting for several of George Bellows' paintings including the 1909 *Stag at Sharkey's*, which depicts two white fighters, in a crowd of white faces, and "Both Members of the Club," which depicts Joe Gans battling a white fighter in a segregated club. Indeed, the crowd at Sharkey's was largely comprised of wealthy white men. With his temporary membership to Sharkey's, Dixie Brown knocked out Kid Williams early in the fourth round after giving the white boxer a terrific beating. The *New York Times* covered the card that evening remarking that, "It was Ethiopian night at the Sharkey, for several of the numbers on the bill were black-face acts." The black ring entertainment also included staged bouts between the Mysterious Iopie from the Congo Free State and Kid Sterling of Alabama.[39]

Dixie Kid lost yet another opportunity to fight in 1909. This time it was not the color line or an unexplained cancellation, but a Catholic priest that cost the Kid his fight purse. The St. Lawrence Catholic Church sat just in front of the Plymouth Athletic Club. From the front of the Church the priest watched with great interest as an unusual number of people walked past the church, pretending they were just out for a leisurely stroll. Once at the back of the church, they turned and entered the athletic club. The priest soon heard shouting and watched as clouds of tobacco smoke drifted through the open window. Entering the rectory and grabbing a "hefty stick," the priest headed for the athletic club. A man posted at the door tried to prevent his entry, but the determined priest walked into the smoke-filled room to find a boxing ring in the middle of the crowd. The referee was finishing his introductions of Charles Seiger, known as the Hoboken Iron Man, and Dixie Kid. The fighters touched hands and raised their fists. But before the round started, the priest pounded his stick on the ring floor and announced, "There will be no fight to-night." A reporter at the scene recounted that, "The Dixie Kid started to say something, but some one, who seemed to be in authority, grabbed him by the leg and in a stage whisper said, 'Don't.'"[40] As the two fighters hurriedly put on their bathrobes, the disgruntled crowd filed out. Those not moving quickly enough felt the priest's stick on their shoulders and shins. After clearing the room, the priest went to the police station to report that a prizefight had almost occurred.[41]

This was not the only time an authority ended one of Dixie Kid's fights. On May 23, 1910, the police stepped in to stop a fight between New York fighter Bill Hurley and Dixie Kid in the eighth stanza of a scheduled ten-round fight. This was the third meeting between "Battling" Bill and Dixie Kid that year, and tensions between the two fighters were high. Dixie Kid had already kayoed Hurley once and had one 'no decision.' On their third meeting the fight was stopped as both boxers used "rough tactics," and the bout again ended as a 'no contest,' although the fight was reported to favor the Dixie Kid. The bout was so rough that both men were hurled from the ring four different times, ending up among the spectators. When the police ended the fight, the ring ropes were broken with only two ring posts left standing.[42]

After yet another fight with Hurley in 1911, Dixie Kid sought more lucrative bouts and set sail for Europe leaving behind the pervasive racial segregation in the United States. Word of heavyweight Sam McVey's success in Paris in 1907 caught the attention of many African American boxers who journeyed to the French capital, drawn by the popular myth of French racial tolerance and the country's celebration of black prizefighters. Joe Jeannette and Jack Johnson had also crossed the Atlantic and had become famous on the Parisian sporting scene. Theresa Runstedtler, professor of African American Studies and History, explains that "African American boxers became huge celebrities in France: they challenged white men in the ring, endorsed a variety of products, published articles in sporting magazines, toured the French provinces, participated in the underground nightlife of the Parisian dance-hall scene, and even gained the admiration of the European avant garde."[43] Yet, she cautions that France was not the color-blind nation it was imagined to be. The black boxer's powerful body was viewed through an exotic, paternalistic gaze and was considered a source of intrigue and humor, rather than a cause for alarm. Black pugilists were still depicted through racist tropes of black savagery, and were often represented in the media with "dragging knuckles, exaggerated lips, jutting jawbones, and overhanging foreheads."[44]

In France the most popular bouts were black-on-black matches and white audiences were eager to see brutal exchanges between black fighters. Black pugilists were thought to possess unrivaled, animalistic power. Parisian fans who reveled in spectacles of black strength highly anticipated the first bout between McVey and Jeannette. When the match was not nearly as gruesome as was expected, and ended in a decision, fans felt cheated. A highly anticipated rematch between McVey-Jeannette took place April 17, 1909, in Paris. This time the promoters arranged a "match au finish" that could only end in knockout or submission, rather than the referee's decision. Bouts with such harsh conditions were long illegal in the United States and remained rare in France, yet an exception was made for these black fighters. In front of a large and enthusiastic crowd, McVey, battered and exhausted, threw in the towel after forty-nine rounds.[45]

Dixie Kid arrived in Paris in 1911 to find enthusiastic audiences. He became the toast of European boxing circles where his ring battles made him a sporting idol. Fred Dartnell, a British boxing historian from this era, claimed that, "The Dixie Kid is the most extraordinary fighter I have ever seen, and in some respects the greatest.... He was a quaint personality and in his way as big an attraction for the boxing public as Charlie Chaplin is to the cinema patrons."[46] An indication of his popularity in France is shown by the fact that while a referee awarded a twenty-round bout to his opponent, Willie Lewis, on a foul, "a riotous commotion followed which threatened to end in a general fight."[47] A jury of Parisian sportsmen was formed to review the referee's action. The jury overruled the referee giving Dixie the decision.[48] It was Dixie's fifth-round knockout over Georges Carpentier that firmly cemented his popularity in France. Carpentier, who at that time was fighting as a welterweight, was twenty years old and stood six foot one. Dixie Kid met Carpentier at Trouville, the famous French resort, when Carpentier should have been at the heyday of his career.[49] The loss damaged Carpentier's reputation in France, but sealed the reputation of Dixie Kid as a star. By the time Carpentier challenged Jack Dempsey for his heavyweight crown in 1921, Carpentier was long considered a washed-up fighter.

Dixie Kid's last fight in 1911 was in Liverpool against Johnny Summers, a popular and highly acclaimed British ringman. Dixie Kid knocked out Summers in the second round. It was only the second knock out in Summers' long career. This bout is also noted as Dixie Kid's last victory over a good opponent. One journalist claims that after this battle Dixie's only remaining triumphs were over "third-raters."[50] The decline of Dixie Kid's ring skills coincided with his introduction into Parisian café society where he developed a tragic addiction to cocaine.[51] Dixie Kid's drinking, womanizing and drug use caught up to him in the ring. On May 5, 1912 Dixie Kid arrived in Glasgow, Scotland, to fight Dan Flynn for fifteen rounds. Flynn was also one of Scotland's champion cyclists, and in his later years founded a famous bookmaking business.[52] Dixie reportedly told the fight's promoter that he had a broken right hand and was also suffering from three cracked ribs. The injuries had been sustained in his previous bout. The promoter insisted that Dixie fight, but cut the bout from fifteen to twelve rounds as an accommodation. Dixie Kid lost the match, but went the distance despite his crippling injuries.[53]

Dixie Kid's record became a mixed bag of wins and losses against mostly journeymen fighters. When he did face a legitimate contender, he often appeared worn out. For example, in 1914, Bandsman Blake, the champion English middleweight, soundly defeated Dixie Kid on points in a 20 round battle. Blake was eight years younger, fourteen pounds heavier, and was touted as the latest English "white hope."[54] The *Daily Mail* reported that with the exception of failing to score a knockout, Blake beat Dixie as decisively as it was possible to do. The paper called Blake the "black man's master" in round four, stating that Blake was "pounding him hard with both hands to the jaw, and shook him badly. The Dixie Kid tried all the stock devices from his bag of mystery in the next few rounds."[55] But the trickster could not pull out any of his specialized ring tricks to save himself. Blake continued to punish and manhandle Dixie, even pushing him through and over the ropes on several occasions. After the tenth round, the crowd of 4,000, taking delight in Dixie Kid's beating, shouted, "'Make him fight' as he sprinted or hung on." In the eighteenth round, Dixie Kid, bleeding and groggy, was knocked down but stood up again to finish the last rounds of the fight on his feet.[56]

While in Europe, Dixie Kid also managed and trained another expatriate, Eugene Bullard. Bullard had traveled to Scotland to escape racial discrimination in the United States. After Dixie Kid watched Bullard dominate in his ring debut against Billy Welsh, Dixie offered Bullard the opportunity to train with him in London.[57] Dixie Kid became a surrogate father to Bullard, taking him to fights in and around London each week. Dixie also introduced him to other African American boxers living in Europe, including Jack Johnson, and made arrangements for Bullard to fight in Paris and throughout France[58]. Under Dixie's tutelage Bullard became an accomplished boxer. Bullard also credits Dixie Kid with helping him join a vaudeville and music troupe called "Freeman's Pickaninnies" that traveled all over the continent. After his boxing career, Eugene Bullard went on to even greater achievement, becoming the first African American military pilot and the only black fighter pilot in World War I. However, Bullard did not fly for the United States, the country of his birth, but for his adopted country of France.[59]

At the onset of World War I, Dixie Kid remained in England and continued to fight out of London until 1916. As the war raged on, Dixie's ring opportunities waned. After entering the ring eleven times in 1915, he boxed only a handful of times in the following years. Dixie did make the world news wire in 1916, not for his ring battles, but for his involvement in a case of fraud. Charges were brought against Dixie Kid and Bob Spencer, a featherweight boxer, for falsifying Spencer's application for a passport to the United States. Spencer's application indicated that he was an American citizen, when, in fact, he was Canadian. Dixie had signed the application, vouching for its accuracy and was brought to Scotland Yard under investigation.[60] As a Canadian citizen, Spencer was one of many British subjects who were in a rush to protect themselves against conscription.[61]

In 1917, Dixie Kid and his family were living in Italy, where Dixie participated in "theatrical work," most likely vaudeville-style boxing shows.[62] In 1918, he moved the family to Barcelona, where he had four fights over two years, three against light heavyweight Frank Hoche. It is unlikely that these four fights were enough to sustain him and his family financially. In November 1919, Dixie Kid applied to renew his U.S. passport, indicating he was planning to remain living in Barcelona, Spain.[63] The document indicates that he planned to return to the United States after working for two more years in Spain, Portugal, France and Italy doing theatrical work. During this same time, immigration records reveal that Dixie's wife, Sophie Brown, and her three children, Emma, age eight, Aaron and Lester, aged seven and six respectively, sailed on their own from Liverpool to New York on March 1, 1919.[64] Dixie Kid remained in Europe, taking a bout against Paul Buisson in France, which he lost in twelve rounds. It is unclear whether Dixie Kid returned to his wife and family upon his re-entry into the United States. It is clear, however, that when he did return to America he was broke and had many difficulties in his remaining years. Dixie worked odd jobs, and survived on the donations of his friends. The 1920 census reports that at age 37, Dixie was working as a janitor in San Diego.[65] Dixie also continued to haunt boxing clubs and train a number of fighters. He worked as a sparring partner for Harry Wills during his training camp for the Wills-Madden and Wills-Firpo bouts.[66]

Dixie Kid's cocaine addiction grew out of his playful years in Paris but continued to plague him throughout the remainder of his life. On September 19, 1924, in an Edinburgh courthouse, Dixie stood accused of trying to rob a Lieth chemist of cocaine.[67] During the trial, Dixie explained that he had stowed away in a German freighter temporarily docked in Hamburg, but that he was so drugged by cocaine use that he hadn't a clue where the ship was headed.[68] Glasgow journalist Brian Donald recounts that Dixie had arrived in Leith and made his way to Scotland's oldest amateur boxing club, the Leith Victoria, which was run by former British and European featherweight champion, Tancy Lee. Brown did not disclose his addiction to Lee, who hired the former world champion as a sparring partner for Britain's reigning featherweight champion, George McKenzie, Lee's nephew. But Dixie's addiction drove him to seek a constant supply of the drug. At first Dixie had a prescription from a physician for a week's supply of cocaine to treat an eye problem. After that supply ended, he returned to several pharmacists to obtain more cocaine. This time he was without a doctor's script, and when each of the port-area pharmacists refused to provide the drug, Dixie resorted to threats of violence. The police were dispatched and Dixie Kid was arrested and charged with six counts under Scotland's Dangerous Drugs Act. Dixie Kid was sentenced to a short prison sentence and deportation back to America. One source indicates Dixie was sentenced to 21 days, and a second reports it was a three-month sentence.[69] Nonetheless, Dixie Kid found himself back in a prison.

In that same year, *The Daily Gleaner*, a Jamaican newspaper, ran the following headline, "Dixie Kid, Well Known Pugilist, Coming to Jamaica" in a story that ran in November of 1924.[70] Dixie Kid had arranged travel to Jamaica to offer a challenge to meet any middleweight during his stay. The article also reports that Dixie was planning to travel to Panama and the South American Republics, where he was booked for several engagements.[71] There is no newspaper record in *The Gleaner* of Dixie Kid ever making this trip. However, Dixie was not yet finished entering the roped arena, even though his aging, drug-addicted body whose "broken nose and cauliflower left ear" bore witness to his extensive fight career.[72]

In 1928 Dixie Kid was still not fully retired. He continued to give public exhibitions, including one with Ace Hudkins, who was preparing to challenge Mickey Walker for his middleweight crown. The *New York Times* reports it was Hudkins who gave the clever exhibition, as Dixie Kid's presence in the ring was unremarkable.[73] At this point, when Dixie Kid's name was mentioned in newspapers, the story was often tragic. In 1928, the *Oakland Tribune* recounted how Dixie Kid had wandered, one cold New York night, into the office of a wealthy coffee importer, asking the man to buy a copy of his poem about his last great fight, which he sold for two bits a copy.[74] The man, himself a former boxer, recognized Dixie Kid. After some discussion, the man purchased several copies of Dixie's poem, giving him a generous sum of money. The coffee importer also offered to assist Aaron Brown with making plans to travel to Oakland to see his mother, whom he hadn't seen for twenty-eight years. Enlisting the help of the chief of police to locate the address of Dixie's mother, the generous man also sent Dixie to a dentist to give the toothless man a set of new "store teeth." He sent Dixie Kid to Oakland, paying for his ticket, and provided him with extra money in his pocket and a check for his mother. The article concluded with the following,

"It will be a great reunion today ... when the 'Dixie Kid' walks in all his reconstructed glory, and says 'Hello, ma!'"[75]

Dixie's financial situation remained bleak, and he often relied on the kindness of his friends in the boxing community. At the age of 47 he continued working in Los Angeles as a boxing trainer.[76] Still able to make a little money in the ring, he traveled to Jamaica and in August 1931, gave a two-round exhibition with Sam McVey on the undercard of the Leonard Pitt-Battling Johnny heavyweight title fight.[77] The exhibition reportedly "amused" the audience, and afterward Dixie also received a challenge by Jack Campbell to a future bout.[78] Weeks later, on September 18, Dixie Kid was scheduled to fight Smiling Kid, a promising Jamaican light heavyweight, in a headline bout. Those who had witnessed Dixie's exhibition with Sam McVea, were worried that Dixie was not taking the upcoming bout seriously enough.[79] Perhaps these spectators were correct, as Dixie Kid left Jamaica without explanation two weeks before the bout.[80] The promoter was "put to a great deal of expense" as a result of Dixie Kid's early departure.[81]

On Saturday, September 9, 1933, Dixie Kid attempted to take his own life by leaping out of the second story window of his cheap hotel room near the railroad yards in a rundown district in Los Angeles. He was found early that morning lying in the gutter by a patrolman.[82] Dixie Kid is reported to have said, "I licked everyone but old John Barleycorn. I licked them all," and then his voice faded as he was loaded in to an ambulance.[83] When detectives investigated his room they found drawers of faded newspaper clippings that told of his ring success and fame. The surgeons expected that Dixie would die from his injuries, which included several broken ribs, a broken arm and internal injuries, but he managed to survive.[84] Prior to this suicide attempt, Dixie was a fixture in fistic training camps, and could be seen wearing the last remnants of his lavishly spent ring earnings, his signature "gold-headed cane and a gold stickpin in a necktie worse for the wear."[85] Although he survived this suicide attempt, Dixie Kid did not return to the fistic marts.

Seven months later, on April 6, 1934, Dixie Kid died, reportedly of natural causes, but most likely succumbing to injuries he had sustained in the earlier suicide attempt.[86] He was 51 years old. Dixie Kid had been living in such obscurity that it was a full week before news of his death circulated in the media, which is why some historians, such as Fleischer, incorrectly report his death as April 13.[87] His body, which originally was unclaimed, was destined for Potter's field, the final resting place for those who have no money or loved ones to even provide the dignity of a headstone. Friends from the Los Angeles boxing community rallied and sought donations to provide him with a proper burial.

The pages of boxing history, Gerald Early argues, are littered with the names of tragic men of color.[88] Indeed, Dixie Kid is one of these men. Simply put, Aaron Brown was a bluesman in life, and a jazzman in the ring. Dixie, like a stereotypical blues musician, lived life hard, was a womanizer, and struggled with addiction, poverty, and loneliness in a world that was deeply impacted by the color line. In the ring, Dixie Kid was an inventive jazzman, always on the move, playful one round and fierce the next. Under the pugilistic spotlight he improvised and cleverly displayed his individuality. Yet despite his prolific career in the ring, Dixie Kid has often been missing from the pages of boxing history. The former world welterweight titleholder boasts an impressive pugilistic pedigree and was a fantastically intriguing character outside of the ring. Boxing fans are still waiting for an in-depth portrait of a man known for his legendary ring skills, a man who deserves to be included in the ranks of the best old-time boxers.

NOTES

1. Fleischer, Nat. *Black Dynamite, Vol. IV*, 253–4.
2. Roberts, James B., and Alexander G. Skutt. *The Boxing Register: International Boxing Hall of Fame Official Record Book*. Ithaca, N.Y.: McBooks Press, 2006, 95.
3. "Famous Fighter Dies in Poverty," *The Lincoln Star*. Lincoln, NB, April 14, 1934.
4. This chapter follows examples laid out in historical work on previously overlooked black fighters such as Moyle's (2006) work on Sam Langford and Aycock and Scott's (2008) biography of Joe Gans.
5. The Library of Congress, American Memory, African American Sheet Music, 1850–1920.
6. Early, Gerald. *The Black Intellectual and the Sport of Prizefighting*. 1988, 107.
7. Donald, Brian. "How the Dixie Kid was cuffed by the Leith police," *Sunday Herald—Glasgow*, May 14, 2000.
8. Smith, Kevin. *Black Genesis: The History of the Black Prizefighter 1760–1870*, 3.
9. Fleischer, Nat. *Black Dynamite, Vol. IV*, 253.
10. Ibid., 252–254.
11. Ibid., 254.
12. "Neil Will Fight Tonight," *Oakland Tribune*, September 20, 1903, 13.
13. Fleischer, Nat. *Black Dynamite, Vol. IV*, 256.
14. *Oakland Tribune*, September 20, 1903.
15. "Sporting Memories Recalled By Spink," *Reno Evening Gazette*, March 24, 1920.
16. Ibid.
17. "'Dixie Kid' a Stayer," *Los Angeles Times*, July 1, 1902.
18. Ibid.
19. Fleischer, Nat. *Black Dynamite, Vol. IV*, 259.
20. Ashe, Arthur. *A Hard Road to Glory: The African American Athlete in Boxing*. New York: Warner Books, 1988, 9.
21. "Welter Honors For 'Dixie Kid,'" *The* (Syracuse) *Post-Standard*, February 21, 1910.
22. "Famous Fighter Dies in Poverty," *Lincoln Star*. Lincoln, NB, April 14, 1934; "Body Headed For Potters' Grave Found To Be Former Welter Champion, Dixie Kid," *San Antonio Express*, April 14, 1934.
23. "The 'Dixie Kid' was Best: Colored Lad's Fight with Temple At Baltimore is Described," *Oakland Tribune*, January 10, 1905.
24. Ibid.
25. Thirteenth Census of the United States: 1910—Population: Department of Commerce and Labor, New York, April 18, 1910.
26. Roberts, James B., and Alexander G. Skutt. *The Boxing Register: International Boxing Hall of Fame Official Record Book*. Ithaca, N.Y.: McBooks Press, 2006, 95.
27. John Phillips, "Trouble and Boxers Are No Strangers," *Daily News,* February 13, 1992.
28. Fleischer, Nat. *Black Dynamite. Vol. IV*, 261.
29. Lloyd, Craig. *Eugene Bullard, Black Expatriate in Jazz-Age Paris*. Atlanta: University of Georgia Press, 2000, 164.

30. "Sport Column," The *Daily Courier*, Connellsville, Pennsylvania, March 19, 1906.
31. "Boxing Tonight," *Pittsburg Post*, March 7, 1906.
32. Fleischer, Nat. *Black Dynamite. Vol. IV*, 262.
33. "Langford Defeats 'Dixie Kid,'" *New York Times*, September 29, 1909; Moyle, Clay. *Sam Langford: Boxing's Greatest Uncrowned Champion*. Seattle: Bennett & Hastings, 2006, 110.
34. *The Freeman: An Illustrated Colored Newspaper*, November 13, 1909.
35. "Willie Lewis and Dixie Kid n the Ring," *New York Times*, November 17, 1910.
36. "Dixie Kid Fights Tamely With Lewis," *New York Times*, November 18, 1910.
37. Ibid.
38. "Williams Knocked Out: George Brown Wins Substitute Bout at Sharkey A.C.," *New York Times*, June 16, 1910.
39. Ibid.
40. "Priest Breaks Up Jersey Prizefight," *New York Times*, October 27, 1909.
41. Ibid.
42. "Fighters Break Down Ring Ropes," *New York Times*, May 24, 1910.
43. Runstedtler, Theresa. "Visible Men: African American Boxers, the New Negro, and the Global Color Line." *Radical History Review* 103, 2009: 63.
44. Ibid., 66.
45. Ibid., 66–68.
46. Lloyd, Craig. *Eugene Bullard, Black Expatriate in Jazz-Age Paris*. Atlanta: University of Georgia Press, 2000, 34.
47. Fleischer, Nat. *Black Dynamite, Vol. IV*, 270.
48. "Body Headed For Potters' Grave Found To Be Former Welter Champion, Dixie Kid," *San Antonio Express*, April 14, 1934.
49. "Sporting Memories Recalled By Spink," *Reno Evening Gazette*, March 24, 1920.
50. "Pugilistic Annals," *Trenton Evening Times*, November 6, 1915.
51. Donald, Brian. "How the Dixie Kid was cuffed by the Leith police," *Sunday Herald—Glasgow*, May 14, 2000.
52. Ibid.
53. Ibid.
54. "Latest British Hope Defeats 'Dixie Kid,'" *Indianapolis Star*, January 2, 1914.
55. "English Boxer's Triumph: Easy Win For Bandsman Blake," *The* (London) *Daily Mail*, January 2, 1914.
56. Ibid.
57. Lloyd, Craig. *Eugene Bullard, Black Expatriate in Jazz-Age Paris*. Atlanta: University of Georgia Press, 2000, 34.
58. Ibid.
59. Chicalette, William. "Corporal Eugene Jacques Bullard: First Black American Fighter Pilot." *http://www.airpower.maxwell.af.mil/apjinternational/apjs/2005/3tri05/chivaletteeng.html* (accessed January 7, 2010).

60. "English Pugs Are Now 'American,'" *Oakland Tribune*, December 21, 1915.

61. "Explains Passport Order: Our London Embassy Denies Affront to Americans Abroad," *New York Times*, January 14, 1916.

62. Aaron Lister Brown, United States Passport Application, November 3, 1919.

63. Ibid.

64. U.S. Department of Labor Immigration Services, List of United States Citizens sailing on the S.S. *Adriatic* from Liverpool to New York, March 1, 1919.

65. Fourteenth Census of the United States: 1920—Population. San Diego, January 8, 1920.

66. "Dixie Kid, Well Known Pugilist, Coming To Jamaica," *The* (Kingston, Jamaica) *Gleaner*, November 27, 1924.

67. Donald, Brian. "Age-old Proof That Drugs and Sports Will Never Mix," *The Herald—Glasgow*, May 29, 1999.

68. Ibid.

69. Ibid.; Donald, Brian. "How the Dixie Kid was cuffed by the Leith police," *Sunday Herald—Glasgow*, May 14, 2000.

70. "Dixie Kid, Well Known Pugilist, Coming To Jamaica," *The* (Kingston, Jamaica) *Daily Gleaner*, November 27, 1924.

71. Ibid.

72. Donald, Brian. "Age-old Proof That Drugs and Sports Will Never Mix," *The Herald—Glasgow*, May 29, 1999.

73. "Hudkins Trains For Walker Bout," *New York Times*, June 13, 1928.

74. "Benefactor's Aid Rejuvenates Old-Time Boxing Champion, Here to Visit Mother," *Oakland Tribune*, August 9, 1928.

75. Ibid.

76. Fifteenth Census of the United States: 1920—Population. Los Angeles, May 4, 1930.

77. "Johnny Regains His Heavyweight Crown," *The* (Kingston, Jamaica*) Daily Gleaner*, August 31, 1931.

78. Ibid.

79. "Dixie Kid and Smiling Kid to Meet Shortly," *The* (Kingston, Jamaica) *Daily Gleaner*, September 18, 1931.

80. "News of Interest for the Boxing Fans," *The* (Kingston, Jamaica) *Daily Gleaner*, September 24, 1931.

81. "Kid Silver and Young King to Meet on Friday," *The* (Kingston, Jamaica) *Daily Gleaner*, September 28, 1931.

82. "'Dixie Kid' Recovers From Suicide Attempts," *Nevada State Journal*, Reno, Nevada, September 10, 1933.

83. "Dixie Kid Is Unable to Down Barleycorn," *The Billings* (Montana*) Gazette*, September 10, 1933.

84. "'Dixie Kid' Recovers From Suicide Attempt," *Nevada State Journal*, Reno Nevada, September 10, 1933.

85. "One-Time Fighter Dead: Aaron L. Brown Once Well Known as the Dixie Kid," *New York Times*, April 15, 1934.

86. "Famous Fighter Dies in Poverty," *The Lincoln Star (*Lincoln, Nebraska), April 14, 1934.

87. Fleischer, Nat. *Black Dynamite, Vol. 4,* 251.

88. Early, Gerald. "Battling Siki: The Boxer as Natural Man." *The Massachusetts Review*, Vol. 29, No. 3 (Fall) 1988a, 451.

CHAPTER 10

Jack Blackburn: From Lightweight Challenger to Trainer of Heavyweight Champions

Joseph Bourelly

For a man known best as a boxing trainer who taught former heavyweight champion Joe Louis how to fight professionally, the word "almost" would best describe the fight career of Charles Henry Blackburn. While it may be a simple word in the English language, it is synonymous with disappointment and unfulfilled dreams, especially in the world of sports and particularly boxing. In fact, "almost" does not cut it in any society that rewards only its best performers regardless of the field or industry.

Coming close to curing a disease or getting a job simply will not do the trick. Having success or glory in the grasp of one's hands but letting it slip through is heartbreaking. For that reason, most people become comfortable living in mediocrity, but few take the risks necessary to dare to be great. Although never reaching his goal of becoming a world champion, Charles Henry Blackburn, better known by the name Jack, dared to be great.

It is hard, if not impossible, for common folks to remember the runners-up in professional sports like baseball, basketball or football even last year, much less three or five years ago. What about the second or third best boxer in a division for a given period? They are so faded from our collective memory it is as if they never even existed at all.

The Period

Jack Blackburn's infancy, the post–Reconstruction South which followed the Civil War in the United States, occurred during a time when being given an opportunity on a level playing field in America was practically non-existent. Depending on the area of the country, a person was literally nothing unless he or she was of the right race, religion and family. Self-made men were few, and to put it mildly, people of African ancestry were not the right anything, especially former slaves and their children, many of whom had to deal with the ramifications of being "free" in a dangerous and violent South. With the exception of very few cases, outside of poorly written slave documents, government census records and oral history, these represent the only remnants of America's forgotten people; a people that more often than not were denied opportunities to finish in the top rungs of society.

In Kentucky alone, over one hundred people were lynched, mostly black, between 1865 and 1874.[1] During the period, a culmination of death and destruction took place with a flurry of Ku Klux Klan precipitated violence during the spring of 1871 in the town of Frankfort, Kentucky.[2] The incidents which included black people being lynched, tarred, feathered and beaten, prompted a group of former slaves to send a letter to the U.S. Congress pleading for protection the state was either unwilling or unable to provide.[3] The help never came.

The early 1880s were interesting times and saw Jesse James, the most famous outlaw America has ever known, gunned down by a member of his own gang; the feud between the Hatfields of West Virginia and McCoys of eastern Kentucky was in full swing; the first Vaudeville theatre was established; and the Brooklyn Bridge was opened.[4] In the world of boxing, a sport which was virtually illegal throughout the entire country, John L. Sullivan defeated Paddy Ryan to become the last of the bare knuckle heavyweight champions.[5]

On May 3, 1883, only eighteen years after the abolition of slavery, Jack Blackburn was born in Versailles, Kentucky.[6] While he would eventually become relatively well known as a boxing

Jack Blackburn in his prime (Bains News Service, George Grantham Bain, Library of Congress).

trainer, Blackburn also happened to be one of the greatest boxers the world has ever seen. As fierce outside the ring as he was inside of it, Blackburn found himself in serious legal trouble as both a young man and while in his latter years, fighting separate shooting allegations that left a total of two men dead, one woman shot in the back and a young girl seriously wounded. He also would suffer a gruesome gash along the left side of his face, the result of a knife fight in a Philadelphia saloon.[7] Even worse, Blackburn would have his throat slashed and face lacerated by his older brother Fred, who also boxed, following a game of poker.[8] A heavy drinker throughout his life and a man with a fiery tongue, Blackburn was a no-nonsense character who was volatile and intimidating, and scary by any definition of the word. While there are some aspects of his life that beg for more clarity, one thing is for sure: Jack Blackburn could at times be as mean as anyone alive, and that is what prevented him more than anything else from becoming a champion in the ring.

The Formative Years

Jack Blackburn's birthplace of Versailles is located in Woodford County, Kentucky, which is in the middle of both horse thoroughbred and bourbon country. Near Lexington, Kentucky, the area is also ripe in the tradition of slavery, and all of Jack's family members were either former slaves or descendants of them. According to 1880 census records, he had at least three older sisters (Lillie, Eva and Alice) and four older brothers (William, George, John and Fred).[9]

However, the true identity of his biological mother and father is murky. Although it has been reported in multiple sources that he was the son of a preacher, a twenty-five-year-old mulatto named Louis Henry Redd is listed as the father of all Blackburn's siblings.[10] Additionally, a nineteen year old woman by the name of Hellen Redd is listed as a resident of their house, and there is an enfant named John Redd who is also identified as a son of Louis.[11]

So the question is, considering that Louis and Hellen maintained a surname of Redd, and all of Jack's brothers and sisters were named Blackburn, what is their true relation? Also, given the young ages of Louis and Hellen as well as the ages of the Blackburn siblings, which ranged up to fourteen years old in 1880, there is simply no way the two could be the biological parents of all these children.

Everyone in the household is identified as a mulatto and given they all lived together, it is easy to surmise they are related to one another and most probably, Louis Redd is either their uncle or cousin.[12] One certainty is with all of his older siblings to compete with, life must have been very difficult for Jack Blackburn, and the fact that census records also indicate both Louis and Hellen Redd were an illiterate laborer and servant, respectively, times were likely very hard for this family.[13]

Learning to fight is a tradition in the oldest sense for young boys, and there is little doubt Jack Blackburn had to fight for everything being the youngest of seven siblings. His situation is reminiscent of current heavyweight contender Chris Arreola's story of having to fight his own family members for the last chicken wing at the dinner table. Desperate times mean desperate measures, and Jack Blackburn was undoubtedly a desperate young man during his early years in Kentucky.

Although Louis Redd would continue living in Kentucky, the Blackburn children, including Jack, would scatter about the country in search of a better life. Living some of his youth in the area of Terre Haute, Indiana, Jack would end up in the city of Indianapolis, living with his brother-in-law, older sister, a nephew and his older brother John by 1900.[14, 15]

Hard times followed the Blackburn family to Indianapolis, where Jack, his brother John and their brother-in-law James Spalding were registered as being out of work at the turn of the century. At 5'10" tall and skinny as a rail, it wouldn't be long until Jack Blackburn decided to take matters into his own hands and allow his fists to be the moneymakers of his adult life.

Fighting Times

When exactly Jack Blackburn began boxing is not totally clear, but it appears according to the 1907 edition of the *T. S. Andrews' World Sporting Annual* that he did engage in numerous unverified, undated fights as early as 1901. In Richard Bak's book *Joe Louis: The Great Black Hope,* it is indicated he may have begun his boxing career at sixteen years of age in 1899. Blackburn's official record according to Boxrec.com is listed as 37 wins, with 27 coming by way of knockout, against 8 losses and 7 draws. In terms of newspaper decisions, bouts where reporters would deliver verdicts on the fights via their newspaper columns, Boxrec.com has him with 65 wins, 17 defeats and 11 draws. In total that is 102 wins, 25

Jack Blackburn, future teacher of Joe Louis, shows his fighting form (Bains News Service, George Grantham Bain, Library of Congress).

losses and 19 draws. Even more impressive is the fact that Blackburn would often fight men all the way up to the heavyweight division even though he was only a lightweight himself.

According to Jack Blackburn, he competed in almost 400 bouts, which is likely to be closer to the truth, given he fought during a time when boxing was illegal throughout most jurisdictions.[16] Therefore, many bouts were advertised as sporting exhibitions during the first decade of the 1900s to skirt the illegality of such contests. These fights sometimes resulted in newspaper decisions. If no media covered a fight, there would be no written record of any decision at all; thus the discrepancy between the number of bouts via Boxrec.com and Jack Blackburn's recollection of his own career.

Prior to Joe Gans winning the lightweight title from Frank Erne in 1902, no African American had ever laid claim to a world title in the sport of boxing. As a consolation, blacks were often awarded lesser titles designated to Negroes that never translated into big money paydays. Accordingly, the most Jack Blackburn could have imagined achieving as late as 1901 was to become widely recognized as the best black fighter in his weight class.

Of course the scope of what Blackburn believed was achievable certainly changed after Joe Gans won his title. "If Gans could do it, why not me?" he had to ask himself. As it would turn out, the two would fight three times over the course of their careers, between 1903 and 1906, but Jack Blackburn could not get over the hump against his archrival, coming up with a six-round draw in their first bout, a fifteen-round loss via decision in the second fight, and a six-round newspaper decision loss in their third and final match. But before he could even think about challenging a man like Joe Gans, who may have been the greatest fighter to ever live, Jack Blackburn had to earn his way up the ranks like everyone else.

Based in either Terre Haute or Indianapolis, Indiana, and somewhere between the ages of sixteen and eighteen years of age, the beginning for Jack Blackburn was around the turn of the century, fighting on small cards throughout the Midwest. Needless to say, there were very few, if any, members of the media covering these bouts, so no credit was given as far as any newspaper results. Measuring almost six feet tall, the beginning had to be very rough for the 133-pound fighter, due to the fact Blackburn had no amateur experience, which was rare for any boxer at the time, but especially because he didn't have anyone to initially protect his career as a professional. Dealing with shady promoters, he would often not receive any compensation at all for participating in the early, unrecorded bouts of his career.[17]

Nobody should underestimate the importance of a reputable manager and good match-making in the sport of boxing. That was true at the turn of the twentieth century, and it certainly remains true today. The idea is to be matched against men that are naturally smaller, less skilled and with limited experience at the beginning of a fighter's career. This allows a boxer to learn in the ring and gain confidence while racking up some victories at the same time. Without such protection, a boxer could end up fighting someone like an Olympian, former champion or simply a bigger, more experienced, tough S.O.B. in his first few fights. Unprotected fighters are usually chewed up and spit out during the course of short careers, but Jack Blackburn was no ordinary fighter.

He had been fighting and competing with his seven older siblings, and chances are all of their friends, from the time he could walk. Being exposed to this kind of competitiveness under poverty-stricken circumstances was the making of who he would become: a very hungry fighter with excellent defensive skills and a good punch who was willing to take on all comers from lightweight to heavyweight. It just did not matter as long as Jack Blackburn was putting food on his table.

Blackburn was therefore thrown in with anybody and everybody from day one of his career up until his last fight in 1923. For example, according to Boxrec.com, in only his second match where a decision was actually recorded, he was matched against Dave Holly, who sported a record of twenty-four victories without defeat in official bouts. Holly had lost some newspaper decisions along the way prior to meeting Blackburn, but the point is clear; this man was of a higher profile with more experience. Regardless, Blackburn went on to defeat Dave Holly via a six-round newspaper decision.

Although on the surface a fighter with an official record of 1–0 matched against another man who is 24–0 may seem like a total mismatch, remember by the time Jack Blackburn entered the ring for his second fight of record, he had already engaged in possibly hundreds of underground bouts. Despite the likelihood these fights were in cellars, on docks, in open fields, on barges or even over a game of cards, the fact is Blackburn had already been in very tough fights against other roughneck types looking to pay some bills or just make enough money to get drunk on a given night. The match-ups did not count on his record, but they certainly made him a hardened fellow to contend with by the time of the Dave Holly fight in 1903.

His style in the ring rarely incorporated a swinging punch.[18] Similar to Joe Gans, he preferred to stay in close and throw short, straight punches.[19] Blackburn worked tirelessly to perfect his technique to the point where he could almost effortlessly drop opponents with either hand traveling only six to eight inches.[20] His short, straight punches were ultimately his secret to being able to take on much larger opponents with inferior technique. He would always be heavily reliant on his scientific skills in the ring to overcome the brawn that most of his opponents would bring to bear.

The day after the Holly fight, Jack Blackburn fought another six rounder against an officially undefeated boxer named Jack McKenzie, who happened to be a welterweight, winning again via newspaper decision.[21] Such was the life of a fighter in 1903, when men were known to fight several times in one week or more than once during a given night. Jack Blackburn himself is said to have fought six one-round fights during a single night in 1907, knocking out three of his opponents.[22] This was before young, hot prospects were given big signing bonuses, obviously before major sponsorships, radio or television. As a result, boxers had to fight often if they expected to earn enough in purses to make even a meager living or avoid having to work an extra job. Although boxers today more often than not hold down jobs to make ends meet, there were enough boxing promotions during Jack Blackburn's era for them not to have to do so, especially if one happened to be talented and entertaining.

A little over a month later, Jack Blackburn fought a heavier man again, this time two weight classes higher in the middleweight division; Blackburn's era only had eight official weight classes. His opponent, Jack "Twin" Sullivan, was a well-known journeyman fighter who amassed a career record of 73–36–42.[23] Blackburn earned a draw against his larger opponent via a newspaper decision.[24]

One of the more interesting evenings for Blackburn during 1903 had to have been three months later when he took on two men in one night (he would do it again in 1908). First up was lightweight Tommy Cleary, who retired in the first round after being on the receiving end of a terrible low blow.[25] Given the fight ended so abruptly, the promoters of the State Athletic Club in Philadelphia decided to throw the vastly more experienced lightweight in against a green heavyweight named Tommy Daly, out of Nebraska. While it was Daly's first verified professional fight, the result was still impressive, with Jack Blackburn proceeding to knock out a man four divisions higher than his normal fighting weight inside of three rounds.[26]

By the time November 1903 rolled around, Blackburn had amassed a record of nine wins, one draw and one no contest against men who normally fought from the lightweight to heavyweight divisions. The quality of opposition was generally strong, and he had proven himself by this early point in his career to be among the best lightweights in the world, earning him a first crack at lightweight champion Joe Gans.

Joe Gans is beyond legendary in the sport of boxing, and is acclaimed by many to have pioneered modern boxing techniques in terms of feinting, footwork, parrying, keeping proper balance, counterpunching and straight punching. A defensive master, he was so good that the boxing public demanded reigning lightweight champion Frank Erne either give him a rematch title shot opportunity in 1902 or risk losing legitimacy as a titleholder during a period when the color line almost always prevented black men from getting a world title shot. Gans knocked Frank Erne out in the first round to become the first African American world titleholder in the history of the sport of boxing. Not only did he destroy Erne in the first round, but he did so just outside of the champion's hometown of Buffalo, New York, in Fort Erie, Ontario, Canada.

Joe Gans was so good that whenever he lost, there was plenty of speculation concerning a fixed fight, and no wonder, considering he had career record of 147 wins, 96 of which came via KO, 11 losses and 15 draws.[27] Like Jack Blackburn, Joe Gans fought men in virtually every weight class and almost always emerged the winner. Unlike Blackburn, Joe Gans was not a natural lightweight and suffered tremendously to make the 133-pound weight limit.

Even though Gans was coming off a stint during which he fought three times in four days about a week before he was to meet Jack Blackburn, the lightweight champion of the world was a huge favorite to school the relatively inexperienced contender.[28] The bout itself was a six round non-title fight that took place at the Washington Sporting Club in Philadelphia, on November 2, 1903, and was most likely meant as a test to see what Blackburn had to offer.[29] Although the most telling blow was landed by Joe Gans — a short right hook that dropped Blackburn in the first round — the young upstart from Versailles, Kentucky, was said to have bounced right up and outscored the lightweight champion the rest of the way, mostly utilizing his left jab.[30] From the second round on, Gans suffered from a bloody nose and at least one devastating body shot that caused him to visibly express pain.[31] In the end, the fight was officially ruled a no contest, with four newspapers awarding a decision to Jack Blackburn, one to Joe Gans (*The Baltimore Sun*— Gans' hometown newspaper), and one local paper scored the bout a draw.[32]

Although not viewed as champion by the general public following the match, that did not stop Blackburn from referring to himself as one after his performance against Gans.[33] In his eyes, he didn't need a belt to strap around his waist, but as is true today, having one often means everything in boxing, especially for a relatively young up-and-comer like Jack Blackburn. So while having gained a great deal of respect from fellow boxers and boxing insiders alike due to his performance, Blackburn still found himself a long way from any kind of real fame or big money paydays.

After losing his next bout three weeks later via a very close six-round newspaper decision to Dave Holly in Philadelphia, Blackburn would travel up to Boston and face one of the greatest boxers of all times, heavyweight Sam Langford. Known as the Boston Tar Baby and Boston Terror, Sam Langford finished his career with an astounding record of 202 wins, with at least 127 KOs, 47 losses and 40 draws.[34] Strictly due to the color of his skin, Langford was frozen out of ever receiving an opportunity at the heavyweight championship, even by the first black heavyweight champion, Jack Johnson.

Only six weeks after his initial fight with Gans, Jack Blackburn squared off with Langford at the Central Athletic Club in Boston, on December 23, 1903.[35] While Blackburn had a three-inch height advantage, Langford maintained a significant weight advantage. Despite a lightweight being matched against a future heavyweight, and a very skilled one at that, Jack Blackburn went into Sam Langford's home turf and won a newspaper decision over the course of twelve rounds, according to the *Boston Globe*, *Boston Herald* and *Boston Journal*.[36] The official decision was a draw due to an agreement the bout would officially be scored even if it went the distance, but Jack Blackburn made his point.[37] Considering the weight differential and the opponent, the result is close to impossible to believe and may have been the greatest performance of his career.

By the close of 1903, Jack Blackburn's mind was on another crack at Joe Gans, but this time in a title fight rather than a non-championship affair. However, Blackburn faced a similar problem as that impacting Sam Langford in the heavyweight division. Being a black fighter meant a lack of financial backing to lure a titleholder into a championship fight. For example, Jack Johnson, who fought Sam Langford several times before winning the heavyweight championship of the world, stated he would gladly face Langford for the title if he could guarantee the champion's enormous appearance fee. The same would apply to Jack Blackburn, as he would have to acquire sufficient financial backing from supporters in order to make a championship fight with Joe Gans a reality.

In a sense, this was just another way of drawing the color line against black fighters, and it is ironic black fighters were denying other blacks much deserved opportunities, but the business side of the sport of boxing has often denied the most deserving. The American public, or the global public for that matter, wanted to see white boxers regain the throne of champion. Therefore, a premium was paid to witness such challenges, and white boxers thus had the financial backing necessary to put up considerable sums of money towards purses and side bets. There was very little demand to see a black boxer fight Joe Gans for his title because the idea of white superiority could not be reaffirmed under such a circumstance.

In light of this grim reality, Jack Blackburn would have to again settle for a non-title affair with the lightweight champion on March 25, 1904.[38] This time instead of the match being in Blackburn's adopted hometown of Philadelphia, it was in Gans' hometown of Baltimore and contested at the Eureka Athletic Club, which regularly featured the champion and represented his financial backing. The fight itself was contested seven pounds north of the 133-pound lightweight limit and over the course of fifteen rounds.[39] An obviously better prepared and motivated Joe Gans would show up to this encounter and avenge his poor showing from the previous year, as he easily whipped Blackburn for a fifteen-round decision. Jack Blackburn would complain about the decision and begin referring to himself as the lightweight champion of America, due to his past performances against Gans and the champion's refusal to meet him for the title.[40] In addition, it was Blackburn's belief that Joe Gans could no longer make the 133-pound limit, given the champion had not made that weight in almost two years.[41] Blackburn believed this rationale gave him some sense of legitimacy as champion, but of course that was his belief alone and one not shared by the general public or media.

It would be a little over two years later until he would get another chance to upend the champion, again in a non-title losing effort, and unfortunately for Jack Blackburn, the two would never meet again.[42] In desperate need of money and approaching the end of his career, Joe Gans would shed the pounds and focus his efforts on the likes of top white lightweight contenders Battling Nelson, Jimmy Britt and Kid Herman in big-purse title affairs. Denied a title opportunity with Gans, all Blackburn could do was continue to call the champion out and fight the best willing opponents across multiple weight classes.

Following the final match with Gans, Jack Blackburn went on a tear, going undefeated in his next twenty-four bouts before losing in January 1908 via a big upset to middleweight George Gunter, a sub-par fighter out of Australia.[43] According to newspaper accounts of the match, Gunter jumped out to a big lead over the first three rounds before being floored in the fourth from a Blackburn right hand to the jaw.[44] Blackburn followed up the fourth with a good fifth frame to draw even in the bout but received a beating in the sixth and final round that left the Philadelphia-based fighter wobbled at the closing bell.[45]

Despite the setback, Blackburn went on another impressive streak, going undefeated over the course of nine fights from January through May 1908, which included matches with formidable middleweights Jack Bonner and Mike Donovan, together sporting a combined record of 118 wins, 26 losses and 54 draws at the time of their fights with the Philadelphian, who was now referred to as "the Philadelphia Comet."[46, 47] The impressive run setup a big match for Blackburn against former world light heavyweight champion and world heavy-

Jack Blackburn's face shows a souvenir from a knife fight (photograph by *Chicago Daily News*, 1915, SDN-060115, Chicago History Museum).

weight title challenger Philadelphia Jack O'Brien. The June 1908 match was an all-action brawl, with O'Brien enjoying a fifteen-pound weight advantage and bringing into the fight an outstanding record of 91 wins, 5 defeats and 13 draws.[48] Both men were said to have "landed often enough to settle a half dozen battles."[49] The pace was very fast, with Blackburn hitting the mat compliments of an O'Brien left hook in the first round.[50] The second and third rounds were also won by the light heavyweight, who launched a vicious body attack and hurt Blackburn via an uppercut at the end of the second frame.[51] The last three rounds were much more even and highlighted by the sixth and final frame, which "was exceedingly fast and both landed nearly every blow sent forth."[52] Jack Blackburn would ultimately lose the fight by decision, but he impressed against the much larger and very talented man.[53] To put Blackburn's performance into perspective, Philadelphia Jack O'Brien would go on to fight heavyweight champion Jack Johnson to a six-round draw the very next year.

Jack Blackburn would finish a very busy 1908 with another long unbeaten streak, this time eleven.[54] What started as a disastrous year with a loss to mediocre fighter George Gunter, the year as a whole would be among the best of his career, as the lightweight notched a record of 17 wins, 2 losses, 2 draws and 1 no contest over the period.[55] Going into the new year, Blackburn was riding high on his accomplishments and fearsome reputation for taking on and defeating many of the best boxers in the world without regard to weight class. He didn't possess the lightweight title, but his career was certainly looking up and his talent could not be denied. Jack Blackburn was now among the best boxers in the world. But all of those good feelings and optimism quickly began to crumble before he even had a chance to ring in the New Year of 1909.

During the evening of December 30, 1908, in Philadelphia, a day after Jack Blackburn defeated Harry Mansfield via a six-round decision, while playing a poker game with his older brother Fred and likely engaged in heavy drinking, an argument broke out.[56] Fred Blackburn was also an accomplished boxer and had moved with his brother to Philadelphia in search of glory and riches in the ring. According to newspaper reports and a note on Boxrec.com, the argument was over insulting remarks Fred made about Jack's common law wife, a white woman named Maud Pillian.[57] (It is possible her name was actually Maud Pullian, according to census records around the time. How she actually met and became involved with Blackburn is not known, but her background was similar to Blackburn's. She was likely born in South Huntingdon Township, PA, outside of Pittsburgh.[58] She was a few years older than Blackburn and also grew up poor.[59] Her family lived with her maternal grandmother, and her father John was a coalminer.[60] Jack Blackburn was briefly based in Pittsburgh after leaving Indianapolis as a young man, so it is possible they could have met there while she was in her early twenties before moving to Philadelphia together.[61] During his relationship with Maud, Blackburn was having intimate relations with a black teenager named Ceceil, who gave birth to his son Joseph in 1907.[62] Jack would later end up getting married to Ceceil.[63]

Whatever Fred said to his brother Jack about Maud that evening, it caused a violent escalation in hostilities between the two men, culminating with Fred slashing Jack's face and throat with a knife.[64] Although the wounds were not life-threatening, the injuries did put Jack Blackburn in the hospital.[65] While he was a very tough man, the psychological wounds of being fiercely attacked by his older brother were deeper cuts than those left on his face and throat. His injuries meant a somewhat prolonged absence from the ring was in order, but approximately two weeks later Jack Blackburn's ring career would be the least of his worries.

His actions during the early morning hours of January 14, 1909, in Philadelphia, would forever change the course of the great fighter's life. Jack Blackburn took a taxi cab with his friend Alonzo Polk to a residence at 216 South Camac Street at approximately 3:00 A.M., where the men came upon their wives, Maud and Matilda (Mattie), in a physical altercation.[66] Instead of the men diffusing the situation, their involvement only made it worse. According to newspaper accounts of the event, at some point in the fight Jack Blackburn pulled a revolver on the couple, shooting and killing Alonzo Polk, striking him once in the neck and once in the abdomen.[67] Blackburn's story that he was simply trying to protect his wife may have held water had he not shot Mrs. Polk in the back as she reportedly tried to run for her safety.[68] While Mattie Polk would survive the shooting, her condition was very serious, requiring hospitalization.[69] There are secondary accounts that he also shot and killed his wife Maud during the incident, but primary sources reveal no truth to this story.

Jack Blackburn was booked at Philadelphia's Fifteenth Street Station on a charge of murder and would eventually be transferred to Moyamensing State Prison, where, it was rumored, the pugilist attempted to kill himself on January 30, 1909.[70] Although prison officials denied the rumor, newspaper accounts reported an attempted hanging, while the *New York Times* actually reported him dead as a result of suicide.[71] One thing was for sure, Jack Blackburn was not dead, and he would eventually pled guilty to manslaughter charges in June 1909 and was sentenced to fifteen years in prison.[72] At 26 years of age and in the prime of his career, his dream of becoming a recognized champion was now shattered.

While incarcerated Jack Blackburn did whatever he could to remain fit and was in hopes of receiving an early release. His friends and associates lobbied hard on his behalf for a pardon, among them former boxing adversary Sam Langford and civil rights advocate Booker T. Washington.[73] He reportedly even wrote a letter to heavyweight champion Jack Johnson, a man whom Blackburn despised, to help him win his release.[74] It is unclear whether Johnson ever offered any assistance, as the two had a running feud stemming from a heated sparring session years before that left the heavyweight champion with a bloody nose.[75] Blackburn also detested Jack Johnson's brash lifestyle, feeling the champion's behavior would inhibit black fighters' chances of ever getting future title opportunities in the ring. Serving as a boxing instructor for the prison warden and his three sons while behind bars, he eventually earned the good grace of the one man who could do something about his prison term.[76] As a result, after serving only four years and eight months of his fifteen year sentence, Blackburn was paroled and released for good behavior.[77]

Left to pick up the pieces from what was once a very promising boxing career, Jack Blackburn would continue to plug along in the ring for almost another decade, never being able to regain the fire and ability that inflicted so much destruction on opponents in the ring. Prison life, age and hard drinking had softened him, and in his first comeback fight on April 4, 1914, he weighed almost 20 pounds above his optimal fighting weight.[78] Although he would win the bout via a six-round decision, it would be eight more months before he would be in the win column again, losing five bouts in a row in between.[79] In his following five bouts from January to August 1915, he would win none, losing four, and manage to get one draw.[80] Jack Blackburn's time as a fighter at the elite level was long gone, and it was time for him to ponder a career change.

Years as Trainer

After concluding his fight career in 1923, he made his way to Chicago and went into the business of training fighters. Even though Blackburn was no longer fighting men inside the ropes, his life outside of them was spiraling out of control. Known around the various boxing gyms in Chicago for being a violent man with a terrible temper who always carried a piece, he kept even the most hardened fighters in fear.

Former pupil Joe Gramby said of Jack Blackburn during his training years, "A lot of people were afraid of Blackburn. He was a nice person, but when he was drinking, he was hell. He used to come up on the elevator, and if we heard him talking loud and all, we wouldn't train that day."[81] He began binge drinking often and could not get control of his alcoholism nor the violence that accompanied it.

During his tenure as trainer for "The Brown Bomber," Joe Louis, Jack Blackburn's life of heavy drinking and penchant for violence came to a head on the streets of Chicago's south side. On the evening of October 20, 1935, the former boxer and a man by the name of John Bowman were identified by witnesses as having engaged in a gun battle after the two were involved in a fist fight.[82] Allegedly, the twenty-four year old Bowman got the better of the fifty-two year old Blackburn in an alley before the former boxer and three other men arrived at Bowman's house later that night, where a gunfight broke out in the

Jack Blackburn with his protégé Joe Louis (Clay Moyle collection).

street.[83] Accounts of the incident placed each man on opposite sides of the street during the shootout.[84] Shot during the violent encounter were two innocent bystanders, a sixty-nine-year-old man named Enoch Houser and a nine-year-old little girl named Lucy Cannon, both of whom were shot on the side of the street where John Bowman was located.[85] Houser would eventually die from his wounds, while Cannon survived her own critical injuries. All fingers pointed to Blackburn as the trigger man.

Originally arrested on an assault with intent-to-kill charge, a private investigator hired by the dead victim's family determined Jack Blackburn was only questioned for ten minutes by police before being released on a $1,000 bond and without the signature of a judge, which was contrary to standard procedures and regulations.[86] The police denied the allegations, stating a judge's signature was obtained and Blackburn had been questioned for several hours before his release after posting bond.[87] Regardless of which version of the story is true, the tale of shoddy police work was embarrassing to officials, and Blackburn would be re-arrested on a manslaughter charge — this time being made to post a $10,000 bond before his liberty would be granted pending trial.[88] Although he would be acquitted of the charge the following year, the allegation itself was a dagger due to the likelihood he was involved in the tragedy inflicted upon Enoch Houser and Lucy Cannon.

For Jack Blackburn, his life would go on, and he would become well-known to the public as the trainer of future heavyweight champion Joe Louis. His association with "the Brown Bomber" actually began when the two were brought together a year before his legal troubles by numbers racketeers John Roxborough and Julian Black, both of whom owned a piece of Louis, who at the time was a very talented light heavyweight amateur boxer looking to turn professional. Blackburn was reluctant to take any black fighters under his tutelage due to the extra barriers they faced when it came to making big purses, but he relented and agreed to train the young Louis for his pro debut.

At the time, Joe Louis was known as a stick and move, defensive-oriented amateur boxer taught to fight in a manner to simply score more points than his opponent.[89] Jack Blackburn was charged with completely revamping his style to make it more conducive to the professional ranks. In particular, Blackburn focused on teaching Louis how to better throw his left jab, unleash his powerful right hand with more regularity, effectively cut off the ring and to fight on the inside.[90] As a result, Joe Louis was converted from a mover to a stalker, with exceptional balance in the ring. Blackburn's philosophy was black boxers were fighting with a deck of cards stacked against them, so instead of Louis looking to outpoint opponents and end up at the mercy of the judges, he should be aggressive and always look for the knockout.

The rest is certainly history, as Jack Blackburn would guide Joe Louis to the heavyweight championship of the world as well as twenty title defenses before meeting his own maker on April 24, 1942. Dead after fifty-eight years of life, Jack Blackburn will forever be most remembered for his association with Joe Louis rather than his own fight career, the knife fights or the shootings of Alonzo Polk, Mattie Polk, Enoch Houser and Lucy Cannon. An inductee into the International Boxing Hall of Fame for the work he did with Louis as a trainer, it is important to remember Jack Blackburn in his totality. Blackburn was a terrible drunk, and a brawler outside the ropes, as well as a convicted murderer, but he was also a world-class trainer and a tremendously talented boxer.

NOTES

1. "George C. Wright Entry." *Notable Kentucky African Americans Database.* 02 Jan 2010. University of Kentucky, Web. 2 Jan 2010. <http://www.uky.edu/Libraries/NKAA/subject.php?sub_id=64>.

2. "Frankfort, KY, Klan Violence." *Notable Kentucky African Americans Database.* 02 Jan 2010. University of Kentucky, Web. 2 Jan 2010. <http://www.uky.edu/Libraries/NKAA/subject.php?sub_id=64>.

3. Ibid.

4. "1882 in History." *BrainyHistory.com,* 2009. BrainyMedia.com, Web. 2 Jan 2010. <http://www.brainyhistory.com/years/1882.html>.

5. "John L. Sullivan." *Answers.com.* 2009. Answers Corporation, Web. December 3, 2009. <http://www.answers.com/topic/john-sullivan>.

6. Shaffer, Harry. "Son of a Preacher Man Part I." *antekprizering.com.* Web. December 5, 2009. <http://www.antekprizering.com/blackburnstoryparti.html>.

7. Bak, Richard. *Joe Louis: The Great Black Hope.* 1st ed. Dallas: First Da Capo Press, 1998, 45. Print.

8. Shaffer, Harry. "Son of a Preacher Man Part I." *antekprizering.com.* Web. December 5, 2009. <http://www.antekprizering.com/blackburnstoryparti.html>.

9. *1880 U.S. Federal Census, Woodford County, Versailles, KY.*

10, Ibid.

11. Ibid.

12. Ibid.

13. Ibid.

14. Kirsch, George B., Othello Harros, and Claire E. Nolte. *Encyclopedia of Ethnicity and Sports in the United States.* 1st ed. Westport, CT: Greenwood Press, 2000, 66.

15. 1900 U.S. Federal Census, Marion County, Indianapolis, IN

16. "Charles Henry Blackburn Entry," *Notable Kentucky African Americans Database.* 02 Jan 2010. University of Kentucky, Web. 2 Jan 2010. <http://www.uky.edu/Libraries/NKAA/subject.php?sub_id=64>.

17. Bak, Richard. *Joe Louis: The Great Black Hope.* 1st ed. Dallas: First Da Capo Press, 1998, 44.

18. "Straight Punch Too Much Neglected Blow." *Anaconda Standard* March 30, 1913, morning ed.

19. Ibid.

20. Ibid.

21. "Jack Blackburn." *Boxrec.com.* 2009. Boxrec, Web. December 13, 2009. <http://boxrec.com/list_bouts.php?human_id=11022&cat=boxer&pageID=2>.

22. Bak, Richard. *Joe Louis: The Great Black Hope.* 1st ed. Dallas: First Da Capo Press, 1998, 45.

23. "Jack Blackburn." *Boxrec.com.* 2009. Boxrec, Web. December 13, 2009. <http://boxrec.com/list_bouts.php?human_id=11022&cat=boxer&pageID=2>.

24. Ibid.

25. Ibid.

26. Ibid.

27. "Joe Gans." *Boxrec.com.* 2009. Boxrec, Web. December 13, 2009. <http://boxrec.com/list_bouts.php?human_id=9026&cat=boxer>.

28. Ibid.

29. Ibid

30. "In The Boxing World." *Racine Daily Journal* November 3, 1903, afternoon ed.

31. Ibid.

32. "Joe Gans." *Boxrec.com.* December 13, 2009.

33. Smith, Eddie. "Blackburn Will Claim Gans' Title." *Oakland Tribune* June 6, 1906, Afternoon ed.

34. "Sam Langford." *Boxrec.com.* 2009. Boxrec, Web. December 15, 2009. <http://boxrec.com/list_bouts.php?human_id=11023&cat=boxer&pageID=4>.

35. "Jack Blackburn." *Boxrec.com.* December 13, 2009. <http://boxrec.com/list_bouts.php?human_id=11022&cat=boxer&pageID=2>.

36. Ibid.

37. Ibid.

38. "Joe Gans." *Boxrec.com.* 2009. Boxrec, Web. December 13, 2009. <http://boxrec.com/list_bouts.php?human_id=9026&cat=boxer>.

39. Jack Blackburn." *Boxrec.com.* 2009. Boxrec, Web. December 13, 2009. <http://boxrec.com/list_bouts.php?human_id=11022&cat=boxer&pageID=2>.

40. Smith, Eddie. "Blackburn Will Claim Gans' Title." *Oakland Tribune* June 6, 1906, Afternoon ed.:

41. "Joe Gans." *Boxrec.com.* December 13, 2009. <http://boxrec.com/list_bouts.php?human_id=9026&cat=boxer>.

42. Jack Blackburn." *Boxrec.com.* December 13, 2009. <http://boxrec.com/list_bouts.php?human_id=11022&cat=boxer&pageID=2>.

43. Jack Blackburn." *Boxrec.com.* December 15, 2009. <http://boxrec.com/list_bouts.php?human_id=11022&cat=boxer&pageID=1>.

44. "Gunter Gets Decision — Bests Jack Blackburn in a Fast Six-Round Battle." *Washington Post* January 10, 1908: Sports Sec. Print.

45. Ibid.

46. Jack Blackburn." *Boxrec.com.* December 15, 2009. <http://boxrec.com/list_bouts.php?human_id=11022&cat=boxer&pageID=1>.

47. Kirsch, George B., Othello Harros, and Claire E. Nolte. *Encyclopedia of Ethnicity and Sports in the United States.* 1st ed. Westport, CT: Greenwood Press, 2000, 66.

48. Jack Blackburn." *Boxrec.com.* December 15, 2009. <http://boxrec.com/list_bouts.php?human_id=11022&cat=boxer&pageID=1>.

49 "Jack O'Brien Won From Blackburn." *Trenton Evening Times* June 11, 1908.

50. Ibid.

51. Ibid.

52. Ibid.

53. Ibid.

54. Jack Blackburn." *Boxrec.com.* December 15, 2009. <http://boxrec.com/list_bouts.php?human_id=11022&cat=boxer&pageID=1>.

55. Ibid.

56. Shaffer, Harry. "Son of a Preacher Man Part I." *antekprizering.com.* December 5, 2009. <http://www.antekprizering.com/blackburnstoryparti.html>.

57. Ibid.

58. 1880 U.S. Federal Census, Westmoreland, South Huntingdon, PA

59. Ibid.

60. Ibid.

61. Kirsch, George B., Othello Harros, and Claire E. Nolte. *Encyclopedia of Ethnicity and Sports in the United States*. 1st ed. Westport, CT: Greenwood Press, 2000, 66.

62. *1920 U.S. Federal Census, County of Philadelphia, City of Philadelphia*

63. Ibid.

64. Shaffer, Harry. "Son of a Preacher Man Part I." *antekprizering.com.* December 5, 2009. <http://www. antekprizering.com/blackburnstoryparti.html>.

65. Ibid.

66. Ibid. Camac Street is well-preserved in Philadelphia today. It is America's only wooden block street.)

67. Ibid.

68. Ibid.

69. Ibid.

70. "Jack Blackburn Said To Have Attempted Suicide." *Daily Kenebec Journal,* February 2, 1909.

71. "Negro Pugilist A Suicide." *New York Times,* January 31, 1909.

72. Shaffer, Harry. "Son of a Preacher Man Part I." *antekprizering.com.* December 5, 2009. <http://www. antekprizering.com/blackburnstoryparti.html>.

73. Kirsch, George B., Othello Harros, and Claire E. Nolte. *Encyclopedia of Ethnicity and Sports in the United States*. 1st ed. Westport, CT: Greenwood Press, 2000, 66.

74. Shaffer, Harry. "Son of a Preacher Man Part I." *antekprizering.com.* December 5, 2009. <http://www. antekprizering.com/blackburnstoryparti.html>.

75. Bak, Richard. *Joe Louis: The Great Black Hope.* 1st ed. Dallas: First Da Capo Press, 1998, 45.

76. Ibid.

77. Ibid.

78. "Jack Blackburn." *Boxrec.com.* December 15, 2009. <http://boxrec.com/list_bouts.php?human_ id=11022&cat=boxer&pageID=1>.

79. Ibid.

80. Ibid.

81. Bak, Richard. *Joe Louis: The Great Black Hope.* 1st ed. Dallas: First Da Capo Press, 1998, 45.

82. "Joe Louis' Trainer Jailed In Shooting." *Bismarck Tribune,* October 21, 1935: 2. Print.

83. "Blackburn in Pistol Battle." *Hammond Times,* October 21, 1935: Sports sec. Print.

84. Ibid.

85. Ibid.

86. "Louis' Trainer Whitewashed; Probe Begun" *San Antonio Light* November 18, 1935: 9A. Print.

87. Ibid.

88. "Sports of Sports." *Signal* November 23, 1935: 6.

89. Bak, Richard. *Joe Louis: The Great Black Hope.* 1st ed. Dallas: First Da Capo Press, 1998, 48.

90. Ibid.

CHAPTER 11

Sam Langford: Heavyweight Champion of Australia, Canada, England, and Mexico

Clay Moyle

Sam Langford, the "Boston Tar Baby," became a professional boxer at the age of 16. By 17, he had already worked his way up the professional ladder with 26 fights to face his first world champion, the legendary Joe Gans, the "Old Master." Langford fought a second world champion, Joe Walcott, in his 36th professional fight, when he was 18. Langford spent the first quarter of the twentieth century and the rest of his fighting life engaging in over 300 officially recorded professional boxing contests, with numerous other bouts likely lost to history. It is a sad irony that this great ring warrior, who began his career fighting world champions, ended with every boxing title known around the world tacked onto his name except *World Champion*. Langford *was* denied the opportunity because he was, simply, too good.

Short statured at only 5' 7" and weighing no more than 170 to 180 pounds in his prime, the Boston dynamo struck terror in the hearts of most of his contemporaries, including the great heavyweight champions Jack Johnson and Jack Dempsey. In 1910, Langford's billing read, "The Man Jack Johnson is Afraid to Meet."[1] In 1916, when Jack Dempsey was only three years away from defeating Jess Willard for the heavyweight crown, Dempsey was offered the chance to fight an aging — but still dangerous — Langford, but he quickly declined. Recalling the incident years later in his autobiography, Dempsey wrote, "The Hell I feared no man. There was one man, he was even smaller than I, I wouldn't fight because I knew he would flatten me. I was afraid of Sam Langford."[2]

Samuel Edgar Langford was born in the small Canadian community of Weymouth Falls, Nova Scotia, on March 4, 1886. Sam's mother, Charlotte Langford, stood only 5 feet tall. His father Robert, on the other hand, was a big, strapping man, 6' 3" tall and known to possess a quick temper. There is evidence that a Weymouth heavyweight fighter named Michael McGowan died from a head injury suffered in a fight with Robert.[3]

The Langford family's path to Nova Scotia can be traced back to the American War of Independence. During the war, the leader of the British forces promised freedom to any slaves who would flee their masters and fight for the British king. Over 2,000 black slaves accepted the offer. When the British evacuated in 1783, thousands of people loyal to the

Sam Langford: "I carry my own referee," 1913 (George Grantham Bain Collection, Library of Congress).

British crown fled for Europe, and other communities in British North America. Weymouth, Nova Scotia, was one of many coastal towns that received a large number of settlers. Sam's great grandfather, William Langford, enslaved to Captain Langford of Shrewsbury, New Jersey, was one of them.[4]

Sam was only twelve years old when his mother passed away and after one too many whippings from his father he ran away from home.[5] Initially, he found work as an ox-driver and log hauler, but also spent time working as a cabin boy aboard a ship, and later in a logging camp for three years, before accepting the offer of a doctor to work on his farm in New Hampshire. When he lost that job for fighting with other boys on the farm he walked to Cambridge, Massachusetts, where he worked briefly in a brickyard, then in a saloon, and finally in a lumber camp, all the while sleeping in parks, before landing a job as a porter for a small boxing club operated by Joe Woodman. In addition to cleaning and helping set up and break down for shows, for which he was provided earnings and a place to sleep, Sam would occasionally be called upon to serve as a sparring partner when no one else was available.[6]

Finding that he enjoyed the fight game, young Langford asked Woodman for the opportunity to appear on one of the club's fight cards whenever another boxer failed to show. But Joe told him that if he wanted to box with professionals, he first needed to learn how to fight with the amateurs. After earning a few gold watches for his amateur victories, worth a lofty $20 a piece, Sam was hooked. He began sparring with Jimmy Walsh, a Boston bantamweight who later became a featherweight champion. Realizing Langford's talent as an amateur, Woodman declared Sam a professional at age 16. In his boxing debut, April 11, 1902, Langford kayoed Jack McVicker. Sam's ability was so promising that Woodman left his club operations to become Langford's full-time manager.[7]

Langford began his career as a lightweight, but as he continued to mature physically, he worked his way up through the welterweight, middleweight, light-heavyweight, and ultimately heavyweight divisions, despite being no taller than 5'7".

Most of Sam's early professional bouts took place in and around Boston, usually at the Armory Athletic Associations, clubs where billiard tables were removed to make way for ringside chairs and bleacher seats, or in small, private clubs, attended by members and their friends. The vast majority of fights in the early part of the twentieth century took place in these two venues throughout the United States.

On December 8, 1903, Sam shocked the boxing community when he won a 15-round

The Boston Tar Baby in fighting pose, 1909–1910.

decision over the great lightweight champion, Joe Gans, the first African American to win a world championship (a title he won in 1902). In a prearranged agreement for fees, champion Gans was paid $700 for the fight and Langford, $250. Had it not been for the fact that Sam weighed in for the contest a few pounds over the lightweight division limit, he would have become a world champion at the young age of 17. Later that night after the fight, Gans approached young Langford and said, "Boy, you're going to be a great fighter someday. You're the first man that ever puffed my lips. Take care of yourself, don't get a big head and nobody can keep you from being a champion."[8] Gans went on to hold the title for another five years.

Sam was still growing, and after the Gans bout, he decided it was too difficult to make weight for lightweight contests. He moved up to the welterweight division where he continued to hone his skills against a number of tough, seasoned veterans, such as Jack Blackburn, Dave Holly, and George "Elbows" McFadden, men who had campaigned for a number of years against some of the toughest and most skilled competition in the game.

On September 5, 1904, Sam was matched with another world champion, Joe Walcott, the "Barbados Demon," this time for the world's welterweight title. Walcott was only 5'2" tall, but he had long arms, a powerful physique, and a punch like the kick of a mule. Both Langford and Walcott are listed among *Ring* magazine's one hundred greatest punchers of all time.[9] In a newspaper story leading up to the fight, reporter Tad Dorgan (noted for his sporting cartoons and his ability to pin colorful nicknames on many of the fighters of his day), sought out a number of fans and asked who they thought would win the upcoming match. A group of young black women replied, "Why our baby of course." Tad asked, "Walcott?" The girls laughed and replied, "Don't you know that Sam Langford is our baby?" Dorgan combined their tag line with Sam's dark skin and the fact that he was fighting out of Boston to come up with the nickname that stayed with Langford the rest of his life, the "Boston Tar Baby."[10]

After fifteen rounds, the match between the welterweight champion Walcott and Langford was ruled a draw by the referee, at which the majority of those in attendance howled their displeasure. Sam had dominated the first seven rounds, regularly landing his left jab to Walcott's face, and landing right hand uppercuts and hooks to the body, despite the latter's crouching tactics. Although the champion became the aggressor over the second half of the fight, Sam scored heavily with counter blows, and even out-boxed Joe.

Arthur Lumley, editor of the *New York Illustrated News,* who sat ringside that night wrote, "The spectators were much displeased by the decision, as the rounds story was one clearly in favor of Langford. He had earned the right and should have gotten the decision."[11] For the second year in a row Sam had come close, but failed to become a world champion.

Langford never got another opportunity to fight for a world title despite the fact that he was a leading contender for a number of years. The only other world champion that he faced was middleweight champion Stanley Ketchel, in April of 1910, but that was in a pre-arranged, no-decision, six-round contest.

After a relatively tame opening round, the action picked up in the second session, both men throwing heavy blows. Langford staggered Ketchel with a left to the face in this round. He bloodied Ketchel's nose in the third round and began to land hard punches with greater frequency. Late in the round he stunned the champion, but to the crowd's great surprise made no attempt to follow up on his advantage.

Langford eased up in the fourth round. The match was rumored to be a preview for a forty-five round title bout on the West Coast later that year, and he had no desire to jeopardize his opportunity to secure a more lucrative title bout with the champion. But while boxing on the defensive in this session Langford miscalculated, and provided Ketchel with an opportunity to land a vicious right hand underneath the heart. The blow might have cost Langford the fight if Ketchel hadn't allowed him to fall into a clinch and recover from its effects.

Ketchel remained the aggressor in rounds five and six, Langford seemingly content to continue to box on the defensive, occasionally stopping to deliver countering punches, and the contest was ruled a draw upon it's conclusion. Newspapermen covering the fight reported differing opinions as to who the victor was, but the general belief seemed to be that Langford had carried his opponent and had his sights set on a follow-up match for the title. Unfortunately, Ketchel was murdered later that year and it never took place. Sam would never get another shot at a world title.

Some boxing enthusiasts still argue to this day as to who got the better of that short contest. It has been reported that when Sam received the news of Ketchel's death, he said simply, "Poor Steve (Stanley's nickname), he went to his grave thinking he could really lick ol' Sam."[12]

The fact that he didn't end up getting a second opportunity to fight Ketchel and prove his superiority to those who felt Ketchel the better man bothered Sam for many years. In late 1910 Langford got so upset about an article written on the fight by Bob Edgren, reporter and cartoonist for the *New York Evening World,* that he sat down and wrote the sportswriter a letter. Edgren quoted the letter in his November 3, 1916 column:

Dear Mr. Edgren, I am always glad to see you or any other person giving Stanley Ketchel a boost. He deserves it. Your boost for the late Stanley Ketchel last week read all right excepting for the part where you said he nearly knocked me out in our six-round rumpus in Philadelphia. To be real frank with you, I will say that you are greatly mistaken, for the simple reason that he never had a chance. I could say much more, but rest most assuredly I told you a mouthful. Respectively yours, Sam Langford.[13]

Heavyweight contest between Iron Hague and Sam Langford at the London Sporting Club, England, May 24, 1909. When Hague knocked Langford down, the English crowd yelled "Here, here!" When Langford got back to his corner and asked what all this "here, here" was about, he was told that the English were cheering. When he went out for the fourth and final round and knocked Hague out, he yelled to the crowd "There, there!" (Clay Moyle collection).

In December of 1905 Sam was matched against his first heavyweight opponent, a tough, 26-year-old black contender named Joe Jeannette. Joe was only thirteen months into his professional career, but he'd already logged fourteen fights — including three that year against future heavyweight champion Jack Johnson. In Jeannette, Sam found himself facing a man five inches taller and forty to forty-five pounds heavier.

Sam tried unsuccessfully to employ the same tactics against Joe that he'd used so effectively against opponents his own size, and took a real beating until he refocused his attack on the bigger man's body. But the punishment he absorbed in the early rounds proved too much to overcome, and his corner men threw in the sponge at the conclusion of the eighth round rather than risk any permanent damage.

Far from being disheartened by the defeat, Sam felt he had learned how to fight effectively against bigger men. He was confident the result would be different the next time the two met, and he proved it four months later, almost knocking Jeannette out in the final round of a decisive fifteen-round-decision victory.

In an article published by *Boxing Illustrated* Jennette said, "Langford was the greatest fighter who ever lived. Sam would have been champion any time Johnson had given him a fight. And Johnson knew it better than anybody. Man! How that baby could hit," Jeannette often exclaimed while rubbing his oval jaw. "Nobody else could hit like that. Well, maybe Joe Louis could," he conceded in later years. "But don't forget that Sam only weighed about 160 pounds. Louis was about 195."[14]

The Joe Jennette–Sam Langford bouts set the stage for a contest on April 26, 1906, with an even more formidable black heavyweight title contender, Jack Johnson. According to the *Boston Globe* no one expected the bout to last the scheduled fifteen rounds because Johnson would be too big for Sam. And it was true that the 28-year-old Johnson had an advantage of at least five inches in height, and 30 to 40 pounds on the smaller 20-year-old.

Johnson administered what Sam later said was the only real beating he ever suffered in the ring. By the end of the contest there was no doubt that Johnson had won a convincing decision. Sam was exhausted and his face was very badly bruised and puffed, while Johnson, though tired, was relatively unmarked.

Sam won many fans for his performance against the bigger man. The *Boston Globe* wrote that though beaten, he proved beyond doubt that he is one of the gamest fighters that ever stepped into the ring.[15] The *Boston Morning Journal* called it "a superb exhibition of grit and courage, making other local exhibitions of gameness in the ring seem insignificant."[16]

Langford's fighting heart, and the dynamite that he carried in his fists, convinced Johnson that it would be wiser to seek paydays against less dangerous opponents. Approximately two and a half years after fighting Langford, Johnson was in the midst of his pursuit of a title bout with the reigning heavyweight champion Tommy Burns, but found himself stranded in London without the necessary monies to follow Burns to Australia. England's National Sporting Club stepped in to provide the necessary funds on the condition that should Johnson win the title, he would return to make his first title defense before the club against Sam Langford, who had won many fans in England.

Johnson subsequently obtained his match for the title and captured the crown with a convincing 14th round stoppage of Burns on December 26, 1908. However, rather than return to England to face Sam Langford, who had added another 30 pounds of muscle to his frame since their earlier encounter, he immediately backed out of the signed letter of promise he'd provided to the club. Johnson maintained that the money offered by the club was insufficient and that his manager had signed the agreement without his approval. The club countered by producing the document that Johnson himself had signed. But it was to no avail, Johnson had other plans. Over the ensuing years the Tar Baby and his manager,

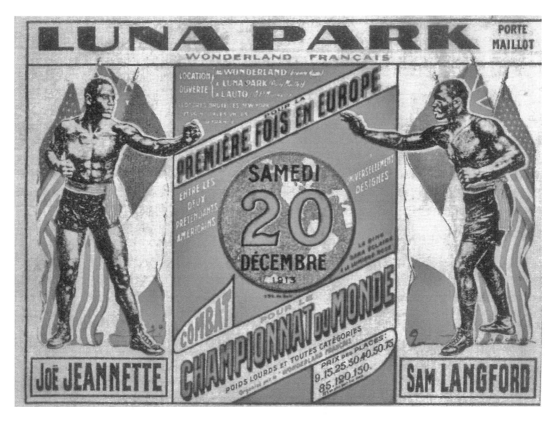

French advertisement for the Sam Langford–Joe Jennette bout December 20, 1913, Paris (Clay Moyle collection).

Joe Woodman, hounded Johnson endlessly in futile pursuit of an opportunity to fight for the title. But the two would never meet again in the ring, Johnson declining all future offers for a rematch with Langford.

"Nobody will pay to see two black men fight for the title," Johnson said. But quickly tiring of the subject, Johnson admitted to one of the many promoters who tried to match the pair, the great Australian boxing promoter, Hugh "Huge Deal' McIntosh, that he had no wish to face Sam again, saying, "I don't want to fight that little smoke. He's got a chance to win against anyone in the world. I'm the first black champion and I'm going to be the last."[17]

Many years later, in a Boston nightclub in the early 1940's, Johnson confided in Kevin Aylwood, a trustee of the New England Sports Museum. When asked what he thought of the Boston pug, "Sam Langford," Johnson replied, "was the toughest little son of a bitch that ever lived."[18]

An Australian trainer named Duke Mullins, the only man who trained both fighters, substantiated in his memoirs what McIntosh said about Johnson's reluctance to face Langford a second time. According to Mullins, Johnson was never anxious to talk about Sam, and always quickly changed the subject whenever Sam's name was mentioned. However, one day when dismissing Langford from a conversation, Johnson said there were dozens of easy money white men for him to meet without having to fight a tough guy like Langford. While Johnson told Duke that he felt heavyweight Joe Jeannette was the toughest man he ever saw, he also admitted to him that Langford was the most dangerous.[19]

Johnson would get no argument regarding Langford's capabilities from Joe Jeannette. Jeannette and Johnson faced each other in the ring no less than eight times prior to Johnson's becoming the champion. Those eight meetings resulted in three no-decision contests, one draw, three decision victories for Johnson, and one win on a foul for Jeannette. But it was Langford, whom Jeannette fought 14 times and suffered his only knockout against, that Johnson held in the highest esteem.

After his match with Johnson, Sam continued to mature physically and although he didn't grow any taller than 5' 7," he filled out considerably, developing into a legitimate light-heavyweight with long arms, wide shoulders, and a deep barrel chest. He proved more than a match for the best heavyweights of his era. In fact, he not only routinely defeated most of the leading contenders of that period, a number of them a full head taller and as much as 30 to 40 pounds heavier, but knocked out many of them. An excellent judge of distance and skilled in the art of feinting, Sam could deliver a knockout blow with either hand.

While he never received an opportunity to fight for another world title after his 1904 contest with Joe Walcott, he did go on to capture the heavyweight titles of countries such as England, Australia, Canada, and Mexico, the last two titles coming while fighting blind in one eye.

Langford permanently lost the sight in his left eye during a 1917 match with Fred Fulton when the bigger man landed a heavy blow to the temple that Langford said felt "like a thousand needles shoved into his skull."[20] He'd suffered a detached retina in a period of time when little could be done to reverse the damage.

Remarkably, Sam fought at least 107 times with only one eye over the remainder of his career. He captured the Mexican heavyweight title when his eyesight was so poor that he had to rely upon his handlers to help guide him into the ring and to his corner. His assistants were so concerned about his eyesight that they wanted to call the fight off. But Sam wouldn't hear of it. He needed the money.

"Don't worry about little Sammy," he said, "I don't need to see that boy, I just got to feel him."[21]

His opponent was 24 year-old "Kid" Savage, the reigning champion of Mexico.

Savage was extremely cautious, running around the ring, and making sure to keep his distance, as Sam struggled to follow his movements around the ring.

He would get a bearing on Savage's location and rush him in an attempt to corner him. He managed to catch Savage near the ropes, and successfully measured him for a right uppercut that landed on the chin, knocking Savage out approximately one minute and forty-five seconds into the first round.

But Sam's best days were well behind him by that time. He fought on for another two years while his eyesight continued to fail, until finally in August of 1926 in his last professional bout he was forced to quit in the opening round of a fight when it became obvious that he couldn't see his opponent at all.

Sam was most likely at his peak from late 1906 thru most of 1914, when he lost only two out of 87 fights, one of those losses a highly disputed bout against Sam McVey in Australia where the referee misinterpreted their rules against infighting, and the other a decision loss to Jim Flynn, which he avenged a few months later.

Almost one-third (96) of Sam's fights (over 300) came against eight large heavyweight opponents. Included among those eight men were Harry Wills, who stood 6'3" tall and weighed 210 to 230 pounds, whom he fought 17 times, and "Battling" Jim Johnson, who stood 6'3" tall and weighed 220 to 240 pounds, whom he fought 12 times, and Big Bill Tate, who was 6'6" and 226 pounds, and whom he faced eight times. These men were legitimate heavyweights, even by modern standards, but little Sam Langford's record boasts victories over every one of them, and numerous victories over others of similar physical stature.

An English depiction of Sam Langford from the magazine *Sporting Budget*, February, 1911 (Clay Moyle collection).

It was a very difficult time for a black fighter, especially if you were very talented. Some states would only allow fights between men of the same race (Tennessee, for example) and a number of white fighters drew the color line, refusing to fight a black man. Even Jack Johnson refused to fight black fighters after winning the title, claiming the public had no interest in paying to watch two black men fight for the heavyweight crown.

Under different circumstances Sam might easily have become a world champion in four, or even five, weight classes. He was often accused of holding back and of participating in a number of fights of dubious nature. Sam always denied involvement in any fixed fights but he did later admit to taking it easy on an opponent from time to time when it made economic sense to do so.

Commenting on the subject and referring to himself in the third person, Sam said, "In all the years that little Sammy was out there strutting his stuff, there was not one time when Sammy had an agreement with the other boy. Little Sammy did do some agreeing about fights, but he did all of it himself. If in some of my fights I didn't try to kill the other boy, it wasn't because I told him I wouldn't."[22]

Sam said that only once did he break his promise when he agreed with himself that he wouldn't hurt the other fighter too much, and that was in the fight where Joe Jeannette suffered the only knockout of his career. Sam was fighting Joe in Rochester and he agreed (with himself) that he wouldn't hurt Joe too much because they were going to have another fight shortly thereafter, and he didn't want to knock Joe and himself out of some additional money.

So he went along doing his best to throw a number of fearsome looking blows and did such a good job of it that even Joe thought he was trying to knock his brains out. Joe attempted to respond in kind, and about the same time that Sam wound up and started a big right from somewhere in the vicinity of the floor, Joe tore in and a punch that Sam meant to miss him with landed flush on the point of his chin. Joe crumbled to the floor and was counted out, and Sam claimed that out of all the surprised people in the place, he was the most surprised of all.[23]

In addition to being a remarkable fighter, Sam was also a very colorful and witty individual with a keen sense of humor. When he traveled to England for the first time in 1907 the matchmaker of the National Sporting Club asked to meet with him regarding the selection of a referee. Sam advised them that he'd brought his own referee. Incredulously, they advised him that was completely out of the question. Sam just gave them a big smile, raised his right fist in the air and announced, "Here's my referee, a referee that can give the right decision every time."[24]

When he first met the 6'3" "Battling" Jim Johnson, the much taller man reportedly looked down upon Sam and remarked, "Look out boy, I is bad medicine. I was born with boxing gloves on my hands." Unimpressed, Sam simply smiled and replied, "That's nothing big boy, the first time I hit you, you is going to die with em' on!"[25]

On another occasion, upon entering a New York arena, Sam came across his opponent, John Lester Johnson, stretched out on a rubbing table with a handler fanning him and inquired, "What are you doing boy?"

"Just taking a little nap," replied Johnson.

"Why now? You're gonna' be taking one in that ring," replied Sam.[26] He stopped him in the first round.

When he fought Andre Anderson in Buffalo, New York on August 17, 1917, Sam called Howard Carr, Anderson's promoter, over for a private conversation twenty minutes before their bout. Leaning in so that nobody else would hear what he said, Sam smiled and said, "I likes you Mr. Carr, and for that reason I am tipping this off to you. Tell your man not to lead with his chin when we get in the ring." Howard laughed and returned to his fighter. Despite reportedly "carrying tons of fat," Sam earned a second round technical knockout against the badly outclassed Anderson. When declared the winner, Sam turned toward Carr and shouted, "Your man failed to follow instructions!"[27]

Joe Louis and Sam Langford, 1935 (Clay Moyle collection).

By 1944, 18 years after his retirement from the ring, Sam was blind, and all but forgotten, living in poverty in a dingy tenement in Harlem. In January of that year a sportswriter for the *New York Herald Tribune* by the name of Al Laney decided to write a story
about Langford, a great boxer who had seemingly fallen off the face of the earth. Since Sam's
last known residence was in Harlem Laney decided to focus his efforts there.

The search proved futile for quite a while. Many people Laney questioned about Sam's
whereabouts were not even aware of who Langford was. At least a dozen others knew who
Sam was, but claimed to know that he was dead. Eventually, Laney learned that Sam was
in fact alive and residing in the city on 139th Street. A woman at the front desk confirmed
that Mr. Langford was, indeed, living there and led him to a tiny dirty bedroom at the end
of a dark hallway on the third floor. It was there that he finally found Sam, just one month
shy of his 58th birthday, sitting on the edge of his bed listening to an old radio.

Laney learned that Sam had all of 20 cents in his pocket and that he was getting by
on a few dollars he received each month from a foundation for the blind. Other than twice
a day when two young boys would come and fetch him to take him to a restaurant for
breakfast and then again late in the afternoon for a second meal, Sam told Laney that he
spent all of his time sitting alone in the dark bedroom, listening to the radio.

When he'd gathered the information he needed for his story, Laney went back to the office and banged out the story on his typewriter for the paper. But he didn't stop there. He was so moved by Sam's situation that he initiated a drive on his behalf in conjunction with a group of New York businessmen and women that ultimately resulted in setting up a trust fund worth $10,892. Included among the 705 individuals who contributed to the fund were men like Jack Dempsey, Beau Jack, Fritzie Zivic, boxing promoter Mike Jacobs, Joe Louis, and famed New York nightclub owner, Toots Shore.

The fund was administered by the Guaranty Trust Company. Sam was provided with an initial payment of $125, followed by $75 per month until April of 1945, after which the balance of $9,000 was invested in an insurance company so that Sam would be provided with an annuity that would guarantee him $49.18 a month for life.

In 1952 Sam moved back to Boston. By early 1953, he was living at the William Tell Hotel, a gloomy establishment inhabited primarily by persons with little means. Located across the street from the hotel was Bill's Lunch, a small bar on Cambridge Street, which served as Sam's last place of employment and hangout for nearly two years. The bar's owner, Phil Barbanti, an ex-fighter himself, idolized Sam. Each day, Barbanti would send a man over to Sam's hotel to pick him up and bring him over for lunch. Sam would sit in a booth drinking beer and spinning tales of his boxing career to the customers. Barbanti had a sign outside the bar advertising Sam as an attraction. In return Sam received his meals, all he cared to drink, and ten dollars per week. Sam didn't think much of the modern crop of fighters, outside of Joe Louis, whom he declared was the greatest counterpuncher he'd ever seen other than Joe Gans. As for the rest, Sam said: "These fellows today don't know how to feint a man. Only a few of them know how to hook. They dance around. They run sideways, but they don't fight."[28]

Sam lived out the last few remaining years of his life being cared for in a private nursing home. He passed away on January 12, 1956, less than two months shy of his 70th birthday, and only ten weeks after being enshrined into boxing's Hall of Fame. At the time of his induction into the Hall, he was the only non-world title holder to be honored in that manner.

Ring magazine founder and original editor Nat Fleischer once said of him, "Sam was endowed with everything. He possessed strength, agility, cleverness, hitting power, a good thinking cap and an abundance of courage. He feared no one. But he had the fatal gift of being too good and that's why he often had to give away weight in early days and make agreements with opponents. Many of those who agreed to fight him, especially of his own race, wanted an assurance that he would be merciful or insisted on a bout of not more than six rounds."[29]

Leading heavyweight contender Harry Wills said that when Sam hit you in the body you'd kind of look around half expecting to see his glove sticking out of your back. He claimed that Sam was the best fighter he ever fought. "He was a real professional," Harry said, "The kind of fighter you'd like to be but know that no matter how hard you try you'll never make it. Sam never made a mistake, he always held command and when he knocked me out in New Orleans in 1916, I thought I had been killed."[30]

"Gunboat" Smith, who faced heavyweights Jess Willard, Frank Moran, Jack Dempsey, Fred Fulton, and Harry Wills, claimed that Langford was the greatest he ever saw, and that nobody else came close to being as good as he was at his peak. He said that Sam ruined him in their last fight, and that he was never the same afterward.[31]

Another of his opponents, "Fireman" Jim Flynn had this to say about Sam's punching power: "I fought most of the heavyweights, including (Jack) Dempsey and (Jack) Johnson, but Sam could stretch a guy colder than any of them. When Langford hit me it felt like someone slugged me with a baseball bat."[32]

The great former lightweight king, Frank Erne, when asked in the 1950's what he thought about Langford replied: "I'd pick him to knock out Joe Louis, Jack Dempsey and Rock Marciano. When he was not under wraps, he was a ring marvel."[33]

Other leading sportswriters of that era had even higher opinions of Sam. Hype Igoe, well-known boxing writer of the *New York Journal,* proclaimed Sam the greatest fighter, pound for pound, who ever lived. Joe Williams, respected sports columnist of the *New York World Telegram,* wrote that Langford was probably the best the ring ever saw, and the great Grantland Rice described Sam as "about the best fighting man I've ever watched."[34]

Sam never regretted his chosen profession and expressed no bitterness or remorse over the loss of his eyesight. He maintained a keen sense of humor and kind disposition throughout his life and always said that boxing provided him with a wealth of memories. In a statement attributed to him a few months before his death, Sam said, "Don't nobody need to feel sorry for old Sam. I had plenty of good times. I been all over the world. I fought maybe 600 fights, and every one was a pleasure."[35]

NOTES

1. "Langford Comes Today: Will Box With Armstrong," *Indianapolis Star,* October 31, 1910.

2. Jack Dempsey, *Dempsey,* 3.

3. J. W. Philbrick, *Descendants of Michael McGowan of Liverpool, Queens County, Nova Scotia.*

4. "Here And There With G.R.T.," *Digby Courier, Canada,* July 22, 1938.

5. "The Greatest Fighter Who Ever Lived," *MacLeans, Canada,* February 1955.

6. "Sam Langford, Heroic Figure ... Tragic Figure," *World Boxing,* July 1973, 24 – 28.

7. Ed Hughes, "Tribute to Sam Langford," *San Francisco Chronicle,* January 18, 1927.

8. The fight between Joe Gans and Same Langford is discussed in detail in: Clay Moyle, *Sam Langford: Boxing's Greatest Uncrowned Champion,* 28–37.

9. "100 Greatest Punchers of All-Time," *Ring Yearbook,* 2003.

10. Robert R. Richards, "The Amazing Langford," *Fight Stories,* Winter 1948, 30 – 63.

11. Nat Fleischer, *Black Dynamite: The Story of The Golden Era of Jack Johnson, Sam Langford and Their Contemporaries,* 133 – 135.

12. For a discussion of Langford's thoughts about his fight with Ketchel, see Clay Moyle, *Sam Langford: Boxing's Greatest Uncrowned Champion,* Ch. 11 "Ketchel."

13. Robert Edgren, editorial, *Syracuse Herald,* November 4, 1916.

14. Sam Laine, "Joe Jeannette," *Boxing Illustrated,* November, 1958, 33.

15. "Decision For Texas Man," *Boston Globe,* April 27, 1906.

16. "Langford Loses In Game Fight," *Boston Morning Journal,* April 27, 1906.

17. "Laughing Sam Langford. The Black Tornado." *Knockout,* 1936.

18. Glenn Stout, "Fighting Blind," *Boston* magazine, February 1987, 91–94.

19. "Was Johnson Afraid of Langford?," *The Sporting Globe,* December 4, 1937.

20. "Sammy Langford Explains Why He Quit to Fred Fulton at Boston," *Halifax Herald,* September 18, 1924.

21. "Sammy Langford Wins Mexican Title by Knocking Out Several Opponents: Blindness Forces Complete Retirement," *Halifax Herald,* September 18, 1924.

22. "Sam Langford Lifts Veil From His Shrouded Past for Herald Readers: Former Nova Scotian A Real Pug," *Halifax Herald,* August 11, 1924.

23. "Langford Says His Knockout of Joe Jeannette in 1916 Was a Miracle: Meant to Swing Wild at Big Black," *Halifax Herald,* September 11, 1924.

24. Nat Fleischer, "The Langford Legend," *The Ring,* March 1956, 44–45 and 59.

25. Bob Edgren, "That's What Made 'Em Champs," *The Ring,* April 1936, 8–9.

26. Clay Moyle, 262–263.

27. *Milwaukee Free Press,* untitled, August 18, 1919.

28. Allan Morrison, "Amazing Career of Sam Langford," *Ebony,* April 1956, 97–98; 101–105.

29. Nat Fleischer, "The Langford Legend," 44–45.

30. "Sam Langford. The Ali of His Generation," *International Boxing,* March 1972, 56–61.

31. Unknown newspaper article source by Alfred Dayton, May 18, 1930.

32. Langford Considered a Terrific Puncher. *Washington Post,* May 6, 1923.

33. Ace Foley, "The Weymouth Wizard," *The Ring*, October 1954, 29, 47.

34. Trent Frayne, "The Greatest Fighter Who Ever Lived. *MacLean's,* February 1955, 28, and 63–69.

35. Alexander Young, Jr., "The Boston Tarbaby," *The Nova Scotia Historical Quarterly*, Vol. 4, No. 3, September 1974, 277–293.

CHAPTER 12

Joe Jennette and Sam McVey: Colored Heavyweight Champions

Alexander Pierpaoli

Heavyweights have always driven the sport of boxing. Heavyweights are the biggest of men, titans capable of separating a man from his senses with a single blow. From the days of the great John L. Sullivan and his proclamation that he could lick any man in the house, it has been boxing's unlimited weight class that captures the public's imagination, transcends the sport, and puts asses in seats. At the turn of the twentieth century, the Heavyweight Championship was passed from the pound-for-pound great, gangly and freckled Bob Fitzsimmons to the beefy and hirsute James J. Jeffries, when Jeffries kayoed Fitzsimmons in 11 rounds at Coney Island in June of 1899. Jeffries held the title for six years and retired undefeated, but just months later he was back in the ring in ceremonial stature, now serving as referee in a bout in Reno, Nevada, between the top contenders for his own championship title. Marvin Hart, the Fighting Kentuckian, squared off against Jack Root, a native of Czechoslovakia, who fought out of Chicago, and in the twelfth round Hart smashed Root with a vicious right to the chest that put Root down. Referee Jeffries counted him out. Thus Hart inherited the title of the heavyweight king, not through blood combat, but by proclamation and by proxy.[1]

It was probably earlier that year, in March of 1905, that Hart had solidified all credibility as heir to the heavyweight throne with his surprising 20-round decision victory over one of the very best of the age, or at least the most infamous, the "Galveston Giant," Jack Johnson. Johnson was a top heavyweight contender who was locked out of the title picture at the time. Johnson was barred from a shot at the heavyweight championship, not due to a lack of pugilistic merit, but because his skin was black.

Although boxing has always been an international sport drawing its champions from around the globe, four of the five men who held the heavyweight title from John L. Sullivan to Hart were Americans by birth—white men, the lot. In the United States, the years between 1889 and 1903 witnessed a period of intense racism when, on the average, two blacks were killed by lynch mobs each week; hangings, burnings and mutilations were commonplace.[2] In large portions of the United States the white establishment used state-

Editors' note: Jennette and McVey, like many boxers of their time, had their names spelled in a variety of ways in the press and elsewhere. The most common variations from the above are Jeannette and McVea.

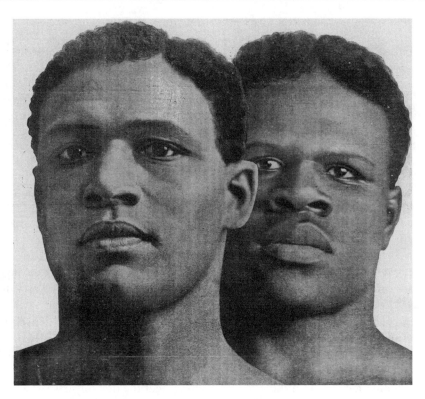

The bottom half of the Big Four, Joe Jennette (left) and Sam McVey, would be forever paired in boxing history (*LaVie Au Grand Air*, Paris, February 20, 1909).

sponsored racism in the form of Jim Crow laws to ensure blacks remained second-class citizens. It was a time of burgeoning empire, and the dark-skinned athletic native existed on the periphery of colonial powers and in the collective unconscious of white America. President Theodore Roosevelt had supported an exhibit at the St. Louis 1904 World's Fair which was said to prove true the theories of Darwin in which Filipinos were displayed as living examples of man's descent from the apes.[3] The exhibit was a gross distortion of the naturalist's theories, but it meshed with the popular sentiment of the age. The U.S. Congress had passed a law annexing the Philippines in 1900, and while American GIs were fighting the rebels in the Philippine jungles, they often referred to the darker-skinned resistance as "niggers."[4] The summer of 1905 saw the U.S. Navy set sail on an Imperial Cruise in which "President Roosevelt agreed a secret treaty that allowed Japan to expand into Korea."[5] Roosevelt's fascination with the Japanese after their victory over the Russians in the Russo-Japanese war made him believe they would be a worthy surrogate to push American interests in Asia. His actions in the summer of 1905 lit the fuse of Japanese expansionism which culminated in their push for a Pacific Empire in 1941.[6] In 1907 the U.S. Navy's "Great White Fleet," consisting of sixteen new warships, was sent on a 14-month-long voyage around the globe in a grand pageant of American sea power. President Roosevelt, a former assistant secretary of the Navy, believed only through a strong navy could America project her power and prestige abroad.[7] The flotilla of warships were all painted white shortly after the end of the Spanish-American War; intertwining whiteness and might together in a display of global dominance.

Joe Jennette (*left*), victor of the great 1909 Paris fight, and Sam McVey (*right*), who battled Langford through 228 rounds, Jennette 111 rounds, and Johnson 53 rounds (photograph dated December 4, 1919; George Grantham Bain Collection, Library of Congress).

Although the general American public was charged with the prevailing sentiments of the time, the athletes, in many cases, respected each other, something unavoidable in a competitive contact-sport like boxing. Fighters develop camaraderie beyond race and ethnicity when they engage in hand-to-hand combat in the squared circle, learning and exploiting each other's weaknesses within the established rules of the game. But the sport has always been steered by what promoters are willing to stage for the public and what will sell. Mixed-race bouts led to problems with local authorities and crowd control, complications that reduced the likelihood of profitable gates. In many places mixed-race bouts were illegal and would be stopped by local authorities and police. In 1901, Jack Johnson spent a month in jail after losing to Joe Choynski when police stopped the bout. Both Choynski and Johnson were jailed together for participating in a mixed-race bout. The pugs ended up trading fight moves and sharing fight strategy; and while spending a month together in the clink, they became friends.

It was a time of white supremacy, and white men dominated boxing's glamour division. There had been great black heavyweights before, men like Thomas Molineaux, Peter Jackson, and George Godfrey, who got close to but were ultimately blocked from competing for the title. The tradition of drawing the color line and barring fighters of color from a chance at the title began with the great John L. Sullivan, who didn't include black men in his open challenge of licking any and every man in the house.[8] Before the bare knuckle days passed to the Marquis of Queensberry rules, the closest any black man came to the heavyweight crown was Thomas Molineaux's defeat at the hands of Tom Cribb and the Englishman's overzealous supporters. But at the start of the twentieth century and with little hope of reaching the pinnacle of the sport, along with Jack Johnson came three other black heavyweight contenders of such skill, character, and physical prowess that they became legendary in the sport.

Together, they were known as the Big Four or the Fearsome Foursome. They were a quartet of heavyweights, all active from 1903 through 1921. Much of their careers are in dispute, from the spelling of their names to the validity of some of their victories. Jack Johnson, the man who did become Heavyweight Champion, was shadowed by Sam Langford, Joe Jennette, and Sam McVey, three greats who were repeatedly blocked from competing in a championship bout, even by Johnson himself.

Through some cosmic dirty trick of birth-timing came four great heavyweights, all active at a time when the boxing establishment was simply unwilling to allow them entry to the championship realms. All great heavyweight champions are defined by the quality of their opposition and the decisiveness of their victories. Heavyweight rivalries capture the imagination. What would Marciano have been without Walcott and Charles, Joe Louis without Schmeling and Conn, Ali without Liston and Frazier, Lennox Lewis without Holyfield and Rahman?

Great heavyweight champions have multiple fights with multiple arch-opponents. They don't necessarily have to be great fights — nothing can stink like a bad heavyweight fight — but they are always dramatic fights. Champions of any weight need to fight the best available challengers in order to maintain credibility in their role as champion. Despite Jack Johnson's tremendous accomplishments as a champion, he failed to do that. In fact he didn't just avoid fighting one of the top contenders, he refused to fight any of the top three.

Johnson vowed to be the first Negro to win the heavyweight title — he also vowed to be the last.[9] Johnson's decision to deny other blacks a shot at his title was at least self-perpetuating, but it cheapened the title and denied boxing history a glimpse of what might have been. In other eras, the Big Four might have swapped the championship back and forth among themselves, with the champion losing to the top-ranked contender only to take on the next challenger. But due to Johnson's insistence on financially unachievable purses, promoters' fears of race riots, and the fragile sensibilities of an American public that feared the potential dominance of a dark-skinned athlete, three of the Fearsome Foursome had to settle for battling each other over and over again, toiling for smaller purses than their white counterparts, and repeatedly fighting other black boxers of the age — competent and dangerous contenders with vivid and active names like Battling Jim Johnson, Denver Ed Martin and Black Bill.

Without a shot at the true heavyweight championship, Langford, Jennette and McVey had to settle for a sort of everlasting, best-out-of-three tourney amongst themselves. And that's exactly what they ended up doing. Among the Big Four, McVey and Langford battled through 228 rounds, the most in total number; Jennette and Langford are second, having warred with each other through 161 rounds; and Joe Jennette and Sam McVey clashed through 111 total rounds. But history places Jack Johnson firmly in the Big Four's number-one spot. It was Johnson who had a 15-round win over Langford, got the better of Jennette in the 53 rounds they battled each other, and bested McVey in the 60 rounds that they boxed.

James Arthur Johnson, known as Jack Johnson, Li'l Arthur, or Papa Jack, was the first black heavyweight champion of the world, and is the most well-known of the Big Four. His impressive strength and size, defensive skills, and smile of gold are emblazoned in the annals of fistiana. Johnson's powerful punch, coupled with his defensive mastery, kept him far ahead of many of the white fighters of the time, who tossed defense aside in favor of aggression and pressure.

Johnson was skilled at in-fighting; the part-grappling, part-wrestling tangle of arms in which fighters, heavyweights especially, try to gain advantage over each other in close, often partially clinched, and using just one arm to tuck uppercuts under the guard to the chin or rip short hooks to the body. Johnson was infamous for mocking his white foes at close-quarters, another sign of his fistic precociousness; he was very much aware of the psychological warfare that should be part of any good fighter's strategy for dominance in the ring.

Sam Langford, a Canadian, the only non–American of the quartet, was likely the most talented fighter of the four. Langford will be remembered, like Stanley Ketchel, Henry Armstrong and Bob Fitzsimmons, in a multi-divisional pound-for-pound class by themselves. Langford started his career as a lightweight and beat some of the best in the world from 135 pounds right on up the scale through the welters, the middles, light heavies and even heavyweights.

Langford had only one bout with Jack Johnson, and when they met, the great Sam L. weighed 156 pounds and Johnson 185 — a middleweight versus a cruiserweight in modern terms. Langford's stocky build, long arms and bone-crushing power in each fist made him a threat to all adversaries who faced him. Even late in his career, when fighting long past his prime and blind in one eye, he was being ducked and dodged by the best fighters in the sport.

The remaining half of the Foursome, Jennette and McVey, fought a five-bout series that must be considered one of the greatest heavyweight rivalries in the history of the prize ring. The 111 rounds Jennette and McVey fought included a 49-round finish fight in Paris in 1909 which became the stuff of boxing legend. Boxing is about styles, and Joe and Sam had the kind of contrasting fighting styles that made for exciting bouts. Jennette was a finesse and an endurance fighter. He wore guys down; he didn't flatten them with power punches. McVey, on the other hand, was a bruiser. Hard charges and wild swinging, coupled with short chopping punches in close, were typical of McVey's style. In short, the fights between Jennette and McVey were the prototypical *boxer versus puncher* match-ups in terms of style, the same that have produced some of the sport's most thrilling bouts through the ages.

Their names were routinely misspelled in newspapers, but worse than that injustice was the dramatic liberty American journalists took to describe non–Caucasians that ranged from the creative to the downright vicious. Words and phrases like *dark-meat, Negro-boy, chocolate-colored, coon, smoke, dinge, ink-spot, black plague, tar-babies, coloreds, Ethiopians,* and *Sambo* were all used to describe any of the Big Four or their African American contemporaries.

The American press was fearful of and fascinated with these exotic looking men who tended to fight more strategically than their white counterparts. Could the white race be the inferior? What did it mean if the black athlete supplanted the white man as the strongest and fastest? White supremacy couldn't be all that supreme if the Big Four were around, right? These questions loomed large behind the boxing coverage of the period, and the fighters helped to answer these questions with their ring tests and toils.

Joe Jennette and Sam McVey were two of the many African American boxers of the age who journeyed "along the routes of imperialism and industrialism" starting their careers "as they labored on commercial and military ships, in the dockyards of international ports, and in the underground life of the city."[10] They turned away from backbreaking manual labor and chose the quicker money in the prize-ring, and as spectacles of athletic power

The man Parisians called "Our Sam" (December 4, 1914, George Grantham Bain Collection, Library of Congress).

"they became ever more ubiquitous figures of fear and desire."[11]

It was into that world of duality for the African American that Joe and Sam first started boxing.

Sam McVey

Samuel E. McVey, or McVea, as the most commonly used alternative is spelled, was born in Waelder, Texas, on May 17, 1884. McVey stood five-foot-ten-and-a-half-inches tall and was thickly muscled. During his fight career, he tipped the scales at two-hundred-five to two-hundred-twenty pounds.

It is unclear as to what McVey sounded like because his speech was usually transcribed in an exaggerated dialect, with "th" used in place of the letter "s" and similar mocking ways in which the American press tried to add auditory verisimilitude to their sports reporting. McVey was dark-skinned and "fierce-looking."[12] His appearance was considered ugly by the Anglo-Saxon, preferred standards of the day, his broad nose, thick lips, and projecting lower jaw all culminating in a look often described as "African Black."[13]

McVey was a man with many crosses to bear. While American society mocked McVey's visage and speech, he suffered the physical insidiousness of bunions and had to wear special shoes both inside and outside the prize ring.[14] As a teen McVey did the work of the California day-laborer, picking beets in the hot sun. But McVey, perhaps realizing the power of his phenotype, learned he could make far more money and make it a lot faster working in the ring instead of working on a farm.

He was just shy of 18 years old when he fought his first bout. He strung together six kayos before the end of his first year as a pro, fighting consistently in Southern California, Oxnard or Los Angeles, where he was a crowd favorite. Sam was a brawler and a knockout fighter from the start. He used aggression and pressure to plow through some of Southern California's best, and in his seventh bout he met Jack Johnson. By then the boxing world was abuzz with the young Californian's early success and considered McVey "a tough customer, capable of taking a good licking and coming back."[15] Jack Johnson had also noticed Sam, as he recounts in *My Life & Battles*:

> I knew perfectly well that Sam McVey was a tough man to beat. I had seen him sparring at the club a number of times and realized that he knew more about boxing than any other pugilist I had fought, with the exception of Joe Choynski. He [McVey] was heavier than me and very quick on his feet....[16]

When they met for the first time, it was over the twenty-round distance, and Johnson came away with the decision, proving far too much for the bullish youngster. But McVey's stock was strong in Southern California, and despite his loss, the regional papers thought him "one of the few men who ever stood up to the mighty boxing champion, Jack Johnson."[17] McVey was so popular that after scoring two more victories, including a first-round kayo of Denver Ed Martin, the betting public was clamoring for a rematch with Jack Johnson.

They got it, and Johnson and McVey met a second time in Los Angeles just a few days before Halloween on October 27, 1903. The bout was similarly one-sided with McVey charging and Johnson parrying, slamming right hands into the onrushing McVey's face. Johnson "punished McVey severely and escaped without a mark" dropping McVey three times with hard rights only to see McVey spring up after each knockdown, "full of fight, forcing it at all times."[18]

Johnson came away with another decision win, but so marketable were the two that they were matched a third and final time just six months later in April of 1904. But McVey's third and final bout with Johnson was less than thrilling, especially for the Oxnard youngster who was stopped by a monster right hand from Johnson at the end of twenty lackluster rounds. Reports suggest the bout was little more than a stinker, with Johnson and McVey doing lots of clinching. McVey fought in a safety-first mode, keeping his chin down below the line of fire of Johnson's right hand as he came forward into clinch after clinch. The crowd saw McVey as completely outclassed and "began to 'boo' Johnson for hanging back."[19] Johnson came alive in the twentieth round to finish McVey just before the final bell. Geoffrey Ward describes the bout's climax and the treatment Johnson received:

> What one newspaper called Johnson's "detachment" so enraged some fans near his corner that between rounds they began flipping lighted matches onto his back. Finally, with just thirty seconds to go in the last round, Johnson mounted a furious assault, sending McVey reeling back toward the ropes. As he bounced off them again, Johnson caught him with a perfect right hand.
> A gang of Oxnard fans who had again bet on their favorite and lost stormed up the aisle, shaking their fists at Johnson and shouting, "Kill that nigger!" As they stepped up into the ring, he hurled the contents of his spit bucket at them, then vaulted out the other side, fled up the aisle "at ten yards per second," he remembered, and escaped into the night. He took refuge in an Oakland sporting house until things calmed down.[20]

With a crowd response like that, it is tempting to speculate as to how much of a beloved fighter McVey really was in California. One wonders whether his largely white audience saw him as anything more than just a betting favorite, perhaps because of his intimidating look.

McVey had five more fights in California, and then in April of 1907 he fought his one and only bout on the East coast. In New York City he battled Joe Jennette for the first time. Choosing to seek bigger paydays in Europe after the loss, Sam shipped out. Eventually McVey would pick up the nickname of the Colored Globetrotter, fighting in France, Australia, Argentina and Panama before the end of his career. By June of 1907 McVey was across the pond in the United Kingdom, where he knocked out Ben Taylor in just three rounds. He fought the Frenchman Marc Gaucher, knocking him out in four rounds in November. McVey stayed in France where he rapidly rose to stardom.

Joe Jennette

Born Jeremiah Jennette in North Bergen, New Jersey, on August 26, 1879, Jennette worked for his blacksmith father, shoveling coal into trucks and delivering it to customers, hard physical labor that paid little. Joe Jennette was a strong and athletic young man who stood five-foot-ten-inches tall and weighed between 185 and 203 pounds.[21] Joe was light-skinned and strikingly handsome. He was described as "a black Adonis; a magnificently proportioned man" who was "never a braggart nor a clown, but led a quiet disciplined life."[22]

Joe had been a success as a street fighter, and on a dare at the age of 25, he passed through one of the only doors open to an athletic black youth — boxing.[23] He was quite the prodigy, starting his career late. He was twenty-five and he learned fast as a pro.

Joe lost his first two professional fights to Morris Harris, another member of the pool of black heavies who fought each other over and over for small purses before small crowds[24]. In his third bout Jennette fought Black Bill, aka Claude Brooks, yet another experienced member of the "dark-meat branch of the swatter's union."[25] Black Bill knocked Jennette out in two rounds, a defeat Joe avenged twice before the end of that first year as a pro. Within just a month and a half Jennette had avenged the defeat to Black Bill by decision, and he fought Bill a third time in less than four months and stopped him in 7 rounds. Before the end of the year, Bill and Joe were in the ring yet again and they settled for a draw after 6 rounds on November 2, 1905.

Such was the norm for the African American pugilists of the day; contenders did battle against each other on multiple occasions often trading victories and defeats according to who was in better condition at the time. Facing the same foes again and again could be dangerous business as the combatants learned each other's strengths, weaknesses, and subtle tricks of the sweet science. The strength of character these men must have had cannot be understated. In Jennette's case, his character was something almost as supernatural as his endurance. Today, a young man who dropped his first two fights by decision and a third by kayo would probably start looking for another career; not so for Jennette. He went on to avenge himself against Morris Harris in June of 1907, the third time they met in the ring.

Jennette learned by immersion, fighting against the top black contenders of the day in Morris Harris, Black Bill and George Cole from the start of his career. From his debut on November 11, 1904, to Christmas day 1905, Joe Jennette went 7–4–1 with 3 knockouts and those seven wins included stoppage victories over Jack Johnson (by DQ) and a kayo win over Sam Langford in the first twelve bouts of Joe's career. Jennette fought out of Hoboken, New Jersey, and he was soon being called the Hoboken Negro in press reports.

From November of 1905 to November of 1906, Joe met Jack Johnson six times; the year before they had fought twice in one month. Jennette finished 1–3–1 with 3 no-decisions with Johnson. Their styles meshed well, making for interesting bouts if not brutal encounters. Johnson even took a liking to Jennette, as is suggested in his autobiography: "Joe and I met up so often that it became a game for us and we genuinely enjoyed it. In our second fight, a six rounder, a very serious match with lots of skill on both our parts, I lost on a foul in the second round. Later on that season, we fought again in Baltimore, and I won in fifteen rounds. I must admit that Joe Jennette fought one of the most terrific fights of his life on that occasion ... then I returned to Philadelphia, where I fought a six-rounder no decision, with Joe Jennette. Jennette was definitely my favorite partner. We put on another beautiful fight for the good people of Portland, Maine; those ten rounds ended in a draw."[26]

Jack and Joe fought mostly "spirited exhibitions" as both men came to learn the "other's style so well that every move called forth the perfect counter-move" moving together "as synchronistically as a man and his shadow."[27] But the prevailing opinion of the day was that it was Johnson who controlled the action; and although Jennette was the "only man of his own color capable of competing with him," Johnson was Jennette's "master at all stages of the game" and "could have done with Jennette just as he pleased."[28] But it was unlikely things would stay that way. Joe Jennette turned to professional boxing late in life, compared to most fighters, and he learned fast. His prime was still to come in 1906 when Jennette fought Jack Johnson for the last time. After that, Johnson wanted no more to do with the Hoboken Negro, and Jennette was forced to look elsewhere for lucrative and competitive bouts. It wasn't long before he found young Sam McVey.

In 1909 Teddy Roosevelt, now a private citizen, went on an African safari and witnessed a lion hunt, which was described vividly in American newspapers, giving readers a taste of life outside the empire's edge where black-skinned men still fought tooth and claw with savage beasts. At the time, France had its own imperial hopes and dreams which included efforts to colonize dark Africa; there were French colonies in Senegal, Congo, Niger, Chad, Guinea and Sudan. Despite France's status as an empire it did not have anywhere near the climate of domestic racism as the United States, perhaps because they did not have a plantation-driven

Tom Kennedy and Joe Jennette (Bains News Service 1910–1915, George Grantham Bain Collection, Library of Congress).

economy like that of the American South. In the U.S. the freeing of the slaves unleashed great fears upon the white status quo. White men were threatened economically as they would now have to compete for jobs with these freed men. More threatening still was the idea of sexual competition; black men competing for white women. But in France there was less of that, and as early as 1848, the abolitionist Frederick Douglass had described the French attitude towards blackness in a speech in New York. Douglass remarked that "in France the Negro was a man."[29]

Atop the heavyweight division sat Canadian Tommy Burns. Burns claimed he would fight anyone for the title, even a black man, but he proceeded to price himself out of a match with Johnson by demanding higher and higher purses as the negotiations got close to a deal. Johnson was in line for a title shot, and of the Big Four, he was the most insistent on getting one and the most deserving. He had beaten Langford, had three wins over McVey, and was 3–1–1 over Jennette. Even though they might not have liked it, "boxing writers were now virtually unanimous that Johnson deserved a shot at Burns' title, just as he had when Jeffries and Hart had held the championship."[30]

Finally, Johnson got a hold of Burns in Sydney, Australia, where an upstart young promoter named Hugh McIntosh was able to put together the place and purses to get Johnson his chance at the title.[31] Johnson lacked the funds to get to Sydney and was loaned the money by Mr. Bettinson of London's National Sporting Club on the condition that Johnson agree to defend the title against Sam Langford should he become champ. Johnson soundly defeated Burns, but the defense against Langford never materialized.[32]

Before the Sydney bout, Johnson had followed Burns to France in June of 1908, hoping a title bout could be made there. Some speculation existed about a title fight in Paris with Johnson's old opponent Sam McVey. McVey had already been living in Paris and was 5–0, all by kayo. While in town, Johnson and his wife, Hattie, went out socializing with McVey. They were photographed making the rounds at Paris nightspots together, the two black fighters towering over French patrons.[33] In France, black prize-fighters were considered more than men, they were athletes who straddled the savage world of the prize-ring where they represented the black-skinned primitive in short-pants, and on the boulevard they cut a striking contrast with the typical white crowd that frequented the cafes and night-spots.

The French light-heavyweight Georges Carpentier was just getting his start in the prize-ring at the end of 1908, and he met Sam and Joe in Paris. Carpentier's take is eluci-dating in that he was a white Frenchman and a prizefighter, a member of the same world as McVey and Jennette, but one unencumbered by the limitations of complexion which they suffered. Carpentier's fascination with color was not as hard-edged as was often seen in American fighters despite the fact that he used the derogatory vernacular of the age to qualify his view of the black American heavies. Carpentier described meeting Jennette and McVey in Paris in his autobiography, *My Fighting Life*:

> From America [came] two remarkable negroes Sam McVea and Joe Jeannette, at that time as near as possible world's champions. They were Negroes of a strikingly different type. Joe Jean-nette would pass for a bronze statue. He was not coal black as was McVea; neither was he so forbidding to look at. McVea was frankly a nigger; Jeannette, dark chocolate. A more attractive, even handsome, Negro I have never seen. And in his ways he had none of the obtuseness of many coloured gentlemen. He was quiet; he did not swagger around the cafes, nor did he go strutting along the boulevards."[34]

Carpentier's description of Joe and Sam was far more nuanced than that of other prize-fighters. Former heavyweight champion, James J. Corbett, who was now writing about box-ing in the *Chicago Daily Tribune*, described Jennette's and McVey's reception by the Parisian public and sounded just as envious as he was bigoted. Corbett wrote that in Paris "the colored man has it all his own way, with both Sam McVey and Joe Jennette heroes in the public eye."[35] Corbett had little respect for Sam McVey, perhaps because of McVey's "African Black" appearance. "I have more respect for Jeannette than I have for McVey," wrote Corbett. "The latter is not worthy the name of a fighter. He has more of the attributes of a swell-headed 'con-man' than a pugilist."[36] Perhaps the idea of McVey dressed to the nines and welcomed at all those Parisian operas was too much for Corbett's small mind to handle. But whether Corbett liked it or not, in Paris, McVey was the toast of the town.

After defeating seven opponents in just over a year, all by knockout, McVey agreed to a mixed-fighting-style bout versus a London-based jiu-jitsu master, Judoka Tano Mat-suda. The fight took place on December 31, 1908, in Paris, and the pageantry lasted far longer than the match itself. McVey charged across the ring at the start of the bout, feinted Matsuda with his left, and ripped a right uppercut to the chin that flattened the jiu-jitsu master. The fight lasted all of ten seconds and added to the mystique of McVey as *L'Idol* of Paris.[37]

Meanwhile, Joe Jennette, hearing of McVey's bankability and soft schedule, headed to Paris "to seriously tap the Paris honey-pot."[38] Upon arriving in France Jennette turned a horse stable into a training camp, and his management organized ladies' teas and charged for graded seating from which to watch the black American train.[39] America seemed sure Paris' females were drooling over Jennette, the strong American Negro, and the virile black man loomed large in white consciousness. At the same time these American fears were being played out in the miscegenation drama that surrounded the persecution of Jack Johnson for his obsession with white women. While in France, the physical appeal and attraction behind McVey's status as the Idol of Paris heralded a "growing fetishism of the black male body."[40] But the Parisian women who visited Jennette's ticketed work-out luncheonettes were less than thrilled. Perhaps having savored McVey's knockout streak, the ladies expected more violence. In one training session Joe went as far as to let one of his sparring partners, Marc Gaucher, a French former champ, hit him in the head without Jennette doing anything to defend himself. Nonplussed female fans "argued that the French champion must be weak: He can't break one of Jeannette's teeth!"[41]

Jennette debuted in Paris against Ben Taylor, who Sam McVey kayoed twice the year before. Jennette stopped Taylor in three rounds, made good money doing it, and decided to stay. Soon Jennette and McVey were set for a rematch.

They had first met at Lyric Hall in New York in April of 1907. Sam weighed 208 and Jennette, 185. The bout had been "an interesting encounter, punctuated with many telling blows and a good show of science."[42] Jennette used movement and did most of his work from "long-range," while McVey used wild rights and "scored at close-quarters."[43] McVey's right eye was cut during the bout, and his "face was puffed and bruised." Joe Jennette had helped make up Sam McVey's mind to set sail for Europe, and now a year and ten months later they were in each other's sights again, traveling gladiators ready to do battle in another of the world's cities.

On February 20, Jennette and McVey met for the second time. The bout was held at the Cirque de Paris and lasted the twenty-round distance. McVey landed the harder blows from the start and dropped Jennette three times enroute to the decision win.[44] But the crowd was less than thrilled. Although the fight had been brutal at times and exciting, it was on the whole "unsatisfactory." There had been boos and rumors started that the two fighters had gone easy on each other.[45] Fixed fights were certainly not unheard of at the time, but the crowd may have mistaken lulls in the action and combat at close quarters for a lack of decisiveness.

Heavyweight boxing is a different type of boxing. Expert boxing commentator Steve Farhood noted how watching the heavyweights is almost like watching an entirely different sport when compared to the other weight classes. He uses as his example the Lennox Lewis versus Michael Grant bout in New York City in which Lewis dropped Grant four times on the way to a second round KO victory. Noting that two of the knockdowns came from blows landed while Lewis was holding Grant, Farhood points out that with heavies, the referee's final instruction of *protect yourself at all times* bears the most weight with the big men. The pure brute physicality of the combatants has an enormous impact on how heavyweight boxing tends to unfold. The big men, when they are exciting, deliver thrills greater than any other weight class. But when the combatants' styles don't mesh well or one fighter chooses to survive rather than compete, fights get rough and ugly and boring. Such was the case at the start of the twentieth century and is still the case today. Nothing stinks like a bad heavyweight bout.

But Joe and Sam always made for competitive fights, and much of the disappointment about their February bout stemmed from the fact that Paris' beloved McVey didn't win and win big as he had every other time through the ropes in Europe. In some American papers the French were mocked for their dislike of a fight that didn't end in a knockout and their passion for McVey's "inaccurate, nasty-whizzing uppercuts with which Sam misses all his opponents" while being unappreciative of "all Joe's splendid science."[46]

The *Washington Post* reported that the referee had announced Jennette the winner that night, but after hearing the response from the crowd, changed his mind and raised McVey's hand to the delight of the crowd.[47] The *San Antonio Light* described it as a great 20-round battle that "sets French sports wild."[48] Writing about Jennette and McVey's first Paris bout in her article "Visible Men: African American Boxers, the New Negro and the Global Color Line," Theresa Runstedtler of the University of Buffalo noted that despite rumors of a fix, the sentiment was not at all unanimous as displayed from letters to the editors of Parisian papers:

> Countering such opinions another fan wrote a blistering defense of the fight, maintaining that those who questioned the match's veracity were simply uncivilized people "whose keen desire was to see a boxing ring transformed into a bullfighting arena." As this fan so astutely observed, underlying this controversy were basic assumptions about the inherent savagery of black men and about the viciousness of African combat, especially since these allegations almost never arose in response to matches involving white boxers.[49]

Whether it was a communal sense of bloodlust or just the need to see McVey drop Jennette and keep him down, the rubber match was to be a fight to the finish. There would be no limit in rounds and the fight would continue until one man gave up. Jennette's record going into the rubber match was 20–9–5[13] while McVey was 24–5[23]. The edge in youth, strength and size all went to McVey, while Jennette's edge was in skill and experience. They were 1–1 against each other and McVey was favored going into their third encounter, primarily due to his popularity in Paris.

On April 17, 1909, Jennette and McVey fought a 49-round bout that according to Nat Fleischer's *Black Dynamite Vol. IV Fighting Furies* included 46 knockdowns, and raged on for 3 hours and 45 minutes into the wee hours of the morning.[50] But could that be possible? How could human beings take that sort of punishment? Perhaps the truth is that they probably didn't.

Despite his position as boxing's sacred cow, the founder of *The Ring*, Nat Fleischer's recounting of boxing history often used enthusiasm to make up for its inaccuracy. Historian Kevin R. Smith, author of *Black Genesis* and *The Sundowners*, the groundbreaking history of the black prize-fighter, comments on Fleischer's accuracy, or lack thereof, in the *Black Dynamite* series: "Fleischer was also unabashed in his use of poetic license, making up sources and fictionalizing events when unable to unearth the true facts. Some of his conclusions are downright ludicrous and have done more to further mystify and confuse the history of several of these fighting men than to clarify their lives, careers and impact."[51]

But whether it was Fleischer who started the rumors about the Jennette-McVey finish fight or not, his book *Fighting Furies* certainly propagated them, and his authoritative reputation made it likely future boxing writers kept looking to Fleischer as a detailed source, thus ensuring the spread of inaccuracies.

Like a "Super-Fight" of today, the organizers and public worried how late the fight would start, just like they worry about with late-starting, modern pay-per-view fights.[52]

Jennette-McVey was the main event of a seven-bout card that featured French regional bouts on the undercard. The crowd was a raucous 2,500, less than half the Cirque de Paris's capacity, as rumors of the first bout being fixed had no doubt hampered ticket sales. Understandably, the 49-round bout took on a legendary quality and with no instant media and no replays, details were lost or misreported almost immediately.

Forty-nine rounds were rounded up to fifty in the headlines of early reports, "the contest lasting for three hours and a half" in a bout that saw Jennette using "effective infighting" to rally back after being "so groggy he could barely keep on his feet," McVey's handlers "threw up the sponge" at the start of the 49th giving Jennette the TKO victory.[53] The *New York Times* of April 18, 1909, mentions no knockdowns at all, and the same story was picked up in papers all across the U.S. but in varied lengths. In the *Atlanta Constitution*, the *Billings Daily Gazette* and in Pennsylvania's *Daily Courier*, there are no mentions of any knockdowns at all. Wouldn't Fleischer's number of 46 knockdowns be a memorable enough detail to have made it into the initial reporting of the bout? Wouldn't it be noteworthy enough to mention even in an abbreviated story on the fight? According to the first press reports Nat Fleischer is off by 15 minutes and about 38 knockdowns, give-or-take.

But confusion seemed to reign. A longer version of the same *New York Times* article appeared in the *Washington Post* and contradicts itself in a count of knockdowns; attributing 3 knockdowns of Jennette to McVey in round 19, only to say they occurred in the 17th three paragraphs later.[54] But the *Post's* article also described the use of oxygen in the corners between rounds by the handlers of both fighters and that Jennette benefited more from the practice. In the *New York Sun*, oxygen was given credit for changing the course of the bout.

Oxygen had first been used in conjunction with boxing just a few months prior, in autumn of 1908. Dr. Leonard Hill of London Hospital had incorporated the use of an oxygen cylinder attached to a rubber bag connected to a hose from which the fighter would breathe between rounds.[55] Dr. Hill believed the oxygen treatment was most beneficial to an athletic man in aiding recovery during strenuous exercise, a practice some felt was unsportsmanlike.[56] But Hill vehemently defended the use of oxygen explaining that it was for the athlete's greater health benefit and recovery: "Almost the whole of modern sport is conducted with artificial aids. The record feats of today are too often not sport but deadly earnest business."[57]

Boxing has often been called the hurt business, and Jennette and McVey's finish fight certainly fell under that umbrella. The *New York Sun* went as far as to suggest the bout had little significance other than serving as a dramatic spectacle.

> The contest will not improve the standing of either man. McVey showed himself slow and lacking in ability to take advantage of openings, while Jeannette demonstrated his lack of a winning punch. As an exhibition of recuperative power on Jeannette's part, however, and of endurance and stamina on McVey's, the contest was remarkable for its brutality. Curiously enough, brutal as it was, it was devoid of ferocity, the men exhibiting an almost friendly spirit throughout the fight."[58]

Jennette and McVey respected each other tremendously and their sportsmanship must have stood in stark contrast to those who expected a vicious, animalistic clash pitting one primitive savage against another. Boxing has always been part sport, part spectacle, and as such it is experienced differently by each individual according to what they bring to the match. With oxygen bottles in the corners, fans hoping for a fierce climax and the absence of boxing's typical rigor of a firm time limit, the Jennette-McVey Finish Fight "linked sport with popular science, politics, and aesthetics," and the Cirque de Paris became "an important cultural contact zone in which all of these racialized themes intertwined."[59]

The French public's appetite for news of these American fistic titans was insatiable, and some of the best accounts of what happened can be found there. The Parisian paper, *L'auto*, included a detailed blow-by-blow account by a ringside reporter that puts to rest much of the controversy over the total number of knockdowns scored and suffered by either fighter.

In the blow-by-blow translation from *L'Auto* that follows, Jennette is referred to as *le negre jaune* or the *yellow nigger*. The word *negre* is considered a derogatory term in modern French, but at the time was used colloquially for someone of African descent. "Yellow one" replaces "le negre jaune" each time it was used. Whether the French intended the same venom in the term *negre* as the American word *nigger* is certainly not apparent in the recounting by French light heavy Georges Carpentier, who was to be ringside for the finish fight. However when Carpentier arrived at the box office with his manager Francois Descamps, the tickets promised them by a promoter were not there, and the two of them were tossed out. Carpentier described what it was like outside the Cirque De Paris where they had to settle for being close to other fans who couldn't get in: "But we consoled ourselves with the knowledge that others could not afford to watch the fight, and we remained in the street content to hear the shouts and the cheers of those at the ring-side. Those of you who know the history of the ring will remember that it was a terrible, fierce fight; a fight to a finish; that Jeannette was knocked down on numerous occasions, only to rise and, eventually, win."[60]

There is a reverence in the tone of the Parisian's recounting of this great battle of Joe and Sam. They are true gladiators, gods of the squared circle. We pick up the action in the Parisian magazine *L'Auto* blow-by-blow coverage in round five. See the appendix for complete rounds.

4/17/1909

Round 5:

Sam, attacking Jennette, stops and lands to the neck; Jennette rushes Sam but lands from too far away, and his blows thus lack the strength to shake this veritable wall that is Sam McVea.

It seems anyhow that Sam, very at ease, is definitely dominating. Twice in a row he lands to stomach and heart. Sam lands a hook to the jaw and his cross sends Jennette to the floor. The yellow one gets up, but very unstable. He tries for a clinch. Maitroit has a hard time separating the two men.

At the end of the round, the brave Jennette attacks again, but has misjudged the distance and stumbles to the ropes while Sam hits him again.

The clear advantage to Sam.[61]

Both the *New York Sun* and *L'Auto* are in agreement that Jennette was first dropped in round five. McVey landed a left hook-right cross combination that put Jennette down in the fifth, while Fleischer's account describes McVey scoring a knockdown in round one. *L'Auto* continues:

Round 9:

After a Jennette jab, a clinch ensues, during which Joe punches, but on the gloves.

Jennette retakes the offensive and lands a jab to the [word illegible] then another to the stomach. In a clinch, he lands three successive uppercuts to the jaw. Sam seems shaken, he is bleeding heavily from the nose, he takes another left jab, followed by a short blow to the stomach. Jennette lands to the heart, and then jumps in to land a jab to the face. Sam then lands to the jaw but without much effect.

During this round the advantage went to Jennette. Just like on February 20, Sam's left eye is half closed.

Everyone applauds Jennette.[62]

The ninth sees Jennette finding success inside, close to the chest of McVey. Jennette's fights often hinged on his skills at infighting, and in the finish fight these skills made the difference as the rounds wore on. Jennette took advantage of the inside versus McVey. Effective in-fighting is a rough and strenuous craft fighters learn in the pro ranks. Former light heavyweight contender and current trainer Iceman John Scully describes it this way: "In-fighting is almost like maneuvering your opponent, knowing how to maneuver your opponent ... pulling people into punches. If I wanna hit you in a certain spot but I can't, I gotta make you go in that direction. I call it manipulation. I gotta manipulate you into that spot. That's what James Toney, Archie Moore and Ezzard Charles and all those old school guys were exceptional at.... It's definitely a skill."[63]

Jennette was a master at manipulating opponents into punches and he was doing it to McVey in April of 1909.

Round 12:
    Sam has got his strength back and it is he who attacks with a cross to the jaw, then knocks Jennette back with a good uppercut. Sam lands again to the heart, then he stops Joe by the throat; they certainly put down too much resin because the two fighters slip and Sam falls several times during the course of the round.
    Sam lands hard with a cross to the jaw and he goes to repeat, Jennette slips and lands to Sam's face.
    Sam's left eye is completely closed.[64]

Both men slip and fall to the canvas and McVey slips more than once before round's end, undoubtedly tiring him if not injuring himself in the falls themselves.

Round 15:
    After a flurry of feints and slips, Jennette lands with a left. He clinches. Sam then lands a jab.
    Jennette now launches an attack which is easily stopped. Sam, who is dominating again, lands twice to the face with short powerful punches; Jennette, totally off balance, drifts more and more.
    Sam's advantage is clear.
    A new discussion about the gloves. Sam's seconds protest, resulting in a new checking of the gloves, this time for Sam's benefit.

Round 16:
    The adversaries shake hands. Sam dodges an attack from Jennette, then tries to land left handed punches to the jaw. He studies Jennette, who attacks with jabs that are slipped. Sam lands a left punch to the jaw, then punches to the body. This round is monotonous, the opponents seeming to want to save strength for later.[65]

In the fifteenth Referee Maitroit worked to get the laces on the gloves in proper order, an official time-out, fighters and their handlers have long attempted to make work to the advantage of a tiring fighter. The sixteenth was less than scintillating but the fans didn't have to wait long for things to get exciting....

Round 19:
    Twice Jennette charges Sam, who half avoids him, without being able to dodge a left jab.

The clinches become more frequent. Suddenly Sam, despite seeming so unimpressive, throws such a ferocious hook that it knocks Jennette to the ground. While the seconds shout loudly, the entire room cheers Sam. Sam, sure of victory, attacks Jennette and knocks him down twice more. Now it's pandemonium. Jennette's seconds throw water on him while he's down, which makes the great Sam furious.

Twice more Jennette has risen. Truly the man is admirable, and it's a big relief to see him saved by the bell.[66]

The nineteenth was a brutal round that saw Jennette on the deck three times, and it was in round 19 where much of the controversy began. When down, stablemate Willie Lewis, working in the corner, dumped a bucket of water on Jennette hoping to help him shake off the knockdowns and keep fighting. This infuriated McVey and his handlers, but the bout continued. Once he got to the corner Jennette was given oxygen by McKetrick and Lewis which, along with the impromptu soaking, revived him.

But how much could the oxygen have actually helped? According to Dr. Leonard Hill it was in just this type of contest that oxygen use would benefit both combatants. But do experts in sports medicine agree with Doctor Hill's one hundred-year-old conclusions?

Dr. Robert Axtell, current professor of Exercise Science at Southern Connecticut State University, explains that McKetrick's oxygen treatment would not be as beneficial as Hill believed.

> Supplemental oxygen would have very little if any ergogenic effects. While it is common to see football players taking supplemental oxygen on the sidelines during a game, there is little physiological benefit, but there could be some psychological benefit (placebo effect). The reason for the lack of physiological effect is that at sea level, hemoglobin is nearly (98 percent) saturated with oxygen, thus the blood cannot be forced to carry any more than it already is.
>
> Additionally, the oxygen would not have helped physiologically with recovery during or after the bout.
>
> However, placebo might not be the right word. This implies that the fighters thought that O2 would help. I'm sure we don't know if the fighters thought that O2 would help. I'm sure it was just their coaches saying, breathe this, it'll help. So the whole mixture was the intervention, not just the O2.[67]

The recovery Jennette experienced from the oxygen treatment may have been based largely in superstition and the fighter's fragile psychology after being dropped repeatedly. Whether a negligible physiological benefit was outweighed by a positive psychological rebound is unclear, but Jennette began to rally.

Round 24:
Some feints, then Sam lands to the face. Jennette then lands with a hard uppercut in a clinch. Poor Sam is bleeding profusely from his hurt eye. A left by Sam, which Jennette counters with a weak uppercut. Sam charges again, but Jennette evades.

Good end of the round. During the rest they blow oxygen on the completely closed eye of poor Sam.[68]

In the McVey corner after round 24, his handlers also used oxygen canisters, but for him they were used to freeze McVey's cut and rapidly swelling eye. The gas in the canisters was probably mixed with an "inert gas like nitrogen" due to the hazards of pure oxygen "in an environment where people are smoking."[69] The inventor, Dr. Leonard Hill, used a rubber bag close to the oxygen canister in order to raise the temperature before breathing it in as it "would have expanded upon release making it cold."[70] Sam's cornermen must have held the canister up close to his face and opened it in proximity to the skin in order to freeze the wound. It is likely that prolonged use of this method would not only be painful, but also quite disfiguring, at least temporarily, as the freezing tissue would no doubt be damaged by the cold gas only to soften up under Jennette's peppering punches, resulting in cuts that froze and then melted, froze, and then melted again as the rounds ground past.

They continued exchanging hard punches — Joe's straight rights and stinging jabs versus Sam's thumping left hook to the body and head. McVey dropped Jennette with a right in the 26th and he is saved again by the bell. Jennette starts the 27th refreshed, but the round is a dull one with lots of clutching and grabbing.

In round 28, Jennette is put on the deck again but rises after a count of nine, and he survives an energized McVey, who tries unsuccessfully to finish him off. Over the next four rounds, Jennette finds success with the uppercut and continues enduring the heavier, punishing blows from McVey. The pace of both men slows as the stakes of the finish fight seem to sink in, neither man knowing how long this will go on. The action was unlike the pressure-cooker pace of a 12 round 36 minute bout of the modern ring. This was undiscovered country, each fighter pushing past physical and mental torment to dig deeper than his opponent to find which of them was made of stronger stuff on this night. By the 32nd round, there are more wild and sloppy moments as exhaustion began to erode the form of each fighter.

In round 33, both fighters start to lose their footings on the canvas covered with excess resin. "Sam attacks and lands a jab to the face, then a left cross that lands to the stomach. Joe dodges Sam's charge; Joe withstands a furious attack, Joe lands right and left to the jaw. Sam slips, then regains his balance, but then in a corner slips again."[71]

In round thirty-three both men slipped on the wet canvas near Jennette's corner and both men hit the deck. Later that round Jennette "fought Sam into the same corner" hoping to use the wet canvas as an aid in scoring a knockdown of his own, but without success.[72]

By round 37 the pace had slackened. Jennette continued landing on the swollen eye of McVey, while McVey used his legs to put some distance between them and regain his wind. "Jennette attacks, but slowly; both are tired; Sam lands two crosses, one to the jaw and one to the heart; Joe lands a left cross to the right eye; The fight is dull; Sam starts to do a little leg work; Joe lands a right to the stomach. At the bell, Sam returns to his corner, skipping a light and elegant polka step."[73]

How McVey still had a sense of humor after 37 rounds of fighting speaks to the character of these men. Psychological warfare is part of any boxing match, and McVey used his jaunty dance-steps to show Jennette and the crowd it was going to take a lot more to finish him.

A shift in the tide of the bout became apparent as Jennette continued landing speedy punches and moving away, and in round 41 he came close to scoring a knockdown after driving McVey into the ropes with a monster right hand. The pro-McVey crowd, having been won over by the smaller man from New Jersey, gives Jennette a standing ovation at the end of the round.

Oxygen is administered to McVey in his corner after round 42 as Jennette has taken command. The uppercuts Jennette landed to McVey's heart and chin in the clinches during the early rounds have taken their toll, and McVey seems a shell of himself. Jennette puts the pressure on and lands frequently but lacks the kayo power to put McVey down and keep him down. McVey's eyes are nearly swollen shut and he staggers about, pursuing Jennette, throwing wild desperate blows at his fresher opponent. In the 48th round, again Jennette lands hard uppercuts while in clinches, and McVey is all but finished.

Here is how the ringside reporter described the end to one of the most famous bouts ever fought in Paris:

> Sam gives up. At the bell for the 49th round, Sam shakes Joe's hand and says he can't go on.
> Sam is unrecognizable. His left eye is completely shut, his face pounded in, he no longer has a human face.
> They give Joe Jennette an indescribable ovation. His fans carry him in triumph; he has well earned his accolades, because through the course of this eternally unforgettable night he has been a paragon of courage.[73]

Jennette carried about the ring in victory, a rather typical celebration "ended the most ferocious battle and sternest test of endurance ever known under Queensbury Rules" before or since.[74] Jennette had rallied, shaking off the effects of nine knockdowns, and pummeled McVey mercilessly until the larger, stronger man could simply no longer function. "He no longer has a human face" read the *L'auto* account from ringside. The tremendous swelling and repeated freezing of the cuts around McVey's eyes by the corner must have resulted in a bruised and puffed-up visage that was absolutely startling. For what it is worth, Fleischer wrote in *Fighting Furies* that for two weeks after the bout McVey didn't leave his bed.[75] If that is so it confirms that Jennette left the Cirque de Paris a winner as he was up and out of bed far sooner than that. The prizefighter Willie Lewis recounted his experience that night with Jennette years later in an elegiac piece in the pages of *The Ring* the month after Joe died. In regards to total number of knockdowns even Lewis was confused, but not about what happened the next morning: "I worked behind Joe that night and it was the most grueling fight I've ever seen. It lasted forty-nine rounds, and what a brawl! There were so many knockdowns, I lost count ... it was 4 A.M. when our happy but weary gang landed back in camp. I had a fight set the next week with Honey Mellody, but this was one morning I wasn't getting up for roadwork. I'd done enough with all that running up and down steps for forty-nine rounds. All I wanted was to hit the sack and stay there. And you'd imagine that Jennette, after that brawl, would have felt like sleeping for a week! Well it was about 6 o'clock when a banging on the door woke me up. Bleary-eyed, I looked up. In walked Jennette, all togged out for the road. Can you imagine the guy! He'd just finished forty-nine of the toughest rounds ever fought, and he should have been snoring his head off in bed. But here he was, looking bright and chipper and ready for a day's work. What's the idea? I asked. I'm a little stiff and sore from the fight, he said, "and thought I'd work some of it out by going on the road with you."[76]

After 49 rounds of combat, a morning jog is unheard of, but that was not the case for Jennette. Later that day, he fired the starting gun to commence a bicycle race in Buffalo, France. If one looks closely at a photograph taken that day, it appears Jennette's left eye and cheek are quite swollen, which should not be at all surprising after absorbing the blows he did from McVey.

During the April 17, 1909, Finish Fight, Jennette did the superior work in close, fighting in partial clinches and out grappling Sam throughout the fight. In their first two bouts it had been Sam who did more damage on the inside, but the reverse was true in their rubber-match. Perhaps Jennette found it safer to stay close to McVey, using chopping uppercuts and flurries before spinning off and circling away only to start all over again on McVey's next charge. They didn't call him McVey, the Bison of the Boulevard for nothing; he could be counted on to keep bringing the fight to his foe.

But Sam McVey gave up too much ground inside versus Jennette, and he must have

Sam McVey poses with referee Reichel in an undated photograph (George Grantham Bain Collection, Library of Congress).

known it as his own comments about in-fighting in the French boxing magazine *La Vie au Grand Air* clearly suggest. McVey watched a film of the July, 1910, bout between Jack Johnson and James J. Jeffries just a year and three months after his forty-nine round defeat, and McVey's description of the action is remarkable for its intuitive clarity. Also worth noting is the descriptive prose used by McVey. These are the thoughts of a boxing insider not the barely coherent ramblings of *yessur-nosur* dialect used often by the American press when quoting McVey.

> But it is above all in the clinches that Johnson won. Oh, the marvelous and educational clinches that took place in Reno! And how mad I would be to hear the unknowledgeable spectators say: "It's great, but there is a little too much clinching." The knowledge of in-fighting is the pinnacle of boxing science, and whoever understands it can witness it with pleasure. Johnson, with remarkable skill, followed the tactic I recommend: "Disarm your opponent before attacking him." Johnson disarmed his opponent by leaning on his opponent's left arm; in each clinch one sees the right hand of the great negro grab the left arm of the white, push it toward the ground, tire it progressively with the most admirable power and certainty, until the numbed shoulder had no more strength to work. From there, he had Jeffries at his mercy. Johnson may have been able to win quicker, but he could not have won more certainly. Jeffries had admirable courage and energy but lacked science.[77]

Despite the facts of the bout and the strategic successes and blunders each fighter made, there was controversy. Just days after the Finish Fight a report in the *Syracuse Herald* stated that Richard Klegin, McVey's manager at that time, demanded a rematch set for "twenty rounds only" that would include "no doping."[78] Klegin believed that the mixture of oxygen, caffeine and ether Jennette received in the corner between rounds along with the "cold water that was thrown on him" had turned the fight in Joe's favor and robbed McVey of certain victory.[79] In August of 1909 Klegin even blamed the oxygen given to McVey for the loss, claiming it had made him groggy so that "he hardly knew where he stood."[80] There had been no mixture of caffeine and ether in *L'Auto*, just oxygen, as was the case in Fleischer's *Fighting Furies* and U.S. newspaper reports; only oxygen had been mentioned. But, would an oxygen, caffeine and ether mixture have changed things all that dramatically? Dr. Robert Axtell attributes some potential benefit to such a mixture:"

> Caffeine would have some ergogenic effects. The effects are mediated by activation of the sympathetic nervous system (sympathomimetic). Activation of the sympathetic nervous system causes a flight or fight response which could enable the boxers to keep fighting even though physically they should be fatiguing.
>
> Ether used to be used as an anesthetic which would blunt some of the pain from the continued punches received during the bout.
>
> Therefore, this mixture enables the athletes to feel less pain and limit fatigue and thus fight multiple rounds."[81]

It seems Joe Jennette may have received some improved performance during the bout due to the mixture he was inhaling. More than the physiological benefit, however, was the psychological boost Jennette likely enjoyed. How much did Jennette believe in McKetrick's oxygen treatment? How often had they tried it, and with what sort of success? It had only been about 6 months since oxygen was first used in this manner, could McKetrick have mastered the technique so quickly? Without the exact amounts of caffeine and ether it is difficult to determine exactly how much of a benefit Jennette might have enjoyed. Perhaps the ingestion of caffeine was responsible for the sleeplessness Jennette seemed to experience after the Finish Fight, which may have been why he was waking Willie Lewis to go running

"Ripley, Believe It or Not," says Jennette was "put down 24 times" in the 1909 battle with McVey (*Syracuse Herald*, September 5, 1913).

so early the morning after. In terms of ether, however, the amount had to be rather specific as "there is a fine line between too little and too much."[82] Assuming Jennette received just enough to benefit him, it is likely some of the sting of McVey's blows was dulled, but not their concussive effect.

Dr. Axtell and his research assistant, Kurt Sollaneck, are specific in mentioning the placebo effect of oxygen used along the sidelines in the NFL. If McKetrick and Jennette had practiced the oxygen treatments, and Jennette had come to believe that he did recover faster and fight better while using oxygen in the corner, then its use in the Finish Fight certainly helped him. Fighters are often superstitious folk, and if Jennette had come to accept the recuperative properties of the mixture it is likely "the intervention" worked.

Wherever the tall tales and legends about the Finish Fight started, America's

Sam Langford and Sam McVey fought each other 15 times (*La Vie Au Grand Air*, March 25, 1911).

racist envy towards the Fearsome Foursome was chronicled in a June of 1909 article in the *Washington Post* which suggested the "gay life in Paris" overwhelmed McVey and mockingly referred to that as the cause of his 49-round TKO loss to Jennette.[83] "They have a way of killing coons with kindness on the other side," the *Post* went on to warn, almost hopefully; "a fact that Johnson, Langford and Jennette may discover when it's too late."[84]

Perhaps there was some truth behind the *Post*'s bigoted warning, as the appetite of the Paris public was still not satiated, and Jennette and McVey met for a fourth time before the end of 1909. On December 11 they fought a twenty-round draw, which like in their first Paris bout, the crowd thought McVey had won. Their styles were such that whenever they fought each fighter would have his share of success in the varying fighting terrain the bouts provided. Joe and Sam didn't meet in the ring again until six years later in Boston where they boxed yet another draw, this time the distance was a more civilized 12 rounds.

As for the heavyweight champion, Jack Johnson finally allowed a black man to make a try for his championship in 1913. Not surprisingly, the fight took place in Paris. Papa Jack agreed to fight Battling Jim Johnson, a popular fighter but little more than a fringe contender or journeyman in terms of skill. The French were thrilled to be hosting the bout, but the fact that both champion and challenger shared the same surname didn't help much in terms of racial sensitivity.

> Because Jim Johnson shared the champion's last name and was also said to come from Galveston, some British reporters suggested that the two men must be related. They weren't, but in the weeks before the fight, the challenger — who was tall and dark, and, like the champion, shaved his scalp — had a fine time signing "Jack Johnson" in autograph books proffered by worshipful but confused Parisians.[85]

Jack Johnson only managed a draw against Battling Jim. It was a dreadful fight in which Jack's arm was broken early in the bout and the injured champion did little more than clutch and grab. But Parisians were thrilled again when a few months later Joe Jennette beat France's darling Georges Carpentier in a fight some reports suggested was a gift-decision victory to the shop-worn black fighter. Referee Franz Reichel, who was the fight's sole judge, awarded Jennette the victory after 15 hard-fought rounds in March of 1914. Jennette weighed in at 183 pounds, and Carpentier just 167½. The smaller, speedier Frenchman scored often with combinations and flurries, yet the aging heavyweight proved his incredible durability yet again.

Carpentier learned training and fighting techniques from Jennette and McVey as he was starting his career, and both Americans were in Paris. The Frenchman's fascination with skin-color was apparent from his recounting of the very start of his fight with Jennette in his autobiography;

> I hurried to shake hands with Jennette, who appeared to me as some great big bronze statue. Fighting a Negro is a weird business, and it was as much as I could do to refrain from dwelling upon the colour scheme which we struck.[86]

Carpentier recounts the fight in detail and was repeatedly stunned by Jennette's ability to absorb punishment and keep coming back. When extolled by his manager to finish Jennette off, Carpentier responded with plenty of emotion:

> "Give him the knock-out," implored Descamps during the interval in my corner. "How can I?" I answered. "You will have to bring the guillotine to finish him. He is many men rolled into one. I hurt him very much one minute; the next I cannot hurt him. Bring me a sledge-hammer!"[87]

Carpentier was thoroughly disgusted with the loss by decision, but he lost no respect for Jennette. Years later in an encounter with a British boxing insider, Carpentier was given one possible explanation for being on the short end of the referee's decision that night against Jennette.

> In a discussion of my many contests, Mr. Bettinson [of London's National Sporting Club] recalled my battle with Jeannette. "Oh, yes," he said, "you beat Jeannette. I was astonished at Reichel's decision, and many times have I tried to understand how he made Jeannette to be the winner. The only explanation I can offer is this: Reichel before the fight must have read *Uncle Tom's Cabin*, and conceived an affection for the black race."[88]

Bettinson's joke about the abolitionist Harriet Beecher Stowe's novel is illustrative of how even after years of fighting some of the very best in the sport, even the members of the Fearsome Foursome, were seen as black men first, boxers second. Yet in total, Carpentier recalled Jennette quite fondly and credited him as the fundamental source and inspiration that made him value fitness and the focused lifestyle of a fighter. Carpentier had even learned a secret training technique Jennette believed improved a fighter's ability to absorb head punches.

> Few men trained like this Negro. It has been repeatedly asserted that his greatness came from his extraordinary stamina and capacity to take punishment. But this is only partially true. Jeannette fell little below a world's champion indeed, had the opportunity been given to him by his brother black, Johnson, the probability is that he would have taken the title, because he fitted himself for fighting by bringing all his intelligence to bear on his training.
>
> It was more than a year before I fought him when I obtained permission to see him in his gymnasium. At that time there was no thought that I would ever meet him. The methods pursued by Jeannette in training were a revelation to me. For hours he would work silently. He was like some black panther; he made me go hot and cold when I first saw him, for at the moment

I walked into his gymnasium he was walking on his hands. At the conclusion of his work he saw that I was thinking and dreaming about it all, and in a quiet, soft way, he came to me and said, "You cannot understand why I think it necessary and helpful to walk on my hands. Wait, my boy, I will tell you. By turning yourself upside down you so employ and test your brain centres that when you are hit on the jaw your head is less likely to go spinning round. No man alive can keep his feet if he is hit properly and heavily on the point; but if you follow this particular exercise, which means that I shoot my feet in the air and walk around on my hands, you become less susceptible to that kind of drunken helplessness which is induced by a clip on the jaw." Jeannette was no student of physiology in the everyday understanding of the term, and yet of all fighters, white or black, I do not remember having met one who broke more completely away from training methods of a stereotyped kind, nor one who showed greater intelligence in the practice of physical culture. History will perhaps have it that Jeannette was only a bruiser; he was more. He was a man with ideas, and in his way a scientist, and the antithesis of the negro as popularly understood."[89]

Carpentier saw Jennette as a sort of boxing guru or shaman, a rich source of fistic knowledge and experience. Whether Jennette's hand-walking really benefited him is unclear, but like the oxygen intervention, Jennette believed in it. Fighters, like so many other athletes, believe in the safety of ritualistic training methods. There may not be scientific proof of benefit, but there is practical and psychological value in the ritualized repetition of training practices and exercise crafted for specific results. Carpentier was able to understand and appreciate that:

Joe Jennette's gravesite at Fairview Cemetery, Fairview, New Jersey. Note the spelling of the family name (photograph by Gregory Speciale, joejennette.com, July 2, 2009).

I shall ever be indebted to [Jennette] for his introduction to training exercises that have been most helpful to me. To win a high position in pugilism a man, whether a fight is pending or not, must always be in training, mentally and physically. As the conjurer, the acrobat, the juggler as, indeed, like every public performer he must be always searching for new ideas. To attempt something new is the surest way of keeping fresh, both in mind and body, and escaping a seizure of that most harmful and heart-destroying thing called staleness."[90]

Joe Jennette seemed at times part conjurer or magician, he'd have to be to survive the nine knockdowns in the finish fight only to come back and win. After emerging victorious from the war with McVey, Jennette was certain that no one could best him in a fight-to-the-finish. In January of 1911 Joe had been brutalized in a twelve-round decision loss to Sam Langford in Boston but wrote to a friend in Paris through the French magazine *Le Boxe & Les Boxeurs* promising a return to France and to glory: "I am sure I would beat him [Langford] in a fight to the finish. The maximum I would ever fight would be 30 rounds and believe me, if an opponent beats me at that distance, I will be the first to shake his hand and congratulate him."[91] Joe Jennette believed in his own preternatural endurance. And so did his manager Dan McKetrick.

Perhaps it had been McKetrick who started the tall tales about all the knockdowns in the Finish Fight in the first place as a marketing ploy. Like so many managers, McKetrick had a flair for hyperbole, and a *Hartford Courant* article in June of 1909 intimates that Parisians were getting wise to the little manager with the large mouth.[92] How far would McKetrick go in order to secure bouts for his fighters? In a 1913 article by T.S. Andrews in *The Racine Journal-News*, McKetrick attributes Jennette's biracial heritage to the fact that he is "such a fine fellow and such a home body."[93] Andrews described Jennette as "more Arabian than Negro," and as such placed him slightly ahead of Sam Langford as heir to the throne of Jack Johnson.[94] That same year McKetrick told Ripley of *Ripley's Believe it or Not* that Jennette had been put down "24 times" in the Finish Fight, and that he had used "two cans of oxygen and goodness knows how much smelling salts and stimulants" to revive him.[95] The intervention McKetrick had devised was certainly one that he himself had faith in, and he hoped for future Finish Fights, no doubt to use his tricks in the corner. In January of 1911, Jennette had lost badly to Sam Langford in Boston, and McKetrick wrote to a Parisian boxing magazine *La Boxe & Les Boxeurs* challenging Langford to a Finish Fight.

Jeannette ... has shown the French public that he is invincible in a finish fight. He has exhibited the courage of a lion. He stopped Sam McVea after 49 rounds, and in these 49 rounds, Jeannette showed his courage by making McVey throw up the sponge in defeat. I later matched Jeannette with McVey, against my will, for a bout of 30 rounds; I urged a finish fight, but McVea wanted nothing of it, and since the club also wanted the 30 round fight, I had to accept it.

Here is what I propose then. I am ready to return to France with Jeannette but on condition that his fight be one to the finish; that is what the French want; and it is the only way to determine who is best of the two ... Jeannette ... wants a finish fight, and I am ready to make such a match with Langford or McVea, winner take all. Langford is an excellent boxer for 12 or 15 rounds. In this type of fight he can get the judge's decision, but in a finish fight Jeannette is his superior, and I am ready to prove this claim and with this letter I hurl a challenge at Langford...."[96]

Like so many fighters and managers before them and since, Jennette and McKetrick's confidence came from shared experiences in the ring and from the toils of training they shared in the gym.

Today, Jennette's career record ranks among the top 25 to 30 all-time best in the heavyweight division, even though he was never champion.[97] His was a career with 79 wins.

Fighters don't fight that many total bouts anymore, let alone win that many. He had twenty-one career losses which include seven to the great Sam Langford, three to Jack Johnson, one to McVey, and one to Harry Wills. Joe Jennette's record was 79–9–6 157 total bouts 66 ko's, 8 wins by decision, 5 wins on fouls, 6 draws, ko'd 2 times, lost by decision 7, 62 no decisions and 1 no contest.

After his career as a fighter ended, Jennette was still not finished with boxing. In February of 1923, he was appointed referee and judge by the state of New York and became the first African American to hold these positions.[98] Jennette also ran a garage in Union City, New Jersey, and upstairs from Jennette's Auto Service was a boxing gym where he trained neighborhood kids. Jennette aged into a "quiet, absent-minded man" who ran a limo service, often driving one of his cars to weddings and funerals himself. He considered Sam Langford "the toughest of the lot" when asked about the Big Four in 1946.[99]

Joe finally got to throw punches at Johnson, but there were no titles at stake, and certainly no prize money. In 1945 the two boxed three rounds in the ballroom of the Henry Hudson Hotel to raise money for Liberty Bonds, an almost supernatural feat for men of their age. Johnson was 67 and Jennette was 64.[100] Little footage remains of the two weathered-looking warriors, all smiles and jocularity as they go through the motions, feinting and pursuing, old rivals throwing punches again after more than four decades. One can fantasize how Jennette must have felt to finally be able to land blows on the ribs of Jack Johnson, the man who kept him from the greatest prize in sport, a prize that would likely have been his if only he'd been given his night to try.

Jennette married Adelaide Atzinger, a white woman, in 1906 and the couple had two children, Joe Jr. and Agnes.[101] Jennette died at the age of 78 "in the North Hudson Hospital in Weehawken, New Jersey."[102] He was inducted into the International Boxing Hall of Fame in Canastota, New York, in 1997, and a historical marker was placed in his honor in Union City, New Jersey, in April of 2009, a few blocks from where his gym and auto-service station stood.

Without Jack Johnson, Jennette, McVey and Langford were stuck with each other. Jennette fought McVey once more in 1915 and Langford nine more times over the next nine years, averaging 12 rounds a year. Although Jennette and McVey's Paris slugfests were over, the wars between the Sams, of the Big Four were yet to begin.

Sam McVey finally met Sam Langford for the first time April 1, 1911, and they fought 15 bouts in total, with McVey finishing at 2–6–5 with 2 no contests between the two of them. Sam McVey retired with a career record of 63–12–7 (48 ko's) in a 97-total bout career. Fourteen of McVey's wins came by decision, 1 win by foul. He fought 7 career draws, was knocked out 5 times, lost by decision 7 times, fought 13 No Decisions and 2 No Contests throughout the period of April 12, 1902, through August 2, 1921.

Sam McVey did meet Jack Johnson in the ring again but only in an exhibition. The day before Johnson's bout with Jess Willard, McVey sparred with the champion in Havana, Cuba. The bout "was a joke" and Johnson's "lack of condition and neglect of training was glaring."[103] McVey scored with several thudding left hooks that stunned the champ, but in all the bout was dreadful and did little more than convince bettors to back Willard versus Papa Jack. McVey worked in Jack Johnson's corner the next day and was not at all surprised when Willard defeated Johnson by 26-round knockout.

McVey insisted that Johnson had "faked with Jess Willard."[104] He described Johnson's demeanor before and after meeting Willard, saying the Galveston Giant "never seemed to be worried about anything before the fight and was just as happy afterward as ever."[105]

McVey didn't think very highly of Willard's skill, insisting that "leaving out all us black fellows" he could "name four white men" who could beat him.

McVey couldn't stand seeing Johnson lose in the hot Havana sun, not when he was certain Johnson "could have done better."[106]

Back in the states after the bout, McVey was forced to cancel a fight with Sam Langford after contracting malaria in Cuba while working with Jack Johnson.[107]

McVey lived just six years longer, dying at the age of 37 of pneumonia in a Harlem hospital. Papa Jack Johnson came back into the picture after Sam McVey's death and Johnson described the circumstances in his autobiography,

> When Sam McVey the noted pugilist with whom I had several ring contests, died in New York City of pneumonia, I was playing a show in Cincinnati, Ohio. I learned of his death, and that a fund was being raised for the purpose of burying him. I wired to New York and stopped the raising of the fund, closed my show and followed my message to the metropolis, where I paid all of the funeral expenses and disposed of the bills that had accumulated during McVey's illness. Friends of McVey and the attending undertakers will confirm me in this statement.[108]

McVey was a rugged and exciting fighter who always pressed the action. He would have been a top contender in any era of the heavyweight division and may just have been able to put together a winning effort to become champion had Johnson given him a title shot at some point between 1909 and 1915. McVey finishes at fourth among the Big Four, going 1–2–2 versus Jennette, 2–6–5 with 2 no decisions versus Langford and 0–3 versus Jack Johnson. Like Jennette, despite never becoming champion, McVey ranks among the top 25 to 30 all-time best in the heavyweight division.[109] Sam McVey was inducted into the International Boxing Hall of Fame in 1999; and along with heavyweights like Ray Mercer, Ron Lyle, Jerry Quarry and Earnie Shavers, McVey was a perennial top contender who could be counted on to give the division's best a difficult and dangerous trip every time through the ropes.

Had Joe Jennette and Sam McVey been granted return matches with Jack Johnson after he'd won the heavyweight championship, it is likely their names would be among those giants from Sullivan to Lennox Lewis. Instead, there is no heavyweight mega-star status for Jennette and McVey, it's just Joe and Sam. Not because they did not at one time or another deserve such a moniker, but that they were never granted the fruits of their ring labors. Joe and Sam would have likely beaten Jack Johnson in the months after the Jeffries fight. Johnson had been dreadfully inactive, fighting twice in three years, his personal life was imploding, and there was no way he could have sustained the focused training camp that would have been needed to prepare for Langford, Jennette, or even McVey. Becoming a champion is often about being the best in one moment, on one particular night. Despite numerous occasions when they shared the ring with Jack Johnson, they were not allowed to try besting him when the greatest prize in sports was at stake. It is assumed the best fighter of any age wants to prove himself against the very best of that age, but Johnson knew the risks for any heavyweight — one well-placed blow could change everything. And there was safety in denying Langford, McVey and Jennette the opportunity of ever landing the blow that could wrest Johnson's title from him.

In the end boxing is business and that was how Johnson saw it. Perhaps he was a pioneer. It is not unheard of today that would-be super-fights, that seem like done deals for days, end up crumbling in endless negotiations and pre-fight conditions. Johnson went through the motions of negotiating bouts with all of the other members of the Big Four, bouts that never became reality. Johnson avoided three-fourths of the best heavies in the world to preserve himself. He, simply, came first. That is often the case with many fighters. But in the age of the Fearsome Foursome, Johnson's pride kept the public from seeing anything more risky than Battling Jim Johnson's draw.

Even without winning the heavyweight championship, Sam Langford, Joe Jennette and Sam McVey won their immortality in the quality of their competition — each other. Paris of 1909 was a special era in heavyweight history. It was when the great Joe and Sam traded bragging rights back and forth through eighty-eight rounds. Joe was the endurance-fighter, punching machine, not a hard puncher but a consistent, up-close, in-your-chest puncher, an athlete with freakish courage and strength of will and character to keep rising and keep on keeping on. And Sam was a ring immortal, the image of menace, a pressuring, crowd-pleasing, aggressive fighter who boxed a bit too long and died far too young, too broke and too alone. Joe and Sam finished numbers three and four of the Fearsome Black Foursome, and there they will forever stay. Such was the age when James Arthur "Jack" Johnson drew the color line on the rest of the Big Four.

NOTES

1. "Marvin Hart is Champion," *New York Times*, July 4, 1905.

2. Zinn, Howard, *The People's History of the United States*, New York Perennial Classics: 1980, 315.

3. Cockburn, Alexander, "War and Peace," *Counterpunch* October 9, 2009 Counterpunch.org *http://www.counterpunch.org/cockburn10092009.html*

4. Zinn, Howard, 319.

5. James Bradley, *Imperial Cruise*, lecture C-SPAN2/Book-TV.

6. Ibid.

7. "Great White Fleet (16 Dec 1907- 22 Feb 1909)," Maintained by John Pike GlobalSecurity.org 2000–2009 *http://www.globalsecurity.org/military/agency/navy/great-white-fleet.htm*

8. Smith, Kevin R., *The Sundowners: The History of the Black Prizefighter 1870–1930*, iUniverse, 8–9.

9. Moyle, Clay, *Sam Langford: Boxing's Greatest Uncrowned Champion*, Seattle: Bennet & Hastings, 2006, 257.

10. Runstedtler, Theresa, "Visible Men: African American Boxers, the New Negro and the Global Color Line," *Radical History Review*, 103, Winter 2009 (MARHO: The Radical Historians' Organization, Inc.) 61.

11. Ibid.

12. Laine, Sam, "The Passing of Joe Jennette," *Boxing Illustrated*, Vol. 1, No. 1, November 1958, 33, 55.

13. Roberts, Randy, *Papa Jack: Jack Johnson and the Era of White Hopes*, New York: The Free Press 1983, 29.

14. Moyle, Clay, 199.

15. Fox, Richard K., *Life and Battles of Jack Johnson no. 22* Franklin Square, NY: Fox's Athletic Library, 1910, 15.

16. Johnson, Jack, *My Life and Battles* edited and translated by Christopher Rivers Washington, DC: Potomac Books, Inc, 2009, 39.

17. "Sam McVey high in ranks of pugs," *The Press-Courier* (Oxnard, CA) 60th anniversary commemorative edition, June 29, 1963.

18. "Johnson beat M'Vey," *National Police Gazette*, Nov. 14, 1903.

19. "Johnson puts out M'Vey in the Twentieth," *San Francisco Examiner*, April 23, 1904.

20. Ward, Geoffrey C. *Unforgivable Blackness: The Rise and Fall of Jack Johnson* New York: Alfred A. Knopf, 2004, 66–67.

21. "Joe Jeannette," Box Rec, *http://boxrec.com/media/index.php/Joe_Jeannette*, Accessed January 10, 2010.

22. Batchelor, Denzil, Weidenfeld, and Nicolson, *Jack Johnson and His Times*, London, Phoenix, 1956, 104.

23. "Joe Jeannette; The Boxer Who Refused to Quit," Dvd/video — Amazing Sports Stories Episode 105: Nash Entertainment *http://www.nashentertainment.com.*

24. Ward, 76.

25. "Any First-Class Man Can Beat Munroe, Says Jeff," *National Police Gazette*, January 9, 1904.

26. Johnson, *My Life and Battles*, 45.

27. Roberts, 44–45.

28. Fox, 19.

29. Douglass, Frederick "We Have Decided to Stay," speech to American Anti-Slavery Society May 9, 1848. *http://www.wfu.edu/~zulick/340/Douglass1848.html.*

30. Ward, 102.

31. Moyle, 82.

32. Ibid.

33. Ward, 109.

34. Carpentier, Georges, *My Fighting Life,* Internet Archive archive.org March 2001. *http://www.archive.*

org/stream/myfightinglife00carpgoog/myfightinglife00 carpgoog_djvu.txt

35. Corbett, James J., "Colored Boxers Hold Stage," *Chicago Daily Tribune*, May 30, 1909.
36. Ibid.
37. "Japanese Art Insufficient to Beat American Boxer," *The Lima* (Ohio) *Times Democrat,* January 11, 1909.
38. "Women of Paris Delight in Seeing Prize Fight," *The Ogden* (Utah) *Standard-Examiner*, March 23, 1909.
39. Ibid.
40. Runstedtler, 63.
41. "Women of Paris Delight in Seeing Prize Fight," The Ogden (Utah) *Standard-Examiner*, March 23, 1909.
42. "Boxing at the National," *New York Times*, April 16, 1907.
43. Ibid.
44. "M'Vey Whips Joe Jeannette," *The San Antonio Light*, February 21, 1909.
45. "Sam M'Vey is Real Noise in Paris Ring," *Anaconda* (Montana) *Standard*, February 26, 1911.
46. "Women of Paris Delight in Seeing Prize Fight," *The Ogden Standard-Examiner*, March 23, 1909.
47. "To Meet In Finish Match," *Washington Post*, April 13, 1909.
48. "M'Vey Whips Joe Jeannette," *San Antonio Light*, February 21, 1909.
49. Runstedtler, 67.
50. Fleischer, Nat, *Black Dynamite Volume IV, Fighting Furies: The Story of the Golden Era of Jack Johnson, Sam Langford and their Negro Contemporaries* New York: C.J. O'Brien, 1939, 182.
51. Smith, Kevin R. *Black Genesis: The History of the Black Prizefighter 1760–1870*, iUniverse 2003, 3.
52. "Tomorrow Night's Big Match," *L'auto* (Paris), April 18, 1909.
53. "Jeannette beat McVey. New York Fighter Wins in Fiftieth Round in Paris," *New York Times*, April 18, 1909.
54. "Ends in Fifty Rounds," *Washington Post*, April 18, 1909.
55. "Add Oxygen Tanks to Boxer's Outfit," *New York Times*, November 22, 1908.
56. "Oxygen's Use in Athletics," *New York Times*, October 4, 1908.
57. Ibid.
58. "Oxygen a Factor in Fight," *New York Sun*, April 18, 1909.
59. Runstedtler, 64.
60. Carpentier, Georges *My Fighting Life* Internet Archive archive.org March 2001 *http://www.archive. org/stream/myfightinglife00carpgoog/myfightinglife00 carpgoog_djvu.txt*
61. *L'auto*, April 19, 1909, translated by Mark Scott. See Appendix.
62. Ibid.
63. Interview with "Iceman" John Scully, *Mohegan Sun*, January 29, 2010.
64. See Appendix for round-by-round translation.
65. Ibid.
66. Ibid.

67. Dr. Robert Axtell and Kurt Sollanek, of SCSU, personal Email dated November 2 and 3, 2009.
68. See Appendix.
69. David Wallace, Personal Email concerning oxygen canisters.
70. Ibid.
71. "Oxygen a Factor in Fight," *New York Sun*, April 18, 1909.
72. See Appendix.
73. Ibid.
74. Batchelor, 108.
75. Fleischer, 182.
76. Williams, Billy, "Joe Jeannette, Last of The Big 4" *The Ring*, September 1958, 22, 47.
77. McVey, Sam, "How Jack Johnson Won," translated by Mark Scott. See Appendix.
78. "Challenged Jeannette," The Syracuse Herald, April 24, 1909.
79. Ibid.
80. "Parisian Promoter Here to Get Dates," *The Anaconda Standard*, August 4, 1909.
81. Dr. Robert Axtell and Kurt Sollanek, of SCSU, personal email, November 2 & 3, 2009.
82. Ibid.
83. "Negro Pugilists Accused of Having Yellow Streak," *Washington Post*, June 13, 1909.
84. Ibid.
85. Ward, 353.
86. Carpentier, Georges *My Fighting Life* Internet Archive archive.org March 2001 *http://www.archive. org/stream/myfightinglife00carpgoog/myfightinglife00 carpgoog_djvu.txt*
87. Ibid.
88. Ibid.
89. Ibid.
90. Ibid.
91. Letter from Joe Jeannette dated January 18, 1911, *Le Boxe & Les Boxeurs,* translated by Mark Scott.
92. "Frenchmen Getting Wise to Boxing Fakes," *Hartford Courant*, June 7, 1909.
93. "Joe Jeannette, Who Claims Title, Not Full Blooded Negro," *The Racine* (Wisconsin) *Journal Times*, June 18, 1913.
94. Ibid.
95. "Joe Jeannette Tells Ripley," *The Syracuse Herald*, September 5, 1913.
96. "Jeannette Challenges Langford, a Letter from Dan McKetrick," *Le Boxe & Les Boxeurs*, March 15, 1911.
97. "Heavyweight All-Time Rankings," IBRO, posted by Dan Cuoco, April 20, 2009. *http://www. ibroresearch.com/?p=52*
98. "Joe Jeannette Made Referee and Judge," *The Bridgeport* (Connecticut) *Telegram*, February 27, 1923.
99. "Sam Langford Rated Tops by Jeannette," *Winnipeg Free Press*, December 13, 1946.
100. Ward, *Geoffrey C*, 446.
101. "Biography for Joe Jeanette" Internet Movie Database, *http://www.imdb.com/name/nm1279807/bio*
102. Williams, Billy, "Last of The Big 4," *The Ring*, September 1958, 22.

103. "Willard Favored to Beat Johnson for Championship," *Oakland Tribune*, April 4, 1915.

104. "Sam McVey says Johnson Faked with Jess Willard," *Gazette & Bulletin* (Williamsburg, PA), April 12, 1915.

105. Ibid.

106. Ibid.

107. "Sam Langford to Meet Joe Jeannette—McVey Sick," *The Lowell* (Mass.) *Sun*, April 12, 1915.

108. Jack, Johnson, 243.

109. "Heavyweight All-Time Rankings," IBRO, posted by Dan Cuoco, April 20, 2009. *http://www.ibroresearch.com/?p=52*

CHAPTER 13

Jack Johnson: World Heavyweight Champion

Mark Scott

A Belated Pardon

On June 24, 2009, the United States Congress passed a resolution to clear former Heavyweight Champion John Arthur "Jack" Johnson of a trumped-up 1913 conviction for violating the Mann Act. The authorities of Johnson's time had twisted a law meant to combat prostitution and used it to prosecute Johnson in order to silence him. The legal charade was a poorly disguised campaign to wrest from Johnson the heavyweight championship which was considered the exclusive property of the white race. After years of seeing Johnson publicly cavort with so many white women and thoroughly dominate the prize rings, it took a concerted effort on the part of those who wished him ill, among them federal judges and special agents of the Bureau of Investigation, to bring about his downfall. Upon his arrest, the much-hounded Johnson said plaintively, "You don't have to do this."[1]

Other black boxers of the era, George Dixon and Joe Jennette among them, had white wives. But only Johnson was singled out by authorities. According to the sentencing judge, Johnson and his relationship with white women set a bad example for men of his race. Almost 100 years after Johnson spent his gloomy years in exile and jail, the move to exonerate him posthumously came shortly after the election of America's first black president. Why had America seen Johnson as such a menace? W.E.B. Dubois attributed Johnson's travails to his "unforgivable blackness." But what did Jack *do*, to quote the mournful Louis Armstrong song, "to be so black and blue?"

Jack Johnson was born in Galveston, Texas, in 1878. He became the first black world heavyweight champion, and in his tumultuous career he would become such a thorn in the side of white America that it literally took an act of Congress to dislodge him.

The son of slaves, Johnson's origins could hardly have been more humble: but no man's behavior was less humble.[2] Jack Johnson was the forerunner of men who sixty years later gathered in multitudes to proclaim, "Say it loud, I'm black, and I'm proud." By his actions Johnson did so all by himself, and his pride would cause him as much trouble as did his lust.

Johnson's life was full of adventure, beginning with his teen years. In his highly entertaining autobiography, he tells of himself as a young man harried by police as he sought his fortune from town to town. For the price of a meal and lodging, he took up fighting in

Jack Johnson dominated the heavyweight division for over a decade (Library of Congress).

battle royals, where a prominent referee who saw him told promoters, "The big coon who won it looked pretty good to me."[3] Battle royals were racist spectacles where up to ten black men, often blindfolded, would duke it out until only one was left standing, the winner earning a few coins. Most black men of the era had to apprentice in battle royals before fighting individual bouts for pay. Johnson was soon fighting regularly for pay.

A very scientific boxer, Johnson had studied the trio of black fighters in the lower weight divisions who preceded him. He had worked as a sparring partner for Barbados Joe Walcott and studied the defensive moves of George Dixon and Joe Gans. He developed a style patterned after Lightweight Champion Gans. In fact, before Johnson became famous, a San Francisco artist drew a cartoon of "heavyweight Joe Gans" vs. then champion Jim Jeffries. The depiction is barely distinguishable from later actual photos of the fight between Johnson and Jeffries. [4]

Jack Johnson's Boxing Style

Before Johnson's brash style outside the ring became the source of scandal across America, it was his revolutionary style inside the ring that brought him fame. Johnson was a heavyweight with the grace of a featherweight. If he had not been such a great fighter, his personality never would have become an American obsession. He employed a fencer's stance, with his weight perfectly distributed, and wasted no motion. Counter-punching was the core of his offense, always waiting for his opponent to commit an error and leave an opening. Johnson became so flawless in the ring and so dominant that, in his most famous bouts with Burns, Ketchel, and Jeffries, he appeared bored as he toyed with his rivals. His blasé manner only served to further infuriate the boxing establishment. His autobiography illustrates his ennui with his fistic talents. Whereas Ali, Sugar Ray Robinson, and other top fighters go into detail about their boxing techniques, Johnson's only comments are general. "My defense completely baffled Burns."[5]

Luckily for posterity, several of Johnson's fights have been captured in film during the early days of motion pictures. Watching Johnson, poised with his feet at a perfect 45-degree angle, gloves spinning a web around the space between him and his opponent, one can hear the spider telling the fly, "Come into my parlor...." Johnson's footwork is economical to the point that he was criticized for shuffling around slowly and "loafing."[6] But he was quick and nimble as a cat when the punches flew. By moving only when he had to, he could fight with vigor for 20 rounds or more.

Modern fighters throw right uppercuts and right crosses, the first by throwing their weight up and across the body at an opponent who dips his head or comes in low. The right cross is designed to travel across the puncher's body, often over the opponent's left hand. One of Johnson's best punches was a hybrid of the uppercut and cross. From his chest, Johnson would pump his right fist to his opponent's face, shifting his weight as if throwing an uppercut. The blow was so short and quick that it can scarcely be seen on film. Against heavyweight champion Tommy Burns, Johnson twice in the first two rounds scored knockdowns with this short-arm jolt. Against Stanley Ketchel, the same blow sheared off "Stanbo's" teeth and sent him to dream land for the afternoon.

During his bout with the fearsome Michigan Assassin Stanley Ketchel, Johnson seemed much more worried about making a good show for the motion pictures than he seemed about his opponent. Several times he held Ketchel up, then swatted him around like a toy, causing blood to flow freely from Ketchel's face. At times Johnson, normally a flat-footed fighter, bounced on his toes like an early version of Muhammad Ali. Ketchel and Johnson were in fact friends and gambling buddies. According to Johnson, they had a deal to fight a "close" twenty-round fight, where Johnson would win on decision. The close decision would create a clamor for a rematch, where the two would make a fortune. This deal was worked up by Ketchel's manager Willis Britt, brother of lightweight contender Jimmy Britt. Willis Britt had achieved notoriety regarding a lightweight title fight between Jimmy Britt and Joe Gans. Gans had agreed to let Britt "make a good showing." But Britt went wild and fouled repeatedly, resulting in his disqualification. Britt then attacked the referee in anger and a melee ensued.[7] Ketchel also did not follow the script. In the twelfth round he threw a potent right-handed haymaker that knocked Johnson down. Johnson quickly got up and smashed Ketchel's face so hard that his teeth became imbedded in Johnson's glove. So much for the deal!

Some of Johnson's tactics against Ketchel and others are difficult to explain. Frequently, he would reach across with his right hand and hold his opponent's left arm or shoulder, trying to provoke his opponent to throw a left, so that he could counter with a right. Or, he simply could have been trying to wear down his opponent. Muhammad Ali was notorious for holding down his opponent's head to cause exhaustion of head and shoulders. Johnson's odd tactic may have had the same purpose.

On the rare occasion when Johnson was hit, his perfect 45-degree stance allowed the force of the blow to be absorbed as he rolled back with the punch. His oncoming opponent usually was hit with jabs and Johnson's ferocious uppercut. When viewing his films in slow motion, the uppercut has an explosive effect on the faces of his opponents, distorting their features while twisting their necks like wrung chickens.

Johnson's most famous fight was against Jim Jeffries. Against Jeffries, who was bigger than Johnson, Li'l Arthur snapped in quick left jabs and sharp right uppercuts. Jeffries' face was cut to ribbons. Several times at the end of a round, Johnson scored with a looping right over the top of Jeffries' guard. Johnson outclassed Jeffries so thoroughly that Congress passed a law to prohibit the distribution of the film. But the genie was out of the bottle, and the world knew that the myth of white superiority in the ring had been shattered.

Johnson, who was fond of posing *a la* Napoleon with his hand in his jacket, met his Waterloo in Havana. Despite his claim that he threw the fight, the film of the bout tells a different story. Jess Willard, half a foot taller than Johnson, could not be defeated by Johnson's usual tactics of laying back and countering. He had to take the fight to Willard, which he did quite effectively until he ran out of gas under the Havana sun.

Willard had trained extremely hard for the fight, whereas Johnson had barely trained at all. In the 25th round, Willard was able to tee off with a right hand to Johnson's body that caused him to gasp loud enough for several reporters at ringside to hear. In the next round Willard teed off again and threw his right, this time connecting to the point of Johnson's chin. Johnson, always on the lookout for a deal, may have been approached or himself asked for a quid-pro-quo for losing to Willard. Whatever the case, the film of the fight indicates that Johnson tried to win and was legitimately knocked out by a less skilled but better conditioned opponent. The fact that Johnson, as out of shape as he was, battered the much bigger Willard for 24 rounds is a testament to his great skill.

In Johnson's Own Words

Johnson's life outside the ring was even more intense than his ring battles. In his autobiography he states, "There were few men in any period of the world's history who have led a more varied or intense existence than I."[8]

Johnson writes with a wry wit of his adventures, much in the style of Voltaire's *Candide,* "hiding intellectual hostility under a thin veil of naiveté.'"[9] (Johnson had help from several French friends in penning his memoirs.) His first battle, at age 12, came not in the ring but on a fishing boat, against "a monster shark 23 feet long." Johnson was trying to make enough money so that he could travel to New York to meet Steve Brody, who had gained fame by jumping off the Brooklyn Bridge. As young Johnson fought the shark he worried. "I became convinced that Steve Brody was going to be denied the pleasure of a visit from me."[10]

Not content with the fishing life, Johnson took up boxing. After a handful of fights, Johnson left Galveston. As he said philosophically, "I did not know where I was going, but I was on my way."[11] One of the benefits of "freight train touring," whereby he stowed away to travel for free, was that he gained more fighting skills by defending himself against railroad detectives. Johnson was told by numerous town judges to hasten out of town. He said it was "just exactly what I wished to do, and what I was trying to do when the police interfered."[12] He wound up in Springfield, Illinois, compelled to stop because of the "erratic schedules of the trains" upon which he could ride for free. In Springfield he won a battle royal that gained for him the notice of the local boxing promoters.[13]

From 1894 through 1902, Johnson's record shows that he fought 43 professional bouts, losing only three times. His knockout victims included Jack Jeffries, brother of heavyweight champion Jim Jeffries. One of his losses was to Joe Choynski, a rugged and wily veteran who had fought all of the best heavyweights of the era. Both men were thrown into the Galveston jail for engaging in an illegal prizefight. While behind bars, Choynski tutored Johnson in the finer points of boxing, and Johnson left his cell a much wiser pugilist.

On February 3, 1903, Johnson won the Colored Heavyweight Championship by defeating Denver Ed Martin, a Colorado boxer known for a strong punch and a weak chin. He won twelve more fights before losing a disputed decision against Marvin Hart, who would soon succeed Jim Jeffries as heavyweight champion.

After Johnson became the Colored Heavyweight Champion he was ignored by Jeffries, who adamantly drew the color line to avoid risking his title against black men (although he had been perfectly happy to fight Peter Jackson in 1898 when the latter was wracked by TB.) During his pre-world title years, Johnson had fought the other top black fighters of his era. He defeated Joe Jennette, Sam McVey, and Sam Langford, among others. Johnson usually took it easy on his fellow black men, but there was one opponent he took pleasure in thrashing. Frank Childs had refused to let Johnson sleep inside his house one cold Chicago night, making his soon-to-be ex-friend sleep in the street.

According to Nat Fleischer's rendition of the encounter, Childs told Johnson to get lost in order to make room for his other guests:

"Come on, big fella. Come on. Git you'self out of this bed. I got company here to-night. Mah cousin from Memphis shares the bed with me tonight. Now listen here big boy. Up I say, up. This am no time foh follin.' Out of dis yere bed, I says. Out you come."

And with that he grabbed the blanket off the bed, pulled Johnson by the heels and yanked him to the floor, as big as he was.

Poor Johnson, was dumbfounded. He looked up at Childs with pleading eyes. The warm, woolen blankets felt like a million dollars to him that moment and when he awoke to the realization that he was being kicked out into the cold, blustering, blizzardly night, he remarked: "Please Mr. Childs, don't throw me out in that storm. You hear that storm? Hear that wind? I'll sleep on that floor. I'll do anything you want, but don't let me go out on the street."[14]

Johnson's pleas were to no avail and he was cast out into the bitter cold. He never forgot it and pounded Childs without mercy on the occasions when they fought.[15]

By the time that Tommy Burns became champ in 1906, Johnson was recognized as the top contender by all serious followers of boxing. The King of England called Burns a phony for posing as champ yet refusing to meet the man who was clearly the best challenger. Johnson literally followed Burns around the world before securing a title fight at Rushcutters Bay, Australia. Johnson knocked Burns down twice in the first round and seemingly carried him until the 13th round in order to punish Burns for all of the names he called Johnson. "Yellow," "cur," and worse epithets were spewed by Burns before, during, and after the fight. The police stopped the fight and shut off the cameras to shield

Jack Johnson won the heavyweight title with a 14th-round knockout of Tommy Burns of Australia — on Boxing Day — in Sydney (Studio card, November 1908; Colleen Aycock collection).

the world from the spectacle of a black man standing over his knocked out, white opponent. But Johnson was the world heavyweight champion. He said afterward that the Burns fight was one of the easiest of his career.[16]

The Great White Hopes

In those years leading up to World War I, a Czar or Kaiser claiming the U.S. presidency could hardly have caused more ire than a brash black man in America claiming the heavyweight championship of the world. A cry went out, notably from the pen of America's foremost writer Jack London, for someone to "wipe the golden smile" from Jack Johnson's face. In 1909 Johnson dispatched a half-dozen white hopes before finally obtaining his long sought match with Jim Jeffries on July 4, 1910, Independence Day in the United States. Jeffries, then considered the greatest heavyweight of all time, was favored to beat Johnson despite his advanced age and declining skills. The fight was originally scheduled for California, but the governor's wife was none too pleased with the attention shown to the heavyweight champ, "I declare, the people are more interested in a nigger fighter than their own governor."[17] To ensure the governor's domestic tranquility, the ring hostilities were relocated to Reno, Nevada.

Johnson so out-classed Jeffries that the latter admitted that he could never have beaten Johnson, even at his best. The film footage demonstrates that Johnson's ripping right uppercut spelled *finis* to Jeffries' challenge. In the fifteenth round, at ring center, Jeffries attempted a clinch, but failed to lock up Johnson's right arm. Johnson ripped in an uppercut that jerked Jeff's head up and back. Jeffries was out on his feet from the blow. Johnson followed him to the ropes and landed three left hooks that do not seem like hard punches, but they were enough to put Jeffries down, because of the uppercut that had separated him from his senses. After Jeffries rises, Johnson calmly measures him with his left and then crashes home a powerful right. Jeffries goes down again as his corner-men enter the ring. Johnson has his right cocked but seems worried about hitting the referee or one of Jeffries' seconds. Jim Corbett, the former heavyweight champion, seems to rush at Johnson, who turns as if to fight him off. Finally, referee Tex Rickard stopped the fight and raised Johnson's hand in

Ticket for the 1910 World's Heavyweight Championship title fight.

GAME CALIFORNIAN BEATEN
DOWN, ROUND AFTER ROUND

As Predicted in the 'Chronicle,'
the White Man Had
Lost His Stamina

By BEN BENJAMIN.

FRONTIER TOWN SWAMPED
WITH A FIGHT-MAD ARMY

Railway Yards Jammed With
Trains---Restaurants
Overcrowded

By "CHRONICLE" STAFF CORRESPONDENT.

TENS OF THOUSANDS APPLAUD QUICKNESS OF CHRONICLE'S FINE BULLETIN SERVICE

Top: Stands being built for the Johnson-Jeffries battle. *Bottom:* Not only could the Nevada stadium hold 10,000 people, newspaper offices attracted crowds by the hundreds and thousands, oftentimes, as in this picture in San Francisco, constructing a stadium of sorts that allowed an announcer to call out the ringside coverage via a megaphone.

WHITE GIANT BEATEN DOWN
BY EBONY FIGHTING MACHINE

JEFFRIES SAYS HE HAS
FOUGHT HIS LAST BATTLE

The Strong Back Muscles of the Victor and the Vanquished

Hugh McIntosh Tommy Burns John L. Sullivan Jimmy Coffroth Frank Gotch Billy Jordan Tom McCarry Bill Lang Fitzsimmons Tom Sharkey Geo. Harding Stanley Ketchell

No. 37. At the Ringside, Johnson-Jeffries Contest, Reno, July 4, '10.

Top: Jeffries' massive size and strength proved prior to the event that he was still a formidable champion. *Bottom:* White champions and sporting men introduced before the Johnson-Jeffries match, July 4, 1910. From left to right: Hugh McIntosh, Tommy Burns, John L. Sullivan, Jimmy Coffroth, Frank Gotch, Billy Jordan, Tom McCarry, Bill Lang, Bob Fitzsimmons, Tom Sharkey, George Harding, Stanley Ketchell. Sadly, Joe Gans, who was scheduled to be in Johnson's corner, was too ill to attend and died shortly after (Dana Brothers photograph).

By 1910 the newspapers began to capture the live action for the reading audience.

victory. Jeffries lay in a pitiable state. His nose was broken; his eyes were shut, and his tongue lolled, the color of the amethysts that the medieval soldiers wore into battle, as he gasped for air. Throughout his ordeal he plodded forward as if he had forgotten how to fight, just mimicking the motions of a boxer. Perhaps he believed the sycophantic praise of his followers, convinced that Johnson would surrender at his mere presence. The white sportswriters had claimed that the Anglo-Saxon race, with a legacy dating from Agincourt, was inherently superior on any field of battle. Johnson crushed that illusion forever, and therein lay the real reason for the hatred directed against him.

Before the fight, many threats were made that Johnson would be killed if he beat Jeffries. He was certainly vulnerable in the moments right after victory, standing in the ring. Tex Rickard was known for running a tight ship in his casinos, and his reputation as a straight lawman was known to lend credibility to his fight promotions. Considering the circumstances, the control of the Reno crowd was praiseworthy.

Mainstream America's anxiety over black ring prowess swelled the day after the Great White Hope fight when Jack Johnson's picture appeared on the entire front cover of the *San Francisco Chronicle*.

Riots broke out all over America, pitting jubilant blacks against bitterly disappointed whites. A black man ordering coffee with scrambled eggs and ketchup told the waiter, "I want my coffee as strong and black as Jack Johnson, and my eggs as red and smashed up as Jim Jeffries."[18] Johnson's pride was high and his fall was just over the horizon.

For Immoral Purposes

Between 1910 and 1913, while giant white men were being recruited to learn to box in the hope of some day dethroning Johnson, the government had decided against leaving something as important as the heavyweight championship to the merits and the skills of the fighters. Johnson's fascination with white women was every bit as strong as Achilles' heal was weak and exposed, and therein lay his downfall in Jim Crow America. A federal law passed in 1910, known as the Mann Act, made it illegal to "transport women across state lines for immoral purposes." The federal regulators, knowing that Johnson was in the habit of transporting his white girlfriends from state to state, or at least sending them money to be able to meet him, now decided to use the Mann Act as a tool against "Black Jack" that was more reliable than the sturdy fists of Jim Jeffries. In 1913 charges were soon brought against Johnson for a past liaison. The fact that a law was being retroactively enforced bothered the courts none too much, and Johnson was convicted and sentenced to prison.

The oft-maligned Reform-era legislation known as the Mann Act had an original purpose more noble than removing Jack Johnson from the public eye. Young women in turn-of-the-century America, especially recently arrived immigrants, were prey to white slavers who forced them into prostitution throughout the country. It was felt that federal legislation was needed to combat white slavery, since the states seemed to be ineffective in their efforts.

Johnson was ensnared in a tangled web of the legal system. For federal government jurisdiction to apply, prostitution practices had to be considered interstate commerce, for which the Constitution gave power of regulation to the federal government. Congress decided to target the act of crossing state lines with the intention to engage in prostitution. Although the Mann Act was clearly designed to combat prostitution and not mere sexual licentiousness or "immoral purposes," the authors of the bill felt it would be difficult to prove that prostitution had occurred as a result of or in conjunction with the transport of women. Prostitution flourished in many states but it was not in the realm of interstate commerce. Besides, it was difficult to catch a prostitute in the act. It usually required some sort of "sting" operation. In a similar vein, "pimping" is harder to establish than, to use the British legal phrase, "living off the immoral earnings of women."

To provide adequate protection to young women, Congress felt that the bar for prosecutors should be set low enough to encourage prosecutions. And so America soon became intimately acquainted with the phrase "transporting women across state lines for immoral purposes." Since most of the people who would be prosecuted were in fact pimps and "white slavers," their lawyers tended not to object to the understatement that they had "immoral purposes." The law at first went unchallenged.

Although Johnson had been cavorting from town to town with white women for years, and many were in fact at various times prostitutes, he was never in any way leading them into prostitution. On the contrary, with his hearty appetite he aimed to have them all to himself. The intent of the Mann Act clearly did not apply to Johnson's activities. But this fact in no way deterred the authorities from using the Mann Act against Johnson. To prove "immoral purposes," the government seemed to have employed the expedient of making Johnson prove a "moral purpose." For paying the expenses of his female entourage and carrying them from state to state, Johnson had no satisfactory explanation. And since the public was already preconditioned to the notion that Johnson had an immoral lifestyle, the government succeeded in its case despite numerous problems with the evidence.

Johnson's first alleged victim, Lucille Cameron, promptly married him, and then invoked the right of a married person to avoid testifying against her spouse. A second "victim," Belle Starr, whom Johnson had romanced prior to the effective date of the Mann Act, came forth with accusations. Jealous of Johnson's new wife and desiring to retaliate against him, Belle was held in protective custody while the government carefully coached her in what to say. After the charade of a trial, Johnson was sentenced to a year and a day in federal prison, but allowed a few weeks to file an appeal. He was released on bond and fled to Europe.

There is some evidence that the government was none too sorry to see Johnson flee the country. After his conviction, the FBI relaxed its monitoring of Johnson. Johnson told of his dramatic escape, disguised as a Negro baseball player. He says that he hid on a Negro baseball team's train and made a daring escape to Canada and from there to Europe. But it may well have just been the case of Uncle Sam looking the other way that enabled him to flee to Europe. As a champion in America, he was a threat to white supremacy, but as a convicted felon, fugitive from the law, he was of much less concern to U.S. authorities.

Johnson fled America, first to Canada and then to France, where he managed to defend his title in Paris just before the outbreak of World War I. In 1915, with war raging and feeling homesick, Johnson agreed, according to his claims, to lose his title to Jess Willard if the authorities would drop the morals charge against him. Willard knocked Johnson out under the scorching sun of Havana in 1915, but charges stateside were never dropped against Jack. He would roam the world like Odysseus for five more years before finally coming back to America to serve his sentence.

Johnson had already learned from his voyage to Australia that, although they may speak the King's English, he could not expect a royal welcome in the British Commonwealth. Although his conviction in America was for a non-extraditable offense, his status as a fugitive from justice made him unwelcome in English-speaking countries. And so, he would make his home in the traditional haven for expatriates: France.

The other great black heavyweights of the era — Langford, McVey, and Jennette, had already fought several major bouts in the land of Napoleon. Upon his arrival, Johnson had his picture taken with his hand in his jacket, in the classic Napoleonic pose. Li'l Arthur liked to point out that he too, like Napoleon, had risen from obscurity to great heights. Parisians, much more concerned with the very real German menace to their east than with any imaginary "Ethiopian menace," as blacks were called in America, welcomed Johnson as a top sporting figure and entertainer.

Johnson's private life was not such a contentious issue in Europe. During his adventurous life, he had four wives and probably hundreds of mistresses, but no offspring as far as recorded by posterity. Belle Starr, the femme fatale whose testimony resulted in Johnson's Mann Act conviction, referred casually to traveling with Johnson, "I was pregnant at the time." It is a fairly safe assumption that many, or most, of the pregnancies of the "sporting women" were aborted. In any case, it is worth noting that despite Johnson's Olympian sexual activities, neither children nor sexually transmitted diseases are attributed to him.

The FBI maintained extensive files on Johnson from his championship days throughout

the rest of his life. Johnson was perhaps guilty of more than paying the expenses of prostitutes. The FBI files, with names redacted in many places, charge that Johnson frequently
beat the women of his entourage. According to an FBI report dated October 19, 1937, "Belle
Starr, who later was the victim in a white slave case in which Johnson was the subject,
testified at the trial that Johnson beat her on an average of once a week, frequently blacking
her eyes, and that on one occasion he beat her with an automobile wrench until her body
was black and blue and she had to remain in bed for a time."[19] Given the zeal with which
the government pursued Johnson on the Mann Act violation, the lack of assault prosecutions
against Johnson is noteworthy. The reliability of the accusations may have been too flimsy
even for the overreaching lawmen on the Johnson case. On the other hand, Johnson's second
wife Etta Duryea was hospitalized, apparently from a beating she sustained from Johnson.
She claimed she had fallen, so as to avoid having to press charges against Johnson. Despite
his cool exterior, Johnson evidently had trouble controlling his temper. His apparent rough
handling of women hardened the government's resolve to throw the book at him on the
Mann Act charge.

Johnson hoped to find in Europe a new home free from racism. Although he was
treated with more hospitality in the Old World than in the new, he still had his run-in with
prejudice in England and France, where despite his wealth he was often denied entrance to
the best hotels and restaurants.

Fate found the world's greatest fighter in the powder keg of France at the outbreak of
World War I. According to Johnson's autobiography, he knew war was imminent from the
troop exercises he viewed in and around Paris while he trained there to defend his title
against Frank Moran.

The war to end all wars did no such thing, but the spark that ignited it succeeded in
hastening the downfall of the Galveston Giant. On June 27, 1914, Johnson fought a 20-
round bout against Moran in the City of Light, in the last great European sporting event
prior to the Great War. The morning after the fight, Archduke Ferdinand of Australia was
shot in Sarajevo over nationalist disputes in the Balkans, setting into motion a four-year
orgy of death on the continent.

The Moran bout lasted the full twenty rounds, and Johnson won easily. Many of the
spectators complained that he had taken it easy on his opponent so that the film of the fight
would include the full twenty rounds. But "carrying" an opponent did not violate Queensberry rules nor Johnson's right to his purse, and several newspapers praised Johnson's performance in the fight. Johnson expected to receive approximately $30,000 against the gate
receipts, plus his share of the movie rights. However, the French lawyer who held the money
in trust was called up by the French army and killed by the Germans on the western front,
and Johnson was left high and dry.

The money for the Moran fight may have enabled Johnson to better navigate the events
that followed in quick succession. If the war had not consumed Europe, he may have waited
it out there and "lived a new life in the Old World," as he declared was his intention. In
his autobiography, Johnson recounts that his diplomatic efforts did much to improve Franco-
American relations, and that he was well on his way to becoming a star in Paris. But then
Johnson found himself broke in war-torn Europe, where there was little market for boxing
exhibitions or any other kind of entertainment. Johnson first fled Europe to Argentina, then
Mexico, but found it hard to pay the enormous bills he was so used to running up with his
high style of living.

According to Johnson, he was offered a deal whereby he would lose the championship in Havana to Jess Willard, in exchange for the U.S. government dropping the Mann Act charges. But the government still wanted its pound of flesh, and Johnson would get no commutation of his year-and-a-day sentence. America has not treated black heavyweight champions well. In the 20th century the U.S. government first hounded Johnson on specious Mann Act charges, then drove Joe Louis to financial ruin for back taxes on purses he had donated to the World War II effort, then sentenced Muhammad Ali to five years of prison for "having no quarrel with the Viet-Cong." At the end of the century, Iron Mike Tyson served three years in jail on what many think were trumped-up rape charges. While Tyson served his sentence, a new war in the Balkans was brewing over conflicts similar to those that had ignited the Great War.

Johnson's Color Line

The mantle of representative of his race did not fit well on Jack Johnson, nor did he really want it to. He was an individualist who considered himself worthy to walk with kings. His purpose was always to maximize his own self-expression. Not only did he prefer white women, once he won the heavyweight crown he preferred white opponents to the point that he drew his own color line.

Three fighters in particular were shut out from the heavyweight title picture while Johnson was champion: Joe Jennette, Sam Langford, and Sam McVey. He held victories over all three from his pre-title days. The fights had been more difficult than his fights against white fighters, and he simply saw no reason to risk fighting tough black boxers when the world would pay so much to see him fight, and hopefully lose to, the white hopes of the era.

Of the three black challengers, Langford and his manager pursued a title fight most doggedly. Johnson had won a clear-cut decision over Langford, having knocked him down twice and cut him up severely, but as Langford put on more weight and gained experience, many thought that Langford could beat Johnson. Johnson wanted nothing to do with the fight.

Johnson had knocked out Sam McVey in the 20th round of their fight. Joe Jennette had given him the most trouble in the ring and Johnson was unable to achieve a decisive decision over Jennette.

Once Johnson had let himself go and become lax in his approach to boxing after the Jeffries fight, any of the three fighters would have had a good chance to take the championship. But Johnson, having struggled so long to reach the top, was not about to risk his position for the amount he could make fighting another black fighter. Langford would repeatedly challenge Johnson in public, and Johnson would side step and parry the attempts with all the skill he had learned in the boxing ring. Nobody was going to pin him in the corner!

In the drama of the ring, there had to be a villain, against a hero wearing a white hat. Johnson was convinced that black fighters would always be considered the villains by white Americans, and hence there was no way to stage a money-making drama with two black men.

Johnson's autobiography portrays him as having worked towards international understanding among nations. He writes of his close acquaintance with Tsar Nicolas of Russia, President Carranza of Mexico, and others. While in Europe, Johnson brushed shoulders with the cream of the Old World. On many occasions he would sit down and discuss world issues "man to man" with important Europeans. Johnson at one point opined publicly that France and England had started the 1914 war with Germany. Johnson saw himself as a man at the center of all things when penning his memoirs. "I have been with kings and queens; monarchs and rulers of nations have been my associates."[20]

Johnson in Mexico

His diplomatic skills notwithstanding, Johnson soon wore out his welcome in Europe. He then ventured down to the land of Montezuma. Poor Mexico, as Porfirio Diaz had lamented, so far from God and so close to the United States. During World War I Mexico had flirted with joining Germany against the United States. President Carranza had ultimately decided it was not feasible, but his goal of nationalizing the U.S. oil interests made him quite unpopular north of the border. Not surprisingly, Johnson the fugitive was a welcomed guest of the Carranza regime. In Mexico City he bought a casa and fought exhibitions there and in Tijuana, under the protection of Carranza's generals. He put out a statement urging American blacks to forsake America and come join him in the "free country" of Mexico.[21]

But alas, Johnson's south-of-the-border utopia came to an end when Carranza met the familiar fate of the era's South American potentates and was assassinated. As was customary, the assassin's bullet, though fatal, still left time for Carranza to utter a pithy, final line: "They have already broken my left leg." After due analysis, it was determined that this was a reference to one of his deputies who had been assassinated the previous month. (Of all the last lines uttered by mortally wounded generalissimos, Pancho Villa's surely takes the prize: "I can't think of anything," he admitted, clutching at the blood gurgling from his wound, "But think of something clever and tell them I said it.")

So Johnson, *menos* his *amigo* Carranza, found himself *persona non grata* in Old Mexico. He put out feelers to see if he could get a reduced sentence back in the U.S.

Papa Jack was never shy about doing anything to make a buck. On October 2, 1935, Jack Johnson made his Operatic debut in *Aida*, playing the role of an Ethiopian general (Colleen Aycock collection).

Nothing doing, came the reply. Johnson waited. Within a few months of Carranza's death, Johnson was told that he would have to leave Mexico. With FBI agents following his moves in every border town from Texas to California, he finally submitted to the inevitable, returned to the United States, and served his year at Leavenworth.

But Lady Luck had not entirely forsaken Johnson. The warden of the prison was Denver Dickerson, the former governor of Nevada who had profited handsomely from the Jeffries fight in Reno. He arranged for Johnson to be the athletic director of the prison during his stay. Johnson spent his time training and was in such good shape upon his release that a match with the new champion Jack Dempsey was a serious consideration. However, Dempsey was none too anxious to fight Johnson, or in fact any of the other top black heavyweights.

Johnson as Ex-Champion and His Effect on Other Black Fighters

Through his travels Johnson had acquired quick wits, self-reliance, and often the air of an *artiste*. He even became a moralist. At the age of 50, when he penned an autobiography, he took the time to bemoan the faltering morality of the jazz age.

In later life, he let his presence be known during the career of Joe Louis. To the dismay of Louis's idolizers, he correctly predicted that Louis would lose to Max Schmeling. Johnson said that Louis's stance was all wrong, and that he was open to right hands. His prediction was spot-on accurate.

Before the second Louis-Billy Conn fight in 1946, Johnson, a youthful 68 years old, was on his way to the event when he stopped at a diner that refused to serve him because he was black. An infuriated Johnson sped away so recklessly that he crashed into a tree and was killed. In the end, it was neither lust nor pride, but wrath that was his deadly sin. Today it is perhaps best for his legacy and forgivable that he went out in a fury, before taking on the air of a conquered warrior who plays for dimes in an Old West burlesque show.

An unfortunate result of Jackson's unrepentant lifestyle was that after his defeat by Willard, opportunity for other black fighters all but disappeared. No black heavyweight was allowed a title shot for over 20 years, and even in the lighter weight classes, blacks were for the most part denied championship opportunities. Jack Blackburn blamed Jack Johnson for the plight of black boxers prior to Joe Louis.

Johnson continued to fight until his late forties.

Jack Johnson's gravesite at Graceland Cemetery, Chicago, Illinois (photograph by Tony Triem, 1967, Tony Triem collection).

Today Johnson is remembered as a remarkably talented individualist. In the ring he combined punching power with the scientific defensive skills of the Old Master, Joe Gans. Johnson always admired Gans, and would visit Gans' Goldfield Hotel in Baltimore whenever he passed through. Like Gans, Johnson contributed to the world of music by opening a nightclub, in Harlem, the *Club Deluxe*, that was later bought by gangsters and turned into the Cotton Club.

The Civil Rights movement, the Viet Nam war, and the increasing radicalism of the 1960s eventually rehabilitated the memory of Jack Johnson. When Muhammad Ali challenged white authority by refusing induction into the armed services, comparisons between Ali and Johnson were inevitable. In 1970 James Earl Jones starred in *The Great White Hope*, a popular drama based on Johnson's life.

In the 1960s and 1970s, Muhammad Ali's trainers would shout encouragement from his corner, "Ghost in the house, the ghost of Jack Johnson is watching." [22] And if in fact Papa Jack was somewhere above looking down with his irrepressible golden smile on Ali, the Sugar Rays, Smokin' Joe, and the other ring artists who came after him, one might imagine that he liked what he saw.

NOTES

1. Randy Roberts, *Papa Jack*, 2.

2. Roberts, 145.

3. Geoffrey Ward, *Unforgivable Blackness*, 26.

4. Colleen Aycock and Mark Scott, *Joe Gans: A Biography of the First African American World Boxing Champion* (Jefferson, NC: McFarland, 2009), 239.

5. Dick Schaap, *Jack Johnson is a Dandy, An Autobiography*, 130.

6. Rex Lardner and Alan Bodian, *The Legendary Champions*, 173.

7. Aycock and Scott, 118.

8. Schaap, 17.

9. Ian Davidson, *Voltaire in Exile* (New York: Grove Press, 2005), 54.

10. Schaap, 29.

11. Schaap, 27.

12. Ibid.

13. Schaap, 29.

14. Nat Fleischer, *Black Dynamite, Vol. IV, The Fighting Furies*, 10–11.

15. Schaap, 42.

16. Ibid.

17. Aycock and Scott, 272.

18. Arthur Ashe, *Hard Road to Glory*, 22.

19. Roberts, 212.

20. Schaap, 18.

21. Roberts, 212.

22. Aycock and Scott, 30.

CHAPTER 14

Speedball Hayden: U.S. Army Middleweight Champion

Chris Cozzone

The year was 1916 and the world heavyweight belt was safely strapped around the waist of "Great White Hope" Jess Willard, who, the year before in Cuba, had purged the sport of its only black heavyweight champion, Jack Johnson. Willard was ready to make his first defense against Frank Moran. Meanwhile, perennial contenders Harry Wills and Sam Langford, denied a chance at the real belt, had finished battling one another again (they would do so a remarkable 22 times), for the Negro version of the title. Though the color lines had been redrawn deeper than ever within the squared circle after Johnson had squinted up at the harsh Havana sun the year before, America had more important threats to sweat about than the bang of black fistiana.

There was the growing threat of world war for the U.S.

And there was Pancho Villa.

Sometimes war has a way of tolling the bell for boxing. Other times, as would be seen during World War I, the sport that suffered in civilian quarters not only witnessed a boom in the military, but would later return with a vengeance to, once again, consume the entire culture for decades to come. Sometimes, war has a way of softening the color lines set so harshly in previous years. This was such a time.

Maybe it was a short-lived era, but for a handful of years, during one World War and under threat of another, down at the border, American preoccupation with race eased, long enough to institute a new breed of boxing champions in the Army.

The era gave rise to an elite corps of black fighters who, at least for a time, were forgiven their color long enough to enjoy the limelight as local box-office draws, regional champions and national heroes.

It's been nearly 100 years now, and the public will not recognize the names — Thomas "Speedball" Hayden, Rufus "The Old Master" Williams and Hock Bones, to name a few — but their mention just might ring a bell for some boxing aficionados. If Mark Matthews were still alive, he might be able to tell you a little something about the names. Matthews, who died at the age of 111 in 2005, was the last remaining Buffalo Soldier, which might also have marked him as the last ringside witness to a handful of fights that occurred between 1916 and 1917, in a makeshift ring out in the desert, somewhere in Mexico.

Somewhere in Mexico

As part of the Punitive Mexican Expedition led by Brigadier General John Pershing, Matthews was one of 12,000 soldiers sent into the heart of Mexico to find—and capture—Francisco "Pancho" Villa.

Before there was a reason for such an expedition, there was the hustling, bustling border-town of Columbus, New Mexico. A stone's throw from Palomas, Mexico, and 75 miles west of El Paso, Columbus has dwindled down to a population of 1,800 or so, but once upon a time, it was home to Camp Furlong.

One of several military outposts in southern New Mexico and Texas—others included Camp Cody outside of Deming, N.M., Fort Bayard and El Paso's Fort Bliss—Camp Furlong had been populated to deal with the Mexican Revolution taking place on the opposite side of the border, and to contain the war from spilling onto U.S. soil.

One day, that threat became all too real. While no one can forget what happened on the morning of September 11, 2001, very few people realize that this country had been invaded once before, on the morning of March 9, 1916. Pancho Villa, feeling betrayed by the U.S. government, which continued to recognize Mexico under President Venustiano Carranza, and spurned by a local merchant who had been supplying him with weapons and ammunition, ordered his troops to attack the Columbus outpost. Eighteen men died. Six days later, President Woodrow Wilson ordered General Pershing to capture Villa. Leading 12,000 soldiers, Pershing pushed ahead into Mexico in search of the Mexican generalissimo.

In a way, one can credit General Villa with giving boxing a boost in the arm, for without the invasion, there would've been no Punitive Expedition; and without the Punitive Expedition, there wouldn't have been quite the explosion of sweet science upon Pershing's return, 11 months later. Though it was obviously not his intent to set in motion a sequence of events that would give rise to a boxing explosion, paving the way for otherwise never-heard-of black fighters, Villa was no stranger to boxing.

For several years during the Mexican Revolution while headquartering in Juarez, Villa had encouraged boxing to thrive on his side of the border, assuring safe travel for gringos willing to cross over. In fact, for

Army Champion Speedball Hayden in fighting pose, 1919 (Chris Cozzone collection).

nearly two months, it looked as if the Jack Johnson-Jess Willard fight of 1915 was going to take place in the Villa-occupied city of Juarez.

Promoter Jack Curley not only met with Villa's emissaries, but, with a handshake, established a March 6 date. "General Villa nor anyone connected with him, directly or indirectly, has made any move for any financial gain out of the coming match," Curley told local media. "Everybody connected with Juarez and El Paso has been as enthusiastic as myself to bring the fight here."[1]

Everything was set. That is, until President Carranza, less than thrilled about helping

American General John Pershing headed up the Punitive Expedition, which, beginning in 1916, trailed Pancho Villa into Mexico for over a year (Library of Congress).

his enemy Villa out in any way, threatened to arrest Johnson should he set foot in Mexico. The fight was moved to Havana.

Though known to be an avid boxing fan, Villa could be a bit harsh and heavy-handed in dealing with American *boxeadores*. Top Texan lightweight-contender Bobby Waugh wasn't too happy after fighting long-time nemesis Benny Cordova in Juarez on September 19, 1915. In their third fight together, the two went 20 rounds to a draw in a heavy downpour at the Plaza de los Toros, making him 1–0–2 against the Albuquerque and El Paso favorite. Waugh, who'd given the border town one of the most thrilling wars in its century-long boxing history, when he'd decisioned legendary Battling Nelson just one month before, called it a hometown frame-up. Though the crowd received the decision with cheers, Waugh later said that he'd been given a death threat by representatives of General Villa if he whipped the local favorite. On his way to Shreveport, Louisiana for yet another fight, Waugh told his hometown paper in Fort Worth that he had stalled for the last ten rounds in fear of his life. Waugh, by the way, never was able to put Cordova out; the two fought seven times, Waugh winning four and drawing three times,—120 rounds total during a rivalry that spanned three years.

Another time, Villa threatened to arrest main-event light heavyweights Fred "Kid" George and Bob York when they fought on October, 1915, if there was any stalling during their 20-round affair. In the end, however, it wasn't Villa's attempts to secure Johnson-Willard, or his allowance and promise of safe travel to *Americanos* attending the fights at the local bullring in Juarez, but his own fighting that sparked the boxing revolution seen during the next four years.

Villa was trailed for a year by General Pershing, 400 miles into Mexico, until the failed mission wrapped up on Feb. 7, 1917. Though Pershing deemed the Expedition successful, most others did not, saying that little was seen but "cactus, horn toads, rattlesnakes and thistles."[2] From the standpoint of sweet scientists, however, the Punitive Expedition was a hit. In order to keep soldiers occupied — and entertained — electricity was hooked up for movie shows and vaudeville theatrics. There was also boxing. Of the 12,000 troops assigned to the Expedition, there were a dozen seasoned prizefighters, not to mention rookies willing to learn — and having plenty of time to do it.

One such fighter was San Francisco welterweight Rufus Williams, assigned to the 10th Cavalry, who'd carved out a reputation fighting on the West Coast since 1910. With an estimated tally of 50 fights, the West Coast battler had made a name for himself by taking on guys like the highly-rated middleweight Battling Ortega and heavyweight veteran Willie Meehan, usually by giving up weight. He would later claim that he'd fought "no more than five boys at my weight" during his career.[3]

In 1914, Williams had enlisted, furthering his reputation as a boxer by taking out his Army peers when stationed in Hawaii and the Philippines. After a brief "rest" in San Francisco, during which he fought several times, the last being a TKO loss to Ortega, Williams found himself part of the 10th Cavalry heading into Mexico to join Gen. Pershing. William's company, the 10th Cavalry, and the 24th Infantry, from which a host of black fighters would emerge, were segregated units that had been part of the original Buffalo Soldiers during the Civil War. Stationed back in Columbus, New Mexico, after the Punitive Expedition, both units — especially the 24th — would become hotbeds of fistic talent.

Williams would not only emerge as *the* fighter from the Expedition, but, equally important, would take a young 24th infantryman named Thomas Hayden under his wing. The lives and careers of Williams and Hayden would intertwine for years. In addition to Williams, there was Whitey Burns, Joe (Brock) Blackburn, Bull Foster, Jack Fitzgerald, Fighting Dick

Oleson, Jack Arnold, Kid Carr, Joe Kale, Benny Miller, Young Allen, Jack Mulvaney and Battling Dovitch — all former prizefighters before enlisting.

Boxing legend Jack Blackburn (no known relation to Joe Brock Blackburn, though it's not impossible that the latter assumed a *nom de ring* from the former's influence) also claimed to be part of the Expedition. Blackburn, on his way to solidifying a legendary greatness, had his career sidelined in 1909 when he was convicted of manslaughter and sentenced to 10 to 15 years in prison. After serving nearly five years, he was released and, after another 100 or more fights, would wind up training the great Joe Louis.

The first fight card (there were at least eight total) on the Expedition was staged on July 13, 1916, when "The 20-foot ring was pitched on a knoll said to be the resting place of Aztec chiefs who held sway in this region centuries ago. Members of General Pershing's staff and other officers each carried his own empty gasoline can or wooden box for his ringside seat, while the cheering soldiers squatted on the ground."[4] Six bouts were staged, with the main event between two unidentified black fighters, of which it was written: "A big colored man from the Tenth cavalry was matched against a Twenty-fourth infantryman." Neither a description of the fight nor the winner was named, though the report included that "Several of the white fighters bore army reputations for their cleverness with the gloves."[5]

It is doubtful that the "big colored man" could have been Williams, for just the night before he'd been stopped in the third round by Battling Ortega. By October, however, Williams' name found its way into the boxing reports wired out of Columbus, New Mexico, when he was matched with 47-year-old veteran Joe Brock Blackburn of the 24th. The grizzled veteran, despite his age, won a moral victory by going the 20-round distance with Williams, who was awarded the decision. The two were next matched for December 9, for the Punitive Army's Middleweight Title. This time, however, Blackburn was kayoed in the eighth.

In between the Blackburn matches, Williams was allowed to take a break from the desert to headline a civilian card at the Crystal Theatre in Columbus in a match that saw no color lines. Up against San Antonio's Bull Foster, stationed at Fort Bliss but on his way to an assignment under Pershing, Williams proved himself a superior boxer by winning a 15-round decision. Since New Mexico law capped boxing matches at 10 rounds, the two went ten stanzas, and then quickly signed articles for five extra rounds.)

After a half-dozen shows that netted a $5,000 profit for the camp, the talk of the camp centered around two names: Rufus Williams, and a blond-topped scrapper from the 16th Cavalry, Whitey Burns, who was challenging both welters and middleweights. Burns had claimed the U.S. Army middleweight title in August, by virtue of a 20-round decision over Californian Jack Fitzgerald, while on the Expedition. To satisfy the question of superiority, Burns had been matched with Williams sometime after, and the result had been a 20-round draw.

On Jan. 2, 1917, the two were re-matched,

Rufus Williams, U.S. Army welterweight champion, also known as the "Old Master" (Chris Cozzone collection).

this time for the Pershing-approved U.S. Army Welterweight Title. There was also no question as to whom the winner was, and the wire report citing Williams' championship win made him a national name. Even before defeating Burns, Williams was being called "Pershing's mascot."[6] "Army officers arriving from Mexico say the name of Williams is synonymous with victory among the Punitive Expedition troopers, so much so that Major General Pershing is said to be deeply interested in Williams' success, even if folks do call Williams 'cinder colored.'"[7]

The Expedition was winding down.

After losing to Williams, Burns got a bit of revenge by accomplishing what his nemesis could not do, in knocking out Bull Foster (round unknown), in what was the final fight card on Pershing's Expedition. With Williams and Burns at the helm, the army fighters returned to their posts — from Camp Furlong to Fort Bliss — sparking a new era in local — and soldier — boxing.

Boxing at the Border

It wasn't as if the scene needed that much of a kick-start. The area was thriving. Off military bases, in New Mexico, Albuquerque had been established as the state's headquarters (this, despite Las Vegas' attempts to be the top spot after hosting the Jack Johnson — Jim Flynn World Heavyweight Championship fight in 1912), but there were few towns that did not host monthly fights. As World War I approached, however, fight centers shut down their rings, losing their local fighters to enlistment.

In close proximity to the border, the mining towns continued to plug away with local pugs. Silver City, Deming, Tyrone and Hurley staged shows, though the frequent fight centers became Fort Bliss in El Paso, Columbus, Camp Cody, just outside Deming, and Fort Bayard, as well as Juarez.

When Texas politicians decided to enforce a buried law that made civilian boxing illegal, El Paso promoters got smart and began staging shows at a hastily constructed outdoor arena just over the Rio Grande, just across from El Paso, but technically on New Mexico land. The Smelter Arena — under different promoters and new construction — existed off and on through the early 1930s while Texas struggled with its prizefighting laws.

In Juarez, the Smelter Arena, the mining towns of New Mexico, and the military bases, boxing flourished when the United States entered World War I on April 6, 1917. The camps existed to keep the border secure and to serve as training grounds for soldiers who were shipped overseas. The combination, of small-town fighting and competition between forts — sparked by the return of Punitive fighters — would, over the next several years, transform the sport in the area, providing the stiffest competition ever seen.

Despite the Hispanic population, proximity to Mexico, and sudden influx of soldiers to the camps — a healthy sampling of the American melting pot — local black fighters were prominent on the boxing scene in New Mexico and El Paso.

Black Fighters of Brown Towns

This was long before former World Light-Heavyweight Champion Bobby Foster would bring home the first world title to New Mexico in 1968. For the first 100 years of organized prizefights, there were no black fighters from this locale able to break through to contention, let alone garner the much-coveted Rocky Mountain Regional Championships that decided whether one was worthy enough to "invade" the West or East Coast cities from which rose world champs.

Early fight reports rarely identified black fighters by name, referring to their bouts as unscientific scraps between "darkies" or "coons." In the mid–1880s, John Hogan, fighting out of Las Vegas, New Mexico, took on all comers, winning ten straight matches against both whites and Hispanics, until the town put a temporary stop to prizefighting. "The coon sluggers might as well leave town," wrote the editor of the *Las Vegas Optic*. "The people have had quite enough."[8]

Several years later, Buck Childs of Santa Fe suffered a similar fate. In the 1890s, others appeared on the scene — Happy Jack of Las Vegas and Albuquerque's John Marshall were two of the best — but they were no match to the area's top names: James Flynn, from the Cerrillos mines, Billy Lewis and "Australian" Billy Smith, the latter two from El Paso. It took more than another decade for a black prizefighter to make headlines.

In 1908, Harry Wallace, a seasoned prizefighter from Kansas City, Missouri, claiming 27 bouts with just two losses (one of those being to legend Stanley Ketchel), stopped off at the fight centers while traveling through as a goat herder. Several towns, from Cimarron to Las Vegas, matched him up. Wallace proved too much for the local fighters, until he was matched with William Pettus, a baseball player who was making the transition into prizefighting. When the two fought in Cimarron on March 7, 1909, Pettus nearly knocked out Wallace, but had to settle for a 15-round decision.

Wallace disappeared and Pettus' popularity soared. When he lost a 20-round decision to rising Colorado star "Fireman" Jim Flynn, Sept. 22, 1909, in Pueblo, Colorado, Pettus migrated to the West Coast to make it big. Though he became a regular sparring partner for Sam Langford, Pettus had no luck securing fights and journeyed home, where, after headlining an Albuquerque card and losing to Tony Caponi in a dull match, he returned to baseball, rising to fame in the Negro Leagues in New York.

Though unable to reach stardom as a pugilist, Pettus paved the way for several other African Americans in the Southwest — a list that includes Al Smaulding, the "Clayton Blacksmith," Lefty Floyd, Young Jack Johnson, who rose to local fame in Silver City as "Big Smoke," and Jeff "The Fighting Ghost" Clarke, of Joplin, Missouri. While failing to either reach contention or elevate black fighters from the level of battle royals in which they were mainly utilized, what Pettus, Smaulding, and Clarke achieved was to prepare the Southwest fight centers for headline black soldier boxers.

Reign of Rufus

Rufus Williams, now with the 24th Infantry at Camp Furlong, Columbus, became the man to beat. Williams barely had time to shake off the sand from the Mexican desert when he became the headliner of a card in Columbus, where he was now stationed.

Henry Smith, Williams' manager, had tried to tempt now–U.S. Army Welterweight Champion Johnny Newton — who was all the rage at Fort Bliss — offering $1,000 to fight "the black demon of Columbus." "The Ohio champion has earned much more than a thousand while boxing here, and the fans need not be surprised if the Buckeye slammer takes on the Columbus darkey."[9] Fans, however, were surprised. Passing on Smith's "roll of greenbacks," Newton's manager, Bill Hull, "refused to entertain a proposition calling for his boy to meet the darkey cyclone."[10] Instead, Bart Gordon, a four-year Missouri veteran who'd been fighting out of Roswell, New Mexico, was signed. Gordon, despite a pudgy appearance, was a sponge for punishment, and took Williams the distance.

Making his pro debut on the card — or actually, making the leap from battle royals to a full-fledged prelim — was a youngster under the tutelage of Williams, Thomas Hayden, who would soon earn the name "Speedball," due to his rapid rise and ring speed.

With Columbus civilians unable to slake their thirst for boxing, another card was thrown together six days later, with Williams. At a comfortable 150 pounds, Williams gave up 35 pounds to longtime Colorado veteran Mexican Pete Everett. The Cripple Creek prizefight pioneer had been fighting sporadically throughout the Southwest for the previous year. Though now 42, having first fought in 1894, the well-aged Everett had proven a crafty foe, having scored an upset kayo over Kid George, going 1–1–1 with Silver City's black hope, Young Jack Johnson, in 1916, and decisioning little-known Australian Tommy Dempsey at the Juarez Bull Ring in January 1917. The man who'd gone 20 with Jack Johnson in 1902 and less than three with James Jeffries in 1898 lasted but four, despite the weight advantage, with Williams.

In a rematch from the previous November, Williams was paired with Bull Foster, a favorite at both Columbus and at Fort Bliss where he was stationed. It was another decision-victory, this time at ten rounds for Williams. With no immediate challenge coming from the boot camps and Newton still reluctant, Williams stayed busy by stepping in for his rising star Hayden, when his pupil injured his hand on June 19 against Chicago veteran "Curly" Jack White, who gave up 12 pounds to the local favorite. Unable to land anything on his bigger foe, White resorted to a low shot and lost by DQ early in the second.

On the Fourth of July, Williams obliged Bull Foster yet again, "who did not seem to mind the rain of blows a bit," in a third meeting that ended the same way as the first two — with a decision win for Williams.[11] Despite his several callouts, there were no longer any willing challengers for Williams. Except for one — Speedball Hayden.

Speedball's Rise

Born in Georgetown, Kentucky, and raised in Indianapolis, Indiana, Thomas M. Hayden worked as a hostler until enlisting in 1915. Henry Davis, a Columbus promoter who would become Hayden's manager, was also a former sparring partner for Jack Johnson. He claimed that his charge, 130 pounds, at 15, turned to boxing while being groomed as a jockey in Indiana, clearing out the local circuit and rising to Midwest stardom before enlisting. Hayden, however, never referenced earlier fights beyond a handful of battle royals.

Davis, no doubt to build up Hayden's rep, also claimed that his fighter, while briefly stationed at

Speedball Hayden, U.S. Army middleweight champion from the 24th Infantry (Chris Cozzone collection).

Columbus, Ohio, cleaned house so effectively that he was kept secret while with the 24th Infantry in the Philippines in the boxing circuit. "They considered the young negro an ace and kept him under cover," said Davis. "The matchmaker later refused to put him on, insisting that he start only in battle royals."[12]

Later, while on Pershing's Expedition, Davis claims Rufus Williams attempted to use Hayden as a punching bag but was given such a trouncing that "Rufus called a halt 'because he did not wish to hurt Hayden.'"[13]

The story of Williams discovering and teaching Hayden, rather than picking on or keeping secret a man he feared, is the one told for years at the border. Soft-spoken and respectful, Hayden never disputed the stories.

Hayden might have tried his luck at battle royals in the Philippines, but his name does not pop up until he was with the 24th in Mexico — and Williams is the man credited with not only discovering the soon-to-be "Speedball," but the one who developed him. Under Williams' tutelage, Hayden picked up experience fighting battle royals on several shows staged throughout the Punitive Expedition. Then, on March 3, 1917, just after Pershing's troops had returned, Hayden made his pro debut on a card headlined by his mentor Williams, winning a four-round decision against James Williams, also with the 24th Infantry.

Two more bouts in March — two decisions over Ernest Gill — and a month off in April prepared Hayden for his first title fight. On May 30, Hayden took on the more experienced Gene "Baby" Cabell for the 24th Infantry's welterweight title. Though a "bundle of nerves" in the early rounds, Hayden, "going like a quarter horse," floored the hard-hitting veteran three times before toppling Cabell for the count in round six.[14]

Headlining his second card, Hayden was next matched against the aged veteran Joe Brock Blackburn, former Army Middleweight Champion, who had the year before gone a 20-round distance with Williams. The fight was a disappointment, however, when Blackburn, either in round three or five (depending on the source), claimed a low blow. The referee awarded the win to Hayden, who'd injured his hand in the bout. The injury sidelined Hayden for a June 19 headliner (Williams subbed for his protégé) against Chicago veteran Jack White. Hayden, who was now being called either "Flash" or "Cannonball," had a bad showing in a dull draw with A. B. Harrison, a bout that "was more in nature of a love affair."[15]

Three successive knockouts followed, over black and white soldier-boxers. By the end of October, after a falling out with Williams, Hayden, whose name was now solidified as "Speedball," was being touted as a challenger for the U.S. Army Middleweight Champion, his former teacher, Rufus Williams.

The Teacher Mastered

Though New Mexicans in the civilian quarters might have dubbed the Joe Rivers–Bobby Waugh match, of November 15 in Silver City as the years' biggest fight, with the U.S. at war and the national press given soldier boxers, the November 22 showdown between Rufus "The Old Master" Williams and rising 24th star Speedball Hayden was certainly the most significant fight in the area.

It had all the elements of a classic. Hayden, 8–0–1, with 5 kayos, was the busier, faster, and younger challenger. Williams had far superior punching power, ring generalship, and the experience of half a hundred fights dating back to 1910. Furthermore, Williams had not lost a fight since his 1916 loss to Ortega.

BOXING CHAMPIONSHIP
CONTEST

CRYSTAL THEATRE
Columbus, N. M.
THURSDAY, NOV. 22, 1917

RUFUS WILLIAMS

155 Pounds, "The Old Master"   Middle Weight Champion U. S. Army

vs

THOMAS HAYDEN

145 Pounds. "Speed Ball"   Welter Weight Champion of the 24th Infantry

RUFUS WILLIAMS, (the Old Master) needs no introduction to the sport-loving public, being the undisputed champion of the whole U. S. Army, having successfully defended his title in the Philippine Islands, Hawiian Islands, in Old Mexico with General Pershing's Expedition, and also here on the border. Williams has not lost a decision in the last four years.

"SPEED-BALL" HAYDEN, the Welter-Weight Champion of the 24th Infantry. A young boxer, but has shown more class than any boxer on the border, having won all his bouts with such ease he is better known as Knock-um Dead Hayden. He carries a knock-out punch in either hand, as his record shows his last 7 fights were all won by a knock-out inside of the limit, and it is conceded by the majority who have seen him in action that any man he can hit, he can beat. He will be a worthy opponent for Rufus Williams.

Curtain Raiser

A Grand Battle Royal

Between Five Huskie Battlers
Of the Rough and Ready, Slam-Bang, Go-As-You-Please Style

General Admission $1.00.   Reserved Seats $1.50.   Ringside $2.00

All Seats Reserved and Numbered

Doors Open at 7 o'clock. Bout Starts at 8 p. m. Tickets on Sale at Johnson & Howard Pool Hall and
12th Cavalry Exchange

Come Early to Avoid the Rush and Secure a Good Seat

Grand Ball After Boxing Contest   **Everybody Welcome**

Union
Labor   HENRY DAVIS, Promoter

For the U.S. Army Championship, held in Columbus, New Mexico, November 22, 1917, Williams weighing 155 and Hayden weighing 145. The publicity poster for the Williams-Hayden fight advertises a battle royal on the undercard (Chris Cozzone collection).

The two signed on November 6 to meet on the 22nd for a 15-rounder in Columbus for Williams' Army title. To accommodate El Paso fans, special trains were scheduled. The standing-room-only crowd of 1,200 fans, who packed into the Crystal Theatre the night of the fight, were not disappointed. As several newspapers reported, the fight was a hummer — and one that would be talked about for years. "To the admirer of fisticdom, there was everything — excepting, perhaps — fancy sparring or anything appertaining to it. Just simply two men and the one that landed the greater number and the stronger blows won."[16] "It looked curtains for Hayden" in the first round. After cautious sparring, Williams let loose on his former protégé, flooring him not once, but twice, with lefts to the temple, and an uppercut. In round two, Williams blasted Hayden to the body and the "gong sounded as Hayden was dragged to his corner by his seconds."[17]

But in the third Hayden bolted out of his corner like a bearcat, and the two slugged it out without a moment's rest, the younger man's speed edging the veteran. In the following two rounds, the fight was an even slugfest; but in the fifth, momentum tipped in Hayden's favor. Williams again floored Hayden twice in round seven. Although staggering back to his corner after the bell, Hayden "seemed to have taken a second lease on life," landing almost at will through the next three rounds.[18]

Williams, spent and punished now by Hayden, tried desperately for a knockout in the 11th, but a stiff right hand had the old master staggering across the ring. A shot to the body had Williams tottering, then crashing to the canvas. Grinning, Williams made the count, barely surviving the remainder of the round. "Rufus was out and he seemed to know it — but the smile still remained. The gong sounded for the twelfth round, and Williams, game to the core, tried to rise, but tottered weakly. Hayden came to the center of the ring. Guy Buckles stepped over the ropes, acknowledging defeat for his principal and Referee Dick Monohan shoved Hayden's right arm skyward as token of victory — and a new champion was made."[19]

New Champ

Speedball Hayden was now the bona-fide U.S. Army Middleweight Champion, and also, unofficially, claiming welterweight honors. Solidified with the win over his former teacher, his reputation continued to rise. Williams challenged Hayden to a rematch. He would later get three of them, but for the time being, the star of the 24th Infantry had other fish to fry. Like Johnny Sudenberg.

While Williams had been touted as the top middleweight in Columbus and New Mexico circles, in El Paso quarters the latest golden-haired child was Sudenberg. From Omaha, Nebraska, Sudenberg had since 1913 carried a reputation while stationed at Fort Bliss from several years of fighting on both coasts. His claim to fame had been established in three fights in Nevada against future world champion Jack Dempsey, against whom Sudenberg, giving up weight, had drawn twice, in ten-rounders, before being KO'd in two. In one of the bouts, however, Sudenberg had floored Dempsey a total of nine times. Without a mention of crossing color lines, the two were matched for 15 rounds on Christmas Day, 1917, in an official title fight for Hayden's U.S. Army Middleweight belt held at Columbus' Crystal Theatre.

Before a record crowd, the fight barely went one round. It was a thriller while it lasted, with Sudenberg going down for a seven-count midway through the first. Then in the final minute, after landing his first solid blow — a left hook — Sudenberg followed up with a blow that strayed south of the border. Worse: After Hayden sank to the canvas, Sudenberg, in his eagerness, struck his foe while down. The fight was given to Hayden, who retained his title.

The following year, Hayden went undefeated, fighting five times. Midway through February, Hayden was matched with veteran Hock Bones, who'd been fighting since 1909. After facing the best black fighters in the world (having been denied white contenders), including Gorilla Jones, Sam Langford and Jeff Clarke, the Memphis middleweight was recognized by many as the world Negro middleweight champion. Earning his shot with a third round TKO over Clarence "Kid" Ross, a stablemate of Hayden's, Bones put his mythical title at stake, against Hayden's official one, on February 22. Though the fight went the full 15 rounds, the outcome was an easier-than-expected decision for Hayden, who had Bones' "face beaten to a jelly."[20] The grizzled veteran, unable to do anything about Hayden's jab, went down twice during the fight, from Hayden's measured right. "The Speed-Ball is young and has had but little ring experience, but has shown that he has the stuff to burn that a good fighter is made of and with experience will certainly be a wonder," wrote the *Columbus Courier*.[21]

By now, Hayden was receiving challenges from all over the country. Young Jack Johnson, stationed in Illinois, Eddie Palmer, of San Francisco, Jack Mitchell in St. Louis and Young McCoy, from New Orleans, all wanted a part of Hayden. *Defis* were also issued — and printed in local papers — from the surrounding army camps. Sudenberg wanted a chance at redemption and Ross, who'd felt he'd been bypassed, wanted a shot at championship honors.

At first, long-time El Paso veteran Frankie Fowser was paired up with Hayden. Fowser had just returned from fighting in France for the Army and had, off and on since leaving the border, fought significant matches in the Midwest and East Coast, claiming a draw (actually, it was a decision loss) with future heavyweight title-challenger Bill Brennan in Cincinnati. After two weeks of build-up, Fowser, citing unresolved contractual weight problems, pulled out, leaving a void to be filled by a suddenly eager Rufus Williams.

Williams, however, had been inactive since Hayden ended his reign — so much so, in fact, that in March, the *Columbus Courier* erroneously reported that Williams had passed away. A week later, Williams denied that he was dead, but admitted ill health and a bad heart since the loss. The return to training, though, brought a quick recovery and, when Fowser pulled out of the May 4 bout, Williams leapt at the opportunity to get his U.S. Army title back and fight for World Colored honors.

Another great scrap was expected. Hayden critics surmised that he had been on the floor no less than four times and had taken 12 rounds to stop Williams — and had the teacher not underestimated his former charge, he would have kept his belt. Unlike the original classic bout, the rematch ended in controversial fashion. After a somewhat even first two rounds, Hayden reverted to wrestling maneuvers, pressing down on Williams' windpipe until the veteran dropped to the canvas for the count. The fans at the Crystal Theatre were not thrilled when Hayden was given the TKO win.

Rather than import a civilian boxer, matchmakers in Columbus decided it was time to settle the score between Hayden and Sudenberg. The El Paso press, always critical of Hayden, had been calling for the rematch and on May 29, they got it. Hayden, still really a welterweight and fighting at 150 pounds, would not only defend his Army middleweight belt he'd taken from Sudenberg, but would do it on the Swede's turf — at Fort Bliss.

By now, Henry Davis had given up promoting in order to manage and train Hayden full-time. At the 24th camp, Davis had a full stable that also included Kid Ross, Babe Cabell, and Hard-Hitting Wright, all on the rise. "Davis now entertains the notion that he has a world beater," wrote sport scribe Hy Schneider, of the *El Paso Morning Times*. "If Hayden is not a world beater, he will have to find something better than he has been sent against at Columbus to wreck Davis' theory."[22]

Sudenberg, Schneider believed, would dispel the growing myth that was Hayden. Calling Hayden's win over Hock Bones somewhat competitive (Bones being "a mighty good mixer ... for a semi-cripple and a veteran"), Sudenberg's past bouts with Dempsey marked him as, at least, even money against Hayden. Though favoring Sudenberg, Schneider named it a close one to call, "a one-punch boxer vs. a scientific boxer," but that "once Hayden slings Johnny, the latter will cut loose with his heavier shells.[23]

To keep sharp, Hayden boxed four rounds with Ross on a charity card May 24 in Columbus, resulting in a draw. Sudenberg, likewise, fought an exhibition bout at Fort Bliss. Then in front of a crowd of 2,500-capacity at the Fort Bliss Punch Bowl — Hayden, weighing in the same as Sudenberg, at 158, but in full uniform, outclassed the 7th Cavalry hopeful for a referee's decision. Though he was unable to finish off Sudenberg, Hayden had him in distress for most of the fight. The *El Paso Times* gave Hayden 10 of the 15 rounds, admitting that while Hayden "won by a mile," he still lacked the potential to be a real champion "for the reason that he misses too many punches and lacks the real kayo steam behind those he does land to make him a sensation were he to battle boxers of the real order."[24]

To determine Hayden's next opponent, a 15-rounder at Columbus was set up between Fowser, the El Paso veteran, and Kid Ross, who wanted a chance to fight his teammate. When the fight ended in a 15-round draw, what was supposed to be a build-up fell flat. Despite the draw, El Paso and Fort Bliss fans clamored for Hayden to fight Ross, claiming that the U.S. Army Welter and Middleweight Champion was ducking the 154-pounder who had, at least, gone four rounds to a draw with Hayden in the past. Ross, since transferring to the 24th in Columbus from Fort Bliss, was building steam and Hayden's past excuse that Ross needed to "go earn a reputation first," no longer held. After beating Hock Bones, via unanimous decision (Jack London was one of the judges), on August 26, in a 13-rounder (the fight was stopped short because the fighters had to make check at 11 P.M.), more decisively than Hayden had done, there was no way out for the army champ. The two were matched up at Columbus, first, for October, then November, due to an outbreak of influenza in the army camps. Finally, November 26 was settled upon.

This time, the Crystal Theatre in downtown Columbus was bypassed, and the Regimental Athletic Board of the 24th Infantry took over promoting Army bouts, constructing an open-air arena that would hold bigger crowds and allow longer-distance fights frowned upon by New Mexico politicians. It wasn't the first 20-rounder for Ross — the Clifton, Arizona boxer had been fighting since 1913 — but it was for Hayden. Both fighters vowed it wouldn't go the distance.

They were right — it went 19 rounds, two minutes and 45 seconds. In front of 3,500, a crowd that was still celebrating the end of the Great War, November 11, Hayden proved Ross's master. Though game, Ross showed improvement, but even his greater experience was no match for the Speedball's natural skills. Hayden piled on points through the first 16 rounds, then poured it on the groggy Ross until the 20th, when Ross "took the count of nine, gamely rose, but in the last minute of the bout took the dreamland kayo on Speedball's left jab and right cross."[25]

End of War, No End to Boxing

Even with the end of the war, there was no end in sight to Army boxing at the border. There was a demand for border protection from a still volatile Mexico — and in addition, Hayden was proving to be the best drawing card ever seen in those parts. Challenges came from Bobby Waugh, who figured on giving up 15–20 pounds to fight Hayden. One thing was for sure, the area had been cleaned up by Hayden and tougher imports were being demanded to give Speedball a challenge, even it if came from the lighter Waugh.

Early in 1919, the right man was found to challenge Hayden — an import and a soldier-boxer. From Camp Funston, Kansas, came Chicago's Navy Rostan, (reportedly) undefeated welterweight. The difference in this fight, however, was that this time, Hayden would be forced to make good his claim on the U.S. Army welterweight title, by making 150 pounds. They were both undefeated — Hayden verifiably so — but Rostan's roster of alleged victims outclassed Hayden's. In 13 bouts with 12 KOs, Rostan had claimed to kayo Jack Britton, Morris Lux, and Lee Morrissey, in one round. Rostan's claims made him a favorite when the two met on January 18, 1919, at Camp Furlong's outdoor arena in front of a crowd of 2,500. Using a jab early, Hayden followed up repeatedly with a big right hand that, by the seventh round, floored Rostan for the count. Three gold teeth reportedly fell from Rostan's mouth as a result of the combination that put him down.

The win raised talk of Hayden really being championship material and nearly ready to give champion Mike O'Dowd a run for the money. Seeking another step up the championship ladder for Hayden, promoters considered Battling Ortega of San Francisco, but preferred Albuquerque's Jack Torres, who'd been touted as championship timber before the war. Entertaining a comeback, Torres agreed, then pulled out due to cataracts, retiring from the sport after his six-year run. In Torres' place came a grizzled pug from Pueblo, Colorado.

Fall and Rise

In over 100 bouts since 1905, there were very few lightweights, welterweights and middleweights Eddie Johnson hadn't fought. He'd spelled doom for several New Mexico hopefuls, taking out Las Vegas's Louis Newman in 1912, for the Rocky Mountain Lightweight Title, and Raton's Ev Winters, by 15-round decision, later that year. He'd also defeated Bobby Waugh and had gone the distance with former world champ Young Corbett. For Johnson, Hayden was just another fight, and little threat given his history.

Keeping busy with exhibition bouts against a new crop of rising stars out of the 24th — Hard Hitting Wright and "The Rabbit" Rogers among the notables — Hayden prepared for his first headliner in Silver City.

Despite outweighing Johnson 155 to 147 (and forfeiting his weight money), with youth and speed in his corner, Hayden suffered his first pro loss in what was the border area's upset of the year. "Heralded as the 'speedball,' a marvel of cleverness and speed, Hayden failed to show any speed, except in trying to do a marathon to keep away from Johnson," read the report the next morning in the *El Paso Morning Times.* "Nothing, but the ropes, preventing him from getting out of range."[26] Although not able to keep Hayden down for the fatal ten, Johnson battered his foe down six times in the 20 rounds. Though *The Columbus Courier* hinted that Johnson should've been DQ'd for repeated fouling, neither the *Times* nor the *Silver City Enterprise* mentioned fouls, only that Hayden had been outclassed by a man of more experience — "of ring generalship and grit.... It was no surmise that Wednesday was a dark gloomy day in Columbus."[27]

Hayden's growing mystique of invulnerability was shattered. Hayden, however, picked himself off the canvas. Four weeks later, hoping to change the minds of local fight fans, that the Columbus flash was just a flash in the pan, another rugged civilian veteran was chosen for Hayden's return, May 3, 1919.

Irishman Jimmy Duffy of Oakland was another 32-year veteran, with over 100 fights, who kept as busy as Johnson. In the last 15 months, Duffy had campaigned from California to Pittsburgh to Denver, engaging in 22 bouts. This time with the fight back at the 24th's outdoor arena in Columbus, Hayden, claiming he'd taken Johnson too lightly, prepared seriously, sparring with Ross, Wright, and The Rabbit. Hayden's nemesis, Johnson, picked Duffy to win, though the Columbus fans had Hayden a 3–2 favorite by fight night.

The outcome shocked fight circles more than Hayden's loss to Johnson. Not only did Speedball defeat Duffy, but he did it in two rounds. After out-boxing Duffy in round one, "Hayden angled Duffy into correct position for a terrific left jab and right cross and put both over. Duffy fell face down and remained there while Referee Lieutenant Mike Halloran counted the knockout."[28] With the crowd at 3,500 capacity, plans were drawn to reconstruct the arena, to accommodate Hayden's renewed following. Less than a week after Duffy, the announcement was made that Hayden would rematch Johnson, and the date was set for June 20, 1919, at the Fort Bliss Punch Bowl. Refusing to risk a hometown decision at Columbus, Johnson was demanding neutral ground. "This announcement falls like a bomb among sport fans in this section, many of whom had given up the cherished hope of ever seeing Johnson meet Hayden again." Not only that, but sport promoters at Fort Bliss and other places in the Southwest, at Miami, Arizona, at Deming and Silver City, had all made bids for the return match between Hayden and Johnson.[29]

To show his gameness, and none too concerned that he would lose the rematch, Johnson took on blown-up lightweight Bobby Waugh at Silver City one week before, fighting a fast draw in 20 rounds, at 145 pounds. Five pounds north and seven days later, Johnson entered the ring to for yet another 20-round war. The fight, seen by 2,800, was the expected classic, but on this night, the outcome couldn't have been any different. "At Silver City, the fans say that Johnson pretty well mussed up the Speedball's smiling countenance with a widely varied assortment of tough slams from his active Book of Boxing, but last night it was different. It was so vastly different in fact, that the El Paso and Fort Bliss followers of the game are wondering how Eddie ever managed to beat the Twenty-fourth crack.... Hayden drew blood in the first round with his deadly left jab. Hayden fought in cool style at all times, was ever confident, never exerted himself and finished unscarred."[30] Referee Billy Smith scored it in rounds, 11–1–8, for Hayden. The Speedball was back.

But things were quickly changing on the border.

Army Boxing Falls, Hayden Goes Civilian

First came the official military order from Fort Sam Houston that boxing was no longer being deemed "as being so valuable to the command as other athletic training in which a large number participate. Such contests are, however, of general interest to the command. To avoid any tendency to commercialize athletics in the array admissions will not be charged to any athletic contests."[31]

With the war over, boxing was no longer being used to keep the troops in shape, and fight cards were no longer looked upon as morale-building entertainment. Without charging patrons, big cards — on a consistent basis, anyway — were no longer a possibility. For a fighter like Hayden who'd been groomed under the protection of the generals who, at worst, considered him a mascot beneficial to morale, life was about to get a lot harder.

The fight scene at the border was changing, anyway. While the military promoters still called the shots, civilian boxers — many of whom were former soldiers returning home — were suddenly in vogue. In New Mexico, Albuquerque was back in the groove and smaller venues dotted throughout the state were picking up where they'd left off before the war. Up north, Walter Caldwell, of Springer, a sergeant in the war, was stirring things up while both Benny Cordova, of Albuquerque and Benny Chavez, a Wagon Mound-born former world title contender, were launching comebacks based on stellar careers made earlier in the decade.

Meanwhile, Hayden hadn't given up his goal of becoming a top-notcher — with the military or not. As a soldier-boxer, Hayden fought one more time — and it was on the road in Phoenix against his old mentor, Williams.

Williams was hot on the comeback trail throughout Arizona, having destroyed Johnny Sudenberg in July of 1919, following up with kayos over Hock Bones and Young Jack Johnson. When the two met in Phoenix, October 17, later that year, Hayden could do no better than a ten-round draw. Four weeks later — during which time Hayden had been honorably discharged from the army — they met again. Fighting at 154 pounds, Hayden once again proved his mentor's master by winning an easy decision in a punishing fight.

By now the word was out that Hayden was fair game, and just another black fighter at the mercy of promoters wishing to match him up tough, or against heavier fighters. While there was talk of going east, then west, then to Washington, D.C, nothing materialized and Hayden stayed inactive until March, 1920.

Speedball's Fall

Hayden's speedball rise to national prominence had taken less than three years. His fall into obscurity took less than half the time, with far more bumps and bruises.

Though Hayden was now a civilian fighter, Columbus Army promoters still knew his value as a drawing card at the 24th arena. On March 27, 1920, after four months of inactivity, they were finally able to match up Hayden with El Paso veteran Frankie Fowser. It was a tactical match, fought outdoors during a sand storm, pitting Hayden's superior speed and footwork against Fowser's defensive tactics and heavier blows, resulting in a ten-round draw before a slim crowd of 1,200.

With the war over and Hayden no longer a soldier, the pressure was on for Speedball to seek bigger game, in bigger arenas. For the past six months, Hayden had been quoted as saying he was tired of the same old Southwest fighters and wanted a chance at top-notchers — a list that included Jack Britton, Battling Ortega and Ted Lewis — so Davis took Hayden, along with teammate Hard-hitting Wright, west.

First stop was Douglas, Arizona, where, on May 15, Hayden lost a ten-round decision to fast-rising Italian and local favorite, Italian Andy "Kid" Palmer. Davis cried robbery, claiming his charge had deserved no worse than a draw, when Hayden lost the decision. Davis took Hayden into the land of four-rounders — California — where, for the summer, Hayden fought six times, picking up four wins, a draw and a loss by DQ. Davis then brought Hayden back to New Mexico where, on Oct. 29, in Silver City, the former local favorite stepped into the ring with Eddie Johnson for a third time, this time forcing the fading Pueblo veteran to call it quits in round 11.

The win against Johnson might've shown the locals that Hayden still had it — but, at the same time, it did little to achieve a topnotch rating. That's when Gorilla Jones — longtime middleweight threat to both white and black fighters — arrived from Alexandria, Louisiana, to establish himself as the reigning Colored champion at the border.

In Hayden's absence, the scene at the border had continued to change. Though black fighters were still in demand, local products and Texan contenders were the bigger draw. Against Jones, Hayden would fight his next three bouts — then conclude the series one year later in a bout that put the final nail in the coffin of the Speedball's career.

In the first bout, Nov. 25, 1920, at Columbus, Hayden got lucky, winning by DQ when Jones, ahead on the scorecards, accidentally hit low in round four. The two were rematched for Christmas Day, again in Columbus. This time, Hayden was not so fortunate, for Jones dominated the fight, stopping him for Hayden's first knockout loss in front of a hometown crowd, in round nine.

Sharing local stardom with Fort Worth's "Dandy" Dick Griffin and El Paso's Payo brothers — "Kid" (Cipriano) and "Young" (Angelo) — Jones "both a giant and a gorilla killer" who was "more of the 'man-ape' persuasion" became the dominant black fighter at the border (he was followed by Tiger Flowers, who knocked him out), while Hayden fell off the map.[32]

There were other things going on with Hayden, however — like the death of his wife, Maggie, who was brutally murdered on December 9, 1920, between the first and second fight with Jones. While John R. Peterson was being tried for murder in the second degree (he was convicted on June 16, 1921), Hayden tried to pick up the pieces of his career.

On April 1, in Phoenix, just two weeks after Jones had disposed of Walter Caldwell in Columbus, Hayden out-boxed Jones for a ten-round decision in Phoenix. Though the bout drew little attention back home, the win enabled Hayden to secure a 15-round rematch with Andy "Kid" Palmer (who'd dominated Jones just two weeks before) on a card in Juarez, May 1. Though most saw Hayden winning the bout, the papers reported "At the end of the handshaking parley, Referee Jack McDonald raised a white arm and a black arm skyward," ruling it a draw.[33]

Discouraged, Hayden spent the remainder of the year not straying too far from home and doing little to bolster his claim — or hope — to be a top-notcher. No longer with Davis, Hayden attached himself to former promoter Marshall Jackson, who was also guiding Hayden's nemesis, Gorilla Jones. Jackson, however, was unable to take Hayden to the next level; and in 1921, he drew with journeymen Young Joe Gans and Eddie St. Clair, in Casper, Wyoming, then Leo Matlock in Albuquerque. Two low-key local fights — a KO in 2 over former 24th teammate Digger Smith in Deming, and another decision over Clarence Ross in Columbus — did little but keep Hayden busy.

The turning point came on Jan. 6, 1922, when Hayden was matched, for the fourth and final time, against Gorilla Jones, at Fort Bliss. The fight, a 15-rounder billed as the Negro Middleweight Championship of the Southwest, was seen in local circles as Hayden's desperate last stand. With the win, Hayden was planning to "invade" the eastern cities, having regained "the heights he once mounted." The question remained: "Will Hayden return to his own?"[34] "After my fight tonight with Gorilla Jones, the fans here are going to say: 'Speedball's back,'" Hayden told the *El Paso Times*. "I believe that going the way I am now and with what I have learned about Jones, I will beat him and that after it's over, folks will say like they used to: 'Speedball's the best.'"[35]

The fight destroyed Hayden — or, rather, Gorilla Jones destroyed Hayden. Before he was counted out, at 1:19 of round nine, a humiliated Hayden was floored an unlucky 13 times — twice in the second, twice in the fifth, thrice in the sixth and seventh, once in round eight, and for the count, in the ninth. The finisher was a right hand to the solar plexus that "journeyed not more than six or eight inches from the starting point, but it was sprinkled with poppy dust and the Speedball flashed on into dreamland."[36]

It was virtually over for Hayden, though he would go on to fight sporadically for another ten years. Following the loss to Jones, Hayden drew with Ross in a 12-rounder at Fort Bayard, then was destroyed in two rounds before his hometown of Columbus by journeyman Chihuahua Kid Brown. Losses to Scotty Williams followed in Casper, Wyoming, where Hayden eventually relocated. Though defeating Kid Brown in a rematch, knocking him out in the 21st round on a card in Mexico City in early 1923, then following up with a decision win in Douglas, Arizona, over Dick "Twin" Dundee, Hayden was finished, as far as fighting as a threat to any title, Negro or otherwise.

In Casper, Hayden raised a son, Kenneth, who had been born in 1919 to his first wife. Sometime after moving out of Columbus, Hayden remarried, but a divorce or separation occurred sometime after 1937. Hayden returned to Indianapolis where he died in 1962.

Hayden's last known fight occurred in Ogden, Utah, on September 2, 1932, when he was TKO'd in seven by a local club fighter, Kid Barger. Fighting in relative obscurity — his last big fight had been 1923 — little of Hayden's golden era remained in press clippings, though he was recognized as a former Wyoming Colored Champion.

Back at the border, the name "Speedball" was filed away, as quickly forgotten as the brief, but furious era of soldier boxing that had consumed the area before, during and after the Great War. Black fighters continued to headline shows — but mainly in Juarez where Tiger Flowers rose to prominence (after destroying Gorilla Jones in 1922), on his way to the World Middleweight Championship, which he won in 1926.

Fights at Columbus came to a halt (the last one being Hayden's loss to Kid Brown in 1922), while Fort Bayard continued off-and-on through the mid–1920s. Fort Bliss carried on bouts through the 1930s, finally phasing out pro boxing for military, amateur bouts. Eventually, that too, disappeared.

Without their military umbrella, black fighters at the border declined in number. Homegrown hopefuls — a list that includes the also-forgotten Jose Rivers, Mike Vasquez, Tony Herrera and Babe Colima — battled their way up the ladder while those once famous with the 24th Infantry, or at Fort Bliss, scattered to the four winds, fighting here and there before succumbing to a similar fate met by their helmsman, Speedball Hayden.

NOTES

1. "Jack Curley Reaches Town," *El Paso Morning Times*, Jan. 19, 1915.

2. "Soldier with Pershing in Dash into Mexico is Here on Visit," *Lexington Herald*, Mar. 11, 1917.

3. Hy Schneider, "Just Sport for Just Sport Across the Board and Back," *El Paso Morning Times*, Aug. 13, 1919.

4. "Six Slashing Boxing Bouts Held At Pershing's Camp in Mexico," *The Washington Post*, July 15, 1916.

5. Ibid.

6. "'Bull' Foster Goes Against R. Williams," *El Paso Morning Times*, Nov. 14, 1916.

7. Ibid.

8. "Around Town," *Las Vegas Daily Optic*, June 3, 1884.

9. "$1,000 Purse for Champ Newton," *El Paso Morning Times*, Feb. 14, 1917.

10. "Newton Can't Cross Color Line, Says W. Hull," *El Paso Morning Times*, Feb. 17, 1917.

11. "Williams wins again from 'Bull Foster,'" *Columbus Courier*, July 6, 1917.

12. "Just Sport for Just Sport Across the Board and Back," *El Paso Morning Times*, Feb. 5, 1918.

13. Ibid.

14. "Hayden Wins Welter-weight Title of 24th Infantry," *Columbus Courier*, Apr. 6, 1917.

15. "Boxing Bouts Were Far Below Standard," *Columbus Courier*, July 13, 1917.

16. "Speedball Hayden stops Rufus Williams and Wins Middleweight Army Title," *El Paso Morning Times*, Nov. 22, 1917.

17. Ibid.

18. Ibid.

19. Ibid.

20. "Hayden Wins World Championship from Hock Bones," *Columbus Courier*, Feb. 22, 1918.

21. Ibid.

22. "Fans Dope Out Sudenberg-Hayden Tilt," *El Paso Morning Times*, May 21, 1918.

23. "Just Sport for Just Sport Across the Board and Back," *El Paso Morning Times*, May 24, 1918.

24. "Speedball Hayden Outpoints Sudenberg in Lively Bout at Studorium," *El Paso Morning Times*, May 30, 1918.

25. "Speedball Hayden Knocks Out Ross," *El Paso Morning Times*, Nov. 17, 1918.

26. "Speedball Hayden Meets His Waterloo," *El Paso Morning Times,* April 2, 1919.

27. "Speedball Hayden Loses to Johnson," *Silver City Enterprise*, April 4, 1919.

28. "Speedball Hayden Wins From Duffy in Two Rounds at Columbus," *El Paso Morning Times,* May 4, 1919.

29. "Eddie Johnson to Meet Hayden," *Columbus Courier*, May 16, 1919.

30. "Speedball Hayden Outclasses Johnson," *El Paso Morning Times,* June 21, 1919.

31. "Paid Boxing Bouts Disapproved in Order Issues From Southern Commander's Headquarters," *El Paso Morning Times*, Sept. 5, 1919.

32. "Kid Palmer to go After Gorilla Jones," *El Paso Herald-Post*, April 10, 1921.

33. "Speedball Hayden Clearly Outpoints Kid Palmer," *El Paso Times*, May 2, 1921.

34. "Jones Disputes Hayden's Stand as Favorite in 158-lb. Division," *El Paso Times*, Jan. 4, 1922.

35. "Gorilla Jones and Speedball Hayden Clash in 15-Rounder," *El Paso Times*, Jan. 5, 1922.

36. "Gorilla Jones Floors Speedball Hayden 13 Times to Win," *El Paso Times*, Jan. 6, 1922.

CHAPTER 15

Battling Siki: World Light-Heavyweight Champion

Peter Benson

"To the whole world, I am a savage."— Siki

It's early March, 1925, and fight fans are eager to see a murderous local light-heavyweight in a Madison Square Garden main event. Nobody knows exactly who the "Astoria Assassin" will be fighting. His scheduled opponent has backed out. But he's such a spectacular knockout artist no one cares. The tickets are selling fast, the up-front promotional costs, set-up costs, money to bribe local writers to talk up the fight, you name it, are all paid. When the last-minute replacement winds up being French Senegalese ex-champion Battling Siki, ticket sales pick up. Siki's star has been steadily fading ever since he lost his world light-heavyweight title in a dubious decision, against Irish middleweight Mike McTigue in Ireland two years before, but as an opponent he'll do nicely. He's not likely to back away from combat. Nearly 12,000 patrons will ultimately pay almost $44,000 (roughly $540,000 today) in gate receipts. Pre-fight features trumpet Siki's "speed and improved boxing ability and stamina,"[1] but in fact he only arrived in training camp four days before the bout, for his first real workout in months.[2] In the weigh-in photo, a pudgy Siki bends to study the scales, with his muscular rival bolt upright beside him.[3] Though Siki had never in his career been knocked out, odds are dead even he will be this time. Most expect the bout to go only a few rounds.

Local fans have been enamored of the "Astoria Assassin," Paul Berlenbach, ever since he quit wrestling (he'd been AAU Champion) to take up boxing two years before. Scarlet fever left him deaf in childhood, and he only learned to speak after a freak accident restored his hearing.[4] He left his first six opponents stretched supine on local canvases. Not one of his first seventeen fights (in one of which he'd been stopped himself) went the distance. He was far from the most carefully-schooled, fleet-footed, or subtle of adversaries, but "Punching Paul" had one big weapon: a left hook that landed with about the impact of a load of bootleg whiskey dumped off a dock. He wasn't hard to hit (Paul Delaney pasted him at will in their first encounter,) but that didn't matter. Like Siki himself, Berlenbach kept coming right through whatever you threw.

In a way, no one was surprised that Siki agreed to fight the brawler of ferocious mien and guttural grunts. What else would you expect? Had he ever done anything rational or predictable in his entire brief sojourn in the public eye? They didn't call this guy "the Singular

Senegalese" for nothing. Besides, he seemed to like to fight. Hadn't he been arrested more than once for fighting strangers on the street, some of them in the uniforms of the metropolitan police?

"I sat at ringside and saw," Nat Fleischer intones, framing his images of Siki's ring apotheosis in language that sounds like testimony in court. "In the eighth round, Paul worked the Negro against the ropes just in front of me, and bombarded him with paralyzing rights and lefts to the head." He etches the moment indelibly, an inescapable physical reality, repeating the verb for witness ("I have seldom seen") to bookend his testimony. He tells of a "primitive" African, "only half human," who "rolled his eyes and snorted" in the early rounds of his final match, as if hoping to "terrify" the German-American stalking him around the ring, yet who had within a few rounds "taken so much punishment that his eyes rolled in agony."[5]

Siki, Fleischer confides, was "boxing's harlequin," an "imitation King Kong" in a "flowing French cape lined with purple satin," wearing "bright red gloves and grey suede shoes."[6] His "primitive nature" impervious to civilized influence, he was "three quarters savage." "More than merely different," he was "fantastic," a perfect racial stereotype, a flawless incarnation of the code of race.[7]

Fleischer tips his story's ending and hints its moral: "With his unleashed passions given full sway and amply provided for by his ring earnings, he was bound to come to grief eventually."[8] The match plays out with bleak inevitability. With "only the crudest idea of defense" (defensive skills, like appropriate dress, being marks of civilized sophistication), Siki stuck it out for ten rounds on brute tenacity alone. Then his more skillful rival, "punching with lightning speed, shot home a bone-crushing right to the jaw." The savage usurper "fell forward on his face as if a bullet had struck him and was counted out" in "his last fight in the ring."[9] Fleischer's image is vivid, indelible. Siki pitches face-first, limbs convulsing, as if gunned down on a darkened street, and lies there limp and lifeless as a rag doll. So real does Fleischer's image seem you're surprised to find, when you check his own *Ring Record Book*, that the bout ended not with Siki dropped senseless to the canvas but with the referee jumping in, prying the men apart, and waving his arms to call off a one-sided beating. Yes, Siki lost. But by "technical knockout," a ruling that he was no longer "making a contest of it."

Battling Siki, the man they called the "Singular Senegalese" (Paris, 1922, Peter Benson collection).

When you flip through the daily newspapers of that era you discover not only was Siki not knocked out, he was never even knocked down. "Slugger Batters Senegalese,

But Unable to Score Knockdown," the *Herald Tribune* headlined.[10] Where did Fleischer get it from, his image of a black man falling face-forward, as if shot? Suddenly there it is, in the *New York Evening Journal*—in plain rotogravure. Five photographs line up like cartoon panels.[11] In the first, a black fighter twists under a white fighter's lunging right. In the second, a white fighter misses a hook to the body as the black fighter paws a counter hook to the face. In the third, a black fighter, exhausted, clings to a brawny white. In the fourth, a black man lurches forward, missing a hook to the body that a white fighter, legs awkwardly crossed, blocks with an open glove. The final image seems a culmination of the first four. A white fighter, in mid-follow through, has landed a big right hand. His black opponent sails through the air, ass over teakettle, feet above his head, arms flailing, like a clown acrobat at the circus. He looks exactly like the man Fleischer describes in *Fifty Years at Ringside*. The only trouble is he isn't Siki. That's Siki and Berlenbach in the first four photos, but the final photo is of Frankie Schoell flooring Harlem middleweight Larry Estridge.

Paul Berlenbach, the Astoria Assassin (Peter Benson collection).

A casual observer might easily misread the set of photos, but how could a seasoned boxing writer like Nat Fleischer miss so badly, flail so ineptly? In a hurry to put together his recollections did Fleischer come across the image, fall in love with it, and memorialize an enticing illusion? Is his "I sat at ringside and saw" wishful thinking? Sid Mercer of the *Journal,* who really was at ringside that night might have added to the confusion by mis-wording his lead, saying Siki "was the victim of a technical knockout in the tenth round, but he was soon on his feet groping for Berlenbach."[12]

"Soon on his feet"? He never left them.

This was, Fleischer insists, "his last fight," but Siki fought five more times before his death later that year. The error almost seems deliberate — as if, thirty years after Siki's death, Fleischer wants to finish the job of writing Siki off. But what impelled him to leave as Siki's legacy this comic, belly-flop indignity? Why did he feel impelled to strip Siki of every other virtue than blind obstinacy?

The real story has more elements of tragedy than comedy. On the outs with his manager, out of shape, without having sparred in months, Siki went out to play the role of human punching bag. He fought on bravely, completely outgunned. But to pretend that brutal beat-down was some sort of fitting finale to his career is a gross slander. It was a crude and cynical effort to exploit his name for money. He went along because he needed the big payday. He knew he was likely to get battered. He was not stupid. Jack Kofoed in the *New York Evening Post* offered a contrary moral to the tale: "There may have been men in the history of the prize ring who have stood up more courageously than the Senegalese but it is doubtful indeed. It did not seem possible that any human could be capable of withstanding such hammering. But, though the Astoria Assassin placed every ounce of power behind his blows, and he must have landed several hundred of them, Battling Siki never appeared to be in danger of being knocked out."[13] He might have added there may have been occasions in the history of the prize ring when managers and promoters conspired to stage a more pointless spectacle, but it is hard to think of one.

Two and a half years earlier, on September 24, 1922, then Light Heavyweight World Champion Georges Carpentier had waited in a huge new stadium, anxious to begin what he supposed would be an equally pointless bout. Bored, blasé, he was overheard telling the corner-man taping his hands, "Come on, let's get going. It's going to rain."[14] He would come to regret that utterance. For years he would hear it repeated in mockery, as signaling a soft, egotistic champion. Just before the referee called the fighters to the center of the ring, Carpentier, in an ankle-length silk robe, strode to Siki's corner, gave a quick glove-to-glove greeting, and, the ritual of sportsmanship over, turned on his heel and strode off, cutting his black rival like a chance acquaintance one shouldn't let linger in one's limelight.

When the hammer hit the ringside gong, fans saw a contest that was perplexing in the extreme. You couldn't call it a fight. It was too bloodless and non-belligerent for that. Siki sailed across the ring, without throwing a punch, and planted his forehead on Carpentier's chest, as if he'd signed the handsome boulevardier's dance card. The two hung on like lovers in a clinch that neither seemed in any special hurry to break. When they did step back they didn't even bother to cover up, sidestep, or jab their way out. Carpentier feinted and threw soft flurries of punches that had neither the range nor the velocity to do any damage. Had it been a sparring session you'd have expected the trainer to call a halt and scold both men for conspiring to take the afternoon off.

Then the strangest thing of all happened. After a long *pas des deux* featuring half-feints and jabs pawing empty air, Carpentier telegraphed an overhand right that Siki easily ducked. Then, though the punch had sailed a good foot over his head, he bobbed down on one knee and stayed there, poised like an altar boy waiting for the salver to be slipped under his chin and the Eucharist plopped onto his tongue. "Come on, get up, Siki. You weren't even hit," referee Henry Bernstein snarled. Siki obeyed and the round recommenced. Siki kept going into an exaggerated crouch, posing motionless out of range, as if modeling for an artist's sketch. Carpentier pranced about, feinting, sticking out his jab but never landing it, tossing rights that sailed wide of the mark. Siki's few meaningful blows were wider still. It was one of the most bizarre displays of mutual nonaggression a Parisian fight crowd had ever seen. And yes, it was already drawing calls of "Chiqué! Chiqué!" Fix! Fix![15]

In the second round Carpentier took it upon himself to liven things up. Coming out of a clinch he caught Siki with a flurry of punches. He twice landed his celebrated right that had even stunned Jack Dempsey the year before. Siki merely grinned, but finally threw something more or less credible back. Still, it was a very strange bout — with far too much dancing, feinting, and clinching to satisfy even amateurs of the sport.

The third round featured Siki skipping around the ring, despite the rain pissing down, then abruptly scrunching into that strange crouch, Carpentier giving shoulder feints, but throwing nary a punch. Then finally, near Siki's corner, Carpentier threw a punch with genuine malice, a short right that sent Siki careening to his knees. He popped quickly to his feet, with Carpentier lunging after him, landing a hook, losing his footing on the slick canvas and skidding to his knees himself. On his feet again he went after Siki, who seemed to have rosin or liniment in his eyes, squatting in his corner, rubbing them with a glove, then sliding along the ropes in full retreat as Carpentier, feet skating from under him on the sodden canvas, tossed one, two, three long rights to Siki's head. Then, nearly in Carpentier's corner, came what looked like the evening's inevitable apotheosis. Carpentier stuck out his jab like a stiff arm, measuring Siki, and delivered a swinging right to the neck, his full weight behind it. Siki went down on one knee, as Bernstein backed Carpentier away, waving his arm like an auctioneer, counting "un, deux, trios." Siki put his glove to his face, checking for blood, then at the count of seven jumped up and went after Carpentier, trading toe-to-toe combinations. Carpentier again swung that big overhand right, but Siki shrugged it off, answering with a nasty uppercut and right hand that sent Carpentier staggering across the ring. Siki walked him down, landing a short left hook and two rights. To the astonishment of the crowd this time it was Carpentier who went down. Up at four, he clinched and held on, but Siki straightened him with another vicious uppercut. Carpentier tried to steal the round at the bell, but his blows lacked their usual force. He was in no shape for a war. He knew it. Siki knew it. Anyone who'd set foot in his training camp in La Guerche knew it too.

He had *cojones*, Carpentier! He wasn't the dandy the American public imagined. "The Orchid Man," one scribe had dubbed him (based on his having been photographed in evening dress with an elegant boutonniere stuck in his lapel). But he'd grown up a miner's son in Lens in Northern France, dropped out of school, and had, like Siki, been destitute when he first found his way into a gym. In Carpentier's case the gym had been mostly dedicated to gymnastics, run by erstwhile prestidigitator François Descamps, who trained the future boxing champion at first for the gymnastics salon, then to assist his magic act.[16] By the time he was fourteen, however, young Carpentier was fighting professionally as a lightweight against grown men. His early training as an illusionist would not desert him on that night in 1922 when, spent, dazed, and battered, he saw his world title slipping away. When physical strength failed him, he tried to preserve his title by sheer sleight of hand.

At the start of the fourth Siki swung for the floating ribs, bringing Carpentier's gloves down, then whacked a right to the chin. Carpentier answered with right of his own, straight down the pike, stunning Siki, followed by a flurry of body blows and uppercuts, backing him across the ring, trying to turn the tables and avert disaster. But after two months of doing little more than rapping the speedbag and tossing a medicine ball, he wasn't strong enough to knock out a fighter as tough, seasoned, and physically fit as Siki. Siki battered the title holder to the ribs, caught him with hooks to the head, snapped back his head with uppercuts. By round's end Carpentier, bleeding from nose and mouth, was hanging on for dear life, nearly out on his feet. At the bell he brought his forearm down across the back of Siki's neck, a blatant rabbit punch. Referee Bernstein ignored the infraction.

In the fifth, his ribs aching, face a bloody mask, both eyes nearly beaten shut, Carpentier clung to Siki's muscular arms, his torso hunched forward in an almost fetal arc, hoping for something, anything, to extricate him from this miserable, ill-considered mistake Descamps had gotten him into. "I began to feel sorry for him," Siki would later relate. "And whispered to him to quit."[17] Carpentier responded by, six, eight, a dozen times, ducking his head and bringing it up abruptly, crown first, towards Siki's face, hoping to inflict the same injuries he'd suffered, by means outside the rules of the sport.

Siki knocks out Carpentier in the sixth round of the light heavyweight world championship fight in Paris, September 24, 1922 (Peter Benson collection).

When Siki pulled himself free, Carpentier, wobbly with exhaustion, lowered his head, and charged, like a boy playing the bull in a game of toreador. Siki shoved him away, extending his arms, appealing to referee Bernstein, who responded by warning not Carpentier but both men for dirty tactics. Carpentier went right back to playing the bull in his private *corrida de toros*, as Siki answered with crisp uppercuts and swinging blows to the ribs. He met one rush by lowering his shoulder like a rugby player, lost his footing, and went skidding on his ass to the ropes. When he crawled upright, Carpentier lowered his head and charged again, lost his footing on the slick canvas, and fell to his knees. Siki crouched behind to lift him to his feet, wrapping his arms around the battered champion as if he were a nurse in an orthopedic ward. Carpentier responded by sucker punching him, as tactic that had salvaged a losing cause for him once before, against Ted "Kid" Lewis.

The end came moments after the bell for the sixth. Siki went after Carpentier with both hands, loading up on uppercuts, rights to the ribs, and a final overhand right that sent Carpentier stumbling towards his corner. Siki scrambled after him, swinging wildly. Falling in, tied up in a clinch, he tried to yank a glove free to punch and lost his balance, jerking his leg up, kicking Carpentier inside the left calf. Regaining his footing he caught Carpentier with a final swinging right to the body, sending him sprawling sideways, to lie with one bent leg in the air, clutching his calf, gasping in pain. His face streaming blood, white trunks spattered with it, Carpentier looked more like a steer being dispatched by inexpert slaughterhouse workers than a fallen fighter.

Bernstein sauntered towards the fallen champion, ignoring the wild celebration among Siki's handlers across the ring. Rather than starting a count, he waved towards officials and handlers at ringside, as if to efface this ghastly, unforeseen reality. The announcer leapt into the ring, hoisting a huge megaphone, to proclaim — not a knockout but a disqualification for unfair tactics. And not of Carpentier, but Siki! Never mind that Carpentier had spent the last couple rounds fouling Siki blatantly and repeatedly, without a single point deduction. Fans on the arena floor were having none of it. They rushed the ring, shouting and knocking over chairs. The president of the French Boxing Federation, Paul Rousseau, seated at ringside, intervened. Three Federation officials would retire to a nearby hotel to reconsider the ruling.[18] Never mind that no provision in Federation rules permitted such a thing! Eventually, they returned to declare Siki the new champion. What other choice had they?

Sportswriter André Glarner, waiting for round-by-round reports by telephone at the sporting café La Régence in Les Rues Basses, Geneva, Switzerland, recalled the reaction when the news came that Carpentier had gone down in the fourth. Patrons were stunned. They'd met earlier reports of Siki's knockdowns with a wry shake of the head. Well, what did you expect? What was Carpentier doing fighting the raw, unpolished ex-soldier anyhow? Then came the stunner: Carpentier knocked out in the sixth. "What?" they shouted. "Chiqué! Chiqué!" (Fix! Fix!)[19]

They were sure Carpentier had taken a dive. But they were wrong. The fight had been set up for a fix, but Siki, not Carpentier, was the one who was supposed to lose. Descamps, alarmed his fighter wasn't training, had gone to Siki's manager, Charlie Hellers, and proposed, instead of a boxing match, a well-remunerated, but challenging acting job. He offered the entire winner's share, 200,000 francs, for a nice artistic dive. Siki was to fake knockdowns in the first, second, and third rounds, then go down for good in the fourth. Descamps even specified that Siki was to contrive to land flat on his back, arms stretched out in the shape of a cross.[20] His showman's instincts had gotten the better of him. Newsreel cameramen were to be on hand to film the fight, from a raised crow's nest above the ring.

Actually Siki was suffering in the early rounds not from fear or self-doubt, but stage fright. Descamps and Hellers were asking a lot. Three knockdowns and then a spectacular pratfall? Who did they think he was, John Barrymore? Carpentier, who had experience in feature films, had to carry the stage-struck novice by himself. He'd done his best for the first round, skipping lightly around the ring, giving new meaning to the term "shadow boxing," as he tossed flashy combinations whose shadows didn't even touch Siki's. But by the second, goaded by the fans' jeers, he'd traded fake belligerence for the real thing.[21] If the first knockdown had been ludicrously fake, the second was genuine. He'd surprised Siki, still playing a role, with a real right hand. Was it his fault if Siki had forced him to quit pulling his punches?

Unfortunately, Siki didn't appreciate being turned into a stage prop. "Those punches hurt," he later told a cameraman he befriended, working on a German feature film. "I decided to punch back."[22] "His punches aren't like mine," Siki said days after the fight. "They come very fast, like this." He demonstrated, stepping around to snap a short hook. "He lifts an elbow and they're there right away."[23] He'd approached *Monsieur Carpentier* at the weigh-in with all the deference of an autograph seeker. It had become a running joke among the writers, much as would be the patent hero worship of Jean Pierre Coopman, the "Lion of Flanders," for Muhammad Ali before their 1975 fight. But hearing Carpentier snarl, in the clinches after the fourth round, "Bastard! Bastard! Go down now! Go down!" cured Siki of that.[24]

He'd gone along with the fix in the first place, Siki said, with great reluctance. When Carpentier didn't keep his end of the deal, pride rebelled. "Hellers said to me: 'By fighting Carpentier, you might get a lot of money, but you'd better go along.' I came to the ring with the intention of going down as they ordered me to. In the first round, in the second, in the third, I went along, but in the fourth round,[25] when I was on my knees, in front of fifty thousand people, I thought like this: 'Look at you, Siki, you've never gone down before any man, you've never been on your knees in public the way you find yourself at this moment,' and my blood only circulated once before I was on my feet and punching."[26]

The resulting scandal, *L'Affair Siki*, would be raised as a point of debate before the French National Assembly prior to a vote over the funding of national sports programs. It would leave Carpentier sputtering, "I don't understand why the press publishes all the declarations of the Senegalese who, in order to revenge himself for his disqualifications, amuses himself by demolishing the sport of boxing."[27] For fifty years Carpentier would repeat that mantra. He'd been out of shape, overconfident, had lost through unfair tactics. There had been no fix, no arrangement, nothing of the kind. It was all a smoke screen raised by that dirty clown Siki, in an effort to distract attention from his own scandalous behavior.

Finally, at the age of eighty, in his final autobiography *Mes 80 Rounds*, he would recant. Yes, he'd admit, it had been set up for a fix. Siki had indeed agreed to *jouer la comédie*. But pride would still prevent him from accepting full blame for the betrayal of public trust. No, no, he insisted, it hadn't been his idea but Siki's. Siki had been terrified of fighting the great Carpentier. The only way to get him to go through with his contract was to agree to stage a fake knockout.[28] That explanation, of course, was palpably absurd. Siki would go fifteen rounds against the great Kid Norfolk at Madison Square Garden just one year later, after only a couple weeks of training, and put on a display of ring courage New York boxing writers labeled the most brutally inspiring performance of the year. Late in his career he would fight on just five days notice, and no training, one of the most vicious punchers the light heavyweight division ever produced, Paul Berlenbach. He was not the sort to duck tough opponents — especially when a large payday was involved. Besides, what earthly motive would Carpentier have for taking such a deal? If Siki backed out, Descamps could have found a half-dozen other fighters to step in and take his place, including Carpentier's sparring partner, René De Vos, who'd given Siki one of his toughest fights two years before.

To this day, it's hard to get the boxing fraternity to listen to Siki's charges — though Carpentier himself admitted they were true. When Siki won the title, the backlash was widespread and immediate. With his blonde-haired, blue-eyed Dutch wife, Siki reminded people far too readily of Jack Johnson. American sportswriters fell over each other in their alacrity to turn him to ridicule, dismissing him as an illiterate freak, though he spoke, read, and wrote several languages, delighting in tales of all-night drunks in the demi-monde of Montmartre, though Siki wasn't up to half the stunts laid at his door. He did not peddle cocaine on the streets, or make sexual overtures to minors, or "assault" a rival manager in the ring (the transgression that cost him his French boxing license). Yet the press played up every Siki libel it got its hands on, and concocted a few others out of thin air. Siki-the-savage-primitive made terrific copy. Later, when Siki deliberately got himself arrested in Memphis, Tennessee, in defiance of America's apartheid system, they somehow talked themselves into believing his protest had been just a drunken blunder.[29]

His real origins were reworked to fit the stereotypes. Milton Bronner, who wrote a column from London for NEA (forerunner of UPI), patched together a putative "autobiography" shortly after Siki won the title, a strange amalgam of facts that could only have come from Siki himself and worn-out misinformation and inside jokes from the French working press. Siki was no stickler for accuracy where his life story was concerned. He gave more than one account of how he'd come to leave Senegal and how he'd won his medals in the war. But Bronner has him alleging Siki is "a 'love word' [in Wolof] like 'darling' in English, or 'cherie' in French,"[30] nonsense it's unlikely he got from Siki. The French press had been similarly mocking his name and ancestry for months. A pseudoderivation had been tossed off, for instance, in the French sporting paper *L'Auto*. Siki, the writer jibed, is a name reserved in Africa for babies who "are chubby cheeked, very black, who have frizzy hair and wide noses. Thus Siki, in Senegalese, is a synonym for pretty, or cute, and all the French diminutives used to designate a charming visage."[31] Actually, the fighter

Despite being lampooned in the press as a savage, Siki was more often than not dressed like a veritable Beau Brummell of the ring (photograph 1923, Peter Benson collection).

probably borrowed his ring name from a Nyamwezi leader who had, from his Tabora strong-hold in what is now Tanzania, led a bloody revolt against German colonial rule.[32] But that explanation wouldn't have played very well in 1922.

Bronner gives Siki's name at birth as "Baye Phal,"[33] but in fact the Baye Fall (the normal spelling) is an aggressively militant Islamic sect, acolytes of Senegalese mystic, poet, and anticolonial activist Cheikh Amadou Bamba. One of Fall's cousins was a *Bamba talibé* (child follower), so Siki might have suggested this name as an inside joke. *Baay* (same pronunciation) is also the Wolof word for *father*, applied in their extended family system equally to paternal uncles and cousins. Bronner has Siki laughing at the idea, floated by journalists, that *Fall*, one of the most common names in Senegal, was associated with Senegalese royalty: ("If I am descended from kings, I never knew it before"). Actually, the name is linked to descendants of black slaves of Arab Mauritanians. Family tradition in Saint Louis, in Northern Senegal, where I met descendents of Siki's first cousins, still living on the site of the house where he was born, holds that Siki's given name was Amadou. His childhood nickname was *M'barick*, from the Toucouleur word *m'bare*, to kill, which gave rise to a Wolof derivative, *béré*, to wrestle. Fall's cousin Lamine Gaye told Mamadou Niang that Siki was a very, very turbulent child, suggesting the nickname *M'barick* marked childhood truculence.[34]

Siki told Bronner his parents were "poor working people," who struggled to put food on the table. Family sources say his father, Assane, a fisherman, died in an accident at sea, leaving Siki's mother Oulimata to care for the boy on her own. He may have picked up the Christian name Louis attending mission school (there were two in his home city during his childhood), or later, in France, when he enlisted to fight in the French army at the outbreak of World War I.

Whatever his origins, he was eager to leave them behind. Various contradictory accounts, several apparently originating from Siki himself, explain how he came to meet the woman who would take him to France. Bronner identifies her as "a German woman who called herself Mme. Fauquenberg, a dancer, who had lots of money." Elsewhere she is identified as Elaine Grosse,[35] an actress,[36] dancer,[37] singer[38] — of Dutch,[39] French,[40] or German[41] origin. One account[42] says Siki himself had no idea whether she was German or Dutch. "She saw me, a kid of eight," he told Bronner, "looking up at the ship. She took my hand, and had me show her about the city. Then she asked me if I wanted to ... sail to France and see other lands." Gaston Bénac offers a more dramatic introduction. Siki, he says, was one of a group of boys diving for coins as her ship docked at Saint Louis. So impressed was she with his agility and impish personality ("he was a resourceful, eccentric, and a devilish liar")[43] that she offered to "make of Siki an educated and well-mannered little boy."[44] Other accounts have her impressed by the naked child's anatomical development. (Pahl, more than one writer would jibe, was an adopted name, chosen "for reasons based on Classical Greek.")[45]

"I didn't take time to tell my family goodbye," Bronner has Siki say, "for I feared the dancer would change her mind. In France the dancer got me nice clothes, and daily taught me to read and write. She danced in many European cities, and I would go on the stage as her little servant, dressed in red velvet."[46] It sounds plausible except for the appearances in "many European cities," for in the next breath Bronner will have Siki lament being left behind when his new friend "went to Germany, but couldn't take me without a passport." One wonders how he got to "many European cities" without a passport. The red (or some-times "bottle green") suit became a universal element in the Siki origins myth, along with the job he was forced to take to survive on his own, as a dishwasher. French writers had great fun mocking the *plongeur* (literally "diver") turned fighter, who'd once appeared on stage in an absurdly emasculating toy boy costume, and been picked out in the first place from among a pack of wharf rats only because of his precocious sexual development. It was all too perfect — the fighter as a once vulnerable sex toy and innocuous underling. It made his brutal triumphs in the ring seem vaguely unreal, unthreatening. They'd been won by a freak, an outlandish non-person, despite his outrageous overdevelopment, both of musculature and sexuality.

Sports writers nicknamed him "the championzee," ridiculing his alleged primitive origins. Bronner gives Siki's reaction: "A lot of newspaper fellow have written that I have a jungle style of fighting, and that I am a sort of chimpanzee who has been taught to wear gloves. I was never in jungle in my life." Siki would more than once, in late night bars or on the street, resent similar insults with his fists. That was the other familiar representation — of Siki the hair-trigger belligerent, so enamored of fighting that he mugged innocuous strangers, fought taxi drivers for the fare, even assaulted the minions of the law. He did get in his fair share of brawls, but Siki had plenty of provocation for his tussles with strangers — in the form of the demeaning language the press had taught the general public to repeat.

The writers similarly shaped into legend Siki's wartime heroism (he won the Croix de Guerre and Médaille Militaire for valor). He told Bronner he'd gotten his medals for the exceptional distance he could throw a grenade — a full seventy-five meters. His trick had been to sneak out at dusk, in the awkward crouch he'd learned in Paul Latil's boxing studio, to lob those skyrocket grenade tosses of his. It's pretty implausible stuff. What likelihood would you have of doing any damage from that range, in the dark? And who'd give you a medal just for throwing things a long way? But take it for what it's worth. Try to ignore the sneaking suspicion that it's just claptrap gotten up to explain the strange crouch Siki went into in the early rounds against Carpentier. He hadn't gotten around yet to saying that fight had been set up for a fix. Other versions of how he won his medals had him single-handedly capturing, in no-man's land, nine German soldiers and slaughtering them with grenades, or wiping out machine gun nests.[47] The truth might have been too sad to sell to the general public. In fact, as the slaughter wore on, the generals handed out medals, antidotes for poor morale, by the "bucketful."[48] Black soldiers won theirs most often not for cinematic derring-do but dumb, steadfast obedience. One *tirailleur sénégalais* won his medals "for remaining upright under fire after an officer told him not to break a basketful of eggs, another for continuing to obey his lieutenant's order to bring him water hours after the lieutenant was dead."[49]

Siki enlisted in the Eighth Colonial Regiment of Toulon, the only black face among thousands of men. He fought with them through terrifying encounters in Champagne on the Western Front, in the charnel house of Gallipoli, and in the second wave in the bloodiest offensive of all, the Somme in July 1916, a ghastly "using-up" campaign in which whole armies were left on the assault for weeks, without relief, under constant shelling and terrifying mustard gas attacks. Pulled out of the Somme for good in September, the Eighth Colonial hardly deserved to be called a regiment. One casualty was Private Fall, both calves shredded by shrapnel.[50] Sent to a hospital north of Paris to recover, he was reassigned to the 73rd Regiment of Heavy Artillery. A better fed and supplied English regiment, garrisoned nearby, welcomed him to their regimental smokers. From them he learned a rugged stand-up style, featuring a now outlawed blow, the "right hand swing," thrown by extending the arm like someone throwing a hand grenade, rotating it to strike with the back of the knuckles, thumb pointing down. A number of top fighters of that era featured the roundhouse blow in their repertoire. Dixie Kid used it with great success before the war. Marcel Petit was still teaching it in 1972, long after it was illegal.[51]

The Ring magazine founder Nat Fleischer's role in defending black boxers (when it suited him) and defining their legacies should not be underestimated, though he was far from immune to the temptations of slipshod reporting in that era of ballyhoo, to stereotypical representation, or to wishful thinking in pursuit of a good story. He bought wholesale the image of Siki the savage clown with a childlike mind, labeling him "a veritable jungle-child, a throwback to the primitive"[52] and even going so far as to add, "Perhaps Siki was only half human."[53] Several iconic elements in the Siki legend come from Fleischer, who seems to have been fascinated by images of Siki in eccentric costume, accompanied by exotic pets. Siki really did own a menagerie of animals in France: Great Danes, a donkey, a Percheron, lion cubs. One of the cubs even bit him on the hand, postponing a scheduled fight.[54] But don't let anyone sell you the idea he walked full-grown big cats. At his training camp for the Louis-Firpo fight, Jack Dempsey was photographed with his pet ocelot on a leash. This did not, however, inspire Fleischer to conclude that Dempsey was a "throwback to the primitive."[55] Siki may in fact have gotten the idea of adopting the cubs from the American pilots of the Lafayette Escadrille, stationed southeast of Paris at Chaudon, whose squadron mascots were a pair of lion cubs named "Whiskey" and "Soda."[56]

Siki's 42nd Street apartment boasted, in addition to dogs, cats, and parrots, a noisy spider monkey who liked to come along on walks. This was towards the end of his American sojourn, after he'd remarried and set up housekeeping there. Fleischer's favorite Siki story has him drunk, at the main Times Square intersection, in an opera cape lined in red velvet, red gloves, grey suede shoes, silk topper, and cane, childishly playing traffic cop in the middle of the road. Accosted by a real policeman, Siki bows, and out from under his cape leaps a monkey—"onto the head of the officer, who almost fainted with fright."[57] In a version written fifteen years later, Fleischer will have Siki manhandled and hauled to the station by the flustered officer, belatedly identified as "Big Pat McDonald," former Olympic hammer thrower—possibly for the sake of suggesting that the fearsome savage isn't so fearsome after all, that the white world had its own powerfully muscled champions. This all took place, Fleischer notes, shortly after Siki came to America, before Siki really owned the monkey.[58] But minor slips can be forgiven, thirty-five years after the alleged incident. More troubling is the furnishing of Siki with a costume straight out of a minstrel show. With a few notable exceptions, nearly every surviving photograph of Siki in street dress shows him in fashionable, well-cut clothing. And if he did appear on the streets of Manhattan in evening dress, would that have been so remarkable in 1923?

Fleischer situates his other favorite monkey tale shortly before Siki fought Paul Berlenbach, in 1925, when he really did own the little spider monkey. This time Siki accosts three female bystanders and mutters something in "his native tongue" to the monkey, perched on his arm. Again it leaps, landing on a lady's back, sending her into shrieking hysterics. Again a patrolman appears to cow and control the absurd primitive, loose on the city sidewalks. "What are you doing with that scarecrow around here?" he grunts. "You come along with me." He hauls Siki off to face charges for molesting innocent white females. "Eet is not my fault," Siki protests. "Eet is my monkey. He likes charming ladies." The "charming ladies" in question, flattered, cave in. They won't press charges.[59] Of course, if Siki really had been apprehended for any crime or misdemeanor—never mind one involving sexual harassment—do you really think he'd have gotten off so lightly? And that not a single paper in New York would report it?

The only actual monkey tale involving Siki to be independently reported in the daily papers is more mundane. In it, Siki is on the way to watch a big fight between Sid Terris and Johnny Dundee, with his monkey in tow, when passengers bursting out of the train at the Thirty-Fourth Street station startled the beast, which leapt from Siki's arm and scuttled out of the train. Siki got off at the next station and returned to recover his animal, but when efforts to find it proved futile, he shrugged his shoulders and went on his way.[60]

No screaming ladies, no Big Pat the Hammer Thrower. Just a lost monkey and a fruitless search. Most searches for Siki atrocity tales end with such anticlimax.

Fleischer was also fond of retelling, as if it exemplified Siki's perplexity with civilization, a story he'd heard Bob Levy tell. In it, a narcissistic savage, upset his name isn't in the Memphis papers prior to a fight, heads down to the wharfs, grabs a bunch of bananas (yes, that's "bunch"—the whole six-foot stalk you cut from the living plant, not that little thing, a "hand" of bananas, you buy at the corner grocer's) hoists them onto his shoulders, and strolls down the street singing that year's Tin Pan Ally hit, "Yes, We Have No Bananas." Arrested by a couple of mounted cops and hauled before a bemused magistrate, Siki is let off with a warning, in return for favoring the court with an a-cappella rendition of the ditty.[61] Classic stuff! But what does it prove? Only that Siki had a flair for publicity and nothing to see but a ludicrous caricature of himself. A year later, after a falling out with Levy, he would slip off to Atlanta on his own to try to set up a fight with future middleweight champion Tiger Flowers, and pull the stunt with the bananas again — along with some other publicity gimmicks Levy had invented on his own.[62] When notoriety is all you have, you work it for all it's worth.

Past prejudice constrains us to talk about the three fights in Siki's career that writer after writer posits as meaningful — against Carpentier, McTigue, and Berlenbach, three white fighters. Siki wanted to fight whites. He told one interviewer, "I don't like fight colored man; can't get big money."[63] In the public mind, Gerald Early says, Siki was "never even quite a man but rather a being who approached being a man."[64] He was a foil, in other words, used to define others' selfhoods. Seldom awarded the subject role in the narrative, he was relegated to the role of adversary, alien other. Yet Siki's most fiercely competitive ring ordeal wasn't against any of the white fighters who figure in every retelling of his ring career. It was against an African American named Willie "Kid Norfolk" Ward.[65] For fifteen rounds those two fierce and determined ring warriors went at it. Sent out to battle once again on minimal training, Siki got the worst of it. But though he was bleeding from nose and lips, with one eye battered shut, in the final round he had Norfolk staggering along the ropes, within one concrete whisker of being knocked out. The *New York Times* called the fight "a privilege" to watch.[66] Both men, the *Chicago Defender* said, "gave and received blows that should have killed an ordinary man."[67] It had been the most memorable back and forth slugfest of the year, reminiscent of the great battle between Joe Jennette and Sam Langford.[68] Boxing writer Sid Mercer said it best: "Battling Siki ... displayed one quality that won the hearts of nearly 13,000 boxing fans.... That quality is gameness. Siki has plenty of it. He proved it during the Great War when he was twice decorated for courage. Last night he proved it again when he endured a fearful beating, yet never took a backward step except from sheer weariness."[69] Siki "would make it interesting for anyone of his weight in the world," added George B. Underwood. "He would be no cinch for Gene Tunney, Tom Gibbons, or Harry Greb. Make no mistake about that."[70]

Perhaps the most pernicious slander of all about Siki is the persistent misrepresentation of how he died. The usual fable has him murdered following a fist fight in a bar. No witness

Siki's punching power came from his extraordinary build. Paris, 1922 (Peter Benson collection).

saw such a fight, but that fantasy has become gospel truth to boxing writers. The real story begins just past midnight on December 16, 1925. John J. Meehan, the cop on the beat on 41st Street, comes across a familiar sight: a drunk wobbling along, like a wagon with a warped wheel. The sight is commonplace in the region near Times Square, as well-known for clip joints as glittering movie palaces. It wouldn't be worth a second glance but for two things: The drunk staggering down the street is black, in a neighborhood where black men are not warmly welcomed, and the drunk staggering down the street is famous. He's the boxer Battling Siki. The cop knows him. He lives just a block away.

"Hello," the blear-eyed drunk mutters. "I'm on my way home."

"You'd better keep going in that direction," Meehan enjoins.

"Don't worry," says Siki. "I will."[71] And off he trundles, more or less homeward.

Four hours later Meehan comes across what he takes to be someone passed out drunk in the gutter at 354 West 41st Street, thirty yards from the Ninth Avenue elevated train. He sees it's Siki and gives a shove to rouse him. Then he sees the bullet holes, both in the back. He's sleeping, okay — the final sleep. Detectives arrive on the scene, prowl the block looking for clues, and find a rusty Saturday night special, flung hastily to the curb about halfway up the block, near a puddle of blood. They'd passed another blood spoor fifty yards downhill. They imagine a likely scenario: Someone had come up behind Siki and shot him without warning. Wounded, he'd staggered downhill, followed by the killer, who plugged him again and saw him plunge face down. He ditched the weapon and took off running, leaving Siki for dead. But Siki wasn't dead. He somehow struggled to his feet and stumbled another twenty yards, nearly to the corner. Then he pitched forward to the grimy pavement for good.[72]

It didn't take Sherlock Holmes, the cops decided, to figure this one out. Siki had a bad habit of pushing white men out of his way on the sidewalk, one detective said, daring them to do something about it. And a worse one of starting scraps in bars. That had to be what happened.[73] That's where they left it — for weeks, while the press had a field day building up a purely imaginary version of Siki's death. The *Evening Journal* ran a cartoon strip featuring one box with "poor deluded Siki," in overcoat and fedora, grinning as he leaves a speakeasy, as a white man, hair mussed, tie loose, fists cocked, glares at his back. Then you get the same white guy, coat collar pulled high, hat brim tilted over his eyes, pistol in hand, ready to follow Siki down the darkened street.[74] In France they so loved that tale they embroidered it, concocting a version where the gunman timed his shots to the passing rumble of overhead trains.[75] They had not the least evidence it had happened that way — and trains don't run minutes apart in the wee hours of a Wednesday morning, but that story too is relentlessly repeated to this day. *Le Petit Journal* ran an elaborate cover illustration of the imaginary confrontation everyone by now was certain had led to Siki's murder, with Siki outside the brightly lit window of a saloon, cracking a brawny white across the face with his fist, another victim of his punches at his feet, a third reeling along the curb, wiping a bloody mouth.[76] In fact, no one had seen Siki in a fight that night, but the imaginary scene fit everyone's stereotypes so neatly, who could resist it? Apparently, the French editors had forgotten that saloons had disappeared with the passage of the 1919 prohibition amendment, and that speakeasies didn't exactly advertise in neon lights.

He'd brought it on himself, writer after writer urged. "What had to happen has happened," wrote *Paris-Soir*, "Siki is dead, and dead in circumstances that the whole world foresaw."[77] That judgment lies heavily on Siki's legacy to this day, even though an enterprising undercover cop eavesdropping on a young punk at a pay phone in a seedy dance hall would find out otherwise. "The bulls are wise to who killed Siki," the punk at the payphone whined. "They're close on our trail. But what can I do? I can't get out of town. I've got no money."[78] The cops kept at it for a while. They put a tail on the punk at the payphone, a street hood named Martin Maroney. They had a few witnesses. One man had seen Siki walking down 41st Street with three other men just before the shooting.[79] Another heard the pop, pop of a low-caliber revolver and seconds later saw a young guy in a light-colored coat dashing towards him down 41st Street, coattails flying.[80] Detectives had learned earlier that Siki had been in a little "Coffee Pot" on Eighth Avenue minutes before the shooting, so drunk he'd spilled his coffee and tumbled to the floor.[81]

Eventually, when Maroney led them nowhere interesting, they hauled him in. The Coffee Pot witnesses gave a positive identification. This very Martin Maroney had walked out the door of the café with Siki just before the murder. Under police questioning Maroney spilled what really transpired — or anyway a lot of it. For all of it to spill out you'd have needed a district attorney like Thomas E. Dewey. Manhattan's political system in 1926 was corrupt through and through, dependent on mob enforcers for its everyday functioning. What came out was this: Two accomplices had sent Maroney to lure Siki into the open with a promise of a drink. Maroney led him down the darkened side street, where two accomplices fell in with them. When they reached a good dark spot, one of them emptied a couple rounds in Siki's back. No fist fight, no personal grudge — just a quick execution.[82]

Maroney was a bit shy about revealing who was paying the three of them to murder Siki — and perhaps the police were a bit shy about asking. But the answer was obvious. Just five months earlier three strangers had jumped Siki and tried to slit his throat on the same street corner where Maroney and his friends gunned him down.[83] Ten years later Gaston Bénac overheard Siki's manager Bob Levy, over drinks, let slip the real reason for Siki's murder. On the tail end of his career, unable any longer to attract big purses in major arenas, Siki had agreed to carry up-and-coming opponents, to please their mob sponsors. But he'd failed to come through. Finally, as Bénac puts it, "The Senegalese had just, as was his habit, played around with a novice who was very much promoted by the gang of the night clubs of Broadway. The fight should have gone the distance and been very equal to justify a draw and launch the career of the new heavyweight, but Siki had stretched him out for the count of ten, during the first round, laughing as he did so, "Here's what I do, me Siki, to your hopes."[84] The fight in question is almost certainly one Siki contested at the West New York Playgrounds, against Jimmy Francis (actually a light heavyweight), a fighter whose record is dotted with fighters known to be mob-affiliated. Siki not only beat the young hopeful, but draped him artistically, dangling by the neck, over the ring rope.[85] That was just four days before those three guys tried to slit his throat in July. The cops actually caught one of his assailants, but although Siki recognized the guy, he refused to press charges. He was afraid for his wife's safety, he ingenuously disclosed.[86] Who other than gangsters would threaten such things?

Were the three guys who shot Siki the same ones who tried to slit his throat? Probably not. He wasn't stupid enough to turn his back on the same guys twice. But almost certainly the mobster who ordered the botched execution in July also ordered the successful one in December. Both Hell's Kitchen and North Jersey were full of criminals flush with cash from the alcohol trade. North Jersey headquartered both the biggest nationwide gambling cartel, the so-called Horse Bourse, and the bootleg whiskey industry.[87] One estimate had something like forty percent of America's illicit hooch passing through Hudson County.[88] The boss of this illicit trade was Jewish gangster Long Zwillman, a passionate boxing fan who'd gotten his start in crime working the Newark numbers racket. If it was someone in North Jersey who decided to teach Siki an indelible lesson they couldn't have made that decision without clearing the matter with Zwillman, whose biggest claim to fame was his origination of the syndicate headquartered on Broadway that controlled crime in the entire met-

"I sometimes let them believe that. But ... it's not at all true." 1923 (Peter Benson collection).

ropolitan region. One of his partners in that venture was the crime boss whose word was law in Hell's Kitchen, Owney Madden — also deeply involved in boxing.[89] Nothing happened in Hell's Kitchen without Madden's okay. Whether he ordered the hit on Siki or not, he knew about it.

That might explain the sequel to the story. Maroney cooled his heels in the lockup for seven months before he was brought before a judge. You'd figure he'd get at least twenty years, right?

He got the gate. The handcuffs came off. He was walked to the door. Charges dismissed. "Lack of evidence."[90]

"Lack of evidence"? What did they want, a film of the crime, shot from different angles? The guy had confessed!

If it's not surprising that, as Gerald Early put it, "nobody really cared very much" who murdered Siki,[91] it is surprising that, even now, nobody wants to hear the news that Siki wasn't to blame for his own death, that it wasn't his own clownish belligerence that killed him, but the machinations of a corrupt boxing underworld.

Or maybe it isn't so surprising after all. Did anyone listen to Siki himself when he said it? No, I am not a savage. No, I am not an illiterate. No, I am not a cannibal. No, I'm not a clown and a joke.

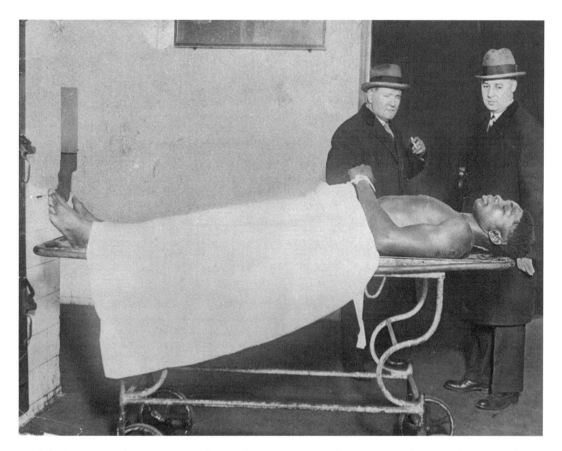

Siki's corpse in police morgue, with two detectives, New York City, December 1925 (courtesy of Mamadou Niang).

In 1922, Parisian papers had been playing hilarious changes on a favorite Siki gag—the one where he disappears for days on end, and no one can find him. One newsman finally tried the obvious expedient of knocking on the door of Siki's home in suburban Vanves—where in fact he'd been all along. "To the whole world I am a savage," Siki said to him. "I sometimes let them believe that. But ... it's not at all true. Yesterday, once again, they were saying that I had disappeared. I was right here, where you see me now, with some friends and the grandchildren of a friend, and, mister, if you have a home like this, you probably did yesterday the same thing I did."[92] He wrote in a letter to *L'Auto*, "First of all, I am not a cannibal. An evening newspaper, recently, seized the occasion of an interview to have me speaking pidgin ["petit négre"]. That's ridiculous. I speak and I write French like the average French person."[93] He told a white journalist, "You put rings in my nose, rings in my ears—I give you some news and you write much that is wrong and in the wrong way too." To a black journalist he said, "You got a statue in New York, Liberty you call it—hah. It mean nothing. No freedom here—no, no, no—not for you—me."[94]

The tragedy is not only that Siki's voice was silenced late one December night in 1922 by a man with a rusty revolver, but that even earlier it had been effectively silenced by a lot of other men with typewriters. Sadder still, the cacophony of their nonsense continues to drown out Siki's voice to this day.

You have to wonder what he would have said about the way even his death was worked into the same sorry joke. Its taste ought to have gone sour in our mouths long ago. It says something about us that it seems it still hasn't.

NOTES

1. *New York Times*, March 13, 1925, 17.
2. *New York Evening Journal*, March 13, 1925, 10.
3. *New York Daily Mirror*, March 14, 1925.
4. Vernon Pize, *Glorious Triumphs: Athletes Who Conquered Adversity*, 114–124; A national amateur champion, Berlenbach went to the 1920 Antwerp games as a representative of the New York Athletic Club, though an injury prevented him from competing—Pete Ehrmann, "Setting the Record Straight on Paul Berlenback," *The Ring*, February, 2005, 69–70.
5. Nat Fleischer, *Fifty Years at Ringside*, 93.
6. Nat Fleischer, *Fifty Years at Ringside*, 92.
7. Nat Fleischer, *Black Dynamite: The Story of the Negro in the Prize Ring from 1782 to 1938, Vol. III*, 88.
8. Nat Fleischer, *Black Dynamite*, 71–72.
9. Nat Fleischer, *Fifty Years at Ringside*, 93.
10. *New York Herald Tribune*, March 14, 1925, 14.
11. The photos appeared on the front page of the sports section, March 14, 1925, over Sid Mercer's column on the fight.
12. *New York Evening Journal*, March 13, 1925, 10.
13. *New York Evening Post*, March 14, 1925, 15.
14. George Carpentier, with the collaboration of Jacques Marchan, *Mes 80 Rounds*, 193.
15. The account of the fight is drawn primarily from the still extant news-reel film, supplemented by accounts in Carpentier's *Mes 80 Rounds* and newspaper round-by-round accounts in *L'Echo de Paris*, September 25, 1922, 1; *L'Auto*, September 25, 1922, 1; *Le Matin*, September 25, 1922, 1; *Le Miroir des Sports, Le Petit Parisien*, September 25, 1922, 1; *L'Humanité*, Sep-

tember 25, 1922, 2; and the New York *Herald*, Paris, September 26, 1922, 6.
16. Carpentier describes Sunday café shows that began with gymnastics ("balancing on chairs and tables, dangerous leaps, juggling exercises"), followed by boxing exhibitions. Later Descamps would bring Carpentier along to help in his magic act and fake spiritualist séances. Georges Carpentier, *Mon match avec la vie*, 32.
17. *Boxing Blade*, December 16, 1922.
18. *Echo des Sports*, September 25, 1922, 2; *Le Matin*, September 25, 1922, 4.
19. *Miroir des Sports*, October 12, 1922, 226.
20. *L'Echo de Paris*, December 6, 1922, 1; *Boxing Blade*, December 16, 1922, 12; *New York Evening Journal*, December 6, 1922, 1.
21. Carpentier, *Mes 80 Rounds*, 193–194.
22. Niek Koppen, *Siki* (Documentary Video Production, Amsterdam, 1993).
23. *L'Echo des Sports*, September 26, 1922, 1.
24. *L'Auto*, December 5, 1922, 1.
25. He mistakes the round. He means the third.
26. *L'Éclair*, December 5, 1922, 1; *L'Auto*, December 5, 1922, 1.
27. *L'Auto*, December 6, 1922, 1–2.
28. Carpentier, *Mes 80 Rounds*, 191–192.
29. *New York Times*, December 22, 1924; *Memphis Commercial Appeal*, December 22, 1924, 14; December 23, 1924, 15; *National Police Gazette*, January 17, 1925, 11.
30. Milton Bonner, "Battling Siki's Autobiography,"

Bellingham (Washington) *American,* November 10, 1922; rpt. Boxing Biographies. Internet. *http://boxing biographies.com/bio/index.php?option=com_content&task =blogcategory&id=17&Itemid=30*

31. L'Auto, October 1, 1922, 1.

32. Robert July, *A History of the African People,* 4th Ed., 281, 352.

33. *Le Matin* also gives "Baye Fall" as Siki's "*vrai nom*" (real name), September 25, 1922, 4.

34. Koppen, *Siki.*

35. Nigel Collins, *Boxing Babylon,* 59.

36. John D. McCallum, *The Encyclopedia of World Boxing Champions,* 92; John Lardner, "The Battling Siki Murder," *New Yorker,* November 19, 1949; rpt. *Negro Digest* 8, 6 (April 1950), 54; Ocania Chalk, *Pioneer of Black Sport: The Early Days of the Black Professional Athlete in Baseball, Basketball, Boxing, and Football,* 164.

37. Gaston Bénac, *Champions dans la coulisse,* 100; Georges Peeters, *La Boxe: 'noble art,'* 67; Nigel Collins, *Boxing Babylon,* 59; Ocania Chalk, *Pioneers of Black Sport,* 164; *L'Auto* Special Edition, September 24, 1922, 1; G. De Lafrete, *L'Echo de Paris,* September 25, 1922.4.

38. Benny Green, *Shaw's Champions: George Bernard Shaw and Prizefighting, from Cashel Byron to Gene Tunney,* 122.

39. Bénac, *Champions dans la coulisee;* François Terbeen and Claude Brezner, *Les Geants del la boxe,* 126, n.; Green, Shaw's *Champions,* 122.

40. Fleischer, *Black Dynamite, III,* 74; Lardner, "The Battling Siki Murder," 54.

41. Ocania Chalk, *Pioneers of Black Sport,* 164; *L'Auto* Special Edition, September 24, 1922; G. De Lafrete, *L'Echo de Paris,* September 25, 1922, 4.

42. Albert Stol, interviewed by Niek Koppen, *Siki* (Video).

43. Bénac, *Champions dans la coulisse,* 100.

44. Ibid.

45. A reference suggesting the word *phallus;* See John D. McCallum *The Encyclopedia of World Boxing Champions,* 92; Lardner, "The Battling Siki Murder," 54.

46. Milton Bonner, "Battling Siki's Autobiography."

47. Fleischer, *Black Dynamite, III,* 75–76; McCallum, *The Encyclopedia of World Boxing Champions,* 92; Harry Mullan, *The Illustrated History of Boxing,* 167.

48. Feuille, *Face aux turcs: Gallipoli,* 153–154.

49. Du Bert, Marthe [Pseud. M. Dutreb], *Nos sénegalais pendant la grande guerre,* 100–102.

50. Bonner, "Battling Siki's Autobiography."

51. Jean Auger, *La boxe anglaise,* 41; Petit, *Boxe: technique — entrainement,* 48.

52. Fleischer, *Black Dynamite, III,* 70.

53. Fleischer, *Fifty Years at Ringside,* 93.

54. *L'Auto,* April 5, 1923, 4; May 17, 1923, 3; *New York Times,* May 17, 1923, 16.

55. Nat Fleischer, *Jack Dempsey,* 65.

56. "The Lafayette Escadrille — Americans Prepare to Enter the Air War," January 4, 2010. Century of Flight, Internet. *http://www.century-of-flight.net/*

Aviation%20history/airplane%20at%20war/Lafayette %20Escadrille.htm

57. Fleischer, *Black Dynamite, III,* 89–90.

58. Fleischer, *Fifty Years at Ringside,* 92.

59. Fleischer, *Black Dynamite, III,* 90.

60. *New York Times,* June 10, 1925, 18.

61. Fleischer, *Black Dynamite, III,* 91; *Fifty Years at Ringside,* 94.

62. *Atlanta Constitution,* January 18, 1925, 1C.

63. *Chicago Defender,* September 29, 1923, 1.

64. Gerald Early, "Battling Siki," *The Culture of Bruising: Essays on Prize-fighting, Literature and Modern American Culture,* 68–69.

65. A complete description of the Norfolk fight is in Peter Benson, *Battling Siki: A Tale of Ring Fixes, Race, and Murder in the 1920s,* 73–88. Those interested in a full account of the Siki-McTigue fight will find it in Benson, *Battling Siki,* 1–22, an edited version of which appeared as "The Savage Battler and Clever Little Mike," *The Ring,* December 2006, 66–75.

66. *New York Times,* November 22, 1923, 23.

67. *Chicago Defender,* November 24, 1923, 9.

68. George B. Underwood, *New York Evening Telegram,* November 21, 1923, 10.

69. *New York Evening Journal,* November 21, 1923, 1.

70. *New York Evening Telegram,* November 21, 1923, 14.

71. *New York Post,* December 16, 1925, 1; *New York Times,* December 16, 1925, 3; *New York Evening Sun,* December 16, 1926, 1.

72. This description is drawn from the *New York World,* December 16, 1925, 1; *New York Evening Sun,* December 16, 1925, 1; *New York Telegram,* December 16, 1925, 1; *New York Post,* December 16, 1925, 1; *New York Daily News,* December 16, 1925, 3; *New York Times,* December 16, 1925, 1,3; and *New York Herald Tribune,* December 16, 1925, 1.

73. *New York Evening Sun,* December 16, 1925, 1.

74. *New York Evening Journal,* December 17, 1925, 2.

75. Francois Terbeen and Claude Brezner, *Les Geants de la boxe,* 126; Benac, *Champions dans la coulisse,* 118.

76. *Le Petit Journal,* December 20, 1925, 1.

77. *Paris-Soir,* December 17, 1925, 4.

78. *New York Times,* March 9, 1926, 8; the description of Maroney's capture follows this source.

79. *New York Daily News,* December 16, 1925, 1.

80. *New York Telegram,* December 16, 1925, 1.

81. *New York Evening Journal,* December 17, 1925, 2.

82. John Lardner, "This Was Pugilism: Battling Siki," *New Yorker,* November 19, 1949, 108.

83. *New York Evening Journal,* July 27, 1925, 18.

84. Bénac, *Champions dans la coulisse,* 117.

85. *Jersey Journal,* July 23, 1925, 12; July 24, 1925, 17, 19; *Hudson Dispatch,* July 23, 1925, 17.

86. *New York Times,* July 27, 1925, 15; July 28, 1925, 23.

87. Summary Report, December 27, 1957, Federal Bureau of Investigation (FBI), Abner Zwillman file, Part 2, Bu file nos. 92–3105, 62–36085, 58–441);

Summary Report, June 18, 1958, Federal Bureau of Investigation, Abner Zwillman file, Part 2, Bu file no. 58–4441.

88. Mark A. Stuart, *Gangster #2: Longy Zwillman, the Man Who Invented Organized Crime,* 194.

89. Graham Nown, *The English Godfather,* 9; Abner "Longy" Zwillman interviewd by Special Agent in Charge A. P. Kitchin, Newark, NJ, November 9–

10, 1938 (FBI, Abner Zwillman file, Part 2, Bu file nos. 92–3105, 62–36085, 58–4441).

90. *New York Times,* October 5, 1926, 8.

91. Early, *The Culture of Bruising,* 82.

92. *L'Auto,* December 12, 1922, 1–2.

93. Battling Siki (Louis M'barick Fall), "Résumé aux lecteurs de *L'Auto, L'Auto,* September 29, 1922, 1.

The Great Fights, Round-By-Round

George Godfrey vs. Peter Jackson (American Colored Heavyweight Championship, August 24, 1888)

George Godfrey, Champion of the United States vs. Peter Jackson, Champion of Australia, Hyram Cook, referee, August 24, 1888, San Francisco, California Athletic Club (reported by the *San Francisco Chronicle*, August 25, 1888, "GODFREY GIVES UP: Jackson Batters Him for Nineteen Rounds: Game and Exciting Fight to the Close: The Bostonian Is Badly Injured by the Australian's Heavy Blows")

Round 1. As the men put up their hands for the first round the contrast of their styles was seen. Jackson held his guard rather low, and moved in the style made so general in the Australian colonies by the example of Jem Mace. Godfrey held his hands a trifle high and his feet wider apart.

The round was opened by the Australian, who felt for his opponent's ribs with his left, but was short. Light and harmless exchanges followed in the middle of the ring, and then the Bostonian showed his hand. He had come to make it a rushing fight, and he went at his work in a way that must have electrified some of the slow-going local sloggers staring at him from the benches.

Jackson from the very first proved that he possessed a most telling left, and after the first preliminary feeler he went in to use it with serious intent. His first determined lead was cleverly stopped by the Bostonian, who, in return, administered him a smash on the jaw that made his ivories rattle. The rest of the round, with the exception of one short breathing-spell of a few seconds, was of the whirl-wind order.

Aiming a hot left at Jackson's jaw Godfrey followed it up with a right-hand swing that would have knocked down an ox. The tall Australian, however, met the onslaught like a genuine Master of the manly art. The left-handed caromed on his chin, but the terrible right missed fire, and as he ducked he caught the Bostonian on his hip, and had the battle been under London prize-ring rules instead of Marquis of Queensberry would have given him a fall he would have remembered.

This beginning of the round showed that the contest was to be a desperate affair, and as it progressed it lost nothing of its determined character. As soon as Jackson released Godfrey from the impending cross-buttock the men sparred a moment at long range. Godfrey landed a light left-hander on the tall fellow's nose, and Jackson retaliated with a smack on the Bostonian's nasal organ, but neither received any injury till Godfrey resumed his tactics.

Jackson, after poising himself on his toes in his peculiar fashion, let go with the left, following it with the right, intending to get in to infighting, in which he is a master. His shorter antagonist was right with him, however, and one of the most exciting rallies ever fought in the California Athletic Club followed.

The exchanges were so rapid and the repeated right-handers of the Bostonian so savage that a knock-out at the very opening of the battle seemed likely. Again and again he rushed at Jackson, only to receive the tall Australian's left flush on his face. He reached his antagonist repeatedly, however, but the tall antipodean managed to elude the fatal smash on the jugular, and plied his left and right in such piston-rod style that the Bostonian was driven to the ropes.

He looked for a second as if he had been dazed, but he rallied instantly, and another series of terrific exchanges followed in such lightning style that when "time" was called every man in the hall was standing. The excitement was intense.

Godfrey had shown himself a most formidable pugilist, but even at this stage there was no gainsaying the fact that he was outclassed in size and reach if not in actual boxing skill. His infighting had been most effective, but though unmistakably a hard and determined hitter and very skillful at ducking to avoid punishment, he did not move with the almost machine-like precision of the Australian, who followed every advantage in a most systematic, scientific and thoroughly workmanlike fashion.

Round 2. The Bostonian did not seem at the beginning of the second round as if he had fears of having met his superior. He came up smiling, and in fact almost to the last laughed through his terrific punishment. He tried with his left but missed, as the Australian was very shifty. He tried left and right, and was topped cleverly. Then Jackson assumed the offensive, and following a straight shot on the chin with the left by a rib roaster with the right, he crowded his man towards the ropes, and administered some heavy punishment. Godfrey never flinched, however, but took his medicine gamely, and tried manfully to floor his tall opponent with one of his right-handed swings.

After the first rally Godfrey sparred at long range a second, and rushed in to half-arm work, but miscalculated the size of the opening, and got a left-hander on the jaw that floored him neatly. He was on his pins in a moment, however, as spry as a lark and apparently not dismayed in the least by the mishap. He dashed his left at the elevated chin of this opponent, and hot exchanges followed, Godfrey missing one well-intended right that would have put a different complexion on the round if it had reached the target.

In this round, as in the other, Godfrey experienced the disadvantage of fighting with a man not only very clever with his hands and feet, but some inches taller, and many pounds heavier. He led time and again, only to be short, while the straight left of Jackson flew out with discouraging regularity, and was planted with telling effect on the Bostonian's face and stomach. Godfrey never tired of trying for a knock-out blow with his right, and the Australian, whenever the opportunity offered, followed up his leads with effective right-handers on the ribs and a rally in which the Eastern man was generally forced toward the ropes, receiving considerable injury as he went, but still fighting.

In the first two rounds there was more punishment administered and taken without flinching than in some of the longest drawn out fights in the club. At the end of the second round both men were short of wind and time was called.

Round 3. The third round was much the lightest fought so far. Godfrey came up fresh and smiling and led, but was short with his left. Jackson then led and planted his left in the Bostonian's stomach in vigorous style and following it up in his now accustomed manner with a right on the ribs, did some lively in-fighting till the Bostonian was close to his own corner. There was very little clinching in any of the rounds, the men standing up gamely to their work and giving the referee very little trouble.

After a clinch in the third round in Godfrey's corner, the men sparred a moment, and then Jackson landed such a heavy left-hander on the Bostonian's collar bone that the blood appeared. The blow was a punishing one, and the smile which had illuminated the small man's face vanished for a few minutes. It was thought that his collar-bone was broken, but his subsequent movements showed that it was not.

The remainder of the round was marked by none of the ferocious fighting of the previous rounds. Jackson kept on using his left at long range, as if sparring for wind, and, just as time was about to be called, landed a blow on Godfrey's mouth that drew blood. The Bostonian laughed as he went to his corner.

Round 4. The fourth round was a hot one. It seemed as if Jackson fought by alternate rounds, and after each unimportant one went in to use up his man in vigorous style. Both men were not over lively to respond to the call of time. Jackson opened hostilities with his left, but was short. He followed with his left and right, but was neatly stopped. The Bostonian, encouraged by this success, took the offensive in determined style, and supplemented a vigorous left-hander on the jaw with a right-handed smash on the Australian's neck that made the kangaroo hunter a couple of inches shorter. The Bostonian's friends, who throughout, seemed to be most numerous, gave votes to a cheer of triumph, and, one excited individual yelled, "A hundred on Godfrey!" A cheerful and unanimous response of "Shut up," "Put him out," spoiled the speculation and the men went on with their work.

They sparred for wind till Godfrey led and got a heavy counter for his trouble. Nothing daunted he led again and got his dose repeated. Then Jackson tried a left-hander and succeeded so well that he rushed in and another hot rally took place, the Bostonian again striving manfully to plant a knock-out blow, but getting badly used by the in-fighting. A clinch took place, and then, after some more sparring, Godfrey tried with his left with business intent, and got so heavily countered on the left eye that it bled during the remainder of the fight.

Round 5. The fifth round was a sample of fighting such as has seldom been seen anywhere. Godfrey began by spitting out a mouthful of blood as soon as he toed the scratch. It was thought that he had lost some teeth, but this was not so. Jackson seemed eager for business and Godfrey accommodated him by trying a left and right-hander, the first of which went home, but the second did not. Jackson caught his man with both fists before he could recover and the Bostonian's chances for the next minute looked blue. Smash after smash from the huge Australian's fists sounded on his face till he changed to the color of an Indian, and Jackson's gloves grew carmine. It looked as if the Bostonian could never last out the round. Though fairly slaughtered, he fought like a tiger. Jackson's white drawers were sprinkled with blood by every blow. The Bostonian staggered around the ring, but though it was an effort for him to stand, he still laughed.

It was only a question of Jackson's holding out a few minutes longer for the fight to have ended then and there, but the Australian's lungs were unequal to the demands of the hurricane fight. His blows began to lack force, and in the critical moment time was called.

Round 6. Despite his punishment Godfrey came up smiling for the sixth round, which was marked by shots at long range, followed by sparring and occasional rallies till Jackson worked his man into a corner and went for him to finish the job. It was a question whether the Bostonian laughed or bled the more freely. He grinned as the blood ran down his face and chest and continued to fight like a tiger, but he looked badly dilapidated when time was called.

Round 7. In the seventh round Jackson forced the fighting and tried again to knock out his man. He planted his left on his face time after time without a return. In the middle of the round Godfrey braced up and it was give and take till time was called.

Round 8. The eighth round was also marked by long-range hits, and more sparring than had yet been indulged in. The tide turned slightly in Godfrey's favor, and seemed not yet half over.

Rounds 9–11. The ninth and tenth rounds were not sensational. Jackson still kept the lead, using his left and slowly but surely winding up his man.

Round 12. In the twelfth round Godfrey proved himself a remarkably game man, and only escaped being knocked out by clever ducking and the most persistent courage.

Everyone thought the battle would be ended in the twelfth round. Jackson drove his man into his own corner and fairly slaughtered him, but the plucky Bostonian, by superhuman endurance, held out till the call of time.

Rounds 13–14. The thirteenth and fourteenth rounds were almost repetitions of the others.

Round 15. In the fifteenth round Godfrey had to be assisted to his feet and the battle seemed over, but though a dozen times on the point of being knocked out, he kept ducking and fighting, though barely able to raise his arms.

Round 16. The sixteenth round found Jackson short of wind, and again he failed to deal the coup de grace, though the Bostonian laughed no more, and was bleeding at every pore.

Rounds 17–19. In the seventeenth round, as in the others immediately pending, Jackson had it all his own way, and it was only a question of how long the Bostonian could endure the frightful punishment. He staggered like a drunken man and was barely able to lift his hands, even for defense, but the end of the seventeenth round found him still on his feet He astonished every one by remaining on his feet till the nineteenth round, when Jackson, after the usual tactics of drawing him back to the ropes, delivered a right-hander over the region of the heart which ended the contest. The plucky Bostonian dropped his hands and gave up the fight.

George Dixon vs. Jack Skelly (Carnival of Champions, September 6, 1892)

George Dixon vs. Jack Skelly of Brooklyn, Prof. Duffy, Referee, September 6, 1892, New Orleans, Louisiana (reported by *The New Orleans Times Picayune*, "The Black Wins," September 7, 1892)

Round 1. Both men sprang to the center of the ring as the gong sounded. Each paused for a second as if trying to gauge the powers of his opponent and then Skelly rushed in. Swinging his right for Dixon's jaw and meeting the colored fighter's left full on the mouth and chin. The men came together in a clinch but broke away promptly at the referee's command. Again Skelly rushed, but Dixon danced lightly away, Skelly following. Skelly led again ineffectually for the jaw and Dixon's right shot out, catching him sharply on the mouth, and they clenched. Skelly crowding in got a good rib-roaster from Dixon's left, and they came together, Skelly countering lightly on the jaw with his left after the break. Dixon's left again found Skelly's face but lightly, and the Brooklyn boy came back with a light return on the neck with his right. Skelly kept crowding his man, driving him to his corner, but Dixon fought his way out, swinging his left with vicious vigor for his opponent's jaw and meeting a clever stop. Skelly followed him to the center and again led his right to the jaw, but Dixon got cleverly away and coming up again reached Skelly's jaw lightly with his left. A clench followed, succeeded by light sparring which was ended by the gong. So far as the punishment was concerned honors were easy, but the master of strength, sciences, and in agility, Skelly was outclassed, though he had a decided advantage in height and reach.

Round 2. The men stood off at arms length for a little, until Dixon got ready to rush. Skelly got his arms under the bronze battering rams, stopping the onslaught cleverly, and bringing Dixon to a clinch. Dixon rushed again and missed with both hands, finally getting his left into the face lightly. Dixon stood off and looked at his rival, saw that the face was guarded well, and then played for the stomach. He reached it at the first attempt. He made a quick side step, and as he came within reaching distance, he swung his left in, stiffened hard, full upon the stomach. It was Dixon's first good claim for the fight, and Skelly's sympathizers groaned. Dixon stepped in again before Skelly corrected the defect in his guard, and shot the right hand on the ribs. Dixon had struck his gait now, and the left again swung in on the stomach, Skelly jabbing him in the face as they came to a clinch. Dixon again landed the left on the stomach harder, and got a half arm counter on the forehead from Skelly's left. Skelly's left was longer when Dixon next closed in, and both men caught the glove on the cheek. Skelly regained some of his cleverness and when Dixon reached in he caught the black nicely and prevented harm, Dixon was speedy and tried the left for the face again, and as Skelly countered neatly Dixon turned the right shoulder in and delivered a quick swing with the right on the ear. Dixon came on without much delay and planted the left on the stomach. The black swung his right in on the neck. The crowd cried "foul." And Dixon stepped back and made a motion of apology. All through the battle he took particular pains to fight fair. After they got at arms' length, Dixon swung his left up near the ribs, near the heart, a spot which was becoming rapidly rosy and puffed, receiving a left counter on his neck. Dixon rushed without rest, but this once, Skelly stepped away skillfully and shot his right skillfully over Dixon's heart. Dixon came on and Skelly kept out of reach, fighting as he retreated, and as he turned he swung his left around and caught the black a blow on the side. It was almost a pivot. Skelly came in close, when Dixon rushed forward and the black's right swung in on the back. It would have reached the heart otherwise. Dixon had far and away the best of the round. His body punches were terrific, and ribs and stomach began already to show signs of punishment. Dixon's left had also found Skelly's nose, which was slightly swollen and sore from one of the Griffin's blows in training. Skelly on the contrary, proved thoroughly game and while his counters did not seem to do injury, they were persistent, and his one blow on the ribs had force in it.

Round 3. Though Skelly came up readily enough, the effect of Dixon's terrible body blows was plainly apparent. He mixed matters at once, crowding Dixon's back as the colored boy broke ground. Dixon turned on the further side of the ring to avoid being cornered and landed a heavy left hand swing on Skelly's ribs, following it up quickly with a smashing right hander on the jaw, which took Skelly off his feet. The white lad rose promptly — too promptly in fact for his own good — and like a whorl-wind Dixon was at him again and would have fought him down had he not clinched. Dixon forced matters again after the break and twice in quick succession his rights found Skelly's ribs with great effect. Skelly was forced back by the onslaught, but Dixon gave him no chance to get away. He led with his left for the jaw, following it up with his right for the ribs, but Skelly was on the alert, stopped him cleverly and countered on the shoulder as he passed him. Again Dixon's left shot out for the jaw and again he was stopped, but he kept at it, and the next attempt was more successful, and he reached Skelly's jaw with his left, evading a return skillfully. As Skelly came up again, Dixon rushed him, swinging his right heavily on the ribs, and they clinched. Again Dixon forced the pace, giving his man a stiff punch below the heart with his right, and jabbing him in the ribs with his left while they were still at close quarters. He avoided a clinch cleverly and rushing his man landed his right heavily on the jaw, cross countering on the neck with his left as Skelly broke away. Again Dixon played for the ribs, and he landed another smashing right hander on the reddened smarting flesh over Skelly's ribs, Skelly clinching and giving Dixon a chance to hug of which he was not slow to avail himself. They came together again promptly, and Dixon's handy left sounded hard on Skelly's battered ribs. He followed it up with his right below the heart at short range and jabbed him hard with his left in the ribs as they clinched. The gong sounded almost immediately after the breakaway.

Round 4. Skelly stepped up smiling, despite his punishment, and instead of waiting for Dixon, took up the chase, but Dixon was wary, and kept away like a little general. Picking his chance, Dixon stepped in quickly and delivered his left swing on the stomach, taking a jab in the face as he came to a clinch. Skelly buried the monotony by rushing on his own account, but Dixon broke ground with dancing step, and jabbed his left in on the nose as Skelly tried to pin him to a corner. Each rushed in turn, to be neatly stopped and brought to a harmless clinch, and then Skelly cleverly stopped another onslaught. In the next meeting Dixon got in his left on the nose, and as Skelly came back with a left on the temple, Dixon gave him the right on the stomach. Dixon was tireless and his left found the bruised ribs twice in succession. The second time Skelly's left was quicker and swung in hard on Dixon's ear. It did not even cause the dusky champion to pause and he came on fast and shot his left in on the mouth with such force that Skelly staggered away. While Skelly guarded the tender face, Dixon's left once more visited the stomach, Skelly countering on the neck. Dixon closed persistently and as Skelly reached for the clench, the black right swung in hard on the neck. After they parted, Dixon swung the left on the stomach, following, a second later, with a right hander on the neck. Skelly preserved his skill better in the next rush, met it well, and the rush turned into a fierce rally, Skelly dealing blow for blow on neck and side, until Dixon came to close quarters and clenched. When Dixon let go, he did not step back, holding Skelly in the corner and sending the left in on the body and stopping the force of the counter with his right elbow against Skelly's neck, jarring his head. It was also Dixon's round, but Skelly stood his ground bravely, and countered hard in the rally just before the close of the round.

Round 5. Skelly was plainly in distress as he came up, while Dixon was as strong as ever. Skelly was glad to spar for a moment but Dixon was after the battered ribs hard with his left. Skelly stopped him and clenched. Another lead with the left faired no better and brought on another clench. Coming up after the break Dixon sent his left in lightly on the jaw and Skelly clenched. Another light left-hander on Skelly's jaw and another clench followed, and then Dixon got an opening. Rushing Skelly, he landed a straight right-hander on the nose and mouth drawing blood. Skelly was staggered and clenched, but they broke quickly and Dixon seemed about to bring matters to a close. He landed his left sharply on the jaw, and as Skelly swerved from the force of the blow the dusky fighter's right shot out with terrific force, catching him below the left eye, and cutting a gash from which the blood flowed freely. Skelly, dazed, and half-blinded, clenched his opponent and hung about his neck. Again, Dixon worked his right, after the break-away, and, landing again on the battered eye, widened the cut and increased the flow of blow perceptively. Skelly's condition was pitiable, and he took the terrible punishment so gamely that the warmest sympathies of the audience were aroused. The blood flowed freely down his face and neck and over his chest, and a thin stream trickled over his bruised lips. Dixon gave him no rest, but was at him again sharply, landing a right hand swing on the jaw, following it up with a left hander on the neck, which forced Skelly to the ropes, where he fought back gamely, though ineffectively. The gong sounded as they were in this position, and Skelly got a much-needed rest.

Round 6. Dixon came up with nose showing the slightest trace of blood, Skelly with signs of battering plainer on his face. Still the Brooklyn boy maintained his coolness, and when Dixon rushed, Skelly parried the attack with the prettiest art. Skelly took up the aggressive, and tried to crowd the black into a corner, but the latter was very slippery, got away, and came back in time to swing the left in on the stomach, getting his left glove over the eye in return. Dixon freshened up under the work, sent right and left in on the face, and, as Skelly tried to duck away, Dixon got in a terrific upper-cut with the left full on the mouth. Skelly kept away for a little and stopped the next rush. Dixon would not be denied, came again and swung the right on the neck. Skelly countering nicely on the jaw. It did not bother the black, and he shot the left over the guard, making a gash under the eye again. When Dixon closed once more, Skelly's left caught him neatly on the nose, but Dixon's left swung round at close-quarters for a vicious upper-cut over the heart. Skelly tried to ward off the next rush, but Dixon's right was too quick, landing on the mouth with such force that Skelly's head went back. The next rush, Dixon's left caught the same spot before the clench. Skelly met Dixon fiercely the next time, and the clench was as strong as a bear's hug. As soon as they parted, however, Dixon again covered the distance and swung his left in on the neck. Dixon rushed again, but Skelly kept him off and before Dixon could clench, Skelly's left swung hard on the ear and Dixon reeled away a few steps and showed signs of grogginess. He recovered while Skelly was being cheered on, and as the latter advanced Dixon twice met him with his trusty left on the nose. Skelly kept on coming and jabbed in the left, getting a left in return, and as they closed, Dixon got in a half-arm jab in the nose. When at arm's length again, Dixon felt his way and swung the left in on the neck hard, but Skelly got in the left with force on Dixon's neck by way of return. Skelly showed improvement in the round, but Dixon punched hard and often, brought blood from Skelly quite profusely and kept three or four cuts for marks his trusty fist.

Round 7. Skelly came up rather weak and unsteady and clenched at the first lead. As they came up again Dixon led with his left for the jaw and was stopped. He found an opening for his left on the battered ribs and sent it in with force. Twice again Dixon's left shot out for the jaw and each time Skelly stopped him. A drive from Dixon's right was also stopped and the men came together in a clench which did Skelly no good. As they faced each other again, Dixon's lead with his left for the ribs was cleverly stopped, but before Skelly could recover, he landed a stinging right-hander on the eye, and the Brooklyn boy nearly went down. Dixon's right found his jaw, and as Skelly reeled from the force of the blow he upper-cut him with his left bringing him to his knees. Skelly rose very groggy only to be knocked down again by a swing from Dixon's right, which caught him squarely on the jaw. As he rose he clinched and steadied himself. As they parted he landed a stiff upper-cut on Dixon's chin, and the champion came back hard with his right on the ear, repeating as the round ended and all but knocking Skelly out. The Brooklyn boy was quickly helped to his corner by his seconds, and needed all of their care and attention. So groggy had he become from the terrible punishment that he had received, that Police Captain Barrett opened the little gate, stepped into the outer ring, and looked him carefully over to decide whether it was not better to stop the contest, which was so plainly a hopeless one for Skelly. The lad was too game, however, to yield to anything but a knock-out blow, and insisted on continuing the struggle.

Round 8. Skelly was a sorry sight in his corner, and Captain Barrett inspected his preparation as if doubtful whether to let him come out again, but Skelly came up refreshed and game, only to be faced by the wily, slippery, smiling, shadowy, hard-hitter, dusky little whirl-wind. The smile seemed to taunt Skelly. He lost some of his coolness and made a vicious rush at the champion, but the latter ducked beautifully and came up under Skelly's arms. Skelly kept his arms in the way and avoided attack. So Dixon stepped back and at long range shot his left on the cheek and consented to a clench. Skelly's courage asserted itself in another rush, but Dixon's body vanished as before, and as the black came up he delivered an upper-cut on the body while Skelly reached for him. Dixon led with his left then and Skelly in turn showed himself an adept at ducking. Dixon pressed him, however, forced Skelly to the ropes with a right-hander on the neck and a left upper-cut on the ribs. Breaking away from Skelly, he again upper-cut with the left on the ribs and swung the right on the neck as Skelly held him, more for support than for harm. It was now Dixon's fight, for Skelly was gradually sinking. Dixon's left piled against the swollen side again and Skelly almost sank against the ropes. Skelly got away, however, and had skill enough left to keep close to Dixon and avoid his blows, Dixon forcing him to the ropes again without a blow. But Skelly's arms were becoming numb from the exhaustion which was gathering, and he was powerless to keep away much longer. As Skelly stood near his own corner, with his seconds eager to aid, but restrained by rules, Dixon's left caught him on the jaw and sent him down. Dixon did not leave him this time, and as Skelly struggled up and made an effort to straighten out, Dixon feinted with his left, but saw a better chance, and quickly bringing the right into play, delivered a quick, short, sharp, half-arm swing with the right on the point of the jaw and Skelly went down in a heap. Skelly fell in sections, legs, body, arms, collapsing in turn and the head falling back as if the neck was broken. It was a complete KNOCKOUT.

Joe Gans vs. Oscar "Battling" Nelson ("The Fight of the Century," September 3, 1906)

Lightweight Champion Joe Gans vs. Oscar "Battling" Nelson, September 3, 1906, Goldfield, Nevada (reported by *The Baltimore Sun*, "Joe Gans Wins," September 4, 1906)

Round 1. Gans led off with two light lefts for the face and they clinched. Nelson received a right on the body and Gans quickly shot a right and left to the face. He followed it with a right to the face and Nelson sent three left swings for the jaw.

Gans in a mix shot his right twice to the face and out-boxed his man at every point of the game. Gans jarred Nelson with two rights to the jaw and followed with a left to the face.

After breaking from a clinch Nelson walloped his right to the jaw and followed with a left to the same place. Gans then peppered Nelson's face with trip-hammer rights and lefts to the face and jaw and kept this up until the gong rang. Gans went to his corner with a big lead. Blood flowed from Nelson's ears as he went to his seat.

Round 2. Both were up quickly; Nelson was the aggressor, Gans uppercut twice with his right and then jarred Nelson with two terrific punches to the jaw. He followed it with a straight right to jaw. Nelson seemed impervious to punishment and came in all the time.

Gans measured his distance and time and again shot his short-arm rights to the Battler's face. They went to close quarters and Gans uppercut Nelson twice to the jaw. At close quarters he chopped Nelson on the jaw again with a stiff right.

Nelson fought him to a clinch and landed a terrific right to face. In a mixup Gans rocked Nelson's head with two wicked rights to the face and followed it with a short-arm jolt to the ear. As the gong rang Gans worked a hard left to jaw. Gans had a good lead and outboxed and outgeneraled his man throughout.

Round 3. Nelson tried to get close and Gans whipped his right to the ear. At close quarters Gans uppercut twice with his right to the chin, and as they fought at close range Gans swung right and left to the head.

Nelson got in a high right over the eyes and Gans hooked a wicked right to the abdomen and Nelson shot a straight left to the face. Several of Nelson's swings went wild. They went to a furious mix in the middle of the ring, in which Gans drew blood from Nelson's nose with a straight left.

Nelson got in a good right to the face as the bell rang. Nelson was being outpointed, but he never gave ground and seemed to thrive on Gans' punishment. It was Gans' round.

Round 4. Nelson missed a left for the body. Nelson charged Gans, but his blows invariably fell into a clinch. Gans worked his right and left to the face. Nelson went after Gans' body and bored in with his head, the black man backing steadily away, but at the same time peppering his man with right and left to the face.

Nelson caught Gans a terrific swing to the jaw and then drove Gans against the ropes, landing both hands to head. Nelson was then bleeding from the nose. He kept after Gans, but this time Gans shot a straight right to the face, which he duplicated a moment later. Gans then put a right to the abdomen and the bell rang.

Nelson brought the great crowd to its feet as he went to his corner with a faint smile on his face. Nelson had a shade the better of it.

Round 5. Gans shot a left to the nose as Nelson rushed in and they went to close quarters. Nelson swung a right to the ear, forcing Gans about the ring. Nelson drove a right to the kidneys, but the black man rocked Nelson's head with a series of lefts and rights.

Nelson swung back wildly and Gans smashed Nelson's sore nose with a terrific right drive. Gans brought blood afresh from Nelson's sore nose with stinging left punches. In a mix Gans uppercut with his right to the jaw.

Not for a moment did Nelson break ground. He swung heavily to Gans' face with his left, but was rebuked by a stiff right to face. The gong clanged and Nelson went to his seat spitting blood. Nelson was badly punished in this round. The betting was now 2 to 1 in favor of Gans.

Round 6. Nelson rushed Gans, but the Negro smashed him on the face three times with his right and easily avoided Nelson's attempts to land. Nelson bored in, forcing Gans to the ropes.

The crowd objected to Nelson's boring tactics, especially with his head against Gans' chest. After breaking from a clinch Gans planted his right to the jaw and followed it with several terrific right drives to the face, sending blood from Nelson's mouth in a stream.

Gans sent Nelson's head back, hammering his man almost at will. Nelson fought back desperately, but could not locate his antagonist. Nelson was in bad shape when he took his chair. His face was cut into ribbons. Gans had a big lead and here looked a sure winner.

Round 7. As usual, Nelson forced Gans about the ring. Gans contenting himself with watching for an opening. Gans pecked away at the face with left and right blows.

Nelson missed two right swings and Gans met him with a fusillade of right and left punches to the face that staggered the Dane. Gans received a slight punch on the body as they worked into a corner. Gans swung right twice to face and Nelson swung wildly.

Nelson neatly ducked two right swings again and Gans kept up a merciless hammering on his face. The bell rang and Nelson went to his corner with blood streaming from mouth and nose. In spite of all the punishment Nelson did not break ground at any time.

Round 8. Gans had no trouble in avoiding Nelson's onslaught and met Nelson with a right swing over the kidneys. He then swung right and left to Nelson's face and found no trouble in getting away from Nelson's swings.

Gans played with the Dane, sending a raking right to jaw, and then on a shift worked a left to face. Nelson swung desperately for Gans' face, but seldom found the black man. They closed in, mixing it roughly.

Gans swung his right and left with fearful force and Nelson slipped to his knees. He got up in a jiffy and Gans went at him fiercely and landed almost at will. The gong was a great relief to Nelson, as he appeared groggy when he fell into his seat.

Round 9. They stood shoulder to shoulder in the center of the ring. Gans walloped the Dane with right and left to the face. Nelson tried desperately to work in two hard swings to the body and for his pains received wallops of the short-arm variety to the jaw.

At close quarters Nelson swung his left twice to Gans' jaw and a moment later swung right to same place. They mixed it-furiously, Nelson getting four punches to the other mans' one.

Nelson swung right and left hard to Gans' jaw, but Gans more than evened matters by sending the Dane back with rapid-fire rights and lefts to the jaw. Gans bled slightly form the mouth after the bell rang.

Round 10. Gans met Nelson with a straight left to face. "Stay with him; don't let him get away!" was the injunction from the Battler's corner. They went in close and Gans smothered Nelson with rights and a succession of lefts to the face.

Nelson bored in and whipped his right and left to the Negro's jaw. Nelson then brought blood from Gans' mouth in a stream with a succession of lefts and rights to that member.

A terrific mix-up resulted at close quarters. Both men fought at fearful pace. Nelson having the better of heart breaking rally. The men bled from mouth and ears. Nelson had a shade on most of this round.

Round 11. They closed, with Gans fighting hard and with the request of Referee Siler that Nelson stop butting with his head. Nelson apparently realized that his only chance was to fight breast to breast, and, judging from preceding rounds, he was the better man at this game.

Nelson started a stream of blood from Gans' mouth by two wicked uppercuts. They broke from a clinch and Gans immediately whipped in two rights to Nelson's jaw.

Gans was cautioned to keep away, but Nelson kept at close quarters. Nelson finally swung a light left to the mouth as bell rang. If anything, Nelson had a slight lead in this round.

Round 12. Nelson rushed on, and they fought shoulder to shoulder for an advantage. Gans, getting Nelson away from him, whipped a stiff right to face. Nelson forced Gans against the ropes and slipped to the floor. Gans held out his hand and assisted him to his feet, and they immediately renewed hostilities.

Gans rested himself and seemed content to permit Nelson to do the leading. They fought breast to breast like two bulls, and Nelson butted Gans on the jaw with his head. They bent very low, head to head, in a monotonous fashion, each seeking to fight according to the style best adapted to his peculiar style.

The bell rang. Gans had a slight lead of a tame round. Siler said he thought Gans was resting up.

Round 13. Nelson rushed in, sending Gans back with two left and two right swings to the face. At close quarters Nelson uppercut with his left and right to the mouth, and a moment later swung his left to the mouth, bringing blood again from Gans.

Both men resorted to wrestling tactics. Gans being chief offender. They exchanged right swings to face in the middle of the ring and went to a clinch. They again fought breast to breast, and at these close quarters, Gans worked his right and left several times to the jaw.

They went to close quarters again, and Nelson worked in two left uppercuts to the jaw that made the champion wince. The latter, however, had a shade the better of the round.

Round 14. Both men fought at close quarters, but very few blows were landed. In a shoulder-to-shoulder contest, Nelson sent Gans against the ropes with a right to the head. Nelson smashed Gans' body with a right. At the close of the round Nelson Kicked at Gans, and the latter promptly retaliated in kind. The belligerents had to be separated by their handlers.

Round 15. This opened with a clinch, and Nelson butted and elbowed Gans constantly. He was warned to desist by Siler, and the seconds yelled foul in unison. No attention was paid to the claim, and the men roughed it at close quarters, Nelson forcing Gans to the ropes.

The men fought at such close quarters, or, rather, wrestled, that little execution could be accomplished. Nelson, in a break-away, was sent to floor with right straight to face.

Nelson looked a bit shaky, and he got to his feet and immediately went to close quarters to protect himself from further long-distance swats. The crowd cheered Gans lustily as he went to his corner.

Round 16. Nelson missed left and right swings. Gans dancing away. Gans tried to keep Nelson at a distance, but Nelson followed about the ring, trying to land some vicious right swings.

Gans whipped his right to jaw and Nelson wrestled Gans about ring, Gans holding on. Nelson scored with stiff right to the face and once more they leaned one against the other. Gans wrestled Nelson clear through the ropes and in falling Nelson pulled the negro after him.

They were pushed back into the ring and immediately resumed their wrestling tactics. In a mix Nelson drove his right twice to the face and a right to the mouth at close quarters, sending Gans to his corner with blood streaming from his mouth.

Round 17. Nelson landed his left on mouth and they went to a clinch. Siler cautioned Nelson against hitting low. Nelson swung his right to the kidneys and they wrestled about the ring, during which Gans worked in a left uppercut to the mouth and a moment later applied a similar punch.

Gans, after Nelson had twisted his arm, sent the Battler back with two hard short-arm right jolts to the face and a moment later shot his right to the wind.

Both men rested on their oars for some time and the round ended with honors a bit in Nelson's favor.

Round 18. Gans rushed in with straight right to face and Nelson swung two lefts to the negro's face. Siler warned Nelson about using his head. Gans blocked Nelson's lefts cleverly and the latter again bent down.

Nelson sent in two left swings to the face, but Gans retaliated with two stinging rights to the face. Wrestling continued and Gans drove Nelson against the ropes with two right smashes to the face.

Nelson nearly went to the floor, Gans backing away and at the end of the round Gans got in a good right punch to the Dane's face. The men did not hear the gong ring and were pulled to their seats by their seconds. It was a tame round.

Round 19. Siler warned Nelson once more for butting and laid his hand on Nelson's head twice as a reminder that the Dane should cut out this kind of work. Nelson continued to butt and Siler stepped in and pulled Nelson from his reclining position.

The men remained in a locked position, Gans resting and Bat wrestling. Finally Gans sent Nelson back with right and left jolts to the jaw, staggering Nelson.

Just before the gong rang Gans sent in a left and two stiff rights to the jaw and Nelson put in a right on the head. There was more wrestling than fighting in this round and derogatory comments were passed around the ringside.

Round 20. The men rushed together and Siler grabbed Nelson by the head, indicating that the Dane should cease boring in with his head. Gans straightened Nelson up with two lefts to jaw and Nelson landed several lefts to the body.

An exchange followed, both landing lefts to the chin. Nelson pushed Gans almost to the ropes and then missed a left for the face.

In a clinch Nelson landed a severe left uppercut to jaw and they mixed, Gans putting right and left to the jaw. He followed his advantage and sent a volley of right and left swings to the jaw as the round closed.

Round 21. Nelson came up as though nothing had happened. His left eye was badly swollen and his right discolored. They fought to a clinch, and Gans poked right and left to the face.

Gans then sent in a stiff uppercut over the eye. Nelson sent in two right body punches, and at close range Gans hooked his left to the mouth. Then they stood off and Gans trimmed Nelson beautifully with straight rights to face and a left to the jaw.

Nelson missed two vicious swings and Gans shot in a straight left to the face as the gong rang. Gans had a shade the better.

Round 22. Gans sent a straight left to the face, and Nelson retaliated with a left hook to abdomen. Nelson drove a straight right punch against Gans' ribs, and then wrestled Gans to the ropes.

Mixing it, Gans worked in two right uppercuts to the body. They again leaped shoulder to shoulder and did little more than wrestle, Nelson pushing Gans almost through the ropes. This thing continued.

Finally Gans rushed Nelson away, and smashed him twice with his right to the jaw. He followed this with two lefts to the Dane's head simultaneously with the gong. This was the only time during the round that the men had fought, and Gans had the advantage.

Round 23. They rushed to clinch, and Siler warned Nelson constantly about boring in with his head. Gans then crossed with his right to the jaw. Then Nelson drove his left twice to the eyes after the colored man had put two lefts to the face.

At close quarters Nelson put two good rights over the negro's heart, and then followed the usual course of wrestling. They broke away, and Nelson staggered Gas with a succession of hard left swings to the jaw and several hard rights to same place.

Gans did not respond, and Nelson sent the crowd into a frenzy by driving Gans to his corner with a right hook to the body that was a peach. The crowd rose to its feet at the end of the round and yelled "Nelson! Nelson!" It was the Dane's round.

Round 24. Nelson went right after Gans, having received instructions from his corner to go in. They roughed it, and at close quarters Nelson swung his left and right to the face.

Nelson smiled determinedly, and gave Gans no chance to rest. He swung his left hard to the jaw, but Gans retaliated with two wicked right uppercuts to the jaw. Nelson then missed two vicious left uppercuts and they worked in close.

Nelson drove Gans back to the ropes and put in two lefts to the body before Gans clinched. They both missed left swings and a rally followed, Gans landing repeatedly on Nelson's face. Nelson had a shade the better of it.

Round 25. Nelson rushed and swung his right to the ear. They fought and wrestled at close quarters, Nelson breaking away, sent his left to abdomen, and then drove his right to the jaw. He then sent two short-arm jolts to the face, and a moment later whipped a left to the face.

Nelson rocked the negro's head with right and left to the jaw. He followed this with two rights and a left to the jaw. Gans awoke from his apparent somnolence, and more than evened up matters by hammering viciously Nelson's face with right and left punches.

They went close, and just before the bell rang Gans shot his left to the face. Gans was a bit worsted earlier in the round, but had the better of the closing rally.

Round 26. Nelson forced Gans to the ropes, but could not penetrate Gans' marvelous defense while in dangerous positions. They wrestled again about the ring, Gans resting up.

Nelson landed a hard right swing on the head, but two left swings for the same place went glimmering. Then the fighters sparred and Gans landed a left swing over the mouth and followed it with three straight lefts to the face.

Then followed the inevitable clinch emerging from which Nelson uppercut Gans on the jaw with the left. Both men appeared tired at this stage of the contest. It seemed hard to predict the winner at this time.

Round 27. Gans sparred, while Nelson wasted his vitality with useless swings. Nelson pushed Gans against the ropes, and the latter, working himself free, sent his left to Nelson's mouth.

Nelson missed a hard left swing and in a mix Joe put in two light rights to the face. Nelson retaliated with two straight lefts to face, the last one sending Gans head back.

Gans then cut loose. He drove his left to the abdomen with terrific force and then drove right and left to jaw. Nelson, maddened, fought back viciously and gave the negro more than he had received as the round terminated. It was an even round, with both men tired.

Round 28. Gans jabbed Nelson on the mouth with his left and Nelson butted the colored man with his head. Nelson then put left and right to the jaw and shortly afterward swung his left to the body and right and left to the jaw.

Then they closed in and Nelson drove Joe to the ropes with left hook to the face. The men wrestled to the center of the ring and Gans sent two right swings to the face.

Nelson tried to wrestle Gans to the ropes and Gans, like a rejuvenated man, drove Nelson back with several fearful clouts to the jaw, the first of which sent Nelson to the center of the ring, halfway across it. Gans kept at his man when he was groggy and the bell clanged and was welcomed as he went to his corner.

Round 29. Nelson rushed to close quarters, apparently as strong as ever. He followed Gans about the ring, but failed to land. Nelson's recuperative powers seemed almost superhuman.

The men wrestled and roughed it in the middle of the ring and exchanged right swings to jaw. Gans then cut loose again and mercilessly peppered Nelson's face and jaw with right and left jolts.

Nelson merely shook his head and wrestled the black man to the ropes. Gans repeated, permitting Nelson to waste his energy trying to land. Gans was against the ropes as the bell sounded. It was Gans' round.

Round 30. They fell against each other and Siler again warned Nelson to cease fighting with his head. They then fought at close quarters, Nelson doing all the work, but not landing.

Gans then put in two right uppercuts and then stalled and rested, apparently with a view of saving his strength. It is in this manner that Gans displayed his great generalship. Gans then put in a right uppercut to Nelson's mouth, and the Dane missed several vicious left and right swings for the jaw.

As the bell rang Nelson deliberately hit Gans, and the crowd went to its feet in a storm of protest. Someone started three cheers for the negro, which drew forth a rousing response.

Round 31. Gans cleverly blocked Nelson's attempts to land wild swings and again tested, permitting the younger man to do all the work.

Again Siler told Nelson to quit butting, and they went to close quarters wrestling and stalling. The men wrestled for fully a minute without a blow being struck.

Gans sent Nelson's head back with a straight left to the face. The men were locked in a clinch as the bell rang. The fight apparently has settled down to a question of the survival of the fittest.

Round 32. Gans danced away from the Dane's leads and as usual closed in on Nelson's initiative. Siler again and again spoke to Nelson about using his head on the negro's chin. Again came the almost interminable clinching and wrestling.

Finally Nelson swung a hard right to the jaw and quickly followed it with a left swing to the same place. Nelson's left eye was badly swollen and almost closed. Gans sent Nelson back with two straight lefts and three rights to Nelson's sore eye.

Gans caught Nelson a terrific clip on the jaw with a right hook and then sent in a dazing left to the face. Again the gong brought relief to Nelson and saved him from almost sure defeat.

Round 33. They closed in, Nelson butting with his head. Gans peppered Nelson's face to a jelly with terrific right swings. Nelson's left eye was entirely closed.

Nelson punched Gans to the ropes and they fought at close range, Gans resting and saving his strength. Nelson bled profusely as the men worked to the center of the ring. It was a sight to behold.

Gans sent Nelson back with a left to the jaw. Both were very weak as the gong sounded, Nelson for the first time showing great weariness. It was Gans' round. It was claimed that Gans had turned his foot in this round, which may seriously incapitate [sic] him for the remainder of the contest.

Round 34. The men wrestled and stalled in the middle of the ring, both seeming content to rest up. This thing continued, neither landing a blow.

It was wrestle, stall, wrestle and stall again. Nelson forced Gans to the ropes and received right and left swing on the head.

Nelson worked in two short-arm lefts to the abdomen and both men wrestled, Gans nearly putting Nelson through the ropes. Nelson appeared very tired. Joe was the fresher of the two as the round closed the wrestling match.

Round 35. The sun was now going down. It was the same old story — wrestle, stall and rest without a blow being struck.

Gans finally ripped in a straight left to the jaw and again they rested each other's head against one another's shoulders. Gans put in a right uppercut that lacked force and they went quickly to a clinch.

Both men tottered about the ring, not landing a blow. Nelson at close quarters worked two left short-arm blows to face and the bell closed a very slow and tiresome round.

Round 36. Both sparred and then Gans started something with a straight right to the face. Again the wrestling was on.

Nelson missed a forceful uppercut intended for the jaw, and for a brief moment it looked as if the men were going to fight, but such was not the case. Gans cleverly ducked a right swing and then ran into a right hook over the heart.

Nelson hooked a left to the abdomen, and at close quarters got his right lightly to the jaw. Nelson pushed Gans against the ropes, and Gans just did step out of the way of a right uppercut.

Round 37. Nelson was again told to stop fighting with his head. Gans vigorously objecting to Siler against this style of scrapping.

The men again went to the wrestling stunts and Nelson swung his left for the jaw that missed its mark by 3 feet. They leaned up against each other and few attempts to strike a blow were made.

Then Gans whipped a powerful left to the wind and they clinched. Both men were very careful. Gans woke up the crowd by catching Nelson within long distance and putting in several straight lefts to the face. Then came the rest.

Round 38. Nelson rushed in and Gans backed up quickly, trying to keep the Dane at a distance and force him to spar at long range.

Gans complained to Siler about Nelson resting his head on Gans' chin and shoulders. Nelson swung a left to the jaw, and after a clinch Gans put in two rights to the Dane's face. Both men were leg weary and stalled and clinched as much as they could.

It was next to impossible to get the Dane to fight at long range. Gans likewise seemed perfectly content to ease up and rest.

Round 39. Gans jabbed his left twice to the face before Nelson could get to close quarters. Then followed stalling and wrestling, which was broken up by Gans punching Nelson viciously over the heart with right.

Gans followed this with two straight rights to the face, and again it looked as if the deadlock would be broken. It was only a flash in the pan, however, and the men resumed the tiresome stalling, Nelson being the chief offender.

Nelson, by way of variety, sent in a hard left to the jaw and Gans came back with two lefts to the jaw. Nelson's left eye was here closed entirely.

Round 40. They started in at a lively pace, Gans landing his left to the ear. Then they stopped.

In a clinch Gans drove his left to the jaw. Nelson came back with a left uppercut to chin. The men did very little fighting.

Gans got Nelson at arm's length and took advantage of this concession by sending his left twice to the Dane's face. Gans complained again about Nelson's head, and sent Nelson's head back with left uppercut to the jaw.

Round 41. They came up slowly and clinched. Gans asked Billy Nolan facetiously, "What time is it?" Then they resumed the clinching contest. Gans shot a straight right to mouth and Nelson rebuked him with two lefts to the stomach. Nelson whipped his left to face and the men ceased fighting entirely.

Suddenly Nelson landed a hard left hook to the jaw and Gans fought him away, landing two lefts to the face and a right on the body. Both men wrestled wearily about the ring, and it was hard to tell which was the more tired of the two as the men went to their corners.

Round 42. Gans started the round with a straight left to the face and they clinched. As the men broke from a clinch Nelson deliberately struck Gans low and the colored man slowly sank to the floor. The blow was clearly observed by everyone in the arena and there was not a murmur of dissent from the spectators as the long-drawn-out battle was terminated.

Joe Jennette vs. Sam McVey ("Le Grand Match," April 17, 1909)

Joe Jennette vs. Sam McVey, M. Matroi, referee, April 17, 1909, Paris, France (reported from "Le Grand Match," *L'Auto*, a French sporting newspaper, April 18, 1909). French text provided by Theresa Runstedtler of the University of Buffalo; translated from French to English by Mark Scott; "Jeannette" is spelled as in the original.

"Before the Big Match." The room, calm at first, heats up, and the arrival of the boxers is greeted by hearty applause.

Sam McVey is seconded by Scalon J. Styles, Piet, Grognet, and Guiller; Sam is cheered; Joe Jeannete enters, followed by W. Lewis and D. MacKetricke.

M Matroi, referee of the big match, gives the final instructions to the fighters; then each man returns to his corner, consults his seconds, and soon the bell sounds announcing the start of the big match.

Round 1. It is Jeannette who lands first with a light jab to the face. After a clinch (corps a corps) the two champions connect to the jaw; then Sam lands a short left hook to the neck. He repeats the same attack, but Jeannette dodges and counters with a jab. Jeannette pounces on his rival, and attacks with a jab, thrown with extraordinary speed, that Sam blocked just in time. Jeannette dances throughout the end of the first round, and lands jab, while bouncing, to the face. Slight advantage to the "yellow negro" (reference to Jeannette) who is, moreover, strongly applauded.

Round 2. It is again Jeannette who attacks, but Sam dodged; Jeannette attacks again, but slips accidentally, he falls and rises immediately. Extremely fast on his legs, he lands a good jab, then a stiff blow to the face. The fight becomes fiercer. Sam lands a powerful swing; Joe with a new attack slips, turns his back to Sam, and lands a sharp blow, while turning, on Sam's "popular face." (This is a colloquialism that could mean *mug* or some other slang for face.) Twice more, Sam lands two pretty doubles to the face; but his blows perhaps don't carry the desired force, because Jeannette takes them casually; towards the end Jeannette comes up short with a jab to the stomach. This time (round) the advantage also goes to Jeannette.

Round 3. Jeannette attacks again with a jab, parries easily. After a clinch, he charges again and lands a left to the body and right to the stomach. Sam parries neatly. Now it's Sam who throws a powerful hook to the jaw which Jeannette dodges away from, and trying another jab. Jeannette loses his balance and falls to the ropes, where Sam pursues without landing serious punches. Sam attacks hard with a swing, marvelously dodged by Jeannette. Sam continues with a hook to the stomach; Jeannette is doubled over. It is definitely the hardest blow since the fight began. Advantage Sam.

Round 4. Twice in succession Jeannette lands weakly with jabs; suddenly Sam after dodging a hook, very quickly lands a very powerful uppercut; he then throws several insignificant jabs and lands hard on the jaw without even having been attacked; (five words illegible,) that the blows carried, which allowed Sam to throw him off balance and land with left hooks, thrown with such speed that Joe could not slip them. Now Jeannette's jabs no longer landed, because Sam, who caught on to his rival's tactics, slipped them easily. Jeannette goes for the stomach. The edge still goes to Sam McVea.

Round 5. Sam, attacking Jeannette, stops and lands to the neck; Jeannette rushes Sam but lands from too far away, and his blows thus lack the strength to shake this veritable wall that is Sam McVea. It seems anyhow that Sam, very at ease, is definitely dominating. Twice in a row he lands to stomach and heart, Sam lands a hook to the jaw and his cross sends Jeannette to the floor. The "yellow one" gets up, but very unstable. He tries for a clinch. Maitroi has a hard time separating the two men. At the end of the round, the brave Jeannette attacks again, but has misjudged the distance and stumbles to the ropes while Sam hits him again. The clear advantage to Sam.

Round 6. Sam attacks vigorously, he throws a hook to the body that is half blocked by Jeannette, suddenly the latter returns to the offensive but Sam adroitly blocks a jab, counters with a blow to the heart, this counter carried out with such speed that the room shakes with applause. Jeannette lands several times with jabs to the face, but Sam smiles, he takes it without pain, then retaking the offensive, he rushes his rival, who very luckily evades the attack. Sam McVea is more and more dominant, while Jeannette tries to clinch until the end of the round.

Round 7. Sam doesn't actually attack, he is looking for the big punch to get rid of his rival, then holding Jeannette's arm he hits him in the face, which earns him a warning from Maitrot. From the left he punches to the face with stiff blows. He easily dodges all the attacks of Jeannette and counters to the body. Twice Sam lands to the jaw with uppercuts. If these blows had landed more accurately, it is without a doubt that Jeannette would have been knocked out, but the "yellow one" luckily succeeded in blunting the force of the blows.

Round 8. Jeannette misses a well dodged jab, then covers up. Jeannette attacks while Sam avoids him, contenting himself with countering now and then with hooks that thud into Jeannette's body. The battle is truly under way, the two men have us expecting a demonstration of their prowess. Joe Jeannette frequently changes his guard but he takes an uppercut to the jaw; in a clinch, after having slipped, Jeannette breaks and lands a good cross right in the face of his rival.

Round 9. After a Jeannette jab, a clinch ensues, during which Joe punches, but on the gloves. Jeannette retakes the offensive and lands a jab to the then another to the stomach. In a clinch, he lands three successive uppercuts to the jaw. Sam seems shaken, he is bleeding heavily from the nose, he takes another left jab, followed by a short blow to the stomach. Jeannette lands to the heart, and then jumps in to land a jab to the face. Sam then lands to the jaw but without much effect. During this round the advantage went to Jeannette. Just like on February 20, Sam's left eye is half closed. Everyone applauds Jeannette.

Round 10. Sam starts by landing a jab to the face. He doesn't seem to want to show courtesy this time. Jeannette lands a left jab and a right hook, which hits Sam in the eye, which is tightly shut. Jeannette dominates, he lands to the face, then to the body, but always leaping in with straight blows. Sam is shaken, reduced to just defending himself and trying to clinch. When he tries to attack he is hit to the stomach, then he receives a hook to the left ear, followed by an uppercut to the jaw. The fight is becoming frightful, Jeannette lands again to the face. Sam counters with a combination to the jaw, then retakes control. He lands two crosses to the jaw, but they don't prevent Joe from having the advantage (for the round.)

Round 11. Sam dodges twice and then takes one right on the nose. The action has to be stopped to tighten Jeannette's glove. Feinting a left to the face, Sam lands a blow to the stomach and then to the face with all his power. Jeannette lands a jab. Sam counters with a hook to the body and Jeannette lands three times to the jaw. This round, less ferocious than the preceding one, was about even between the two men.

Round 12. Sam has got his strength back and it is he who attacks with a cross to the jaw, then knocks Jeannette back with a good uppercut. Sam lands again to the heart, then he stops Joe by the throat; they certainly put down too much resin because the two fighters slip and Sam falls several times during the course of the round. Sam lands hard with a cross to the jaw and he goes to repeat, Jeannette slips and lands to Sam's face. Sam's left eye is completely closed.

Round 13. At the start, Sam lands a ferocious hook to the stomach, Jeannette takes it and counters to the jaw. Sam responds to the jaw, which Jeannette partially avoids. Twice more Sam lands to the jaw, then lands a serious uppercut. Jeannette is tested again, but still manages to attack with vigor but without the desired effect. Sam lands twice more very hard to the stomach. Once again the advantage to Sam is becoming indisputable.

Round 14. Barely out of the corner, Sam bounds at Jeannette and lands a left uppercut to the jaw. Sam then punches in a clinch, he wants to shake hands, Joe refuses; the battle only gets tougher, three times Sam lands to the stomach and jaw; Jeannette slips a left jab from Sam, but the latter punches in a clinch with a right to the jaw, but it seems to land lightly.

Round 15. After a flurry of feints and slips, Jeannette lands with a left. He clinches. Sam then lands a jab. Jeannette now launches an attack which is easily stopped. Sam, who is dominating again, lands twice to the face with short powerful punches; Jeannette, totally off balance, drifts more and more. Sam's advantage is clear.

A new discussion about the gloves. Sam's seconds protest, resulting in a new checking of the gloves, this time for Sam's benefit.

Round 16. The adversaries shake hands. Sam dodges an attack from Jeannette, then tries to land left handed punches to the jaw. He studies Jeannette, who attacks with jabs that are slipped. Sam lands a left punch to the jaw, then punches to the body. This round is monotonous, the opponents seeming to want to save strength for later.

Round 17. Jeannette attacks, but Sam avoids (several words illegible) After a clinch, Sam lands to the face (several words illegible) ... lands a straight left without being able to land the following right. Jeannette, having barely slipped the blow, Jeannette lands a beauty of a right while charging Sam to the ropes. Jeannette has again made an excellent impression and receives a hardy ovation.

Round 18. This round starts with a long clinch. Then Sam throws a left, then slips accidentally. Jeannette brilliantly evades Sam's attack, McVea lands to the heart, but then Jeannette counters very hard to the jaw. Then he lands a jab while evading Sam's attack. Sam doubles with a left to the jaw and chest, but Jeannette lands a marvelous jab to Sam's mouth. The popular Sam bleeds profusely from the mouth. Jeannette seems very fresh and has pulled ahead during the course of the round.

Round 19. Twice Jeannette charges Sam, who half avoids him, without being able to dodge a left jab. The clinches become more frequent. Suddenly Sam, despite seeming so unimpressive, throws such a ferocious hook that it knocks Jeannette to the ground. While the seconds shout loudly, the entire room cheers Sam. Sam, sure of victory, attacks Jeannette and knocks him down twice more. Now it's pandemonium. Jeannette's seconds throw water on him while he's down, which makes the great Sam furious. Twice more Jeannette has risen. Truly the man is admirable, and it's a big relief to see him saved by the bell.

Round 20. Jeannette has regained his strength and attacks. Sam stops, then slips, looking to land the final blow. Suddenly he lands a jab to the jaw. Jeannette tries to clinch and rest, but Maitroi steps in. Jeannette has nothing left, he punches to the heart without power. Sam loses a good chance to put Joe away. He lands an uppercut.

Round 21. Jeannette takes the offensive. Lands twice to the heart, Sam rears back and bangs to the jaw. Jeannette tries his double jabs of left and right. He hits Sam to the stomach and then throws a left to the jaw. In the clinches, Joe throws two uppercuts that land to the jaw. Sam seems tired, however he punches with a left to the jaw. Joe falls, stays 7 seconds, and gets up a few seconds before the end.

Round 22. Jeannette is again greatly refreshed. After a thorough attack, a clinch ensues, during which Jeannette lands to the jaw, but Sam retakes the advantage and lands twice to the face. Jeannette lands a light uppercut thrown from too far away. Jeannette is really coming back, he lands to the face and then to the neck with a good jab. Sam seems to want to catch his breath.

Round 23. After some feints, Sam punches to the body, then there is dodging, Suddenly Jeannette lands to the face and Sam counters with a left then takes an uppercut after a clinch. Sam lands a hard straight left to the stomach, he seems to hold back. Jeannette lands a good jab that lands with force to the stomach.

Round 24. Some feints, then Sam lands to the face. Jeannette then lands with a hard uppercut in clinch. Poor Sam is bleeding profusely from his hurt eye. A left by Sam, which Jeannette counters with a weak uppercut. Sam charges again, but Jeannette evades. Good end of the round. During the rest they blow oxygen on the completely closed eye of poor Sam.

Round 25. Sam jumps in with a jab to the face. Jeannette totters but then quickly recovers. Then the two men go to clinch but Maitroi briskly separates the two fighters. Sam attacks, and lands to the jaw. Jeannette is slightly shaken but he meets Sam in a corner and hits him three times with lefts and right to the jaw. Sam takes it and attacks, Joe then hits several times to the heart.

Round 26. It is Jeannette who starts out by throwing a jab and a right to the ear. Sam counters and lands with his terrible left to the jaw and stomach. Jeannette however, dances cleverly. He stopped an uppercut that seemed dangerous. Jeannette now thoroughly attacks the great Sam, who is completely surprised by the turnabout. Several clinches, then Sam lands such a good right that it knocks Jeannette down again. The bell saves him from this dangerous situation. What a man!

Round 27. At the start Jeannette is back in it. His endurance is marvelous. Sam lands a terrific left cross that lands to Joe's jaw; then the clinches become numerous. Joe dodges an uppercut, but Sam lands a straight right to the chin. This round is a round of rest.

Round 28. Jeannette, still spirited, no longer has the same nerve, he charges anyway, but hesitantly. And he is hit cleanly in the clinch by Sam, who pushes his advantage with a terrific jab to the jaw. Jeannette goes down again and stays down nine seconds. A return of courage brings him to his feet. Sam, sensing that Jeannette is in his cross-hairs, increases the speed and power of his attack, but Sam can't finish off the extraordinary Jeannette.

Round 29. Jeannette attacks, then a clinch occurs where nothing happens, Sam comes in, but Jeannette stops him with a blow to the stomach. Jeannette rushes after a clinch. Sam hits him with a left and a right to the jaw; then Sam gets in a left hook, that lands lightly on Jeannette.

Round 30. Here Jeannette is back. Sam is forced to be careful. Jeannette lands to the chest, on the second attack Sam is able to evade. Sam attacks and comes up a little short with an uppercut. He retakes the offensive and avoids two dangerous swings, then slips into the ropes while trying to get at his formidable adversary.

This round saw a Jeannette again relatively refreshed and a Sam McVea who is very careful, having decided to take a short rest.

Round 31. Jeannette is a little disoriented by a blow to the jaw. He doesn't attack with the same abandon as in the prior round. In a clinch he hits Sam with an uppercut. Sam counters with a jab to the face, followed by a left cross to the jaw. Prior to the end of the round Sam takes an uppercut and a jab to the jaw.

Round 32. After a calm start Sam lands with a cross to the jaw. He repeats a few seconds later without downing Jeannette. Jumping in, Sam lands to the eye. Poor Joe looks ready to go at any moment, however Jeannette has not yet said his final word; before the end of the round he lands a big swing and succeeds in disorienting Sam, who retreats to the ropes.

The attacks become more numerous and less accurate.

Round 33. Sam attacks and lands a jab to the face, then a left cross that lands to the stomach. Joe dodges Sam's charge; Joe withstands a furious attack, Joe lands right and left to the jaw. Sam slips, then regains his balance, but then in a corner slips again.

Round 34. Jeannette is hit to the jaw coming in, Sam lands again, Jeannette charges furiously (Four lines illegible)

Round 35. Jeannette rushes Sam; in a clinch he lands an uppercut to the jaw; then he feints with a left and lands a straight right to Sam's injured eye. The latter lands a jab leaping in, then continues the offensive. Jeannette wobbles, then steadies himself and chases Sam to the ropes. He lands a light left cross to the right eye.

Round 36. Sam seeks the final blow without finding it. The beginning of the round is nothing but feinting and dodging. Sam is the first to land, it is to the chin. Sam continues to attack but Jeannette without being able to again land seriously. All indications are that the fight will continue for quite a while.

Round 37. Jeannette attacks, but slowly; both are tired; Sam lands two crosses, one to the jaw and one to the heart; Joe lands a left cross to the right eye; The fight is dull; Sam starts to do a little leg work; Joe lands a right to the stomach. At the bell, Sam returns to his corner, skipping a light and elegant polka step.

Round 38. Jeannette charges Sam into the ropes, then the calm returns. Twice Jeannette misses with jabs to the jaw; the third time he lands to the stomach, Sam smiling and pointing to where the punch landed as if to say it was an odd attack. Joe starts up again; Sam fends him off easily and it is Sam who finishes the round with a jab to the face without much on it. Whether they like it or not, the two both show signs of being tired; as can only be expected.

Round 39. Jeannette attacks, he lands a left to the jaw. Sam responds in kind. The punches arrive weakly. Joe throws an uppercut; Sam isn't moved and jumps in with a punch to the jaw. Suddenly Sam takes a formidable right cross to the jaw and slightly wobbles.

Round 40. Sam, trying to land from too far out, is hit by an uppercut. Jeannette sets himself to go again, looking right into Sam's face. But it is Jeannette who gets hit in the jaw, but Sam did not punch hard and Joe is not in trouble. It could go on quite a while like this. The spectators don't think of complaining.

Round 41. Jeannette rushes towards Sam, who stops him with a jab to the face. But Joe attacks , crowds Sam into the ropes, and hits him with a series of uppercuts that hurt Sam, but the latter responds and punches to the jaw, Joe dances away and lands two lefts to the jaw. Then Sam is knocked back into the ropes with a right and staggers, Joe is marvelous, he is given the biggest ovation possible.

Round 42. The great effort that Joe just put out continues with a combination attack to the face and heart. Sam grimaces, he shows signs of certain defeat, so much that the entire room is on its feet cheering Sam on with all their might. Obviously poor Sam is badly shaken. The bell saves him just in time. They give him oxygen to revive him.

Round 43. Joe, attacking, falls and immediately gets up. He seems fresh and hits Sam with two uppercuts to the jaw and a jab to the heart. Sam answers with a punch to the jaw, but Joe counters over it and lands twice to the eye. Sam counters to the heart, but takes another one on his wounded eye. He returns to his corner, visibly tired. His manager, to revive him, gives him inhalations of oxygen.

Round 44. The two men are still going. Of course they are fighting with less vigor and especially less accuracy, but unbelievably the two men have been fighting for almost two hours.

Sam seems to have regained his strength. He barely misses a hard hook to the jaw. Jeannette's slip of the punch is applauded. Joe charges Sam, but he also successfully dodges.

Round 45. Sam seems weak again. He carries his guard low and punches Joe to the body, then with a left to the jaw. Punching is sparse and the blows are light. Only in the clinches, the fighters hit each other in the sides. Joe throws a light double jab to the face and ends the round with a jab to the pit of the stomach. Jeannette seems more with it than Sam.

Round 46. With a series of combinations Jeannette bravely charges Sam. The "yellow one" wants to profit from Sam's weakness and works him over hard. Sam, clearly the weaker of the two at this point, punches without power. He shakes his left arm, as if to show that he can no longer punch with it. Jeannette at the end of the round, follows up hitting Sam twice in the face, without the latter being able to counter.

Round 47. Jeannette takes a left jab to the jaw, however he attacks. Sam attacks lightly, however he lands a right cross to the jaw. Sam is completely out of strength and staggers desperately. Joe pursues the attack and in a clinch hits Sam with several uppercuts. Sam seems completely finished.

Round 48. Jeannette, who wants to end it, again finds the strength to hurt Sam. Unfortunately for him, he no longer has sufficient power to punch hard enough, so Sam once again gets out of trouble. Jeannette, happier in the clinches, throws several uppercuts that Sam can no longer block. In summary very little punching is done in this slow round.

Round 49. Sam gives up. At the bell for the 49th round, Sam shakes Joe's hand and says he can't go on. Sam is unrecognizable. His left eye is completely shut, his face pounded in, he no longer has a human face. They give Joe Jeannette an indescribable ovation. His fans carry him in triumph, he has well earned his accolades, because through the course of this eternally unforgettable night he has been a **paragon of courage**.

Jack Johnson vs. James J. Jeffries (The "Great White Hope" Fight, July 4, 1910)

Jack Johnson vs. James J. Jeffries, Tex Rickard, referee, July 4, 1910, Reno, Nevada (reported by *The San Francisco Chronicle*, "Ben Benjamin Tells Ringside Story of Great Battle, Round by Round," July 5, 1910)

BEN BENJAMIN: The fight was something of a disappointment to many of the spectators. It was not the fast spectacular fight so many expected. There was a sameness about every round that robbed the contest of considerable interest. It was shown clearly in the contest that Jeffries was wild in his delivery and could not reach his clever opponent. He would rush time and time again, but Johnson blocked him with ease and gradually beat down the white man with a succession of upper-cuts. Jeffries was also the victim of poor advice. He failed to make the hurricane battle which might have given him a chance to get in a heavy blow at the start. Jeffries was almost in a state of collapse at the expiration of ten rounds. As outlined, in the "Chronicle" no man can come back after a long absence from the ring. Age also counted as the fight progressed and the defeat of Jeffries was generally prognosticated after the eighth round. Johnson was extremely confident all the way and scored an easy victory on his superior cleverness. Jeffries was a keen disappointment to his admirers and never showed a flash of his old time ability at any stage of the fight. The outcome of the championship fight was strictly in line with my forecast in Monday's "Chronicle."

Round 1. Both advanced slowly to the center of the ring. Jeffries makes a bluff with left for a lead. Both feint. Johnson leads with left, lands on Jeffries' mouth. They clinch. Jeffries feints with the left. Both land lefts. Again they clinch. Jeffries swings with left, but don't [*sic*] quite land. Clinch. Johnson lands, but with no effect. Jeffries comes back toward his corner smilingly and winks his eye. The first round is very uneventful and furnishes no intelligent line on the fight.

Round 2. Johnson comes up looking very serious. He blocks Jeffries' left and both laugh. Johnson slipped a left uppercut. Johnson stops a left swing. Both try short-arm jolts without effect. Jeffries reaches Johnson's bread basket. Fighting very tame up to the present. Both men exhibit extreme cautiousness and Jeff is not making the whirlwind fight so generally forecasted.

Round 3. Jeffries crouches low and feints, but the colored man gets away and lands a left on Jeffries' stomach. They clinch in the middle of the ring. The men fight at close range, and indulge in a little wrestling. Johnson swings a left on Jeffries' neck. It is not very effective. Jeffries rushes and lands a left on Johnson's bread basket. Johnson tries an uppercut with the right, but Jeffries dodges it. More clinching. Both men hanging on a good deal. Jeffries follows up Johnson, but the colored man blocks him. The white man finds it hard to break through the clever defense of Johnson.

Round 4. Johnson rushes Jeffries to a clinch. Jeffries begins to run Johnson more frequently. They both land. Jeffries finds it difficult to reach his opponent, owing to Johnson's clever blocking. Johnson's lips are bleeding. Jeffries rushes at him like a cyclone, but cannot land with any great effect. Johnson lands a left as Jeffries rushes in. They fight at close range. Jeffries jolts Johnson three or four times in the stomach, but the blows lack force. Johnson's mouth is now bleeding. Johnson leads with left, but misses. Fight uneventful up to this period.

Round 5. Johnson is fighting with his open hands. Jeffries rushes in close and several clinches follow. Johnson rushes Jeffries in an amateurish way and they clinch. Some fighting at close range. Johnson lands a left on Jeffries' mouth and it bleeds a little. More clinching. Jeffries lands on Johnson's mouth, but does not jar him. Very little fighting done in this round and it is a repetition of the preceding four rounds to a great extent.

Round 6. More sparring marks the opening of this round. Jeffries continues to chew gum. Johnson swings a left on Jeffries' sore mouth, probably the most effective blow he has yet delivered. Again Johnson lands his left on Jeffries' face and they clinch. Jeffries' cheek is cut. He keeps trying to get in, but is very awkward. More clinching . Jeffries rushes like a cyclone, but his blows lack in accuracy. Johnson is displaying speed and lands several blows. In a hot rally in which both lead Johnson came back with a double lead and landed the second one on Jeffries' eye. Jeffries is fighting aggressively, but is all at sea, and he goes to his corner with his right eye closed. The end of this round was the most effective of the fight and Johnson marking up Jeffries' face. His seconds work on his eye during the round intermission. Johnson has by a long way the best of the round and it looks as if Jeffries' eye is going to worry him.

Round 7. Jeffries crouches lower than at any time previously, but is finding it difficult to land on the colored man. Johnson is now showing more aggressiveness than he did in the opening rounds. Jeffries rushes to a clinch and receives a jolt in the face. Johnson is fighting cleverly and stops both Jeffries' leads. Johnson lands with left on Jeffries' nose. Jeffries is still rushing, but is not displaying the same judgment that he did in the opening. They clinch in the middle of the ring. Johnson leads with left, but misses Jeffries' head. Johnson took a decided lead in this round and Jeffries is showing signs of weariness.

Round 8. Jeffries leads with the left, which Johnson blocks, and Johnson leads a glancing blow on his opponent's face. Johnson lands with his left on Jeffries' face and they clinch. Jeffries tears in, but is apparently not landing with any effect at all. His blows are not well directed. Both welcome clinches. Jeffries still aggressive, but having great difficulty in landing. Jeffries rushes in, but the colored man blocks him. The last part of the round was very slow, consisting principally of clinching. Even money is now being bet at the ringside on Johnson: he is apparently making a winning fight.

Round 9. Johnson lands with left on Jeffries' jaw. They clinch and Jeffries tries a right uppercut, but is cleverly blocked. Both land. Johnson comes back with a second left, but apparently did not hurt Jeffries. Johnson lands his left on midribs of Jeffries. Jeffries is crouching lower than ever. Both land in region of the stomach. Johnson reaches Jeffries' face and he rushes in. There was little fighting in this round. Both men show extreme caution and every round is a good deal like that which went before.

Round 10. Johnson gives Jeffries a slight pat in the face, and follows it with a good jab. Jeffries rushes with his head down, but fails to land. Again he rushes in and swings his right lightly on Johnson's ribs. Jeffries jabs one in on Johnson's stomach. Johnson jolts Jeffries in the face and draws more blood. The colored man is making a careful battle and contents himself by jabbing Jeffries at intervals.

Round 11. The men continue to make the same kind of a fight. Jeffries keeps boring in, but finds great difficulty landing. Johnson jolts Jeffries on the chin. Jeffries receives terrific punishment with right and left. Jeffries rushes Johnson, but lands in rapid succession the most effective blows of the fight. Jeffries is now fighting like a cyclone, but cannot land. They clinch. Johnson upper-cuts Jeffries with two lefts in rapid succession, and again he follows it with another. Jeffries is getting a good bombarding and Johnson swings with left and Jeffries again rushes like a cyclone, but is very tired at the finish. The men were fighting furiously at the sound of the gong, with Johnson doing nearly all the landing.

Round 12. Johnson swings left. Jeffries swings and misses. Johnson leads and lands his left on Jeffries' face and repeats; swings again on Jeffries. Johnson blocks in clever style and jolts Jeffries' jaw with uppercut. Jeffries leads again, but is blocked. Rapid exchange of short arm jolts, but no apparent damage. Johnson swings with left.

Round 13. This round opens up with a clinch. Jeffries still continues to chew gum. Johnson beats Jeffries to the lead; jolts Jeffries with a left in clinch. Johnson lands with left on Jeffries' face. Johnson is now landing pretty much as he pleases. After terrific mix-up, both exchange blows. Jeffries is losing his defense with great rapidity and Johnson appears to be able to land at will. Johnson lands left swing on Jeffries' face. The bear appears to be very tired at this stage of the fight and comes back to his corner bleeding profusely. His face is all cut up. This round was decidedly in favor of Johnson. Jeffries is tiring fast.

Round 14. Johnson lands with his left as Jeffries comes in. Jeffries lands left on Johnson's face, but the colored man blows to the audience and smiles. They clinch. Johnson lands with his left, and follows it up with a right uppercut. Jeffries keeps coming at his opponent, but the colored man lands quite frequently. He seems to be able to block Jeffries' leads with the greatest facility.

Round 15. The men come up slowly. Jeffries rushes, swinging right and left without effect, and in a hot rally Johnson lands right and left in rapid succession. A succession of stiff blows puts Jeffries in a state of collapse. Johnson is lightning fast to take advantage of Jeffries' collapse, knocks the big fellow down for the first time in his career. Jeffries takes the count of nine seconds, although it appeared to be a very long nine seconds, getting on his feet with a great effort. He was not quite steady when Johnson rushed at him like a tiger, landing hot rights and lefts on the face, again knocking him to the floor. He got up for the third time, but Johnson was right on him like a tiger and knocked him clear through the ropes, a badly beaten man. His seconds rushed into the ring, however, and threw up the sponge. Jeffries remained in his chair a few minutes bleeding profusely from the mouth. Long absence from the ring tells the story.

George Harting, "The Official Time-keeper Tells What Watch Showed," *San Francisco Chronicle*, July 5, 1910.

Time was called at 2:45 o'clock. Johnson entered the ring at 2:28 o'clock, and Jeffries entered four minutes later. The fight lasted fifteen rounds. The time for the last round was 2 minutes and 27 seconds. The fight was stopped at 3:41 o'clock. In the fifteenth round there were three knockdowns. The first two of these were each of nine seconds duration; the last one was eight seconds. Then Jeffries' seconds rushed in and the referee gave the decision to Johnson. There is no doubt that independent of this action, Jeffries would have been counted out.

Sam McVea, "How Jack Johnson Won," December 7, 1910 ("Comment Jack Johnson a Gagné Par Sam McVea," *La Boxe et les Boxeurs*). Translated from the French by Mark Scott.

Today we give to our readers for the first time an article of the highest interest: the celebrated champion Sam McVea has actually been so good as to give us his impressions on how Johnson beat Jeffries in Reno.

Sam McVea has watched several times the film of the fight that was shown with amazing clarity by the American Bibliograph *on Taibout street, has been able to follow very carefully all sides and aspects of this famous bout, much more easily and completely even than the spectators at the Reno event, tired by the trip, jostled by the crowd and who obviously could only view the fight one time. If we add to that McVea is as competent as anyone with regard to boxing combat, it is easy to understand that these observations are of an exceptional interest.*

You asked me to give my real opinion of the Reno fight, and it is with great pleasure that I undertake to do it.

I am far from being a passable author or even journalist, I am going to content myself with saying my impressions from my several viewings of the remarkable film of the fight.

I will skip over the training of the two opponents which was without great interest and get right to the fight.

The two men seemed nervous to me at the time they climbed into the ring; which is entirely natural considering the contest in play was of enormous importance and that one of them was risking his title while the other was perhaps going to be defeated for the first time in his career. However the more nervous of the two seemed to me clearly to be Johnson: Jeffries had, in effect, such a reputation, they had so vaunted the irresistible power of his left, that inevitably the conqueror of Burns and Ketchel had to have a strong apprehension.

Jeffries is relatively calm considering such extraordinary circumstances, but although his attitude seems very calm, he is far from having the advantage with respect to form and musculature. While Johnson seems to be in marvelous shape with his supple muscles, light at the same time powerful and cat-like, so to speak, while the anatomy of Jeffries seems forced, hard, artificial, without harmony. The white champion lacks all suppleness, lightness, one senses already that the longer the fight lasts, the less are Jeffries' chances. He does not look at all like a man who can last 20 or 30 and much less 45 rounds.

From the first round it is clear to the schooled eye that Johnson has decided to follow a strict line of attack and not get sidetracked at any cost: gradually weaken his opponent, study him carefully, harass him from a distance, utilizing his reach and tie up in the clinches the very dangerous left, known so well to Fitzsimmons and Corbett, tire him, and stay out of harm's way.

Johnson followed his battle plan point by point throughout the fight; hardly even once or twice did he risk a right hook, he was always as careful as could be.

Jeffries, on the other hand, confident in his star that had never yet let him down, confident in his remarkable power and courage, fought with little method. From the first round, frankly, he attacked with little skill. He tries for his part to tire his opponent with leads and rushes, but soon realizes he has a hard road to hoe, and he is hit constantly in the face with short blows that really get to him; one sees that he changes his guard and his tactics several times; as soon as he adopts a low crouch Johnson's left uppercuts cause him to abandon it; each time he rushes in like crazy he is hit by accurate and slashing left jabs.

Jeffries' long absence from the ring and fighting, has taken away from him his ability to judge distance. His punches fall short, and besides he is meeting for the first time a man taller than he who is just as strong.

From the second round it is clear that, if Johnson continues his efficient and careful tactics, Jeffries' left will never achieve its fatal purpose. Johnson holds his opponent at a distance with his log arm, and every man with a long and effective left could beat Jeffries.

But it is above all in the clinches that Johnson won. Oh, the marvelous and educational clinches that took place in Reno! And how mad I would be to hear the unknowledgeable spectators say: "It's great, but there is a little too much clinching." The knowledge of in-fighting is the pinnacle of boxing science, and whoever understands it can witness it with pleasure.

Johnson, with remarkable skill, followed the tactic I recommend: "Disarm your opponent before attacking him."

Johnson disarmed his opponent by leaning on his opponent's left arm; in each clinch one sees the right hand of the great negro grab the left arm of the white, push it toward the ground, tire it progressively with the most admirable power and certainty, until the numbed shoulder had no more strength to work. From there, he had Jeffries at his mercy.

Johnson may have been able to win quicker, but he could not have won more certainly.

Jeffries had admirable courage and energy but lacked science.

One sees him try all the tactics successively, all the blows in his repertoire; until the last second, he tries to land his left, convinced that a single blow well landed will end the fight, but he should have realized that he had before him an opponent who was too scientific to be caught in a mistake.

From the 1st to the 10th round, Johnson does not cease to harass his opponent as much with his jabs from a distance as with his short left and right uppercuts in the clinches. The rules of boxing allow punching as long as one has a free hand and one can see very clearly that Johnson uses first one hand, then the other, quickly letting go of the arm it is holding, shoot up a rapid uppercut, then grab the arm again; from one end to the other throughout the 15 rounds Jeffries is hammered with short punches that irritate him at first, then daze him, and finally weaken him to the point of being at the mercy of his implacable opponent.

Despite the rough punishment he received, Jeffries did not lose hope, he knew that the slightest mistake could be fatal to Johnson; until the final fall, he still hoped that luck would favor him. However when he returned to his corner after the 9th and 10th round, his bowed head and his anxious manner showed well that he found himself in serious trouble; the negro's defense is impenetrable.

One round follows another and Johnson continues his work. Such a lumberjack chopping down a mighty oak tree, he chops away and his axe (I mean his left fist) weakens the reputedly unshakable trunk with each blow. Johnson also has the prudence of a lumberjack who fears being crushed if the giant tree falls on him. He covers himself with the greatest care, pulls back, dodges and ceaselessly returns to his work. He conserves his strength, because he doesn't know how much longer his task will take. He doesn't waste a step, he doesn't try to "amaze" the crowd with clever leg work, which would be useless and tiring; he has a precise goal; his mind isn't open to any other thought; from afar he punches, in close he still punches with short blows repeatedly and with each of them seems to say, "each chopping blow weakens the trunk." From the 12th round, at any rate, Jeffries is visibly shaken; he abandons all method and no longer blocks hardly any punches; only his courage remains and he stoically takes and takes up until the moment he is knocked down.

In the 14th round, the tree no longer has anything but a questionable foundation under it and yet Johnson still does not hurry. He waits until his opponent is really ready to go down by himself, until he can't even hold up his arms, to give the final blow. Finally the 15th round arrives, the oak sways on its base and a final blow knocks it down.

Bibliography

This bibliography incorporates the resources cited in the chapters, as well as a number of works that may prove useful in researching early boxing history.

Ashe, Arthur R., Jr. *A Hard Road to Glory: The African-American Athlete in Boxing*. New York: Amistad, 1988.

Auger, Jean. *La boxe anglaise*. Paris: Librairie Garnier Frères, 1923.

Aycock, Colleen, and Mark Scott. *Joe Gans: A Biography of the First African American World Boxing Champion*. Jefferson, N.C.: McFarland, 2008.

_____. "The Joe Gans — Kid Herman World Boxing Title Fight: New Year's Day, 1907, Tonopah, Nevada," *Boomtown History III*, Jean Johnson ed., Boomtown History Conferences: Tonopah, Nevada, 2009.

Bak, Richard. *Joe Louis: The Great Black Hope*. 1st ed. Dallas: First Da Capo Press, 1998.

Batchelor, Denzil. *Jack Johnson and His Times*. London: Weidenfeld and Nicolson. 1956.

Bates, H. E. *The Black Boxer Tales* (fiction). London: Pharos, 1932.

Battling Siki (Louis M'barick Fall). "Résumé aux lecteurs de *L'Auto*." *L'Auto*, September 29, 1922, 1.

Bénac, Gaston. *Champions dans la coulisse*. Toulouse: L'Actualité Sportive, 1944.

Benson, Peter. *Battling Siki: A Tale of Ring Fixes, Race, and Murder in the 1920s*. Fayetteville: University of Arkansas Press, 2006.

_____. *Black Orpheus, Transition, and Modern Cultural Awakening in Africa*. Berkeley: University of California Press, 1986.

_____. "The Savage Battler and Clever Little Mike." *The Ring*. December 2006, 66–75.

Bonner, Milton. "Battling Siki's Autobiography." *Bellingham* (Washington) *American*, November 10, 1922. Rpt. Boxing Biographies. January 4, 2010. Internet. http://boxingbiographies.com/bio/index.php?option=com_content&task=view&id=23&Itemid=30&limit=1&limitstart=2.

Bradley, James. Book-TV/C-SPAN 2 program — James Bradley lecture of 12/2/09 in San Francisco at a meeting of the Marines Memorial Club (Bradley is the author of *The Imperial Cruise: A Secret History of Empire and War* first aired on 12/20/09).

http://www.booktv.org/Program/11157/The+Imperial+Cruise+A+Secret+History+of+Empire+and+War.aspx, Accessed January 30, 2010.

Broom, R. "Jackson, Peter," *Australian Dictionary of Biography*, Vol. 9 (1891–1939). Melbourne: Melbourne University Press, 1983: 458–459.

Callis, Tracy, Chuck Hasson, and Mike Delisa. *Images of Sports: Philadelphia's Boxing Heritage 1876–1976*. Charleston, S.C.: Arcadia Publishing, 2002.

Carby, Hazel V. *Race Men*. Cambridge, Mass.: Harvard University Press, 1998.

Carpentier, Georges. *Carpentier by Himself*. Trans. Edward Fitzgerald. London: Hutchinson, 1955.

_____. *Ma vie de boxeur*. Amiens: R.L. Eveillard, 1921.

_____. *Mes 80 rounds*. With the collaboration of Jacques Marchand. Paris: Oliver Orban, 1976.

_____. *Mon match avec la vie*. Paris: Flammarion, 1954.

Chalk, Ocania. *Pioneers of Black Sport: The Early Days of the Black Professional Athlete in Baseball, Basketball, Boxing, and Football*. New York: Dodd and Mead, 1975.

Clark, S. F. "Up Against the Ropes: Peter Jackson as 'Uncle Tom' in America." *The Drama Review*, 44, 1 (Spring 2000): 157–182.

Cockburn, Alexander. "War and Peace," Counterpunch.org, October 9, 2009. http://www.counterpunch.org/cockburn10092009.html, accessed January 31, 2010.

Collins, Nigel. *Boxing Babylon*. New York: Citadel Press, 1990.

Davidson, Ian. *Voltaire in Exile*. New York: Grove Press: 2005.

Dempsey, Jack, Bob Considine, and Bill Slocum. *Dempsey: By the Man Himself*. New York: Simon and Schuster. 1960.

Du Bert, Marthe [Pseud. M. Dutrèb]. *Nos sénégalais pendant la Grande Guerre*. Metz: Maison d'Édition des "Voix Lorraines," 1922.

Du Bois, William Edward Burghardt. *The Souls of Black Folks*. Chicago: A.C. McClung, 1903.

Early, Gerald. "Battling Siki: The Boxer as Natural

Man." *The Massachusetts Review*, Vol. 29, No. 3 (Fall) 1988a, 451–472.

_____. "The Black Intellectual and the Sport of Prizefighting." *The Kenyon Review*, Vol. 10, No. 3 (Summer) 1988b, 102–117.

_____. *The Culture of Bruising: Essays on Prize-fighting, Literature, and Modern American Culture.* Hopewell, NJ: Ecco Press, 1994.

Egan, Pierce. *Boxiana: or Sketches of Ancient & Modern Pugilism from the Days of the Renowned Broughton and Slack to the Championship of Cribb, Vol. I* (orig. pub. London: George Virtue, 1830), facsimile at www.Elibron.com: Elibron Classics. 2006.

Ehrmann, Pete. "Setting the Record Straight on Paul Berlenbach." *The Ring*, February 2005, 66–73.

Farr, Finis. *Black Champion. The Life And Times of Jack Johnson.* New York: Scribner. 1964.

Fields, Armond. *James J. Corbett: A Biography of the Heavyweight Boxing Champion and Popular Theater Headliner.* Jefferson, N.C.: McFarland, 2001.

Feuille, Henri (*Capitaine*). *Face aux Turcs: Gallipoli 1915.* Paris: Payot., 1934.

Fleischer, Nat. *Black Dynamite, Vol. I, The Story of the Negro in Boxing.* New York: O'Brien, 1938.

_____. *Black Dynamite, Vol. III, The Three Colored Aces: The Story of George Dixon, Joe Gans and Joe Walcott and Several Contemporaries.* New York: C. J. O'Brien, 1938.

_____. *Black Dynamite, Vol. IV, The Fighting Furies: The Story of The Golden Era of Jack Johnson, Sam Langford and Their Contemporaries.* New York: O'Brien. 1939.

_____. *Black Dynamite, Vol. V, Sockers in Sepia.* New York: O'Brien. 1947.

_____. *Fifty Years at Ringside.* New York: Fleet Publishing, 1958.

_____. *Jack Dempsey, the Idol of Fistiana: An Intimate Narrative.* New York: Ring Athletic Library, 1929.

_____. *The Ring Record Book and Boxing Encyclopedia, 1961 ed.* Norwalk, CT: O'Brien Suburban Press, 1961.

Fleischer, Nat, Sam Andre, and Nat Loubet. *A Pictorial History of Boxing.* New York: Bonanza Books, 1975.

Fox, Richard, K. *Life and Battles of Jack Johnson, No. 22.* New York: Fox's Athletic Library, 1910.

Fraser, George MacDonald. *Black Ajax, Tom Molineaux.* New York: Carroll & Graf, 1998.

Garraty, J.A. and M.C. Carnes, eds. *American National Biography*, Vol. 11. New York: Oxford University Press, 1999: 761–762.

Gates, Henry Louis and Gene Andrew Jarrett. *The New Negro: Readings on Race, Representation, and African American Culture, 1892–1938.* Princeton, N.J.: Princeton University Press, 2007.

Gilmore, Al-Tony. *Bad Nigger! The National Impact of Jack Johnson.* Port Washington, NY: Kennikat, 1975.

Gordon, Graham. *Master of the Ring: the Extraordinary Life of Jem Mace, Father of Boxing and the First Worldwide Superstar.* Wrea Green (UK): Milo Books, 2007.

Green, Benny. *Shaw's Champions: George Bernard Shaw and Prizefighting, from Cashel Byron to Gene Tunney.* London: Elm Tree Books, 1978.

Greig, Murray. *Goin' the Distance: Canada's Boxing Heritage.* Toronto: Macmillan. 1996.

Grombach, John V. *The Saga of the Fist: The 9,000 Year Story of Boxing in Text and Pictures: The Saga of Sock.* Cranbury, N.J.: A.S. Barnes, 1949.

Hjalmarson, Birgitta. *Artful Players: Artistic Life in Early San Francisco.* Los Angeles: Balcony Press, 1999.

Heinz, W.C. *The Fireside Book of Boxing.* New York: Simon and Schuster. 1961.

Hietala, Thomas R. *The Fight of the Century: Jack Johnson, Joe Louis and the Struggle for Racial Equality.* Armonk, N.Y.: M.E. Charpe, 2002.

Hornibrook, F. A. *The Lure of the Ring.* London: Pendulum, n.d.

"Jack Blackburn." *Boxrec.com*. 2009. Boxrec, Web. December 13, 2009. <http://boxrec.com/list_bouts.php?human_id=11022&cat=boxer&pageID=2>.

Jeffries, James J. "Life and Fights: Colorful Story Told by Himself for 'The Referee,'" *Referee*, August 16, 1927.

"Joe Gans." Boxrec.com. Web. December 13, 2009. <http://boxrec.com/list_bouts.php?human_id=9026&cat=boxer>.

Johnson, Jack. *Jack Johnson Is a Dandy: An Autobiography with Pictures.* New York: Chelsea House Publishers, 1969.

Johnson, Jack and Christopher Rivers. *My Life and Battles.* Westport, CT: Praeger, 2007.

Johnson, James Weldon. *Black Manhattan.* New York: Arno Press, 1968 (1930).

Johnston, Alexander. *Ten—And Out! The Complete Story Of the Prize Ring In America.* New York: I. Washburn, 1947.

Johnston, J. J. and Sean Curtin. *Images of Sport: Chicago Boxing.* Charleston, S.C.: Arcadia, 2005.

July, Robert W. *A History of the African People*, 4th Ed. Prospect Heights, Ill.: Waveland Press, 1992.

Kirsch, George B., Othello Harros, and Claire E. Nolte. *Encyclopedia of Ethnicity and Sports in the United States*, 1st ed. Westport, CT: Greenwood Press, 2000.

Koppen, Niek. *Siki.* Documentary Video Production, Amsterdam, 1993.

Kremer, G. R. "The World of Make-Believe: James Milton Turner and Black Masonry," *Missouri Historical Review*, 76, 2, January 1982: 50–70.

"The Lafayette Escadrille—Americans Prepare to Enter the Air War." January 4, 2010. Century of Flight. Internet. http://www.century-of-flight.net/Aviation%20history/airplane%20at%20war/Lafayette%20Escadrille.htm.

Laine, Sam. "The Passing of Joe Jeannette: The Only Thing that Prevented Him from Becoming Champion Was the Timing of His Birth." *Boxing Illustrated*, Vol. 1, No. 1, November 1958.

Langley, Tom. *The Life of Peter Jackson, Champion of Australia.* Leicester: Vance Harvey, 1974.

Lardner, John. "This Was Pugilism: Battling Siki." *New Yorker*, November 19, 1949, 97–108

_____. "The Battling Siki Murder." *New Yorker,* November 19, 1949. Rpt. *Negro Digest* 8, 6 (April 1950): 52–63.

_____. "The Jack Johnson Era of Boxing." *Negro Digest* 8, 1 (November, 1949), 24–34.

_____. *White Hopes and Other Tigers.* Philadelphia: Lippincott, 1951.

Lardner, Rex and Alan Bodian. *The Legendary Champions.* New York: American Heritage Press, 1972.

Lawless, W. "A Page of Pugilistic History, I." *Boxer and Wrestler,* July 14, 1933: 3.

Lloyd, Craig. *Eugene Bullard, Black Expatriate in Jazz-Age Paris.* Atlanta: University of Georgia Press, 2000.

London, Jack. *Jack London Stories of Boxing.* Edited by James Bankes. Dubuque, Iowa: William C. Brown, 1992.

McCallum, John D. *The Encyclopedia of World Boxing Champions Since 1882.* Radnor, PA: Chilton, 1975.

McCormick, J. B. *The Square Circle: Stories of the Prize Ring.* New York: Continental, 1897.

McFadden, George "Elbows." *Blocking and Hitting.* New York: Richard K. Fox, 1905.

Mead, Chris. 1985. *Champion Joe Louis, Black Hero in White America.* New York: Scribner, 1985.

Mencken, H. L. "Master of Gladiators." *Heathen Days: 1890–1936.* New York: A. A. Knopf, 1943.

Moyle, Clay. *Sam Langford: Boxing's Greatest Uncrowned Champion.* Seattle, WA: Bennet and Hastings, 2006.

Mullan, Harry. *The Illustrated History of Boxing.* New York: Crescent Books, 1987.

Myler, P. "Untwisting the Cyclone." *The Ring* (August 2003): 50–54.

Nagler, Barney. *Brown Bomber.* New York: World Publishing, 1972.

Naughton, W. W. *Kings of the Queensberry Realm.* Chicago: Continental, 1902.

Northrop, H. D., J. R. Gay, and I. G. Penn, *The College of Life: or Practical Self-Educational Emancipator and a Guide to Success.* Chicago: Chicago Publication and Lithography Co, 1895.

Notable Kentucky African Americans Database. University of Kentucky, Web. 2 Jan 2010. <http://www.uky.edu/Libraries/NKAA/

Nown, Graham. *The English Godfather.* London: Ward Lock, 1987.

Peeters, Georges. *La boxe: 'noble art.'* Paris: Vigot Frères, 1944.

_____. *Pleins feux sur les rings.* Paris: La Table Rond, 1970.

Petersen, Bob. *Gentleman Bruiser: A Life of the Boxer Peter Jackson, 1860–1901.* Sydney: Croydon Publishing, 2005.

Philbrick, J.W. *Descendants of Michael McGowan of Liverpool, Queens County, Nova Scotia.* Natick, Mass., 1973.

Phillips, Melvin W., M.D. *Mile Hi Docs.* Prescott, AZ: M & J Publishing, 1996.

Pizer, Vernon. *Glorious Triumphs: Athletes Who Conquered Adversity.* New York: Dodd, Mead, 1966.

Pollack, Adam J. *John L. Sullivan: The Career of the First Gloved Heavyweight Champion.* Jefferson, N.C.: McFarland & Co., 2006.

Reel, G. "This Wicked World: Masculinities and Portrayals of Sex, Crime, and Sports in the National Police Gazette, 1879–1906," *American Journalism,* 22, no. 1 (2005): 61–94.

Roberts, James B. and Alexander G. Skutt, eds. *The Boxing Register International Boxing Hall of Fame Official Record Book.* Ithaca, NY: McBooks, 2006.

Roberts, Randy. *Papa Jack: Jack Johnson and the Era of White Hopes.* New York: Free Press, 1983.

Rose, Al, and Eubie Blake. *Eubie Blake.* New York: Schirmer Books, Macmillan, 1979.

Runstedtler, Theresa. "Visible Men: African American Boxers, the New Negro and the Global Color Line." *Radical History Review,* MARHO: The Radical Historians' Organization, Inc., Issue 103, Winter, 2009, 59–81.

"Sam Langford." *Boxrec.com.* 2009. Boxrec, Web. December 15, 2009. <http://boxrec.com/list_bouts.php?human_id=11023&cat=boxer&pageID=4>.

Saunders, Charles. *Sweat and Soul: The Saga of Black Boxers from the Halifax to Caesar's Palace.* Hantsport, N.S.: Lancelot Press; Dartmouth, N.S.: Black Cultural Centre for Nova Scotia, 1990.

Schaap, Dick, ed. *Jack Johnson Is a Dandy: An Autobiography.* New York: Signet Classics, 1970.

Scharf, Thomas. *Images of Sports: Baltimore's Boxing Legacy 1893–2003.* Charleston, S.C.: Arcadia, 2003.

Shaffer, Harry. "Son of a Preacher Man Part I." *antekprizering.com.* Web. December 5, 2009. <http://www.antekprizering.com/blackburnstoryparti.html>.

Smalls, James. *The Homoerotic Photography of Carl Van Vechten: Public Face, Private Thoughts.* Philadelphia, PA: Temple University Press, 2006.

Smith, Kevin R. *Black Genesis: The History of the Black Prizefighter 1760–1870.* New York: iUniverse, Inc., 2003.

_____. *Boston's Boxing Heritage: Prizefighting from 1882–1955.* Charleston, SC: Arcadia, 2002.

_____. *The Sundowners: The History of the Black Prizefighter 1870–1930: Vol. II, Part One.* www.lulu.com publications, 2006.

Somrack, F. Daniel. *Boxing in San Francisco.* Charleston, SC: Arcadia, 2005.

Streible, Dan. *Fight Pictures: A History of Boxing and Early Cinema.* Berkeley: University of California Press, 2008.

Stuart, Mark. A *Gangster # 2: Longy Zwillman, the Man Who Invented Organized Crime.* Secaucus, NJ: Lyle Stuart, 1985.

Sugar, Burt Randolph. *Boxing's Greatest Fighters.* Guildford, CT: Lyons Press, 2006.

Terbeen, François, and Claude Brezner. *Les géants de la boxe.* Paris: Éditions Mondiale, 1962.

Van Every, Edward. *The Sins of New York: as 'Exposed' by the Police Gazette.* New York: Frederick A. Stokes, 1930.

Voorhis, Harold Van Buren. *Negro Masonry in the United States.* New York: Henry Emmerson, 1949.

Wallace, Maurice O. *Constructing the Black Masculine: Identity and Ideality in African American Men's*

Literature and Culture, 1775–1995. Durham, NC: Duke University Press, 2002.

Ward, Geoffrey C. *Unforgiveable Blackness: The Rise and Fall of Jack Johnson*. New York: Vintage, Random House, 2006.

Williams, Billy. "Last of the Big 4." *The Ring,* September 1958, 22–23.

Wood, Jeremy. *Hidden Talents: A Dictionary of Neglected Artists Working 1880–1950*. Billingshurst UK: Tempus, 2006.

Zinn, Howard *The People's History of the United States*. New York: HarperPerennial, 2005.

Video

Amazing Sports Stories, Episode 105: Joe Jennette; The Boxer Who Refused to Quit. Nash Entertainment http://www.nashentertainment.com

Big Fights: Siki vs. Carpentier, Sept. 24, 1922. Video recording, created from 16 mm. film. Big Fights Inc., New York.

Niek Koppen, *Siki*, Documentary Video Production, Amsterdam, 1993.

Archival Source

Federal Bureau of Investigation. Abner Zwillman file. Freedom of Information Act.
_____. Jack Johnson file.

Periodicals

Albuquerque (NM) *Journal*
Atlanta Constitution
L'Auto (Paris)
Anaconda (Montana) *Standard*
Baltimore Sun
Bismarck (ND*) Daily Tribune*
Boston Morning Journal
The Boxing Blade (St. Paul, MN)
Bridgeport (CT) *Telegram*
Brisbane Courier (Australia)
Chester (PA) *Times*
Chicago Daily Tribune
Chicago Defender
Chicago Times Herald
Columbus (NM) *Courier*
Dagbladet Politken (Germany)
Daily Gleaner (Kingston, Jamaica)
Daily Mail (London)
Daily Republican (Fresno, CA)
Digby Courier (Canada)

Davenport Democrat and Leader (PA)
L'Echo de Paris
L'Echo des Sports (Paris)
L'Éclair (Paris)
El Paso (TX) *Morning Times*
Fitchburg Daily Sentinel
Halifax Herald (Canada)
Hammond Times (IL)
Hartford Currant (CT)
Indianapolis Star
Hudson Dispatch (Jersey City, NJ)
L'Humanité (Paris)
Jersey Journal (Jersey City, NJ)
Las Vegas (NV) *Daily Optic*
Lexington (Ky) *Herald*
Lima (OH) *Times Democrat*
Lincoln Star (NE)
Lowell Sun (MA)
Le Matin (Paris)
Memphis (TN) *Commercial Appeal*
Milwaukee Free Press
Le Miroir (Paris)
National Police Gazette (NY)
Nevada State Journal
New Orleans Times Democrat
New York Daily News
New York Evening Journal
New York Evening Post
New York Evening Sun
New York Herald
New York Herald (Paris Ed.)
New York Herald Tribune
New York Police Gazette
New York Telegram and Evening Mail
New York Times
New York Tribune
New York World
Oakland Tribune
Ogden (Utah) *Standard-Examiner*
Omaha Daily Tribune (NE)
Paris-Soir
Philadelphia Press
Racine Daily Journal (WI*)*
Reno Evening Gazette (NV)
Saint Paul Globe (MN)
San Antonio Light (TX)
San Francisco Chronicle
San Francisco Examiner
Scranton Tribune (PA)
Silver City (NM) *Enterprise*
Sunday Herald (Glasgow)
Syracuse Herald (NY)
(Zanesville, Ohio) Times Recorder
Trenton Evening Times (OH)
Washington (D.C.) *Post*

About the Contributors

Peter Benson lives in Hoboken, and teaches African literature, American literature, and writing at Fairleigh Dickinson University in Madison, New Jersey. His interest in boxing began at the age of seven, hanging around the training room at the Field House at Camp Lejeune, where his father trained the camp boxing team that would win the All-Marine title and ultimately the All-Service title. His first bouts, at the age of eight, were fought in front of an audience of Marines during intermission at the team's tournaments. He is the author of *Battling Siki: A Tale of Ring Fixes, Race, and Murder in the 1920s* (2006), and *Black Orpheus, Transition, and Modern Cultural Awakening in Africa* (1983).

Joseph Bourelly is an avid boxing fan and student of the sport's history, and a member of the Boxing Writers Association of America and the International Boxing Research Organization. He is the national boxing writer for www.Examiner.com and has his own blog www.XLFights.com, and has covered numerous fights as a member of the media. He is a graduate of the American University and George Washington University. Originally from Chicago, he splits his time between the San Francisco Bay Area and Las Vegas.

Bill Calogero lives in the Lake George, New York, area and is the host of boxing's top-rated talk radio program, "Talkin' Boxing with Billy C." The show airs live in the United States and Canada and is accessed worldwide through the website www.talkinboxing.com. He has been involved in the sport of boxing for twenty-five years as a promoter, manager, advisor, historian, and writer. He is a member of the International Boxing Research Organization (IBRO) and is currently working on a biography of Tom Molineaux.

Douglas Cavanaugh is a native of Los Angeles and a sixth-generation Californian, and is an avid historian. He is a member of the International Boxing Research Organization and has written for *Boxing Illustrated, Boxing Scene, Boxing Digest* and *Boxing '96*, and has also written about the history of boxing in Pittsburgh and about boxing's "forgotten contenders," and is the author of the screenplay *Blues in a Mississippi Night*.

Chris Cozzone has been a photojournalist, writer and historian of boxing for the past ten years. He lives in Albuquerque, New Mexico, and travels to Las Vegas, Nevada, to cover the big fights. For ten years, he has worked for Fightnews.com and owned and operated www.NewMexicoBoxing.com. In 2009 his work was recognized by the Boxing Writers' Association of America. He wrote a weekly boxing column in the *Albuquerque Tribune* before the paper's demise. His work has also appeared in *Penthouse, Ring Magazine, Newsweek*, and on ESPN. He is currently at work on a book about New Mexico's boxing history.

Mike Glenn, who lives in the Atlanta area, played for over nine years in the NBA and earned the nickname "Stinger" for his shooting accuracy. He is a basketball television analyst and inspirational speaker. In 1980 he founded the nation's first major summer basketball camp for deaf and hard of hearing athletes, the Mike Glenn Camp for the Hearing Impaired. His non-profit camp is held annually in Decatur, Georgia. www.mikeglenn.com. He is the author of *Lessons from My Library: The Integration of Sports History* (2005).

Clay Moyle is a member of the International Boxing Research Organization (IBRO). He is the author of *Sam Langford: Boxing's Greatest Uncrowned Champion* (2008), available at www.samlangford.com and a biography of Billy Miske. In addition to writing, he is a collector of boxing books, with over 3,400 titles, many dating back to the 1800s. His website is www.prizefightingbooks.com. He lives in Edgewood, Washington.

Bob Petersen was a professor for many years at the University of Sydney, Australia. His research has been among such topics as ancient Greek athletics, the sporting press, masculinities, nineteenth-century boxing and wrestling. He is the author of *Gentleman Bruiser: A Life of the Boxer Peter Jackson, 1860–1901* (2005), the study of a black West Indian who became one of Australia's greatest sporting heroes and whose grave in Brisbane is still a place of pilgrimage. He lives in Sydney.

Alexander Pierpaoli is a writer who lives in Hamden, Connecticut. He has been addicted to the Sweet Science since 1985 and is the owner/operator of two boxing websites: www.KOFantasyBoxing.com and www.FistThingsFirst.com. He has recently co-starred in and co-produced an independent horror film entitled *Family Secret*. He continues to write about boxing history and the "Fearsome Foursome."

Michael J. Schmidt is a lawyer and licensed boxing manager, known in boxing circles as "The Canadian Fight Lawyer." He is a lifelong resident of Kitchener, Ontario, Canada. He boxed as an amateur, beginning at age 8, and compiled a record of 34–1 before ending his boxing career. His "home" gym has produced many well-known champion boxers and as president of Cloverlay Management Corporation (www.CloverlayBoxing.ca) his lifelong passion for boxing continues with a stable of boxers that currently includes four-time world champion Lisa "Bad News" Brown, Canada's most decorated female pugilist.

Kevin Smith was born and raised in Boston. He has researched the history of the black prizefighter for over 15 years. The founder of the Historical Society for Black Prizefighters, he has served as a consultant for the History Channel, the British Broadcasting Company, the British Museum, the National Portrait Gallery (London) and PBS as well as the International Boxing Hall of Fame and several historical societies nationwide. A member of the International Boxing Research Organization, he is the author of *Boston's Boxing Heritage* (2002), *Black Genesis: The History of the Black Prizefighter 1760–1870* (2003), and *The Sundowners: The History of the Black Prizefighter 1870–1930* (2006). He lives near Boston.

Tony Triem, former executive director of the World Boxing Association, lives in Indian Springs, Nevada. He was Golden Gloves Light Heavyweight Champion in Phoenix, Arizona, for three years in the early 1950s. His love of boxing history began when he spent several years traveling with his father Harold J. Triem, also a boxing historian, to visit with some of the great old prizefighters of the past. He has compiled one of the largest boxing archives in the United States with more than 20,000 photographs, books and newspapers. He also serves as publicist for Ring 101, Veterans Boxing Association of Baltimore.

Cathy van Ingen lives in Toronto and is an associate professor in physical education and kinesiology at Brock University. Her passion for boxing came from teaching sport history where she was swept up by the themes of race, gender and nation that underscore boxing. What began as an interest in the broad cultural terrain of boxing quickly led to her stepping inside the ring as an amateur boxer. She has written about the history of unsanctioned women's boxing in Canada and is a founding partner of the "Shape Your Life" project, a recreational boxing program for female survivors of violence in Toronto.

Co-Editors **Colleen Aycock** and **Mark Scott** are the authors of *Joe Gans: A Biography of the First African American World Boxing Champion* (McFarland, 2008). Colleen lives in Albuquerque, New Mexico. Mark lives in Austin, Texas. Mark and Colleen's website on boxers of the past is located at www.JoeGans.com.

Index

Numbers in *bold italics* indicate pages with photographs.